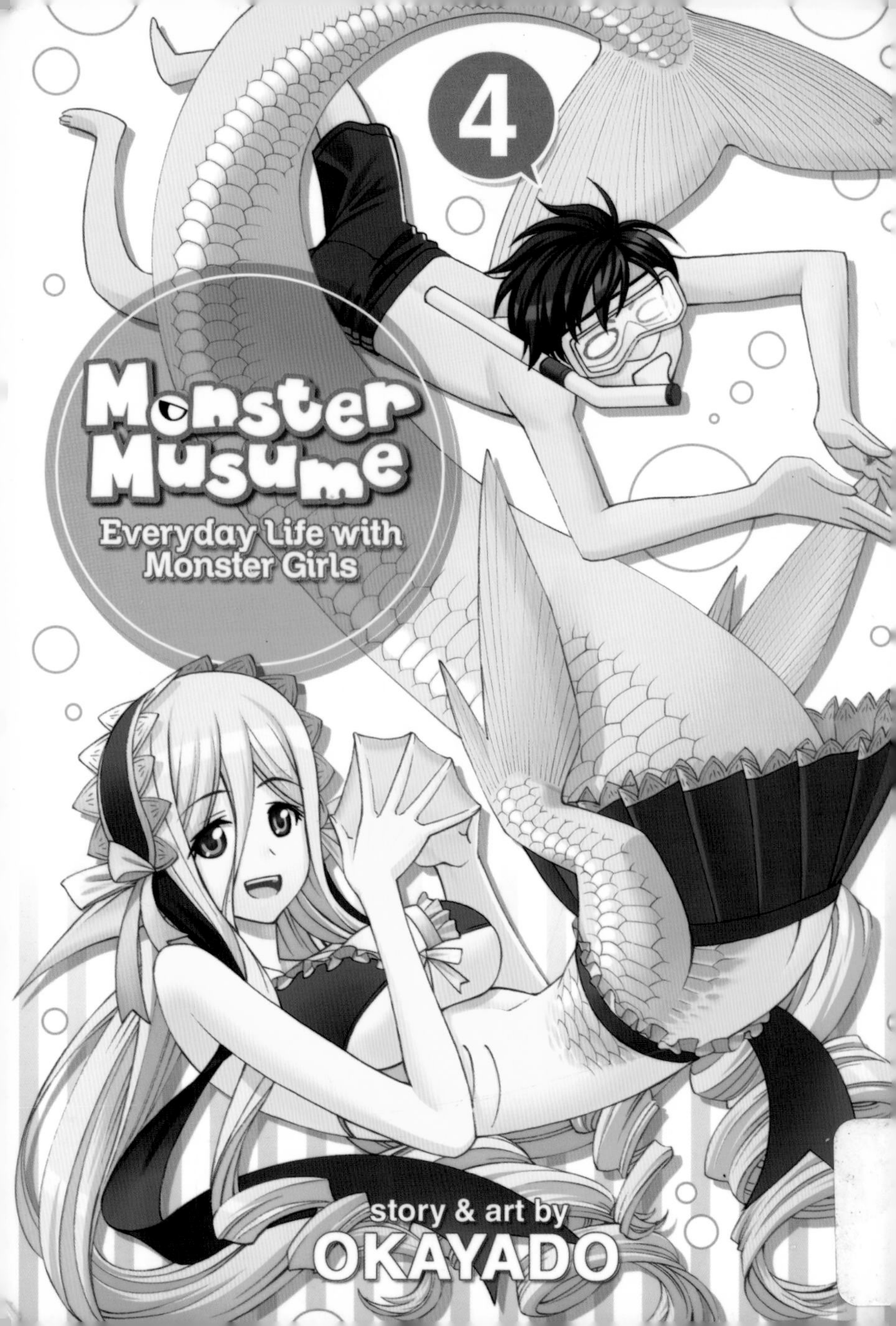
4
Monster Musume
Everyday Life with Monster Girls
story & art by
OKAYADO

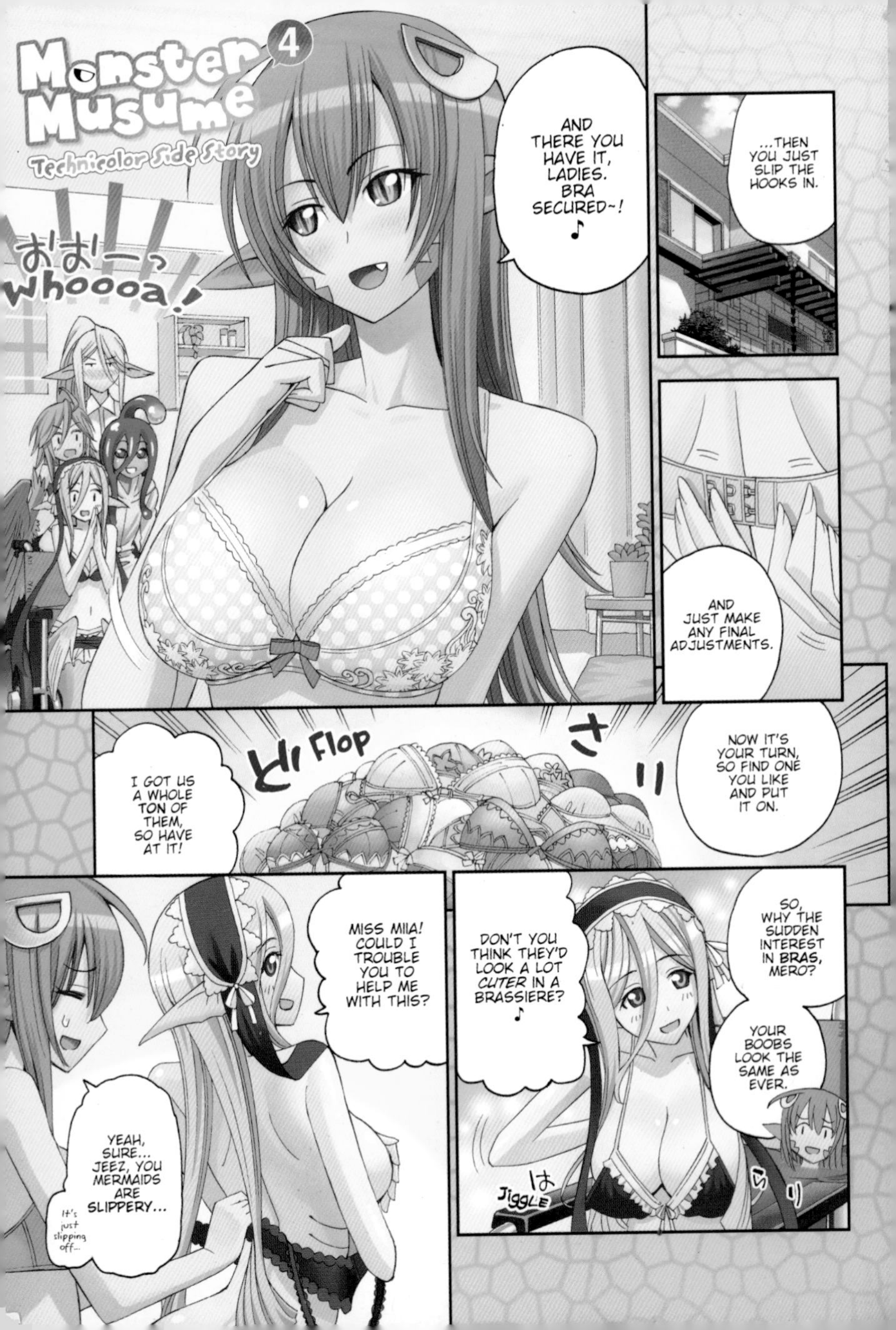
...THEN YOU JUST SLIP THE HOOKS IN.
AND JUST MAKE ANY FINAL ADJUSTMENTS.
Monster Musume 4
Technicolor Side Story
AND THERE YOU HAVE IT, LADIES. BRA SECURED~! ♪
おおーっ
whoooa!
NOW IT'S YOUR TURN, SO FIND ONE YOU LIKE AND PUT IT ON.
Flop
I GOT US A WHOLE TON OF THEM, SO HAVE AT IT!
SO, WHY THE SUDDEN INTEREST IN BRAS, MERO?
DON'T YOU THINK THEY'D LOOK A LOT CUTER IN A BRASSIERE? ♪
YOUR BOOBS LOOK THE SAME AS EVER.
Jiggle
MISS MIIA! COULD I TROUBLE YOU TO HELP ME WITH THIS?
YEAH, SURE... JEEZ, YOU MERMAIDS ARE SLIPPERY...
It's just slipping off...

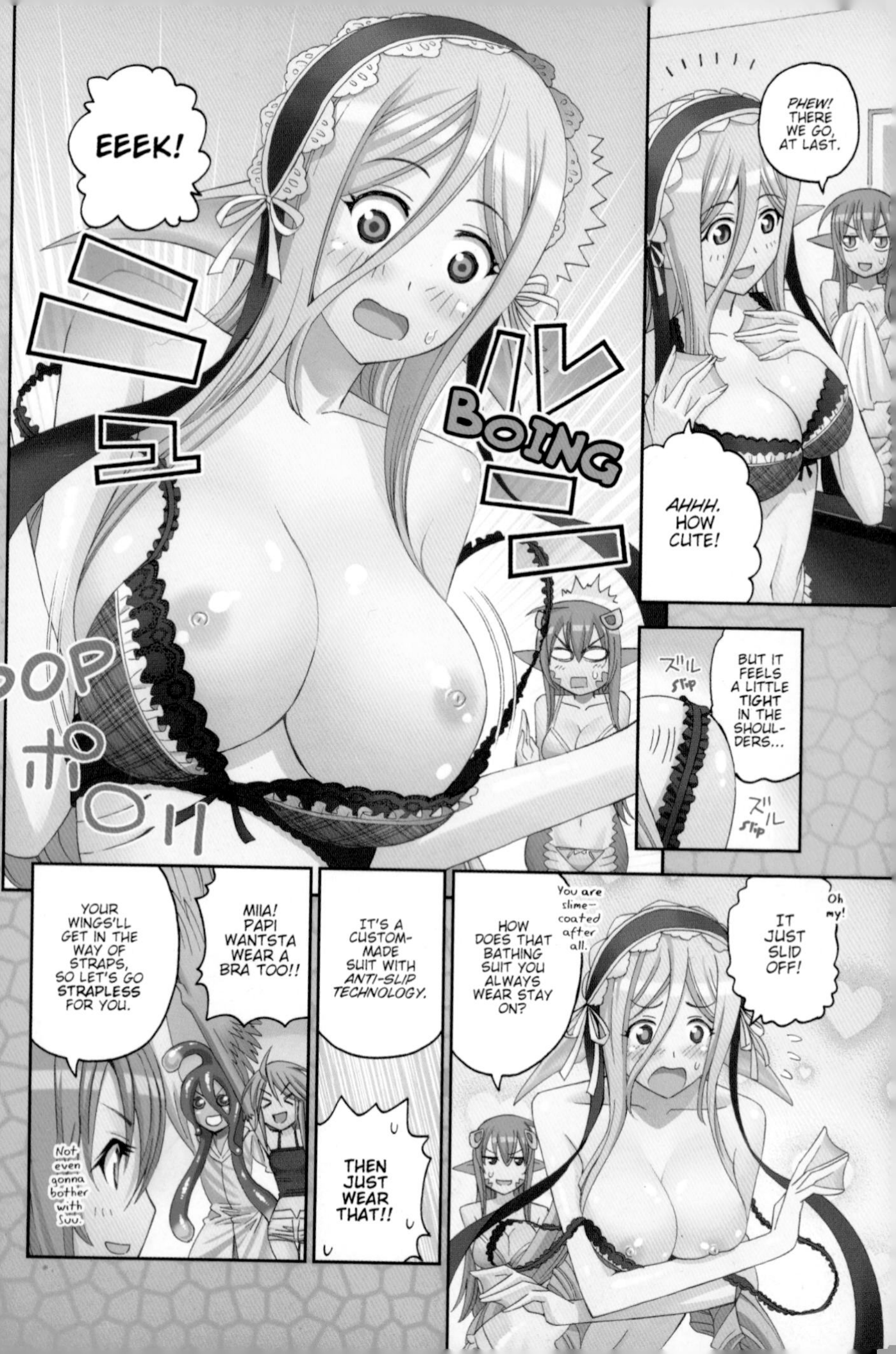
PHEW! THERE WE GO, AT LAST.
AHHH. HOW CUTE!
BUT IT FEELS A LITTLE TIGHT IN THE SHOUL-DERS...
ズル slip
ズル slip
EEEK!
BOING
POP
IT JUST SLID OFF!
Oh my!
HOW DOES THAT BATHING SUIT YOU ALWAYS WEAR STAY ON?
You are slime-coated after all.
IT'S A CUSTOM-MADE SUIT WITH ANTI-SLIP TECHNOLOGY.
THEN JUST WEAR THAT!!
MIIA! PAPI WANTSTA WEAR A BRA TOO!!
YOUR WINGS'LL GET IN THE WAY OF STRAPS, SO LET'S GO STRAPLESS FOR YOU.
Not even gonna bother with Suu.

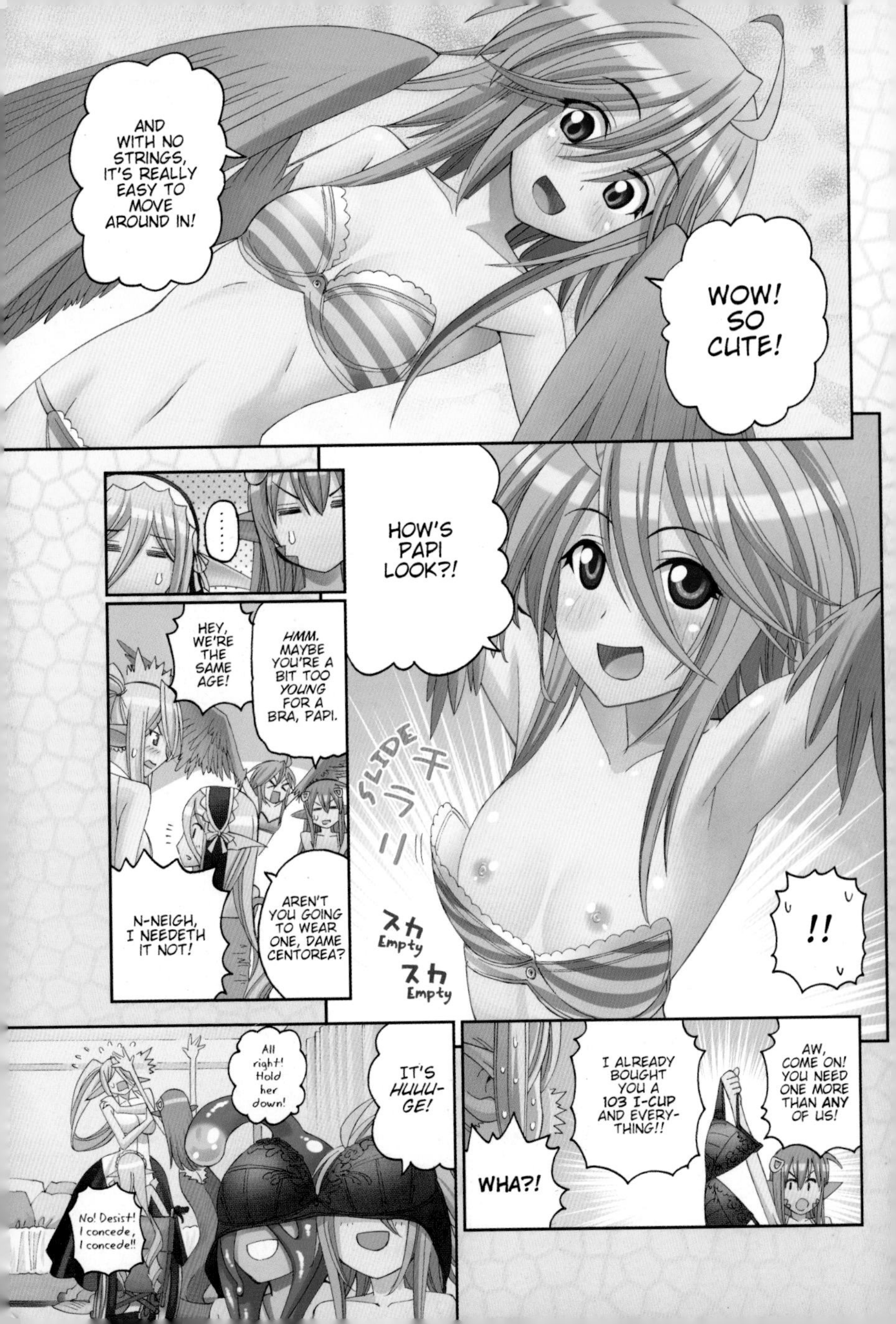
WOW! SO CUTE!
AND WITH NO STRINGS, IT'S REALLY EASY TO MOVE AROUND IN!
HOW'S PAPI LOOK?!
!!
SLIDE チラリ
スカ Empty
スカ Empty
......
HMM. MAYBE YOU'RE A BIT TOO YOUNG FOR A BRA, PAPI.
HEY, WE'RE THE SAME AGE!
AREN'T YOU GOING TO WEAR ONE, DAME CENTOREA?
N-NEIGH, I NEEDETH IT NOT!
AW, COME ON! YOU NEED ONE MORE THAN ANY OF US!
I ALREADY BOUGHT YOU A 103 I-CUP AND EVERY-THING!!
WHA?!
IT'S HUUU-GE!
All right! Hold her down!
No! Desist! I concede, I concede!!

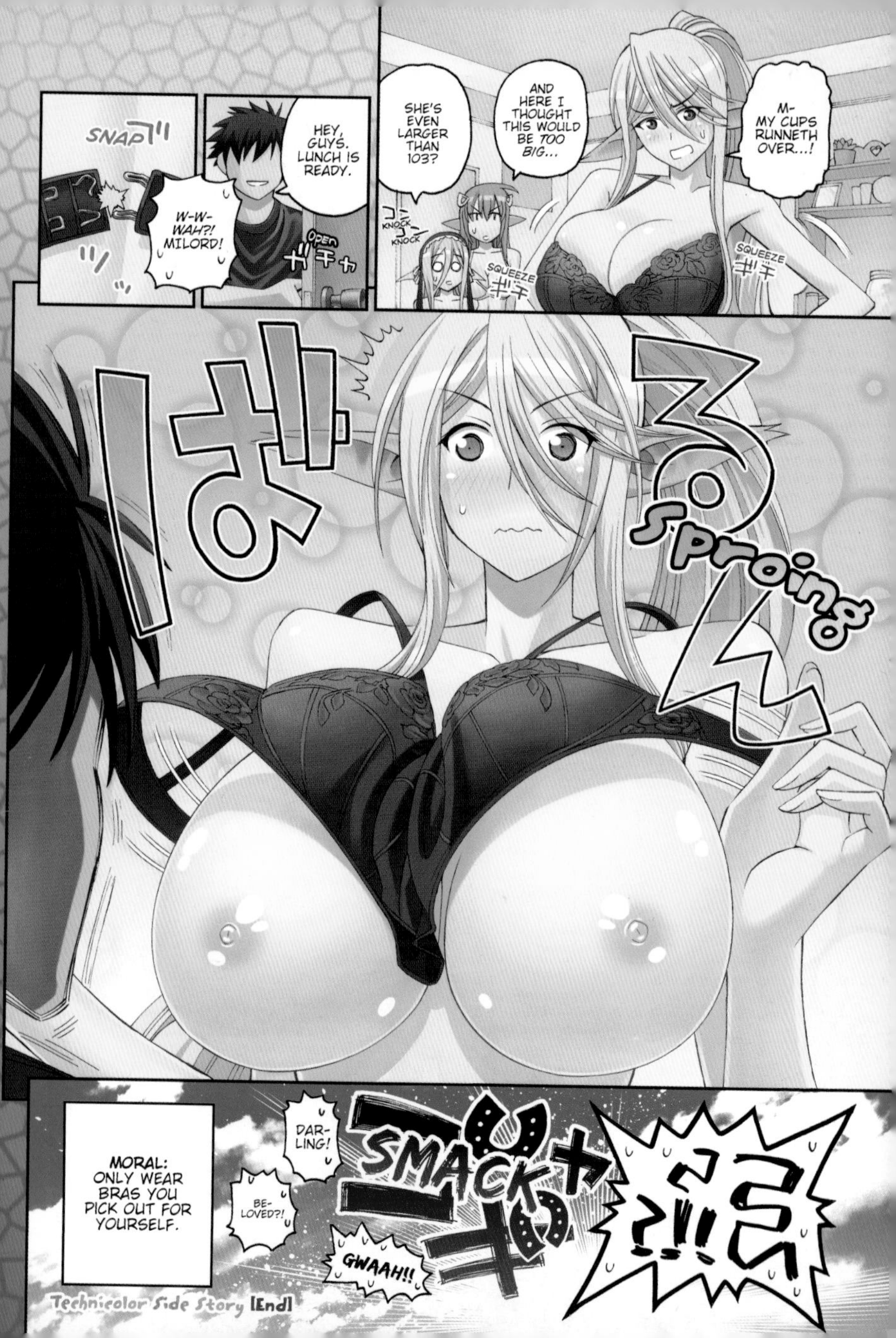
M-
MY CUPS RUNNETH OVER...!
SQUEEZE
AND HERE I THOUGHT THIS WOULD BE *TOO* BIG...
SHE'S EVEN LARGER THAN 103?
KNOCK KNOCK
SQUEEZE
OPEN
HEY, GUYS. LUNCH IS READY.
W-W-WAH?! MILORD!
SNAP
sproing
SMACK
GWAAH!!
BE-LOVED?!
DARLING!
MORAL: ONLY WEAR BRAS YOU PICK OUT FOR YOURSELF.
Technicolor Side Story [End]

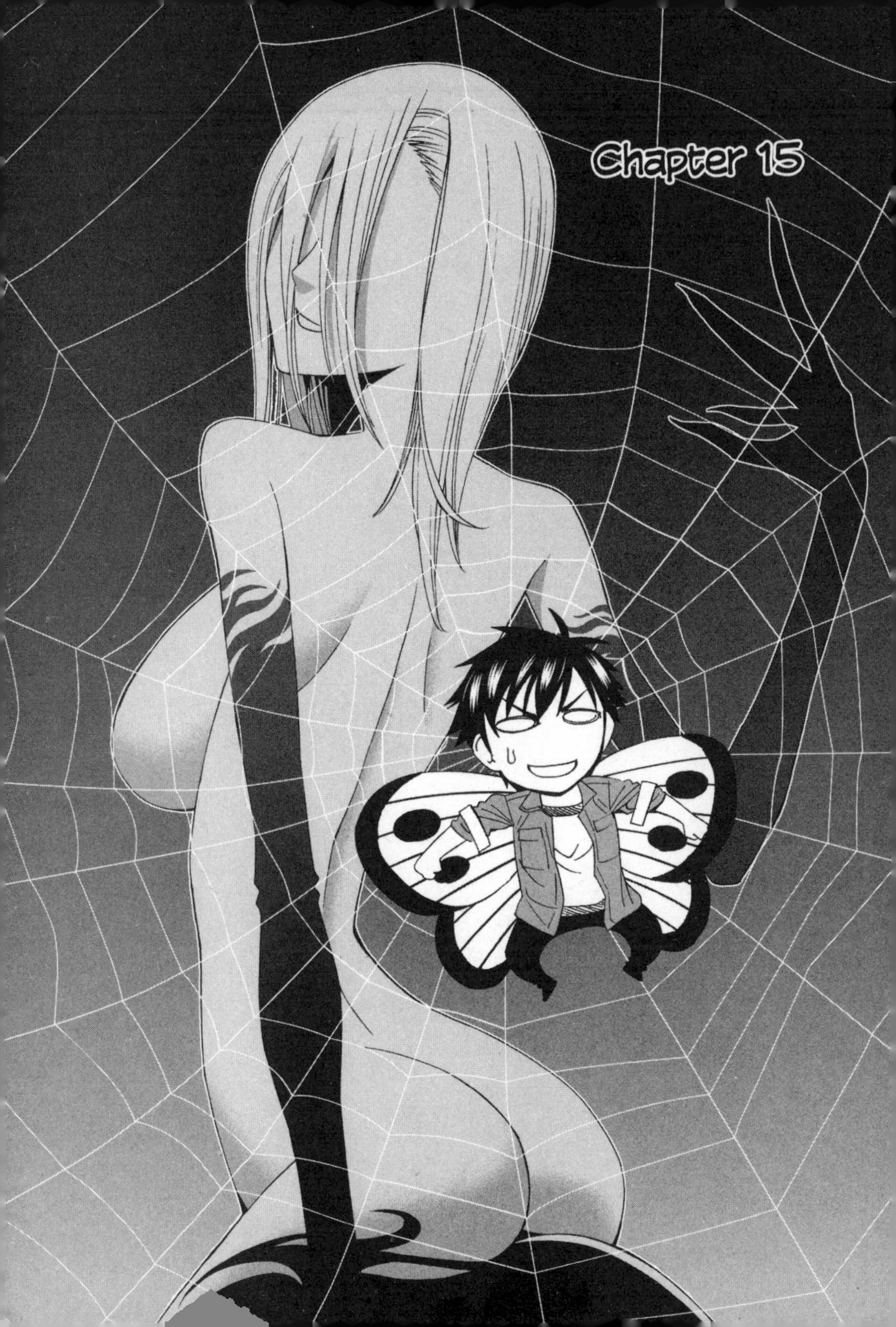
Chapter 15

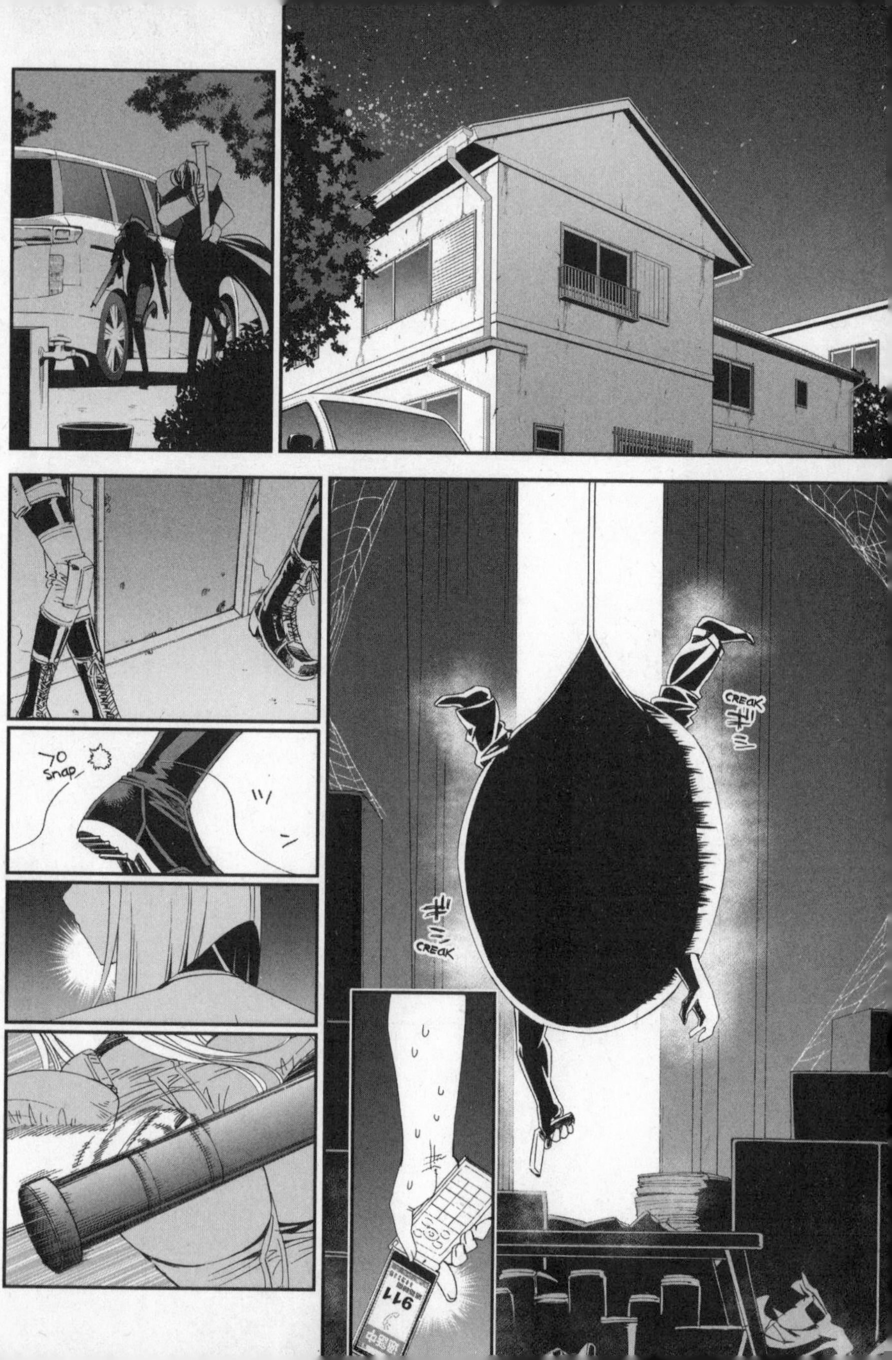
CREAK
CREAK
911
snap

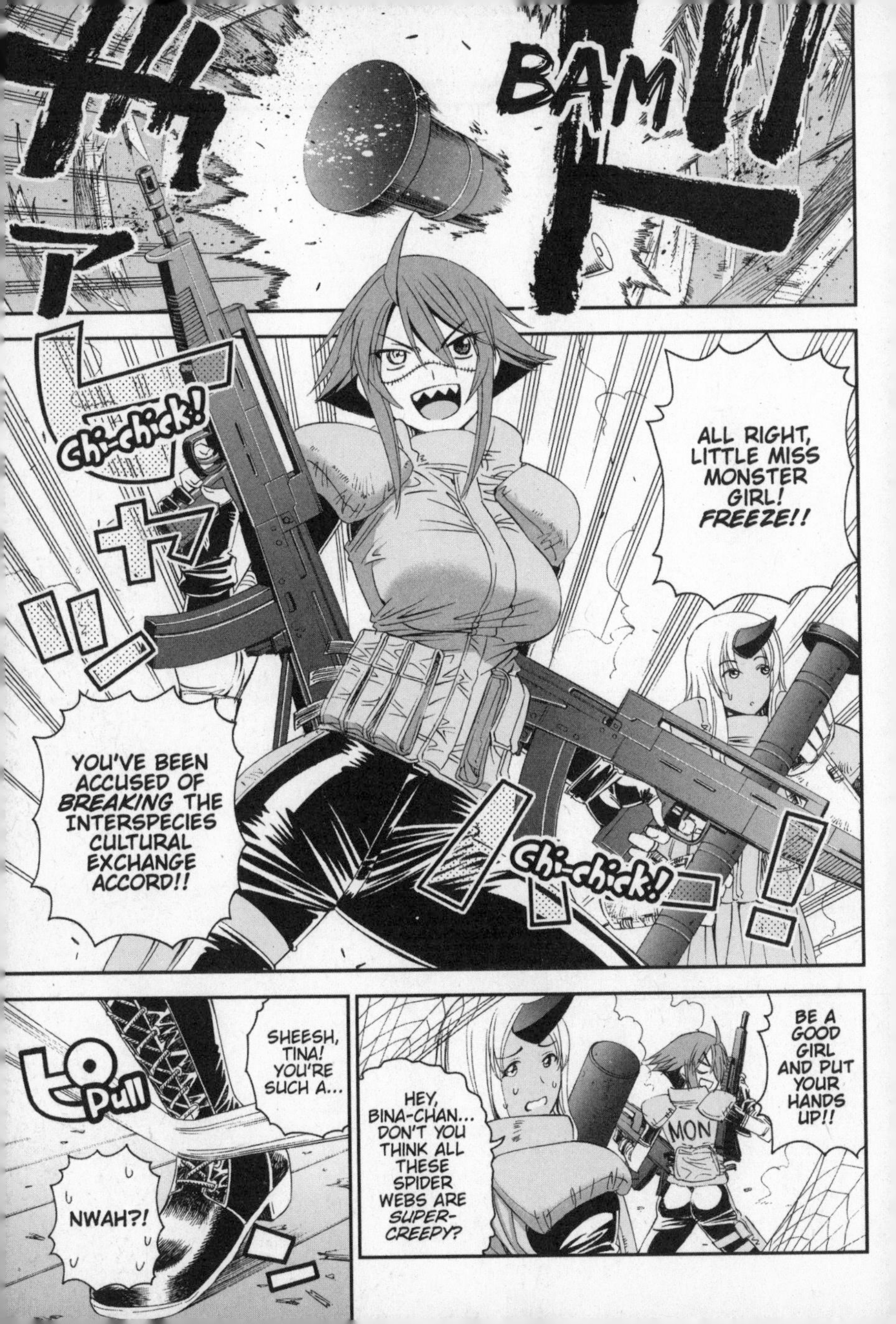
BAM!!
ALL RIGHT, LITTLE MISS MONSTER GIRL! FREEZE!!
Chi-chick!
YOU'VE BEEN ACCUSED OF BREAKING THE INTERSPECIES CULTURAL EXCHANGE ACCORD!!
Chi-chick!
BE A GOOD GIRL AND PUT YOUR HANDS UP!!
HEY, BINA-CHAN... DON'T YOU THINK ALL THESE SPIDER WEBS ARE SUPER-CREEPY?
MON
SHEESH, TINA! YOU'RE SUCH A...
Pull
NWAH?!

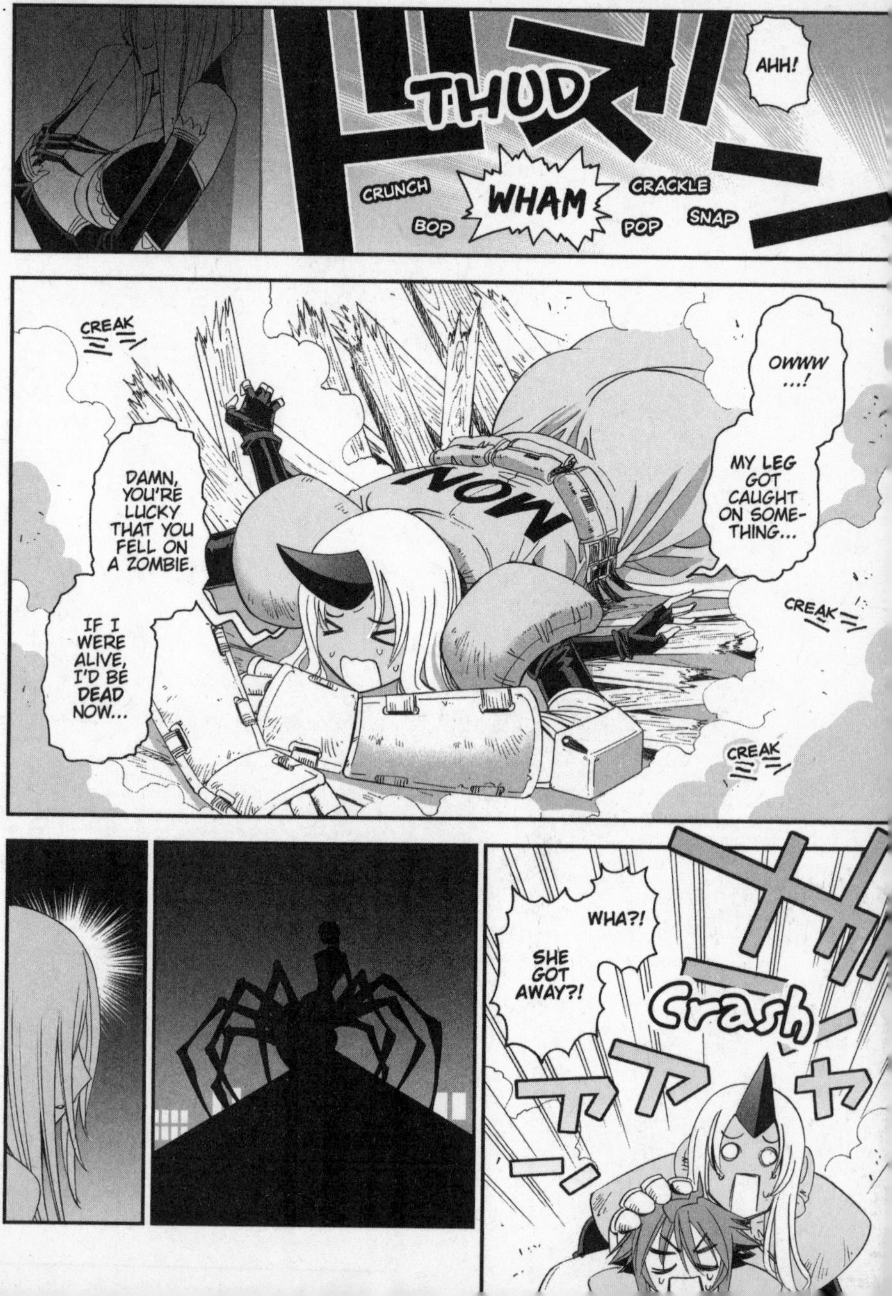
AHH!
THUD
CRACKLE
SNAP
POP
WHAM
CRUNCH
BOP
OWWW ...!
MY LEG GOT CAUGHT ON SOME-THING...
CREAK
CREAK
CREAK
DAMN, YOU'RE LUCKY THAT YOU FELL ON A ZOMBIE.
IF I WERE ALIVE, I'D BE DEAD NOW...
WHA?!
SHE GOT AWAY?!
Crash

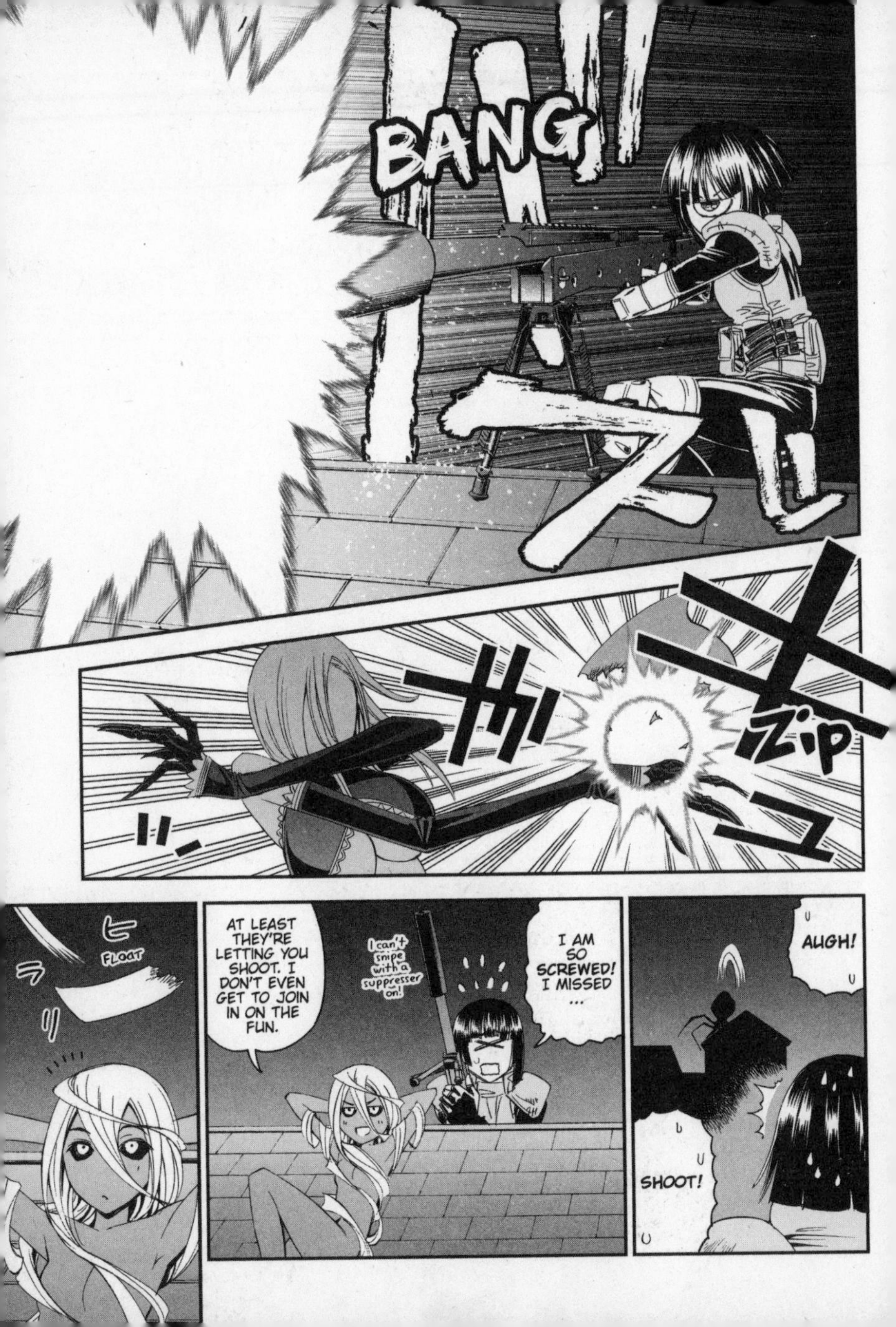
BANG
ZIP
AUGH!
SHOOT!
I AM SO SCREWED! I MISSED ...
I can't snipe with a suppresser on!
AT LEAST THEY'RE LETTING YOU SHOOT. I DON'T EVEN GET TO JOIN IN ON THE FUN.
FLOAT

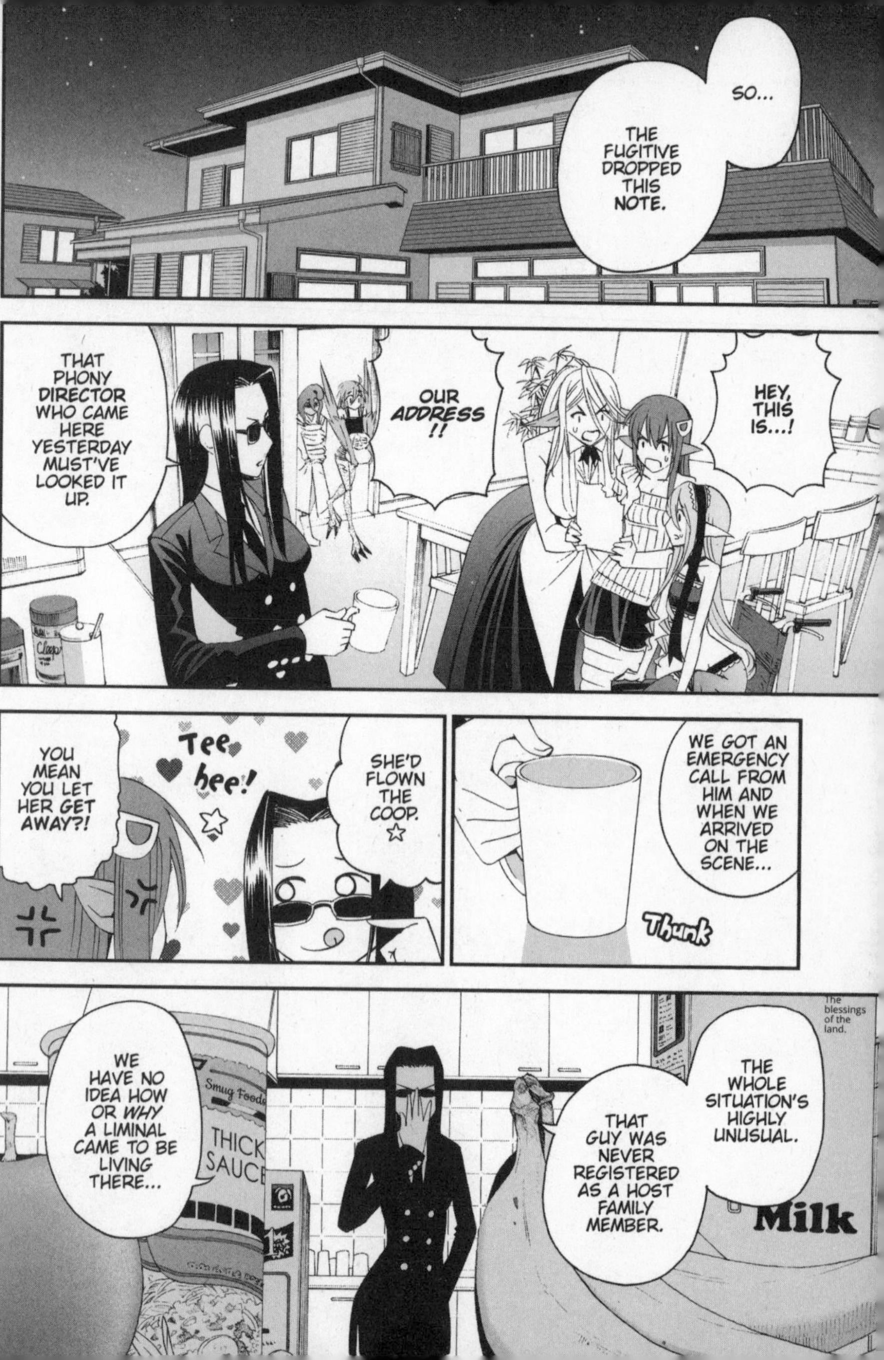
SO...
THE FUGITIVE DROPPED THIS NOTE.
HEY, THIS IS...!
OUR *ADDRESS*!!
THAT PHONY DIRECTOR WHO CAME HERE YESTERDAY MUST'VE LOOKED IT UP.
WE GOT AN EMERGENCY CALL FROM HIM AND WHEN WE ARRIVED ON THE SCENE...
Thunk
SHE'D FLOWN THE COOP.
Tee hee!
YOU MEAN YOU LET HER GET AWAY?!
The blessings of the land.
THE WHOLE SITUATION'S HIGHLY UNUSUAL.
THAT GUY WAS NEVER REGISTERED AS A HOST FAMILY MEMBER.
Milk
WE HAVE NO IDEA HOW OR *WHY* A LIMINAL CAME TO BE LIVING THERE...
Smug Foods
THICK SAUCE

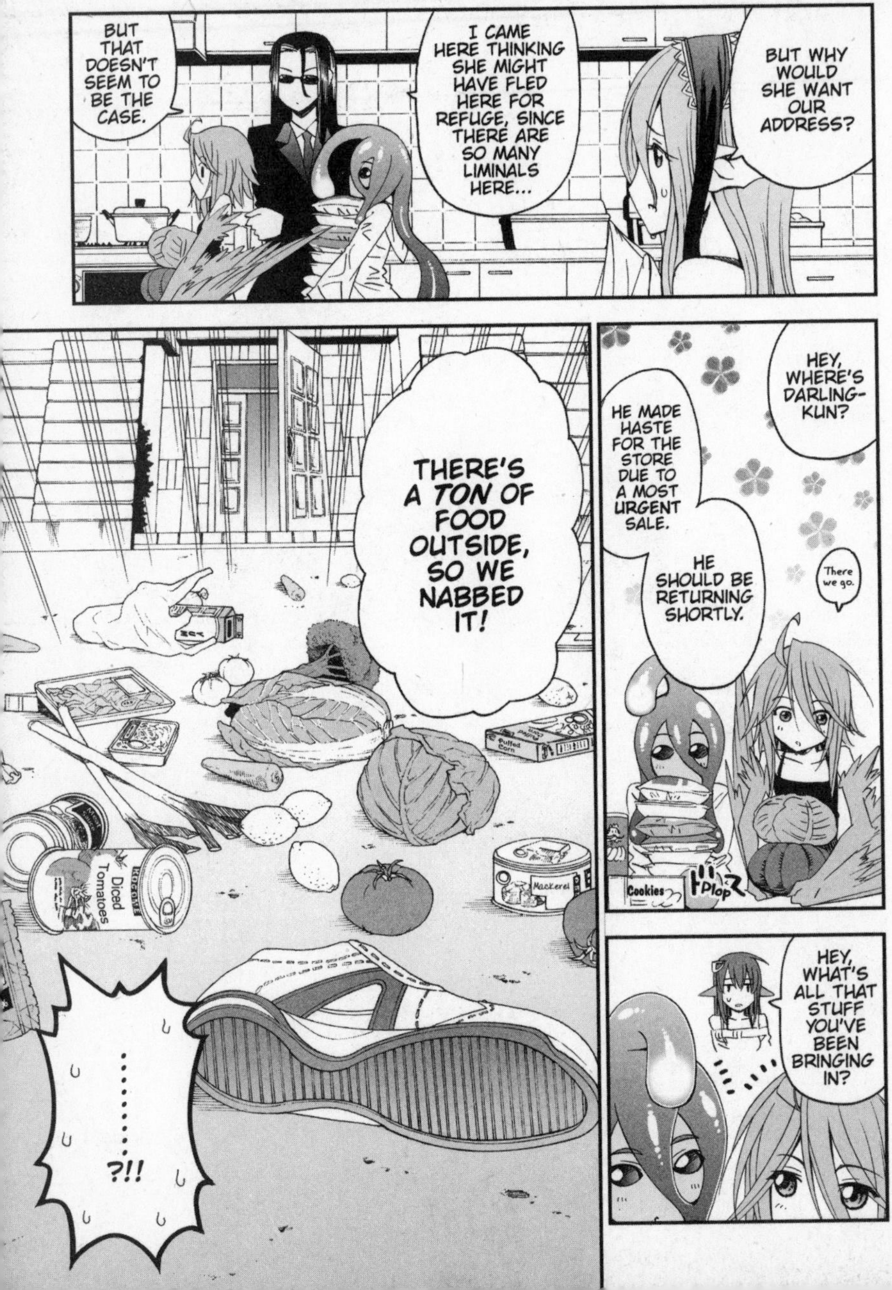
BUT WHY WOULD SHE WANT OUR ADDRESS?
I CAME HERE THINKING SHE MIGHT HAVE FLED HERE FOR REFUGE, SINCE THERE ARE SO MANY LIMINALS HERE...
BUT THAT DOESN'T SEEM TO BE THE CASE.
HEY, WHERE'S DARLING-KUN?
HE MADE HASTE FOR THE STORE DUE TO A MOST URGENT SALE.
HE SHOULD BE RETURNING SHORTLY.
There we go.
Puffed Corn
Cookies
Plop
HEY, WHAT'S ALL THAT STUFF YOU'VE BEEN BRINGING IN?
THERE'S A *TON* OF FOOD OUTSIDE, SO WE NABBED IT!
Mackerel
Diced Tomatoes
......
?!!

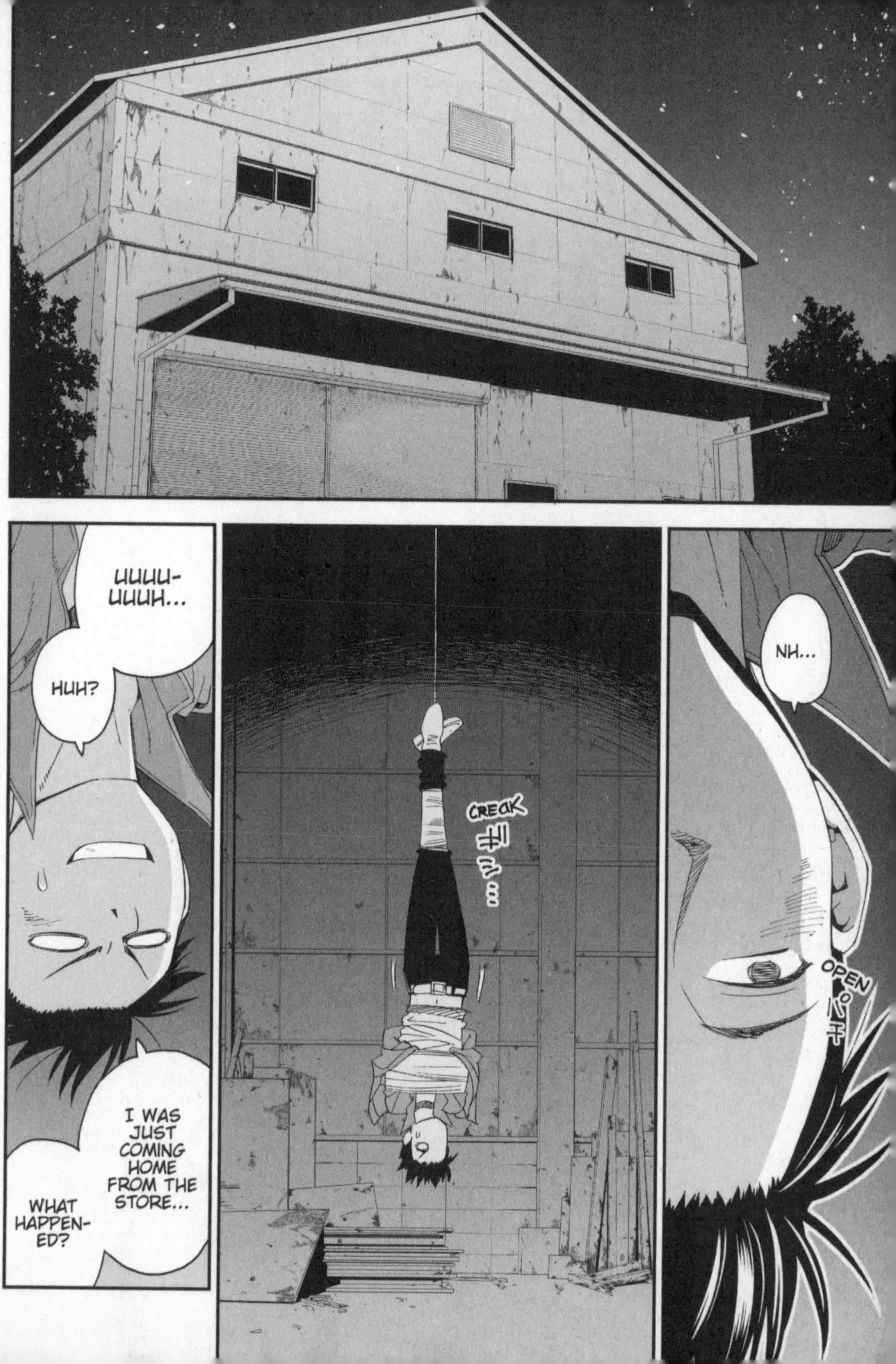
NH...
OPEN
CREAK
UUUU-UUUH...
HUH?
I WAS JUST COMING HOME FROM THE STORE...
WHAT HAPPENED?

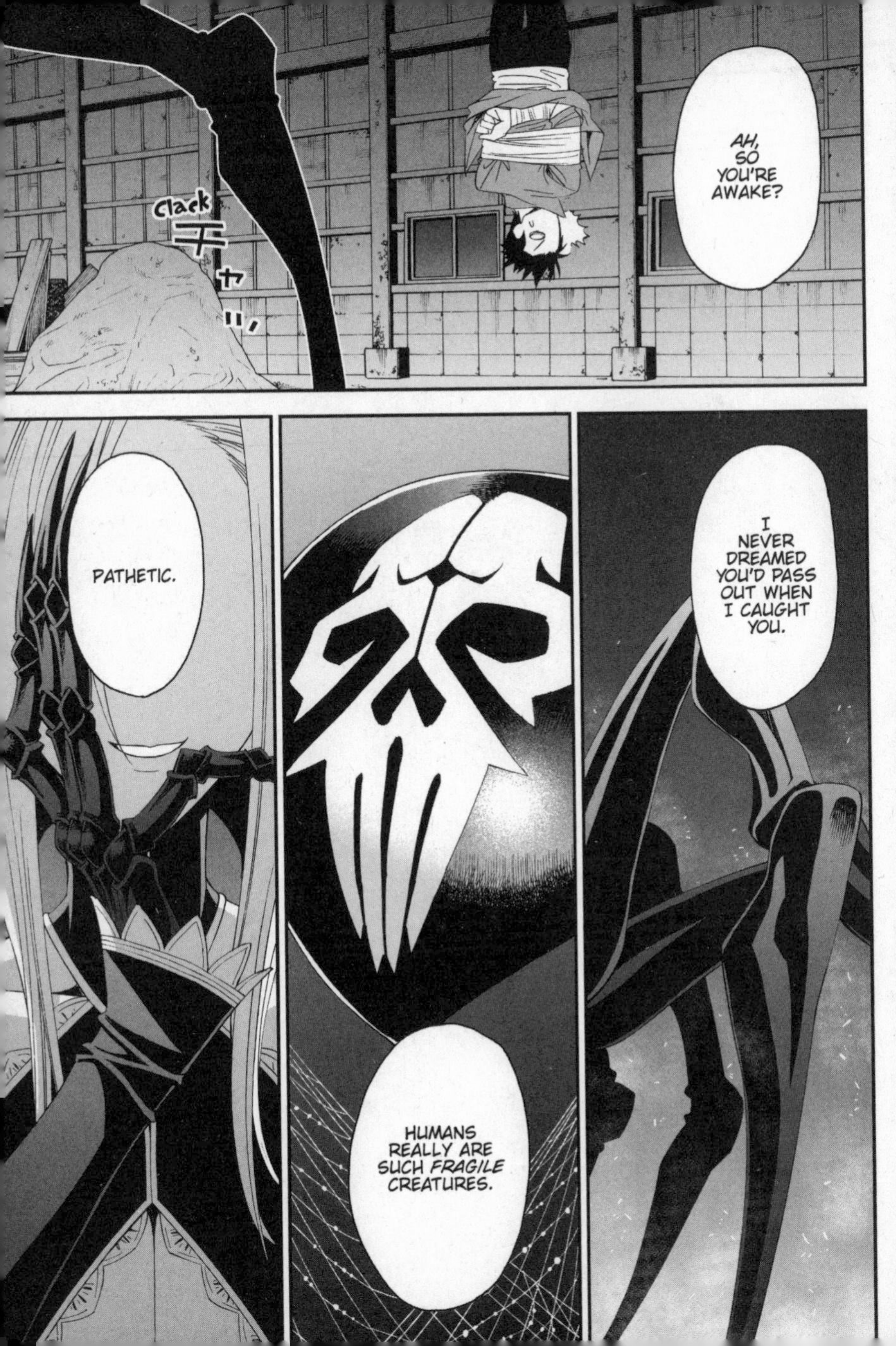
AH, SO YOU'RE AWAKE?
Clack
チャッ
I NEVER DREAMED YOU'D PASS OUT WHEN I CAUGHT YOU.
HUMANS REALLY ARE SUCH *FRAGILE* CREATURES.
PATHETIC.

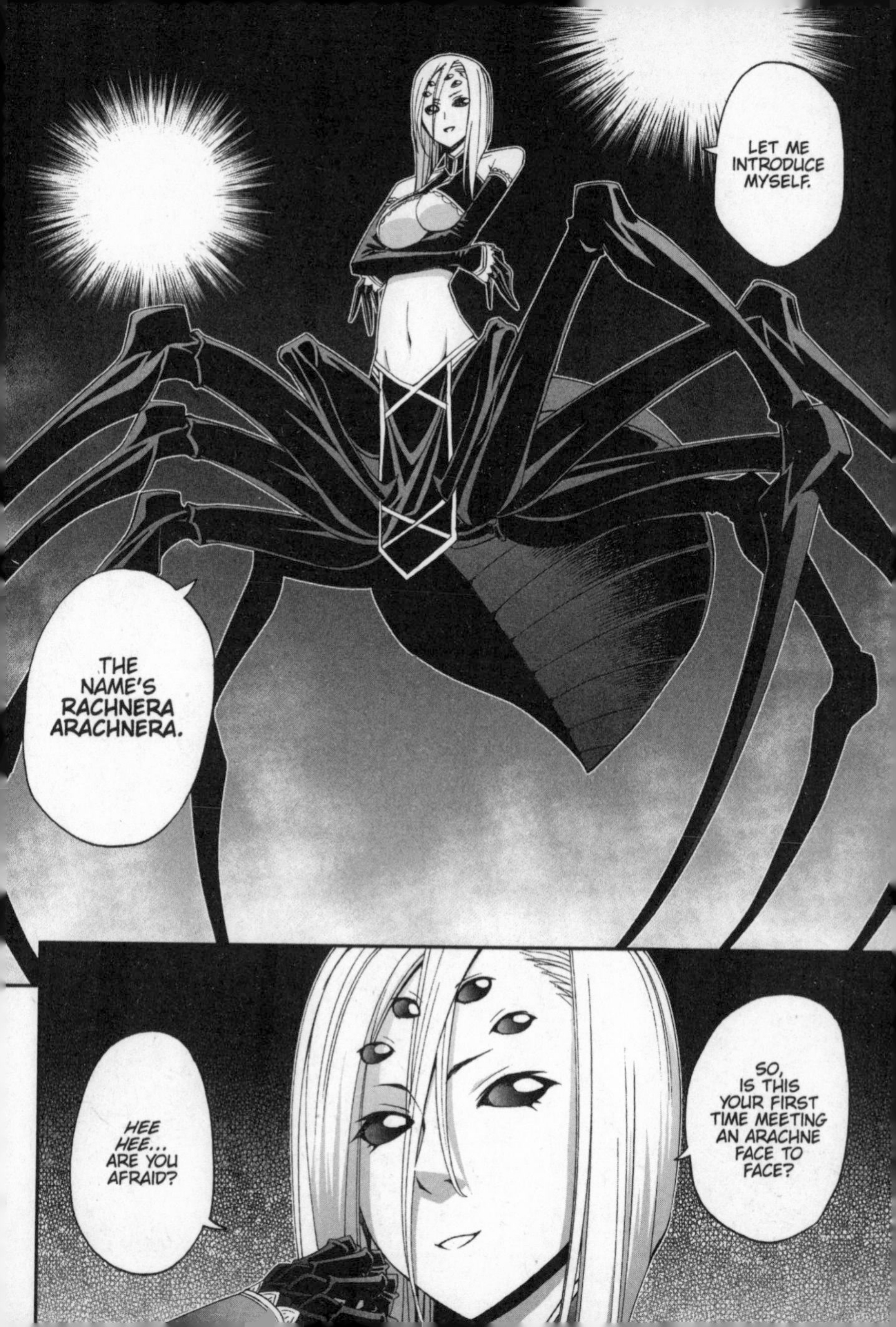
LET ME INTRODUCE MYSELF.
THE NAME'S RACHNERA ARACHNERA.
SO, IS THIS YOUR FIRST TIME MEETING AN ARACHNE FACE TO FACE?
HEE HEE... ARE YOU AFRAID?

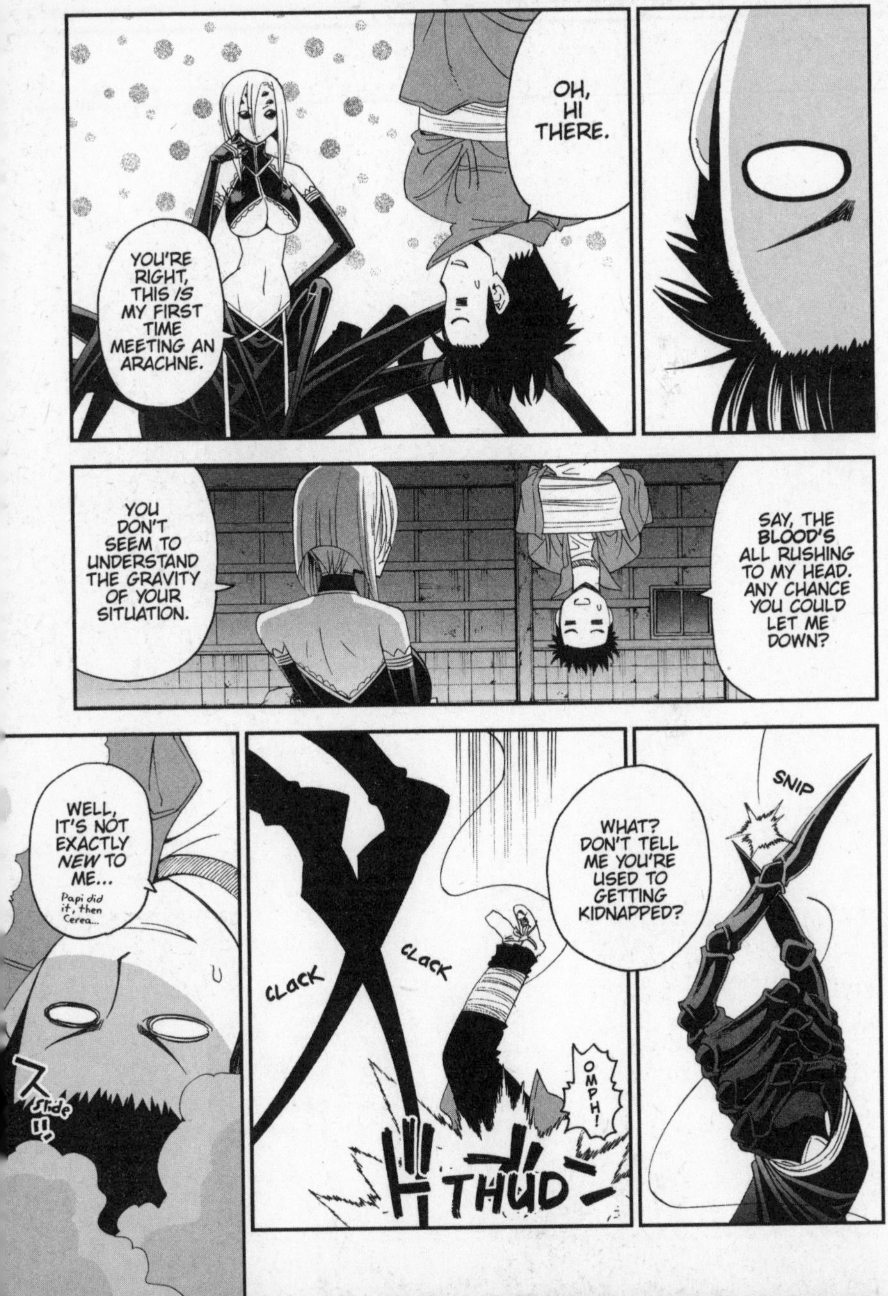
OH, HI THERE.
YOU'RE RIGHT, THIS *IS* MY FIRST TIME MEETING AN ARACHNE.
SAY, THE BLOOD'S ALL RUSHING TO MY HEAD. ANY CHANCE YOU COULD LET ME DOWN?
YOU DON'T SEEM TO UNDERSTAND THE GRAVITY OF YOUR SITUATION.
SNIP
WHAT? DON'T TELL ME YOU'RE USED TO GETTING KIDNAPPED?
CLACK
CLACK
OMPH!
THUD
WELL, IT'S NOT EXACTLY *NEW* TO ME...
Papi did it, then Cerea...
slide!!

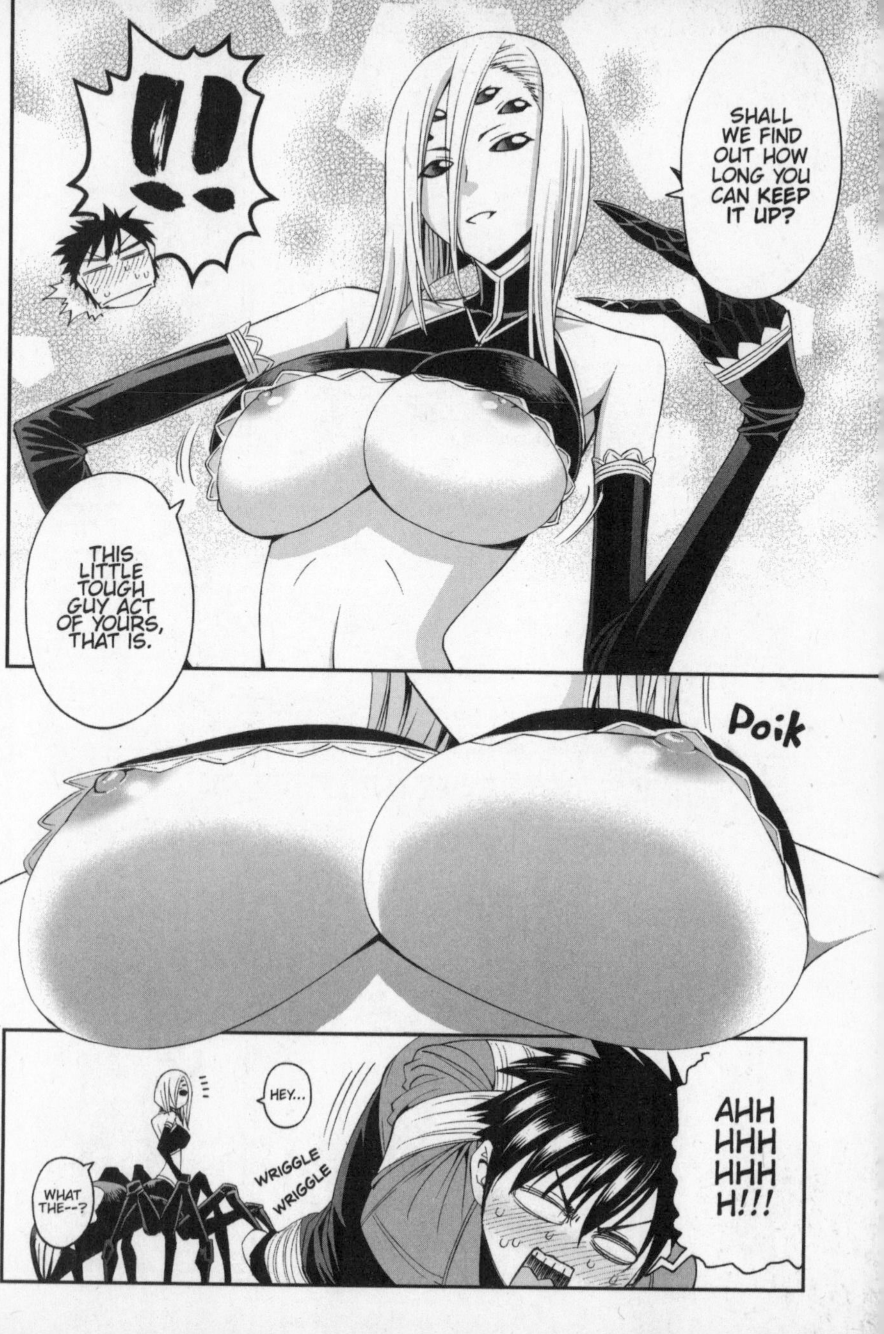
SHALL WE FIND OUT HOW LONG YOU CAN KEEP IT UP?
!!
THIS LITTLE TOUGH GUY ACT OF YOURS, THAT IS.
Poik
AHHHHHHHHHH!!!
WRIGGLE WRIGGLE
HEY...
WHAT THE--?

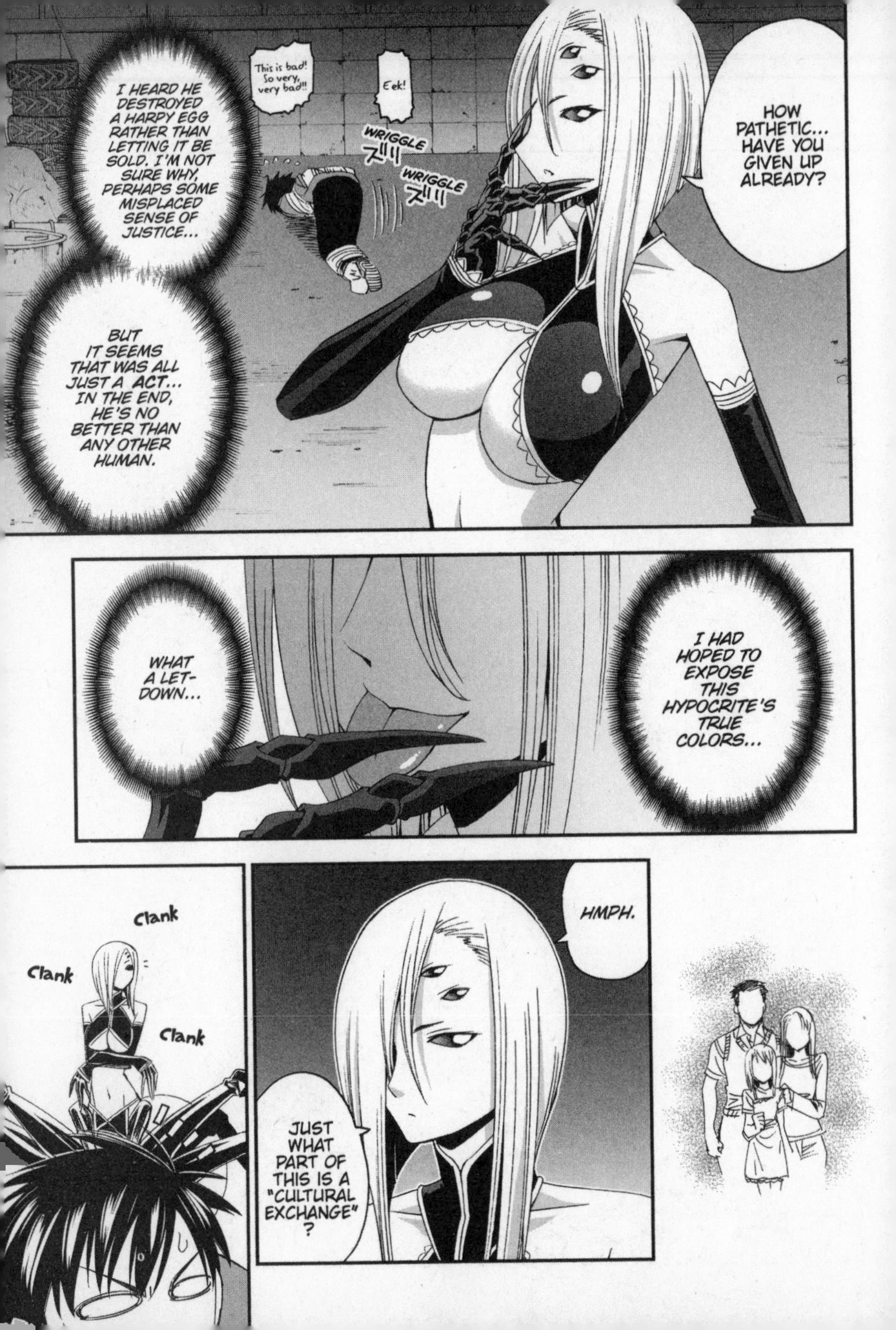
HOW PATHETIC... HAVE YOU GIVEN UP ALREADY?
Eek!
This is bad! So very, very bad!!
WRIGGLE
WRIGGLE
I HEARD HE DESTROYED A HARPY EGG RATHER THAN LETTING IT BE SOLD. I'M NOT SURE WHY, PERHAPS SOME MISPLACED SENSE OF JUSTICE...
BUT IT SEEMS THAT WAS ALL JUST A ACT... IN THE END, HE'S NO BETTER THAN ANY OTHER HUMAN.
I HAD HOPED TO EXPOSE THIS HYPOCRITE'S TRUE COLORS...
WHAT A LET-DOWN...
HMPH.
JUST WHAT PART OF THIS IS A "CULTURAL EXCHANGE"?
Clank
Clank
Clank

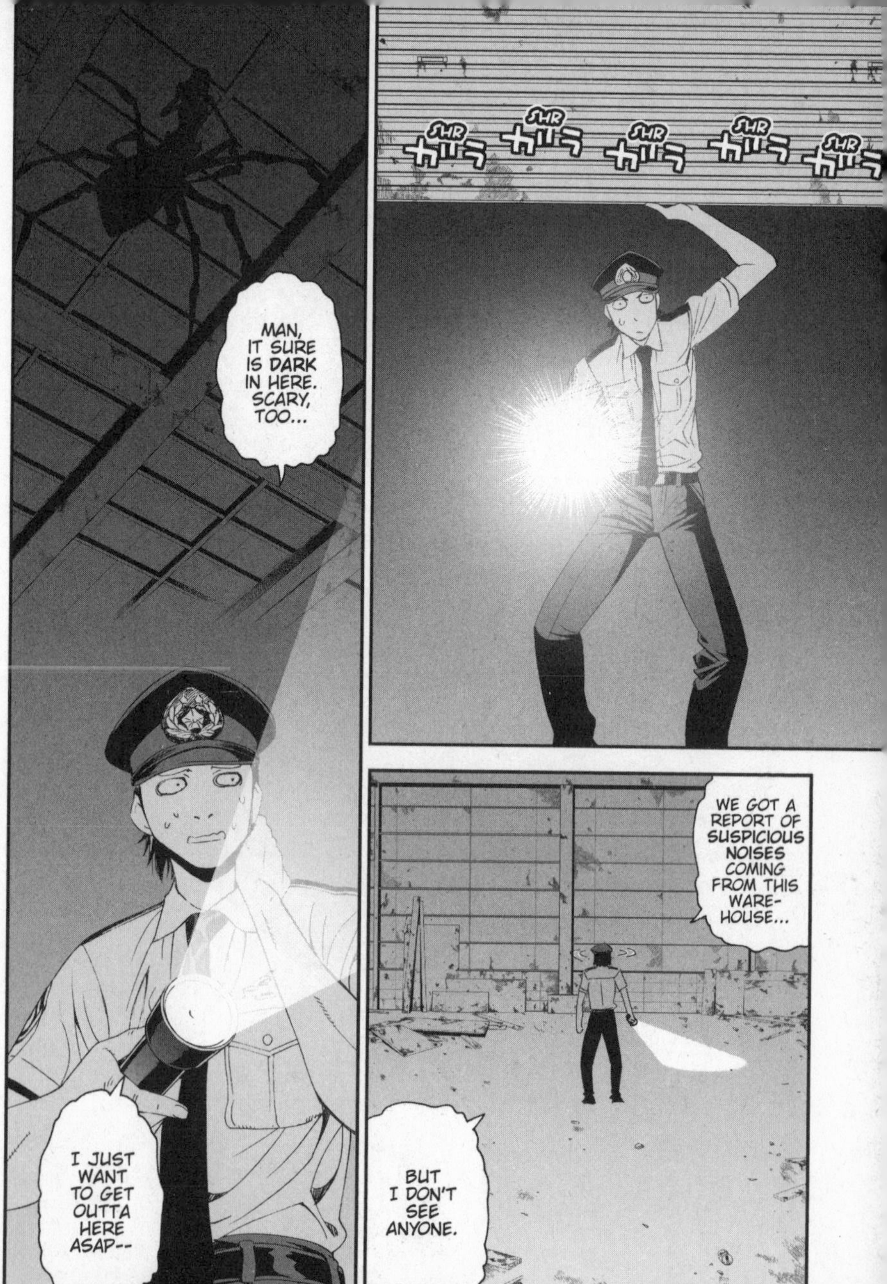
SHR ガラ
SHR ガラ
SHR ガラ
SHR ガラ
SHR ガラ
WE GOT A REPORT OF SUSPICIOUS NOISES COMING FROM THIS WARE-HOUSE...
BUT I DON'T SEE ANYONE.
MAN, IT SURE IS DARK IN HERE. SCARY, TOO...
I JUST WANT TO GET OUTTA HERE ASAP--

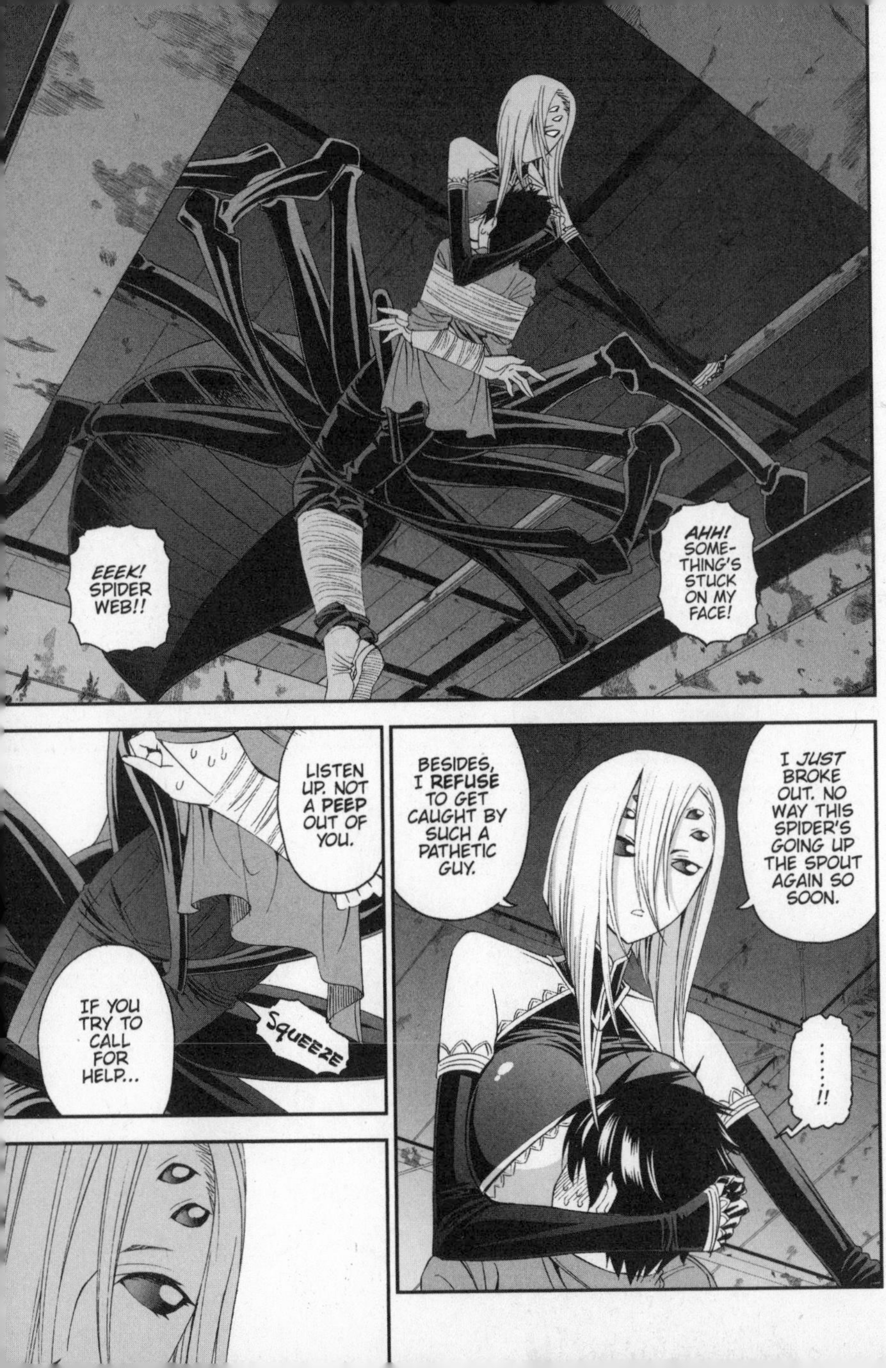
AHH! SOME-THING'S STUCK ON MY FACE!
EEEK! SPIDER WEB!!
I JUST BROKE OUT. NO WAY THIS SPIDER'S GOING UP THE SPOUT AGAIN SO SOON.
BESIDES, I REFUSE TO GET CAUGHT BY SUCH A PATHETIC GUY.
......!!
LISTEN UP. NOT A PEEP OUT OF YOU.
Squeeze
IF YOU TRY TO CALL FOR HELP...

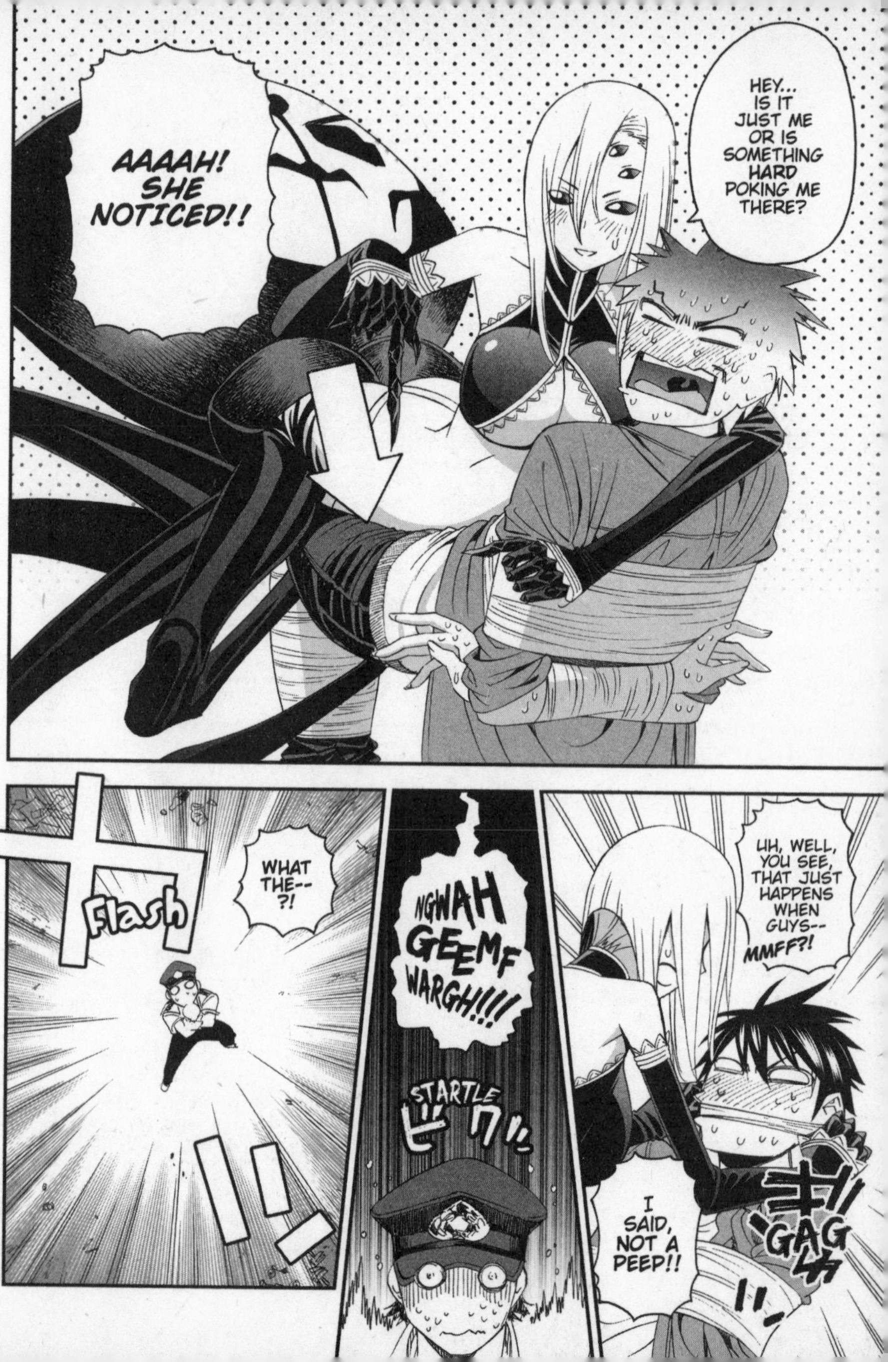
HEY... IS IT JUST ME OR IS SOMETHING HARD POKING ME THERE?
AAAAH! SHE NOTICED!!
UH, WELL, YOU SEE, THAT JUST HAPPENS WHEN GUYS-- MMFF?!
GAG
I SAID, NOT A PEEP!!
NGWAH GEEMF WARGH!!!!
STARTLE
WHAT THE-- ?!
Flash

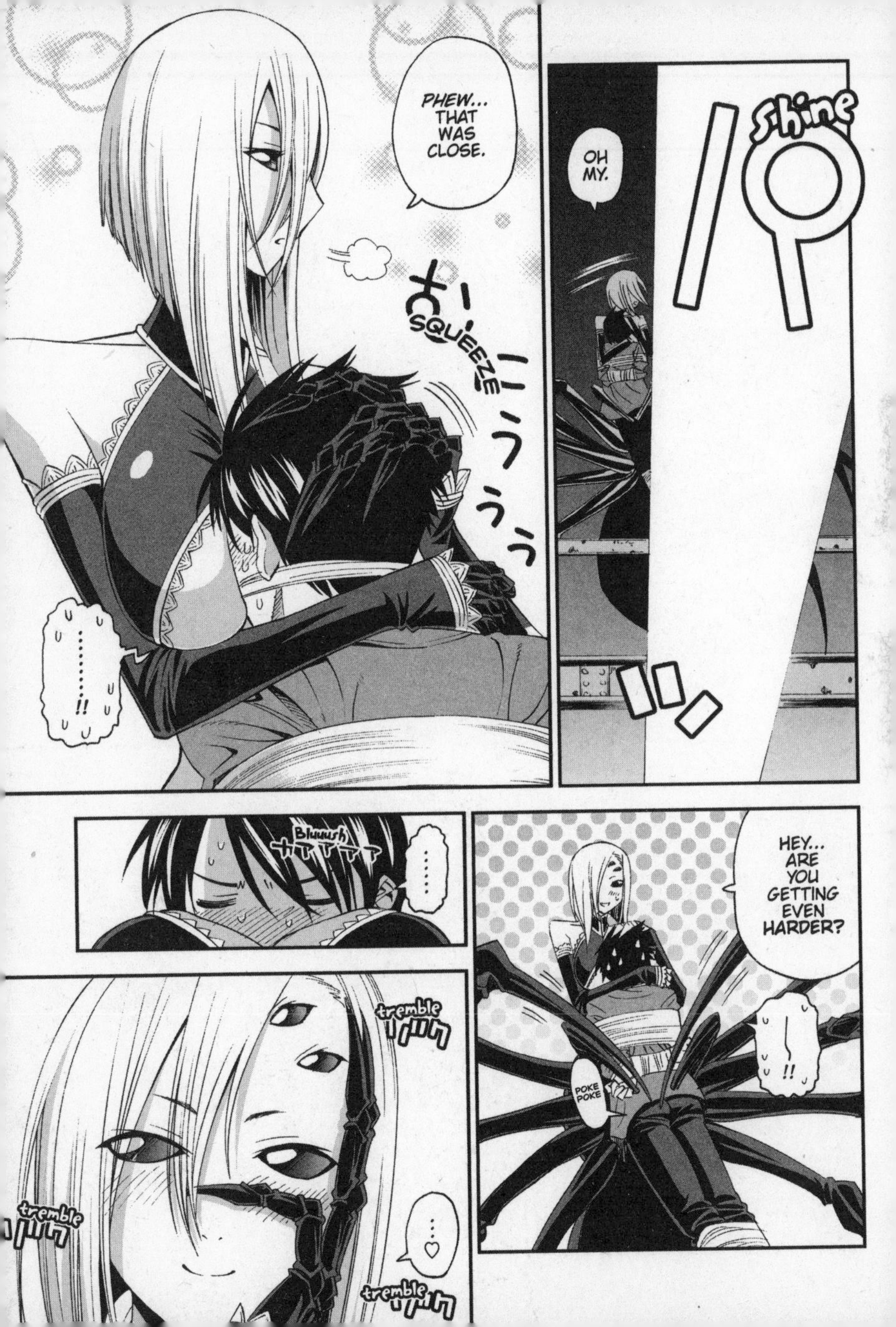

Shine
OH MY.
PHEW... THAT WAS CLOSE.
SQUEEZE
......!!
HEY... ARE YOU GETTING EVEN HARDER?
......!!
POKE POKE
Bluuush
......
tremble
tremble
tremble
...♡

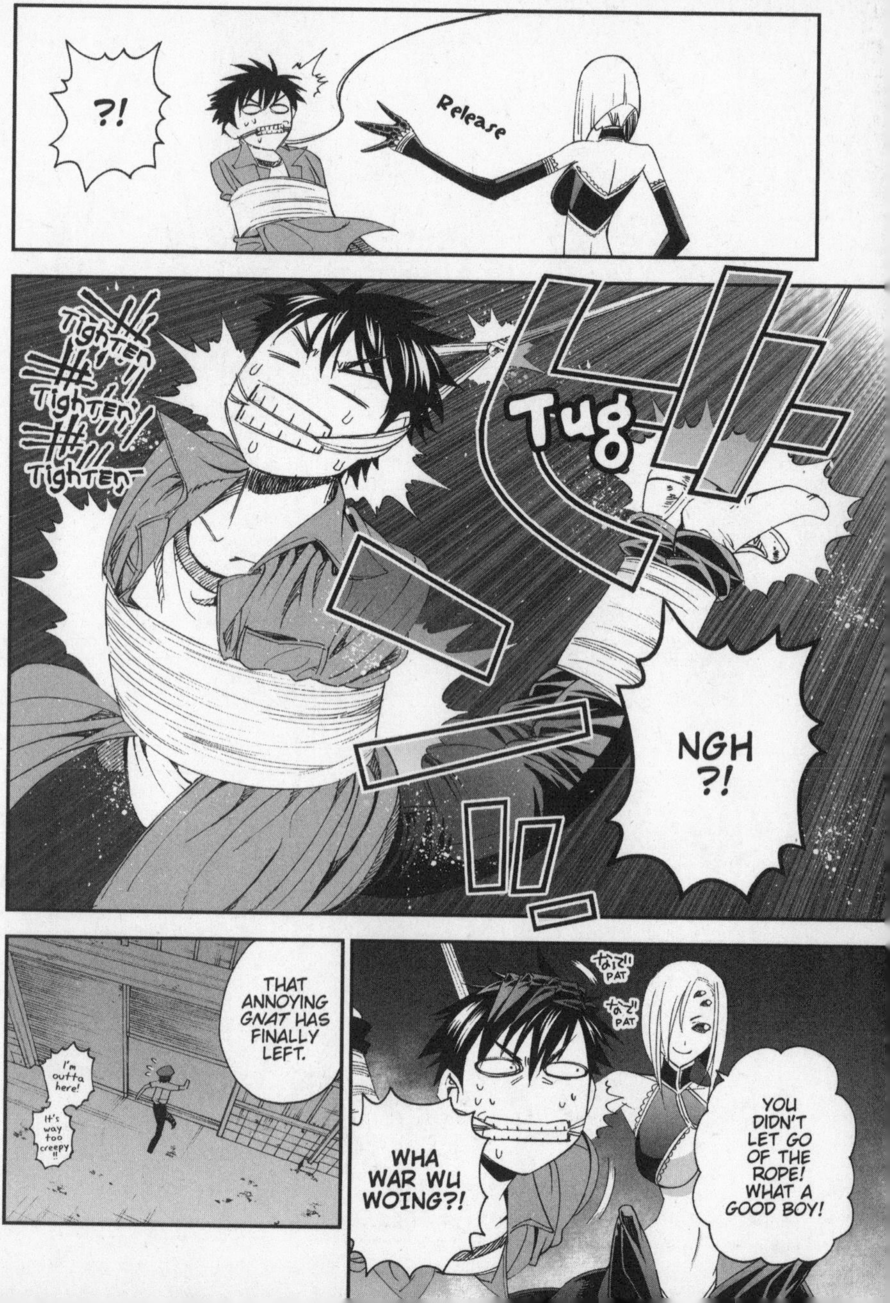
Release
?!
Tug
Tighten
Tighten
Tighten
NGH ?!
なで PAT
なで PAT
YOU DIDN'T LET GO OF THE ROPE! WHAT A GOOD BOY!
WHA WAR WU WOING?!
THAT ANNOYING GNAT HAS FINALLY LEFT.
I'm outta here!
It's way too creepy!!

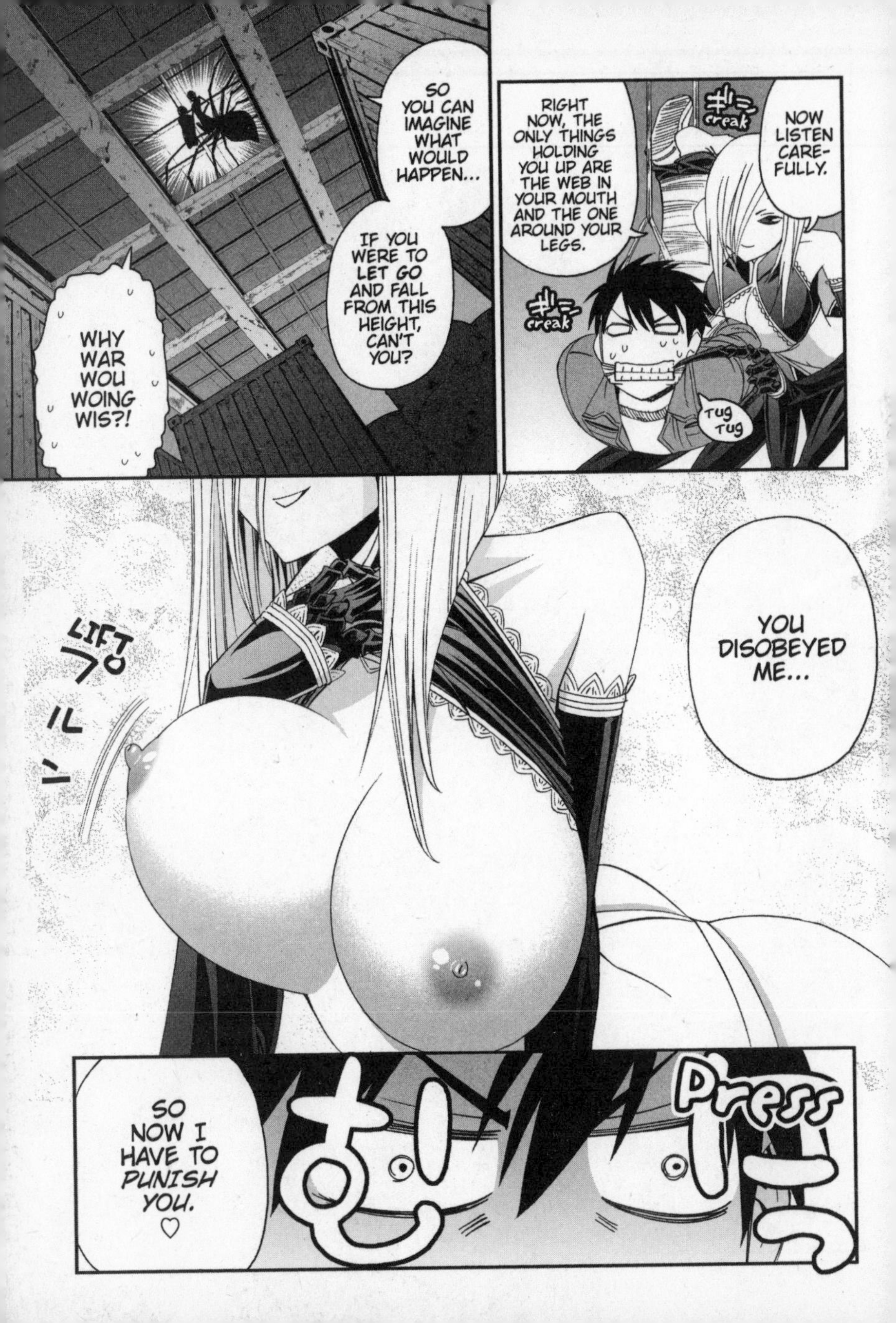
NOW LISTEN CARE-FULLY.
creak
RIGHT NOW, THE ONLY THINGS HOLDING YOU UP ARE THE WEB IN YOUR MOUTH AND THE ONE AROUND YOUR LEGS.
creak
Tug Tug
SO YOU CAN IMAGINE WHAT WOULD HAPPEN...
IF YOU WERE TO LET GO AND FALL FROM THIS HEIGHT, CAN'T YOU?
WHY WAR WOU WOING WIS?!
YOU DISOBEYED ME...
LIFT
SO NOW I HAVE TO PUNISH YOU. ♡
Press

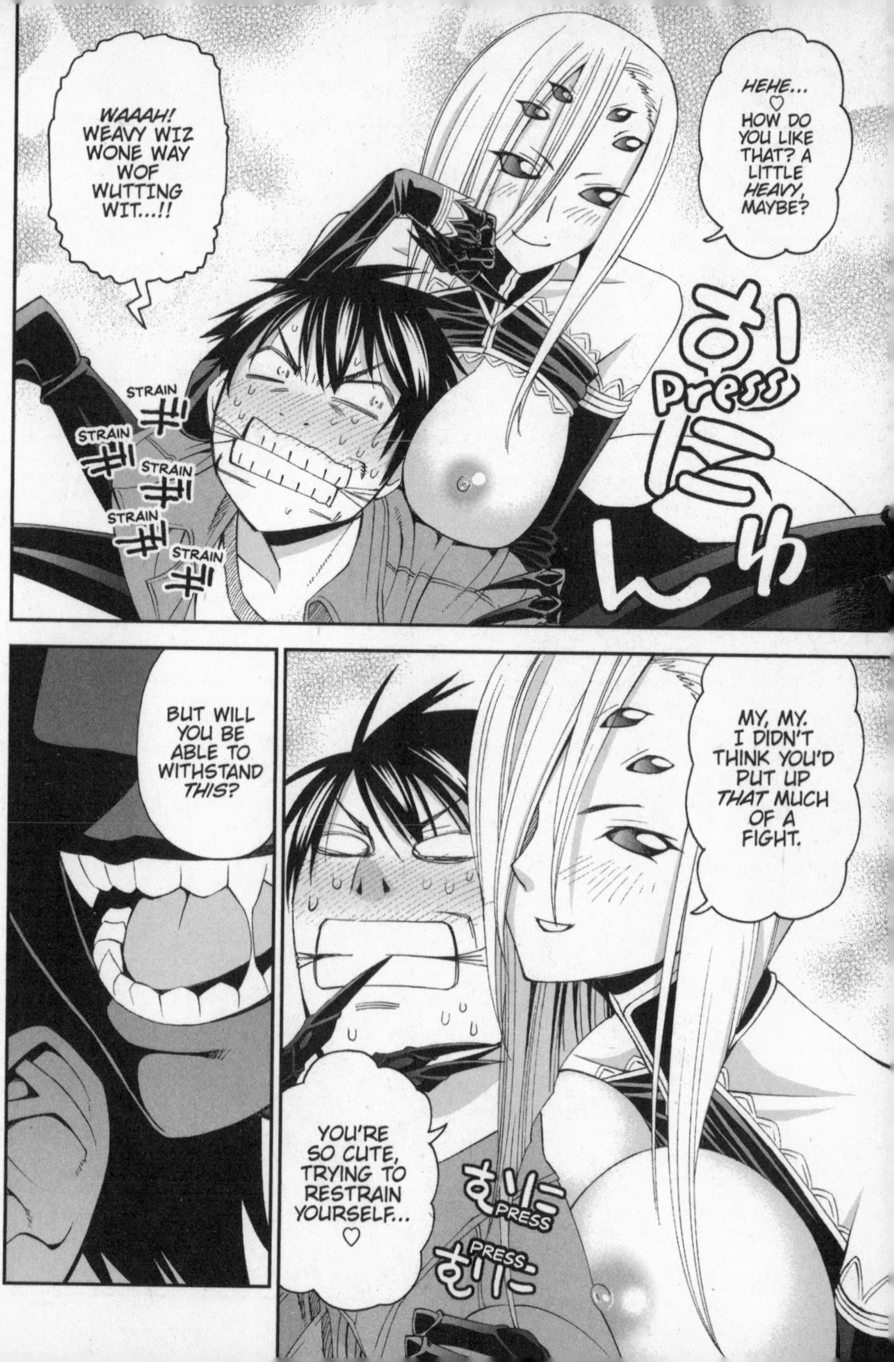
HEHE... ♡ HOW DO YOU LIKE THAT? A LITTLE *HEAVY*, MAYBE?
PRESS
WAAAH! WEAVY WIZ WONE WAY WOF WUTTING WIT...!!
STRAIN
STRAIN
STRAIN
STRAIN
STRAIN
MY, MY. I DIDN'T THINK YOU'D PUT UP *THAT* MUCH OF A FIGHT.
YOU'RE SO CUTE, TRYING TO RESTRAIN YOURSELF... ♡
PRESS
PRESS
BUT WILL YOU BE ABLE TO WITHSTAND *THIS?*

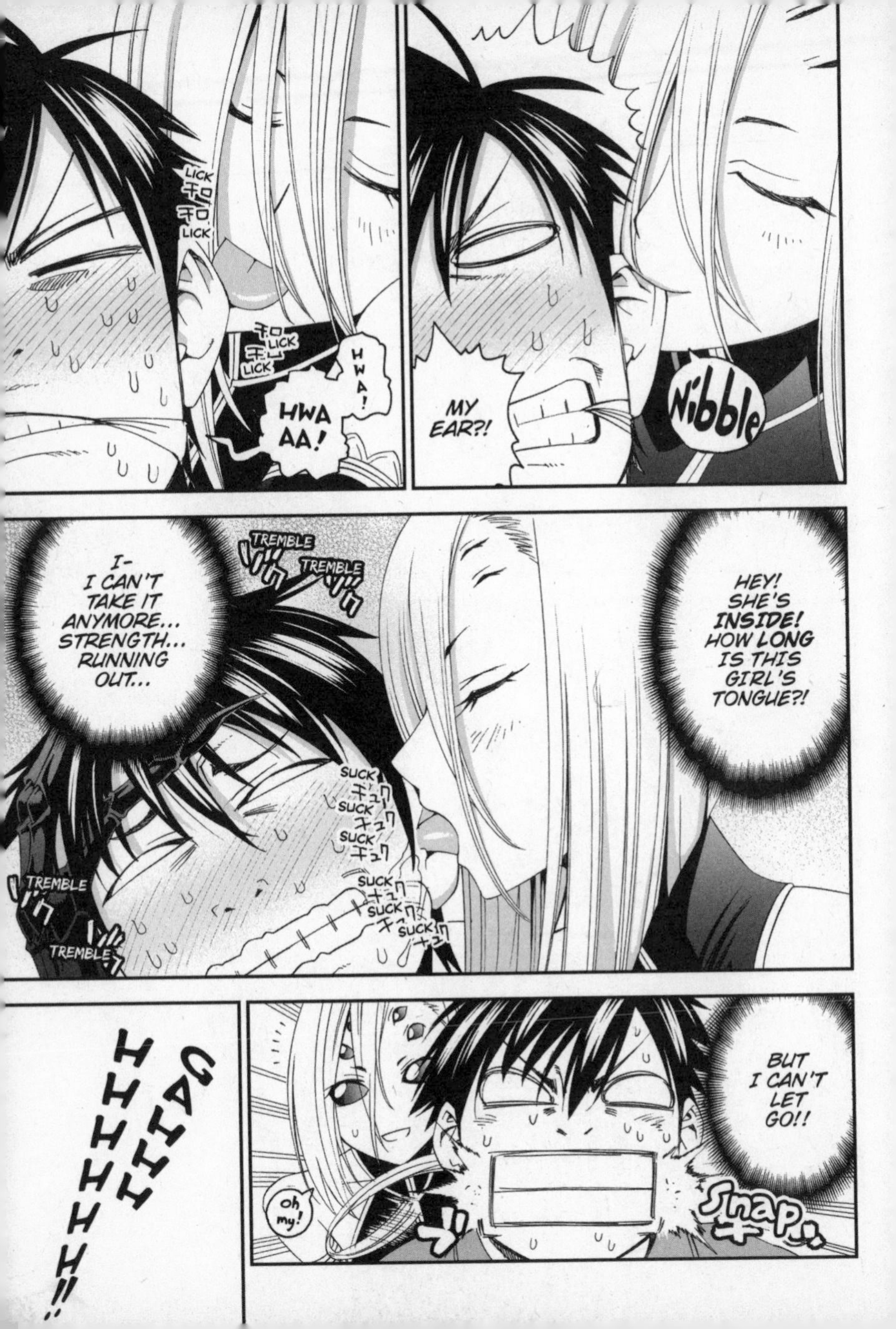
Nibble
MY EAR?!
LICK
LICK
LICK
LICK
HWA!
HWA AA!
HEY! SHE'S INSIDE! HOW LONG IS THIS GIRL'S TONGUE?!
TREMBLE
TREMBLE
I- I CAN'T TAKE IT ANYMORE... STRENGTH... RUNNING OUT...
SUCK
SUCK
SUCK
SUCK
SUCK
SUCK
TREMBLE
TREMBLE
BUT I CAN'T LET GO!!
Snap.
oh my!
GAHHHHHHHHHHHHHH!!

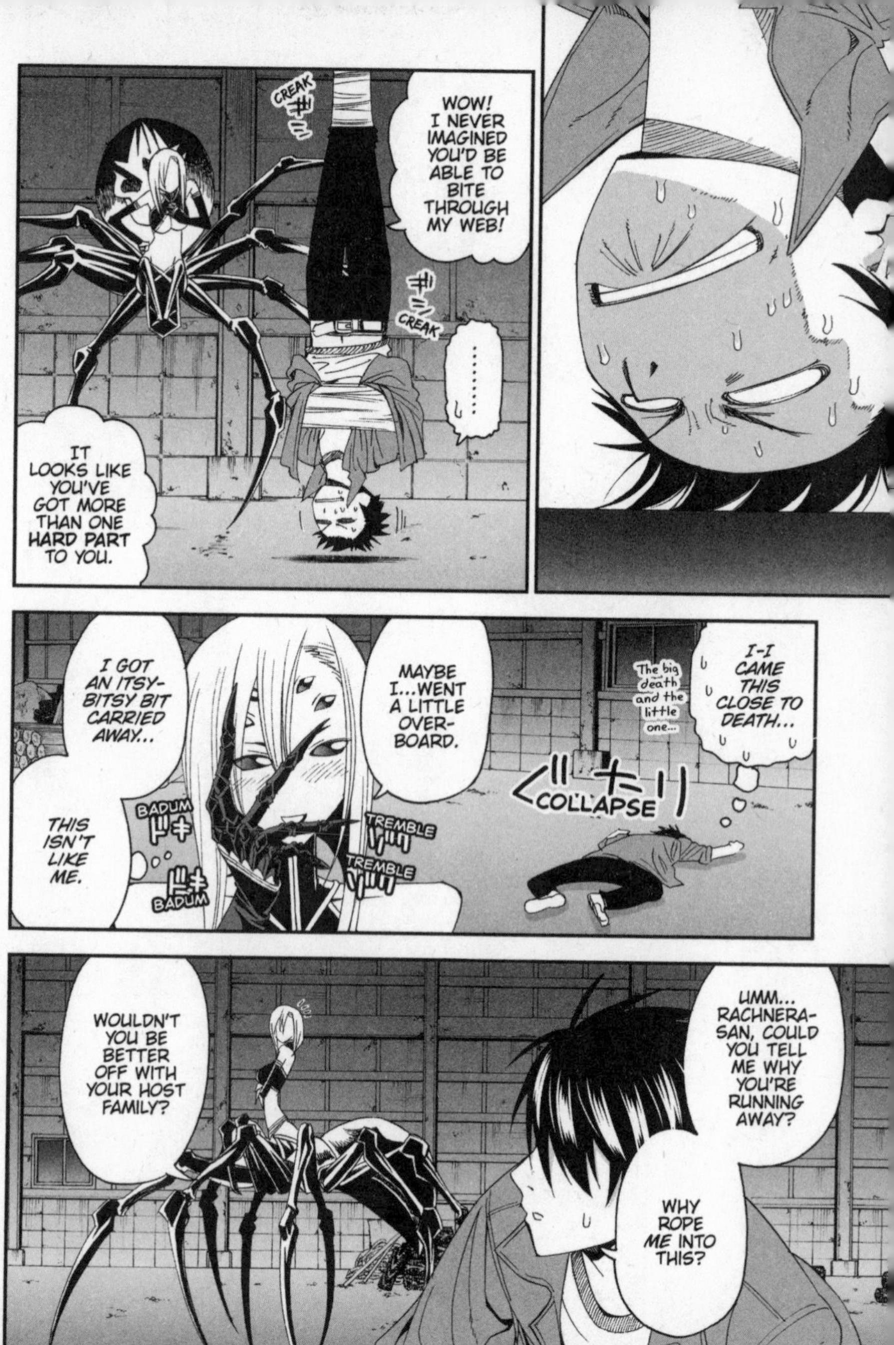
WOW! I NEVER IMAGINED YOU'D BE ABLE TO BITE THROUGH MY WEB!
CREAK
......
CREAK
IT LOOKS LIKE YOU'VE GOT MORE THAN ONE HARD PART TO YOU.
I-I CAME THIS CLOSE TO DEATH...
The big death and the little one...
COLLAPSE
MAYBE I...WENT A LITTLE OVER-BOARD.
I GOT AN ITSY-BITSY BIT CARRIED AWAY...
TREMBLE
TREMBLE
BADUM
BADUM
THIS ISN'T LIKE ME.
UMM... RACHNERA-SAN, COULD YOU TELL ME WHY YOU'RE RUNNING AWAY?
WHY ROPE ME INTO THIS?
WOULDN'T YOU BE BETTER OFF WITH YOUR HOST FAMILY?

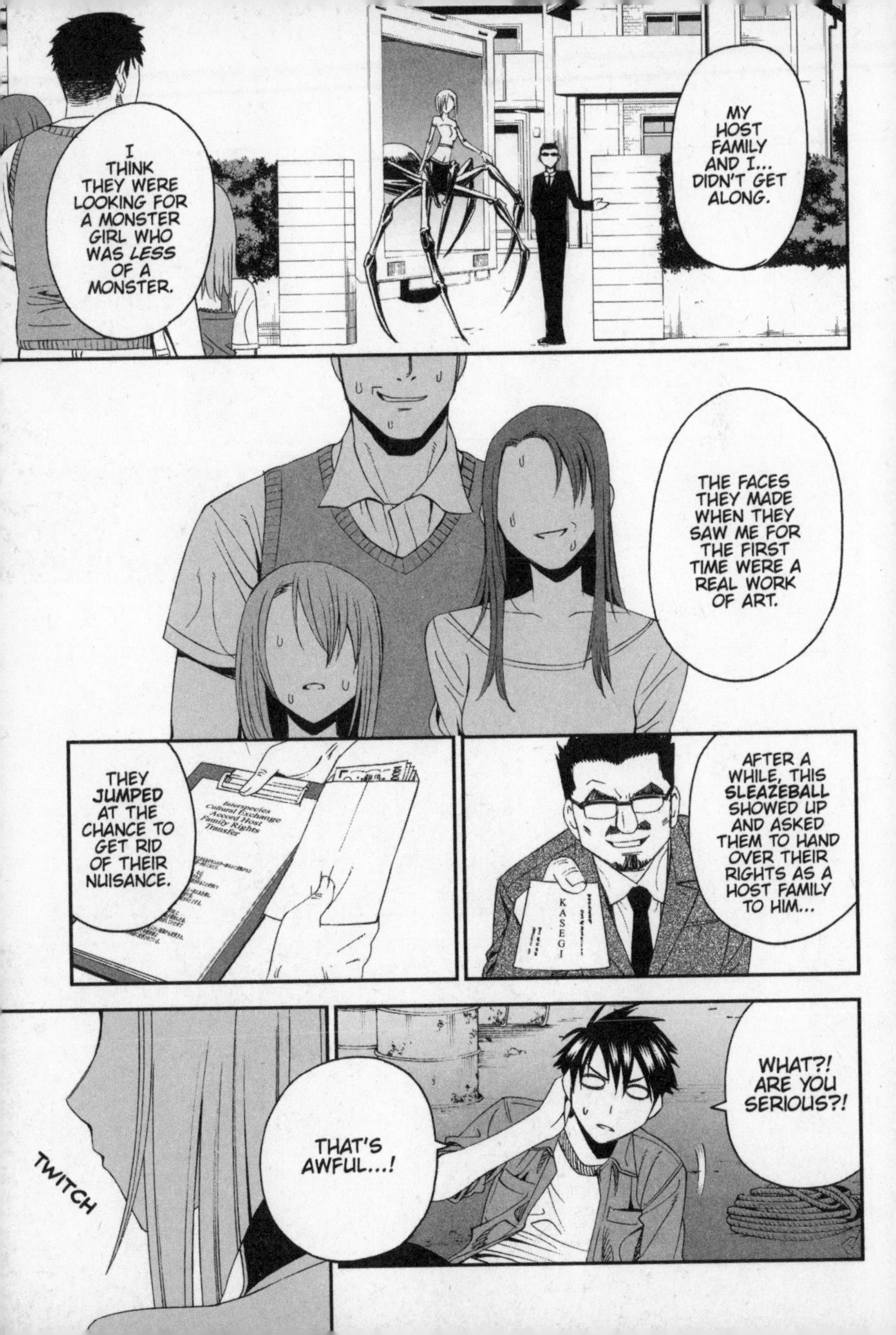
MY HOST FAMILY AND I... DIDN'T GET ALONG.
I THINK THEY WERE LOOKING FOR A MONSTER GIRL WHO WAS *LESS* OF A MONSTER.
THE FACES THEY MADE WHEN THEY SAW ME FOR THE FIRST TIME WERE A REAL WORK OF ART.
AFTER A WHILE, THIS SLEAZEBALL SHOWED UP AND ASKED THEM TO HAND OVER THEIR RIGHTS AS A HOST FAMILY TO HIM...
KASEGI
Interspecies Cultural Exchange Accord Host Family Rights Transfer
THEY JUMPED AT THE CHANCE TO GET RID OF THEIR NUISANCE.
WHAT?! ARE YOU SERIOUS?!
THAT'S AWFUL...!
TWITCH

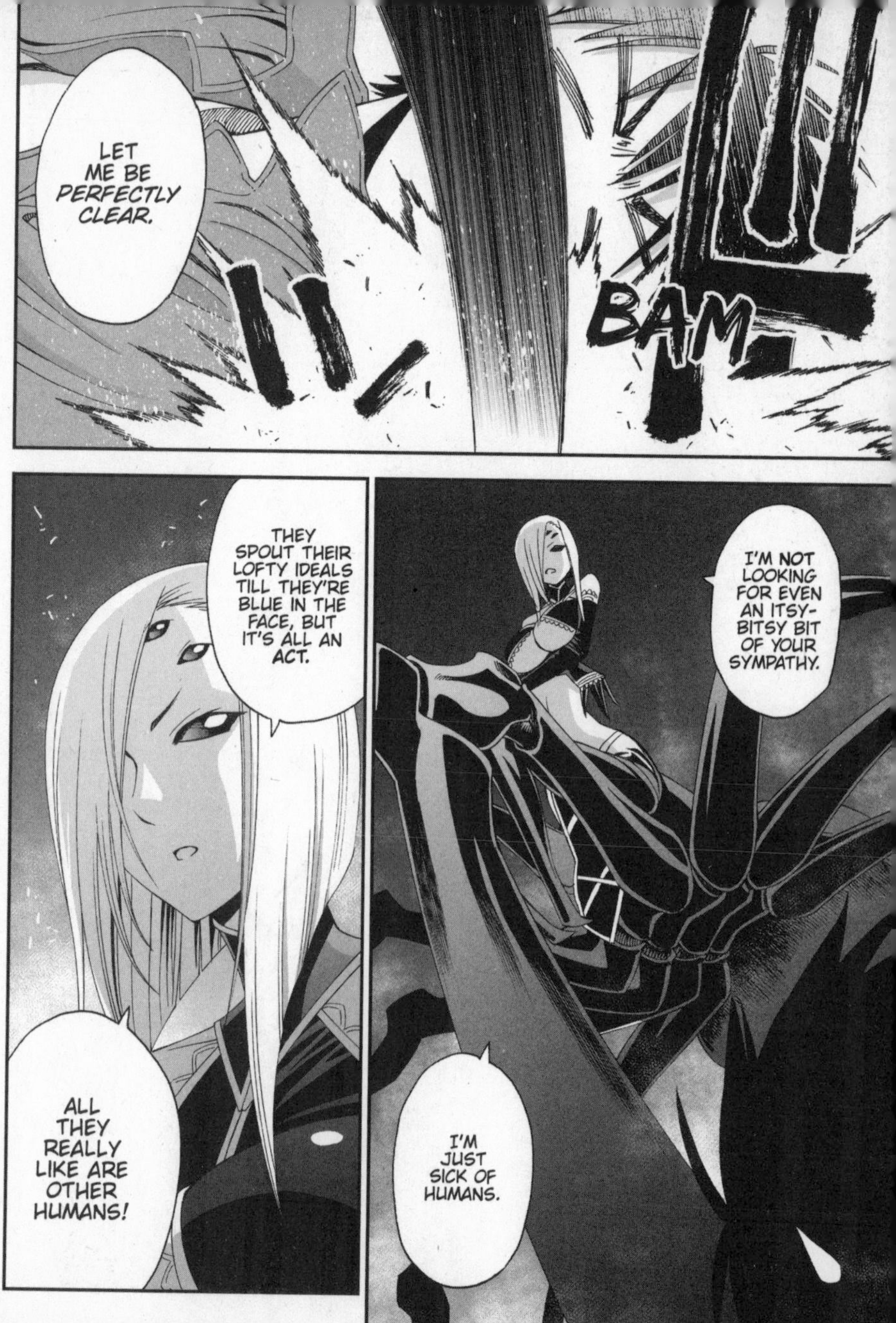
BAM
LET ME BE PERFECTLY CLEAR.
I'M NOT LOOKING FOR EVEN AN ITSY-BITSY BIT OF YOUR SYMPATHY.
I'M JUST SICK OF HUMANS.
THEY SPOUT THEIR LOFTY IDEALS TILL THEY'RE BLUE IN THE FACE, BUT IT'S ALL AN ACT.
ALL THEY REALLY LIKE ARE OTHER HUMANS!

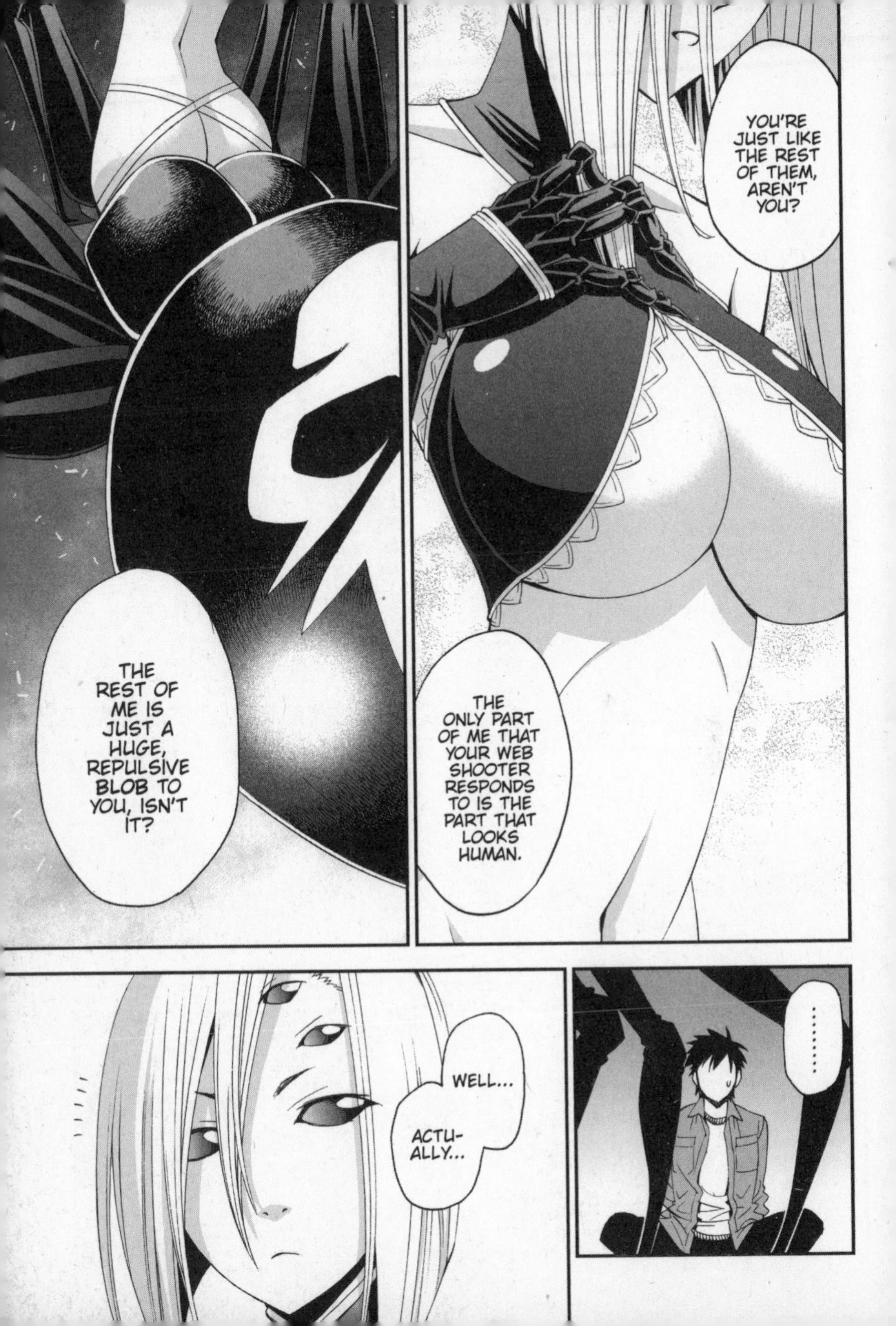
YOU'RE JUST LIKE THE REST OF THEM, AREN'T YOU?
THE ONLY PART OF ME THAT YOUR WEB SHOOTER RESPONDS TO IS THE PART THAT LOOKS HUMAN.
THE REST OF ME IS JUST A HUGE, REPULSIVE BLOB TO YOU, ISN'T IT?
......
WELL...
ACTU-ALLY...

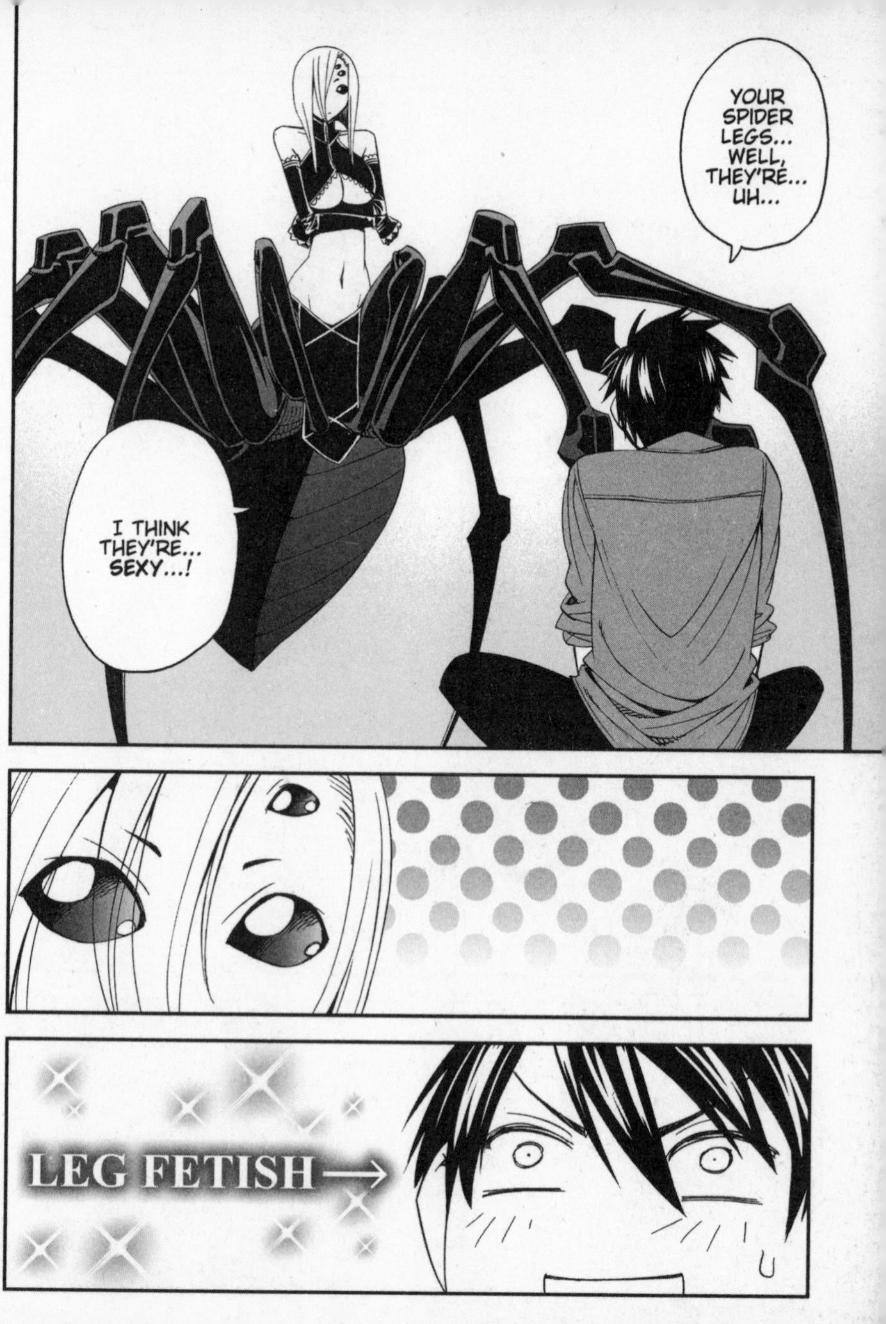
YOUR SPIDER LEGS... WELL, THEY'RE... UH...
I THINK THEY'RE... SEXY...!
LEG FETISH →

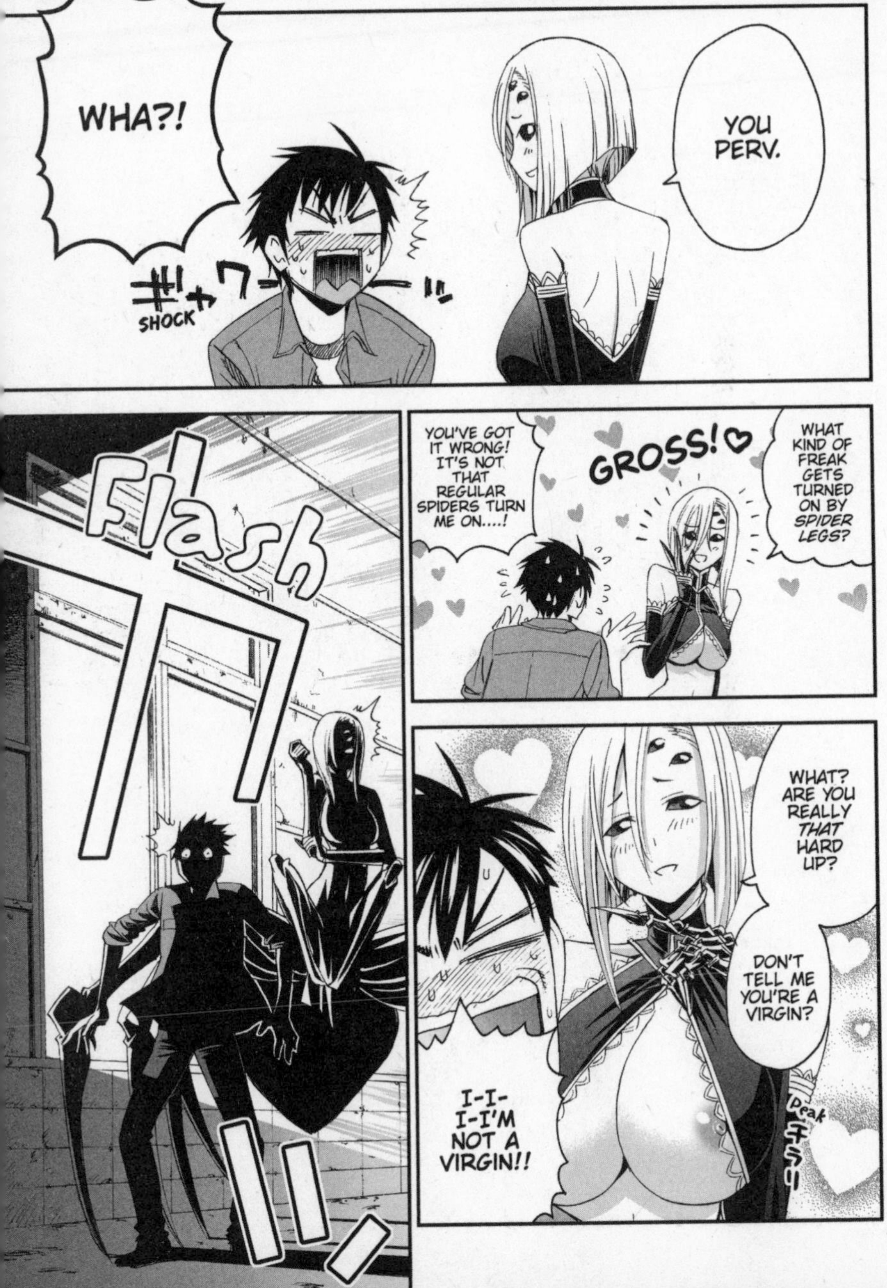
YOU PERV.
WHA?!
SHOCK
WHAT KIND OF FREAK GETS TURNED ON BY *SPIDER LEGS*?
GROSS!♡
YOU'VE GOT IT WRONG! IT'S NOT THAT REGULAR SPIDERS TURN ME ON....!
WHAT? ARE YOU REALLY *THAT* HARD UP?
DON'T TELL ME YOU'RE A VIRGIN?
Peak
I-I-I-I'M NOT A VIRGIN!!
Flash

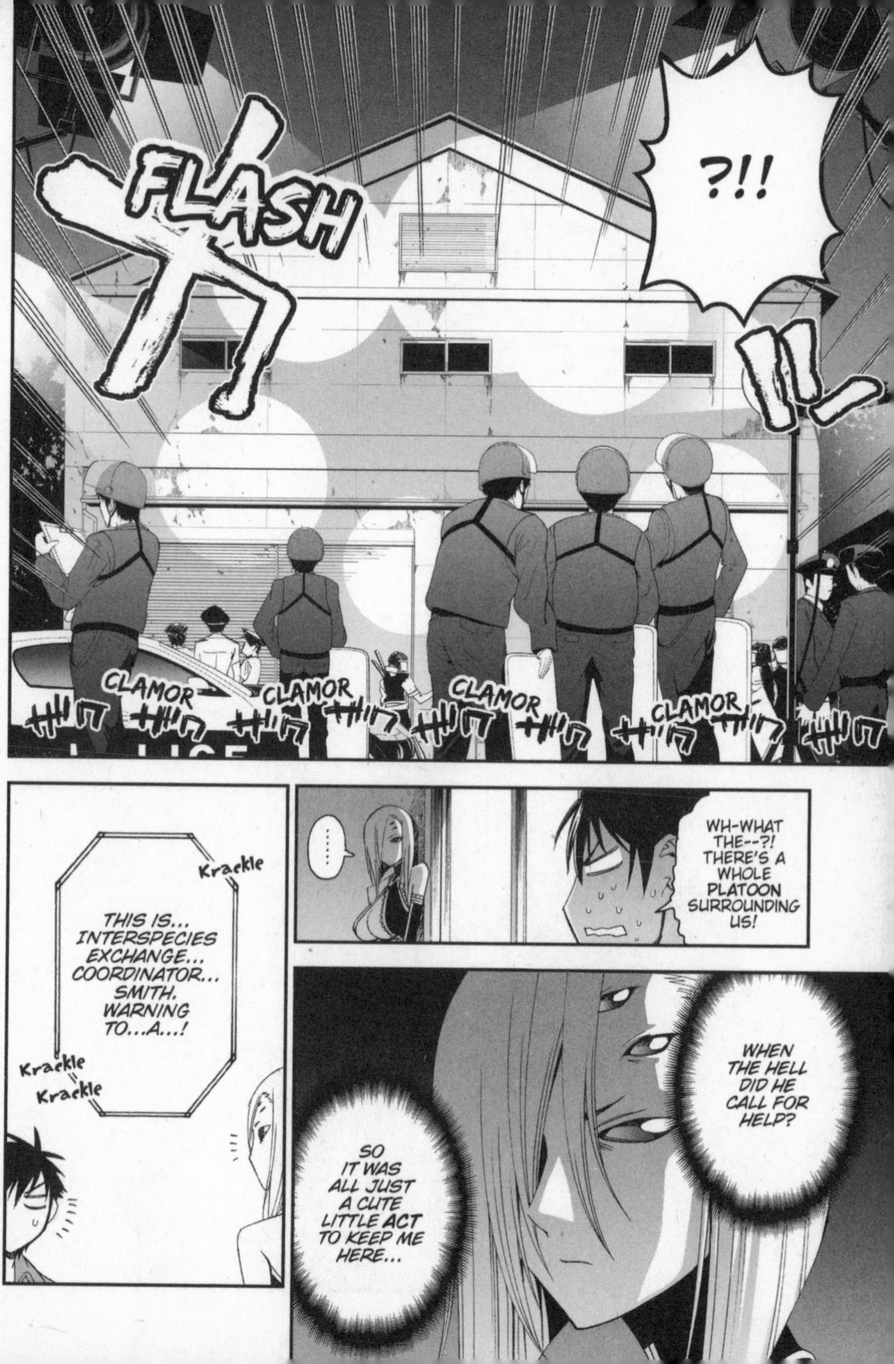
?!!
FLASH
CLAMOR
CLAMOR
CLAMOR
CLAMOR
WH-WHAT THE--?! THERE'S A WHOLE PLATOON SURROUNDING US!
......
WHEN THE HELL DID HE CALL FOR HELP?
SO IT WAS ALL JUST A CUTE LITTLE ACT TO KEEP ME HERE...
Krackle
THIS IS... INTERSPECIES EXCHANGE... COORDINATOR... SMITH. WARNING TO...A...!
Krackle
Krackle

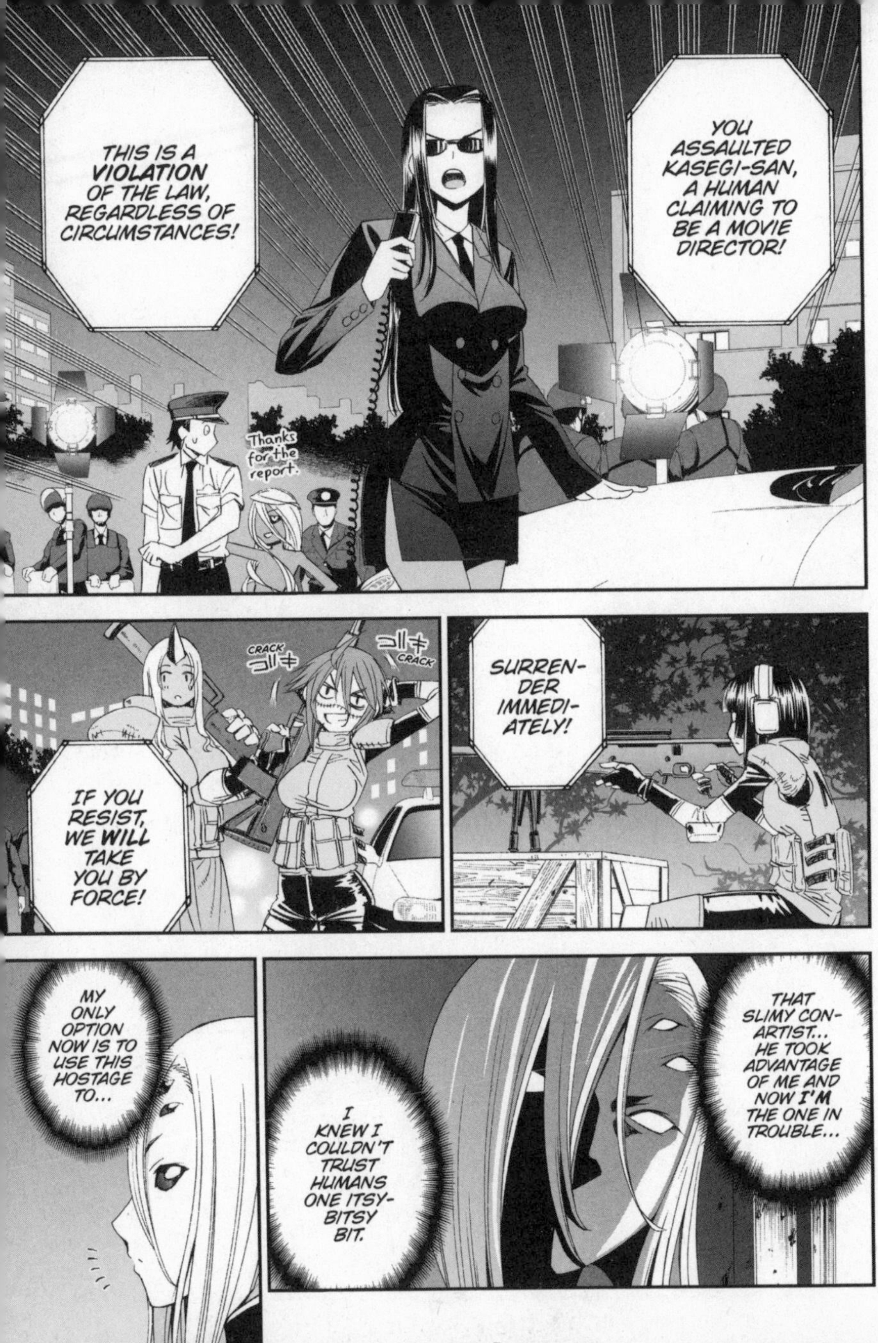
YOU ASSAULTED KASEGI-SAN, A HUMAN CLAIMING TO BE A MOVIE DIRECTOR!
THIS IS A VIOLATION OF THE LAW, REGARDLESS OF CIRCUMSTANCES!
Thanks for the report.
SURREN-DER IMMEDI-ATELY!
CRACK
CRACK
IF YOU RESIST, WE WILL TAKE YOU BY FORCE!
THAT SLIMY CON-ARTIST... HE TOOK ADVANTAGE OF ME AND NOW I'M THE ONE IN TROUBLE...
I KNEW I COULDN'T TRUST HUMANS ONE ITSY-BITSY BIT.
MY ONLY OPTION NOW IS TO USE THIS HOSTAGE TO...

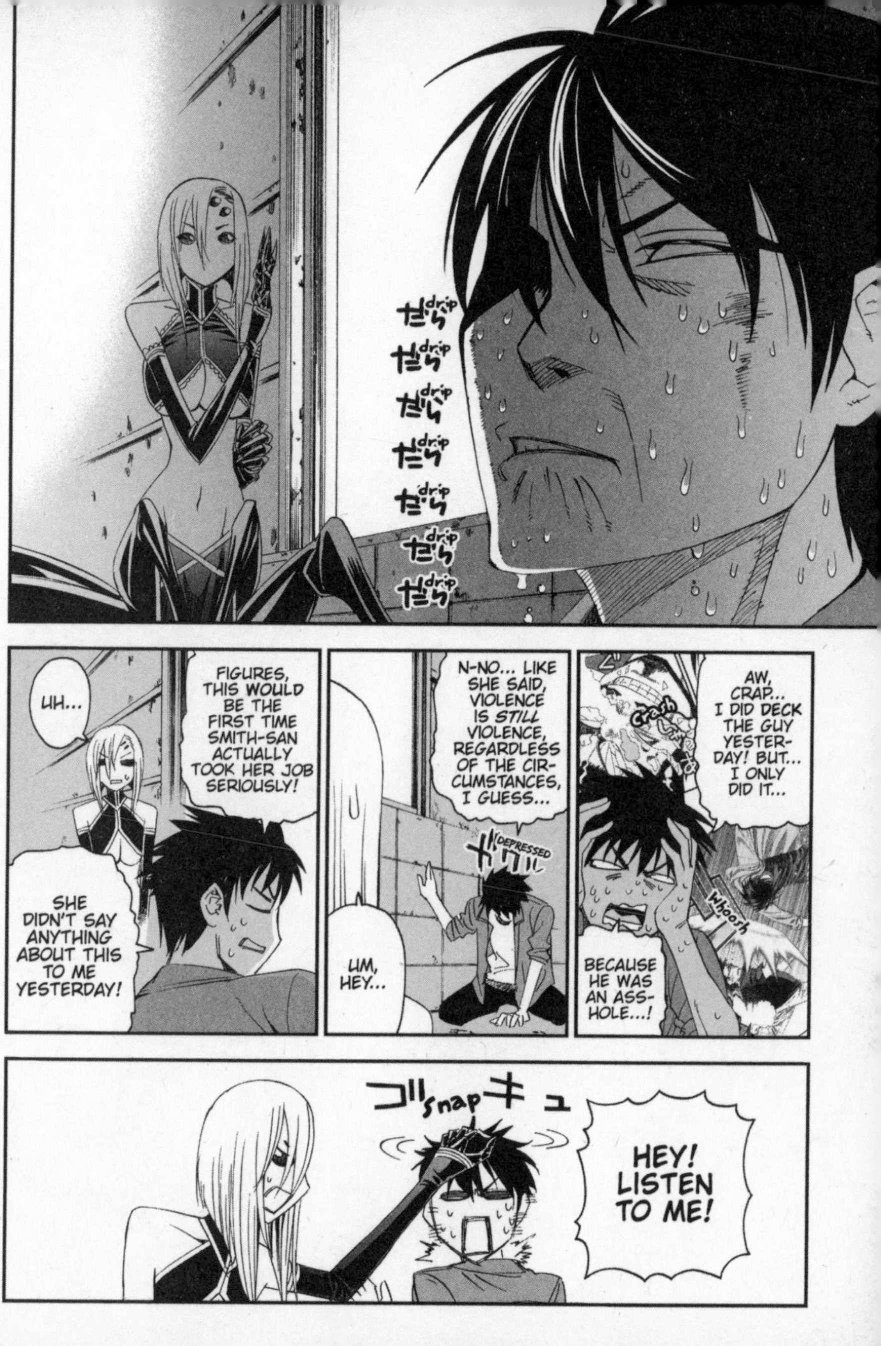

だら drip
だら drip
だら drip
だら drip
だら drip
だら drip
だら drip
AW, CRAP... I DID DECK THE GUY YESTERDAY! BUT... I ONLY DID IT...
Crash
whoosh
BECAUSE HE WAS AN ASSHOLE...!
N-NO... LIKE SHE SAID, VIOLENCE IS STILL VIOLENCE, REGARDLESS OF THE CIRCUMSTANCES, I GUESS...
DEPRESSED
UM, HEY...
FIGURES, THIS WOULD BE THE FIRST TIME SMITH-SAN ACTUALLY TOOK HER JOB SERIOUSLY!
UH...
SHE DIDN'T SAY ANYTHING ABOUT THIS TO ME YESTERDAY!
snap
HEY! LISTEN TO ME!

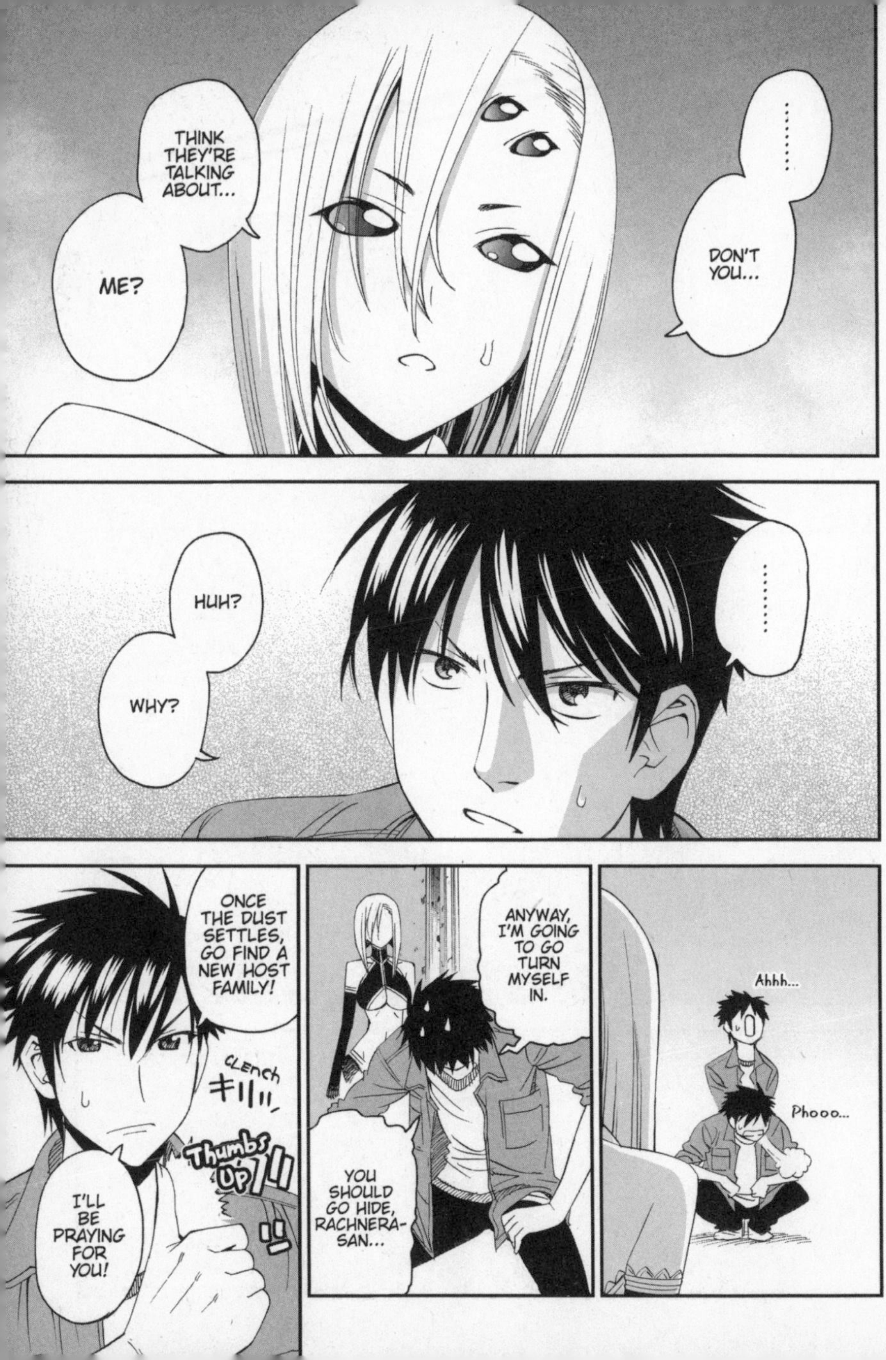
......
DON'T YOU...
THINK THEY'RE TALKING ABOUT...
ME?
......
HUH?
WHY?
Ahhh...
Phooo...
ANYWAY, I'M GOING TO GO TURN MYSELF IN.
YOU SHOULD GO HIDE, RACHNERA-SAN...
ONCE THE DUST SETTLES, GO FIND A NEW HOST FAMILY!
CLENCH
キリッ
Thumbs Up
I'LL BE PRAYING FOR YOU!

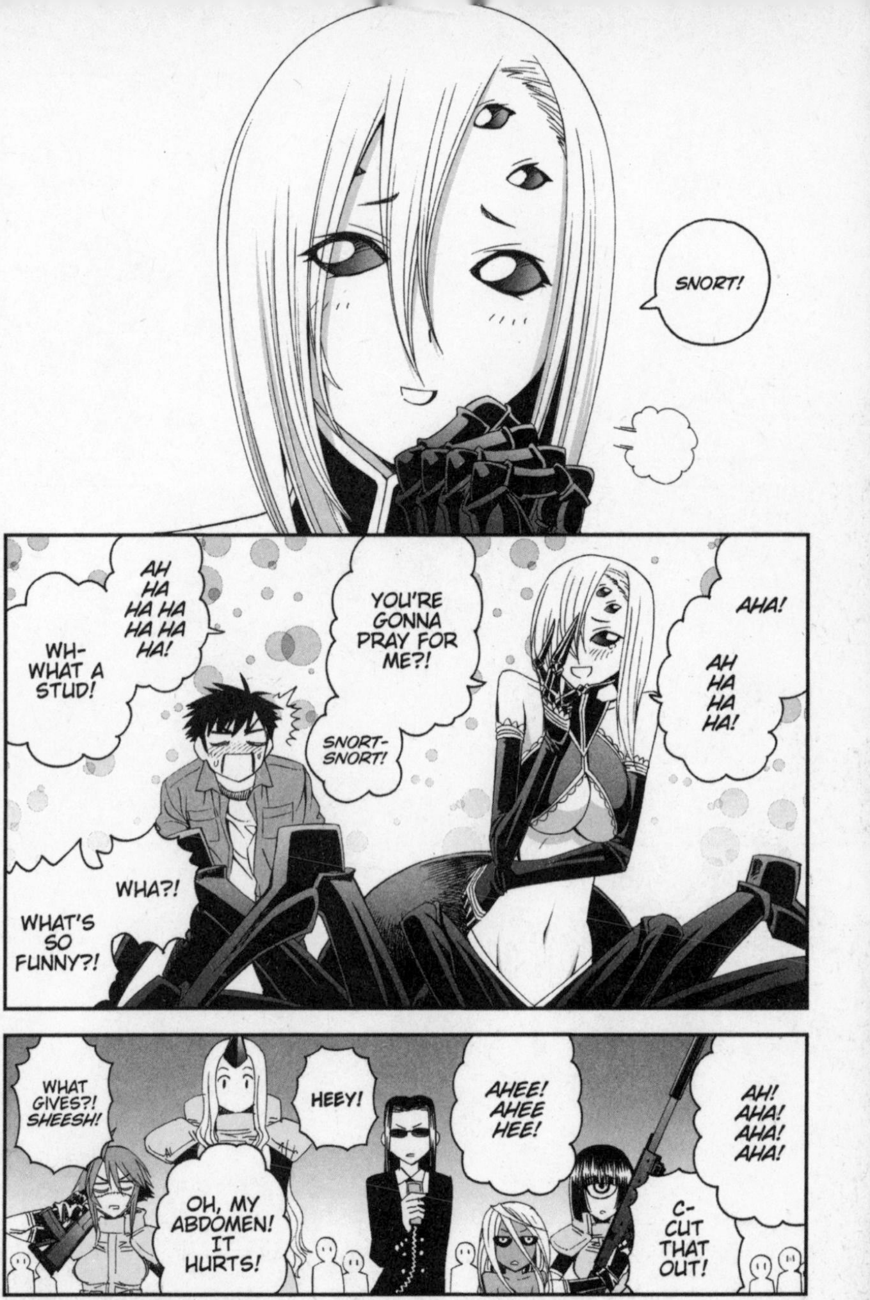
SNORT!
AHA!
AH HA HA HA!
YOU'RE GONNA PRAY FOR ME?!
SNORT-SNORT!
AH HA HA HA HA HA HA!
WH- WHAT A STUD!
WHA?!
WHAT'S SO FUNNY?!
AH! AHA! AHA! AHA!
AHEE! AHEE HEE!
C-CUT THAT OUT!
HEEY!
WHAT GIVES?! SHEESH!
OH, MY ABDOMEN! IT HURTS!

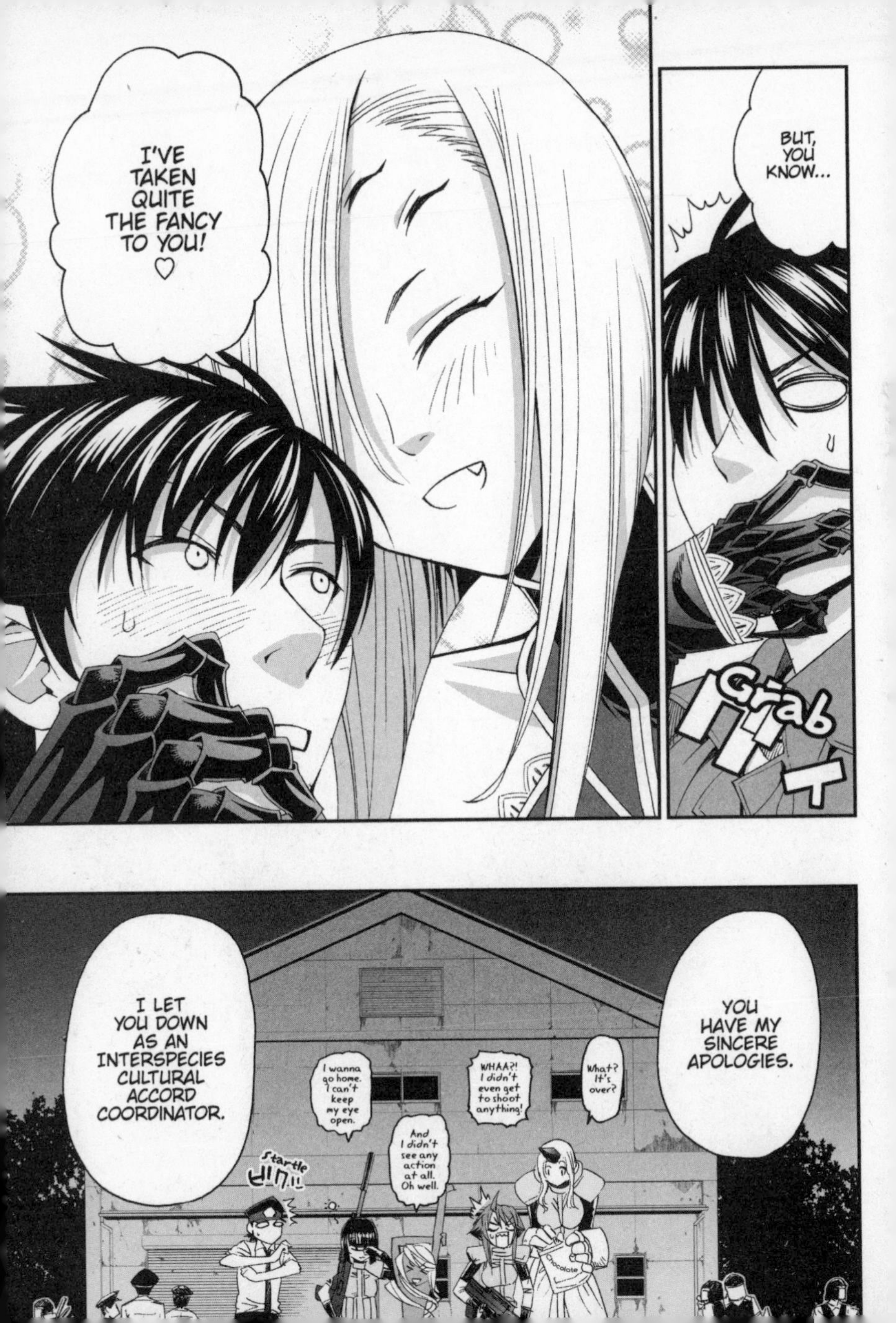
BUT, YOU KNOW...
Grab
I'VE TAKEN QUITE THE FANCY TO YOU! ♡
YOU HAVE MY SINCERE APOLOGIES.
What? It's over?
WHAA?! I didn't even get to shoot anything!
And I didn't see any action at all. Oh well.
I wanna go home. I can't keep my eye open.
I LET YOU DOWN AS AN INTERSPECIES CULTURAL ACCORD COORDINATOR.
Startle
Chocolate

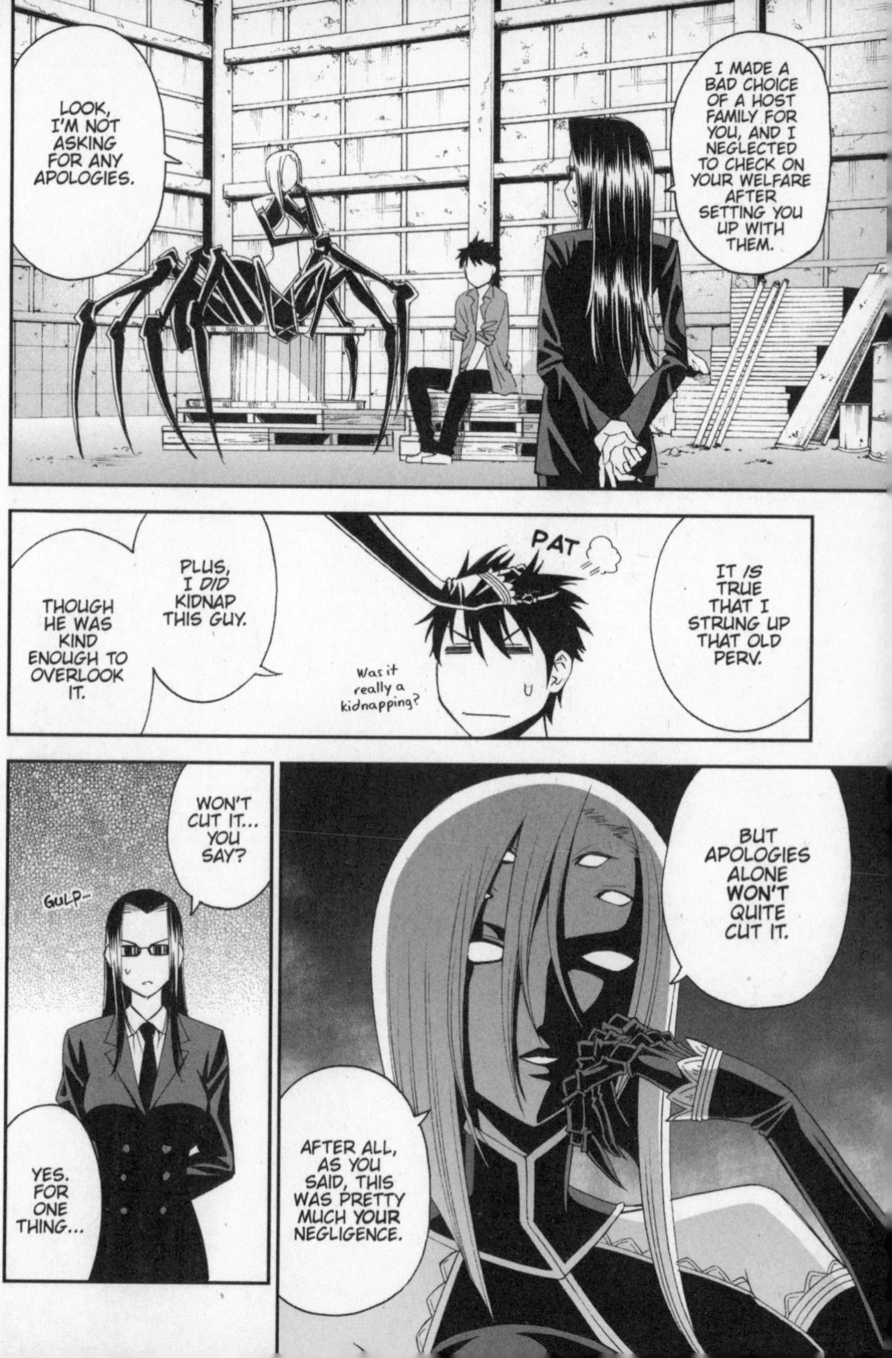
I MADE A BAD CHOICE OF A HOST FAMILY FOR YOU, AND I NEGLECTED TO CHECK ON YOUR WELFARE AFTER SETTING YOU UP WITH THEM.
LOOK, I'M NOT ASKING FOR ANY APOLOGIES.
IT *IS* TRUE THAT I STRUNG UP THAT OLD PERV.
PAT
Was it really a kidnapping?
PLUS, I *DID* KIDNAP THIS GUY.
THOUGH HE WAS KIND ENOUGH TO OVERLOOK IT.
BUT APOLOGIES ALONE WON'T QUITE CUT IT.
AFTER ALL, AS YOU SAID, THIS WAS PRETTY MUCH YOUR NEGLIGENCE.
WON'T CUT IT... YOU SAY?
GULP...
YES. FOR ONE THING...

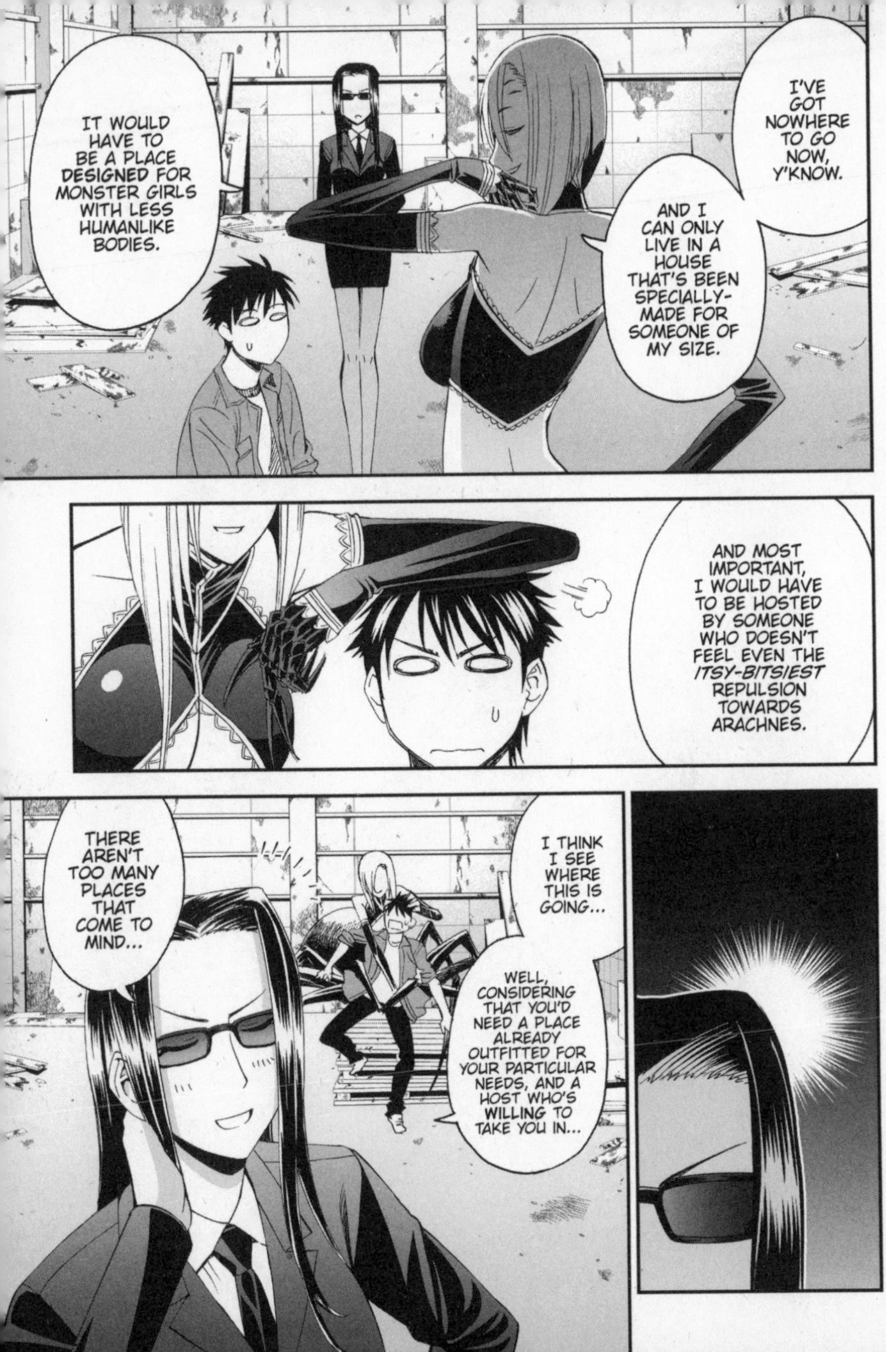
I'VE GOT NOWHERE TO GO NOW, Y'KNOW.
AND I CAN ONLY LIVE IN A HOUSE THAT'S BEEN SPECIALLY-MADE FOR SOMEONE OF MY SIZE.
IT WOULD HAVE TO BE A PLACE DESIGNED FOR MONSTER GIRLS WITH LESS HUMANLIKE BODIES.
AND MOST IMPORTANT, I WOULD HAVE TO BE HOSTED BY SOMEONE WHO DOESN'T FEEL EVEN THE *ITSY-BITSIEST* REPULSION TOWARDS ARACHNES.
I THINK I SEE WHERE THIS IS GOING...
THERE AREN'T TOO MANY PLACES THAT COME TO MIND...
WELL, CONSIDERING THAT YOU'D NEED A PLACE ALREADY OUTFITTED FOR YOUR PARTICULAR NEEDS, AND A HOST WHO'S WILLING TO TAKE YOU IN...

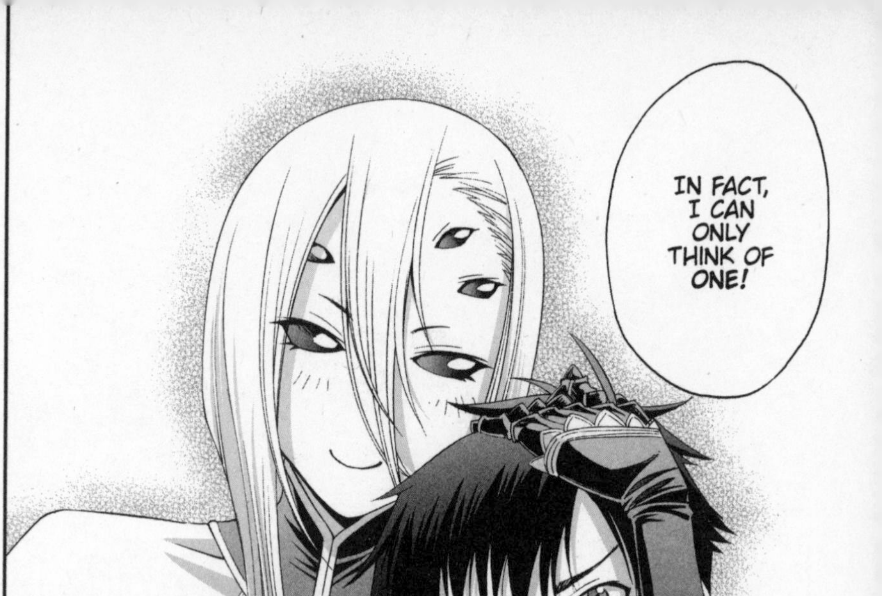
IN FACT, I CAN ONLY THINK OF ONE!
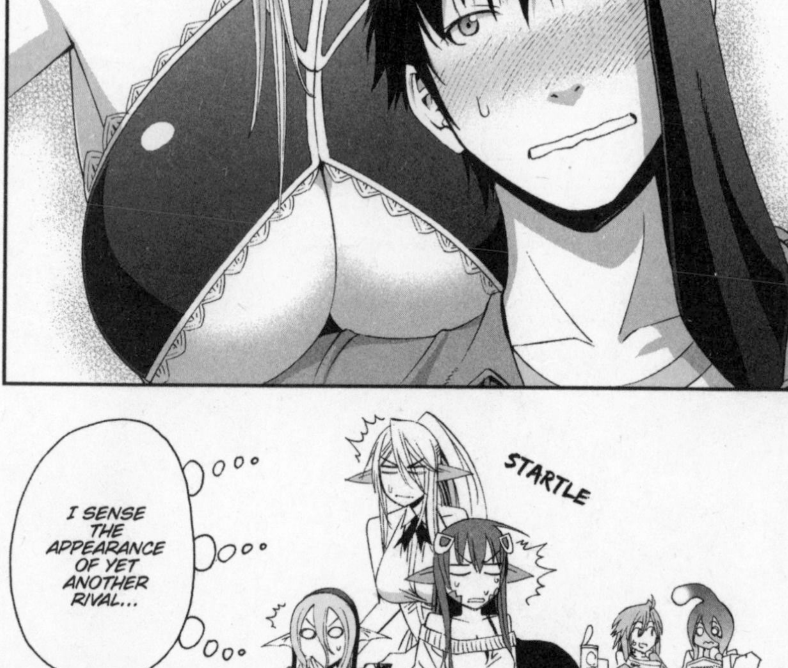
STARTLE
I SENSE THE APPEARANCE OF YET ANOTHER RIVAL...
CHIPS
POTATO

Monster Musume

Everyday Life with
Monster Girls

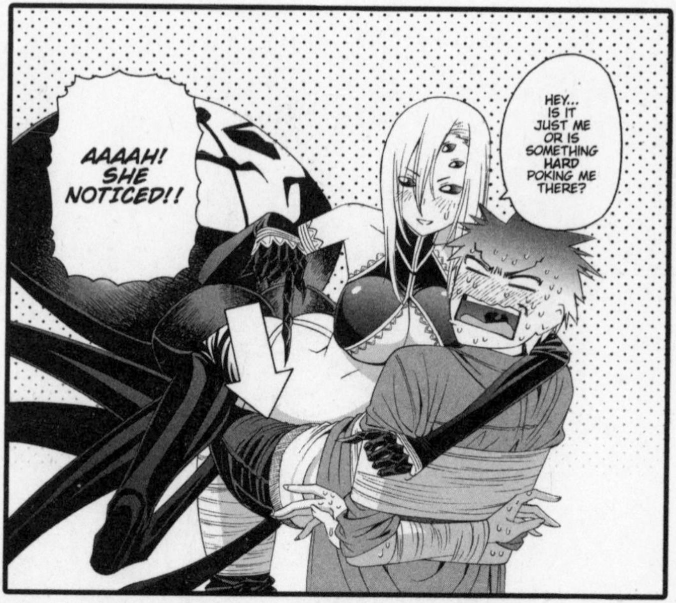
HEY... IS IT JUST ME OR IS SOMETHING HARD POKING ME THERE?
AAAAH! SHE NOTICED!!

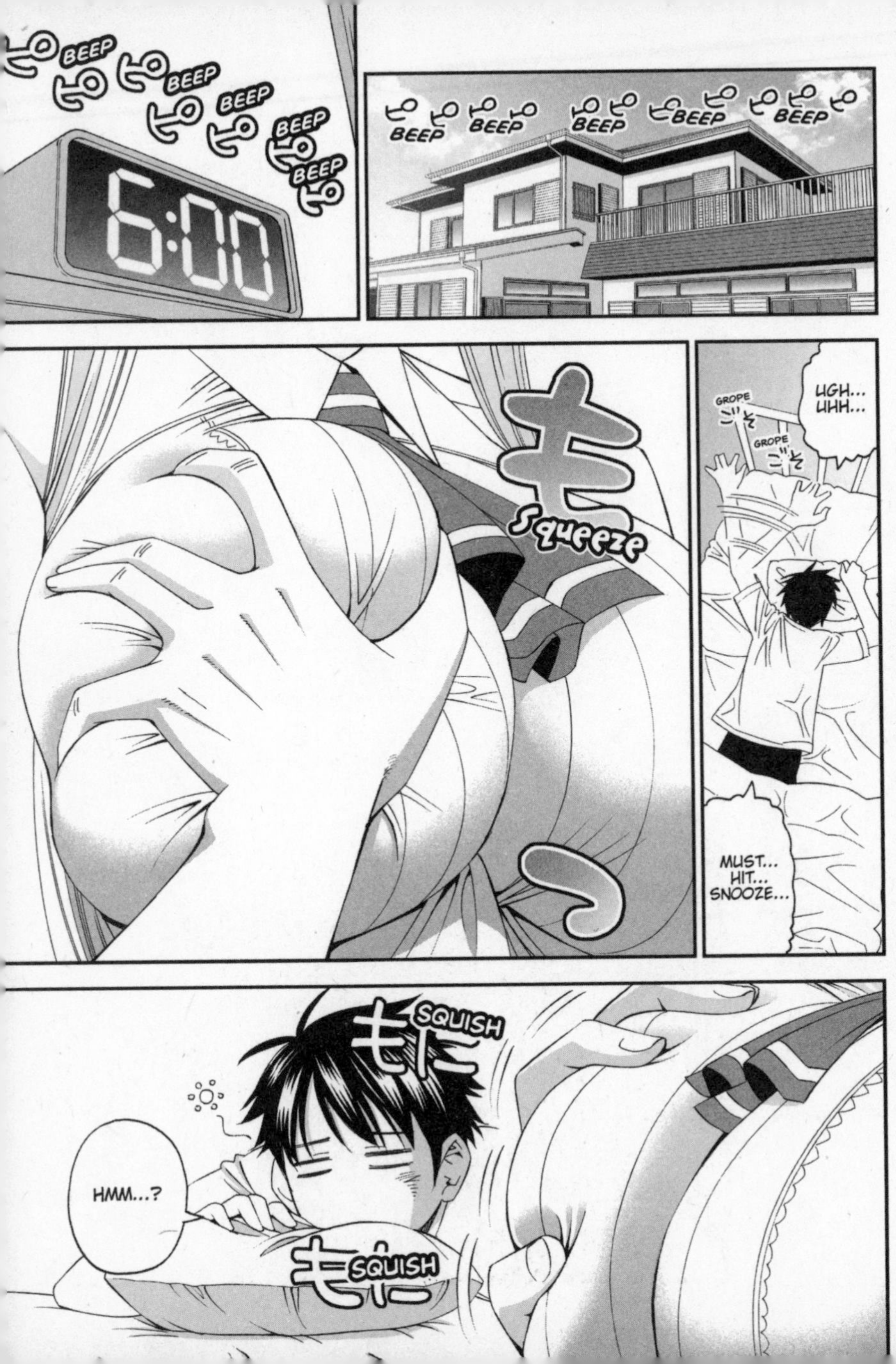
BEEP
BEEP
BEEP
BEEP
BEEP
BEEP
BEEP
BEEP
BEEP
BEEP
6:00
UGH... UHH...
GROPE
GROPE
MUST... HIT... SNOOZE...
SQUEEZE
SQUISH
HMM...?
SQUISH

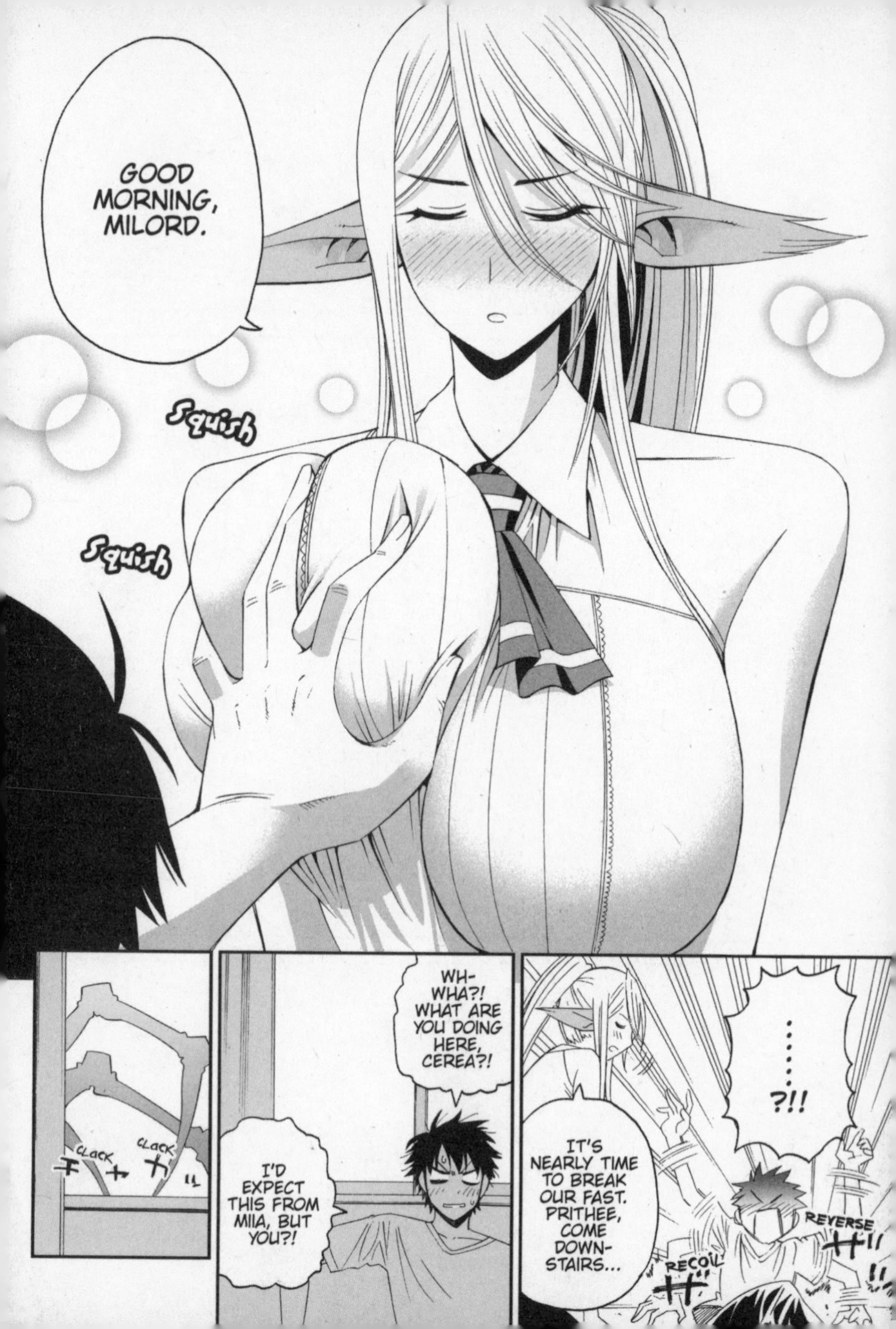
GOOD MORNING, MILORD.
Squish
Squish
......
?!!
IT'S NEARLY TIME TO BREAK OUR FAST. PRITHEE, COME DOWN-STAIRS...
REVERSE
RECOIL
WH-WHA?! WHAT ARE YOU DOING HERE, CEREA?!
I'D EXPECT THIS FROM MIIA, BUT YOU?!
CLACK
CLACK

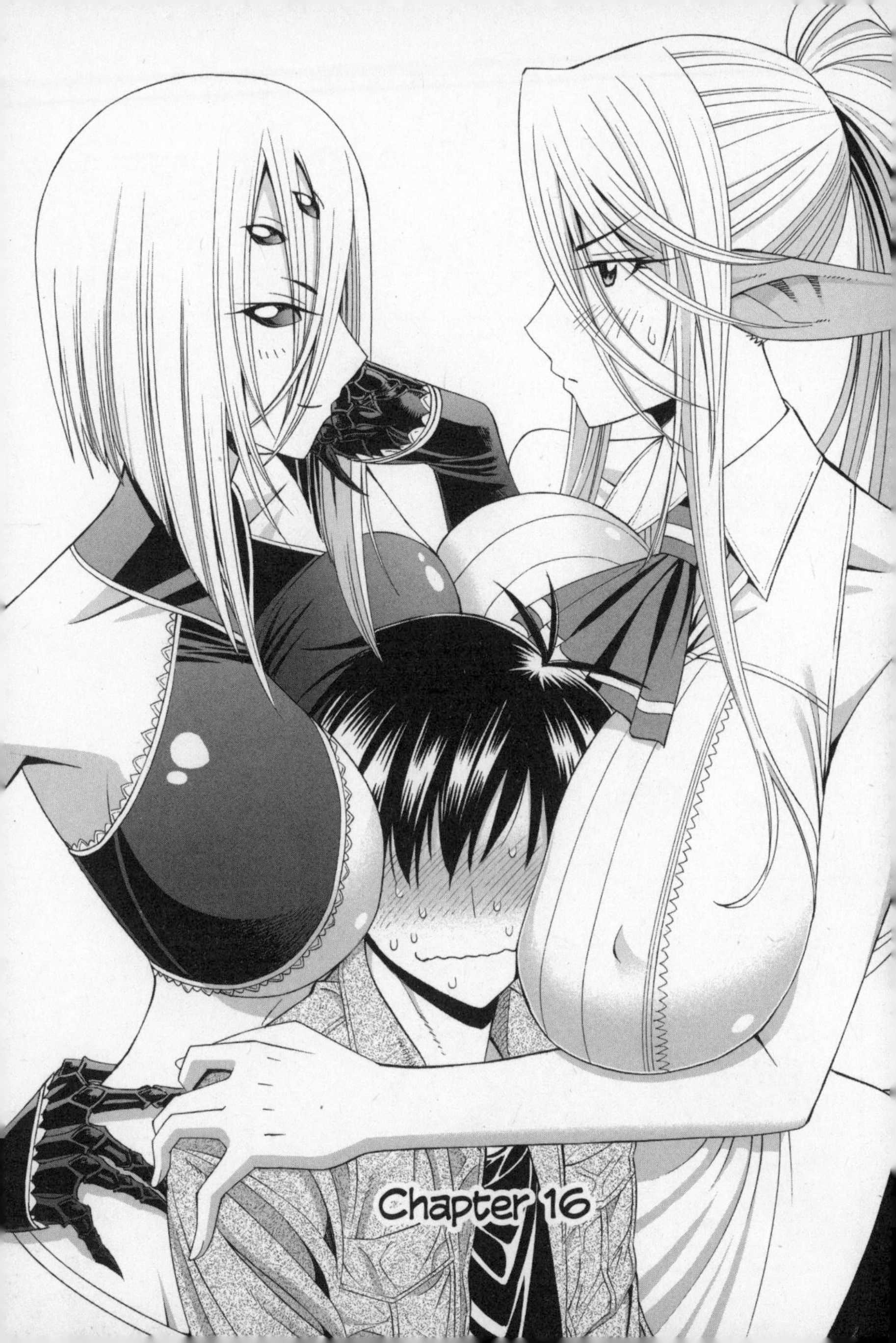
Chapter 16

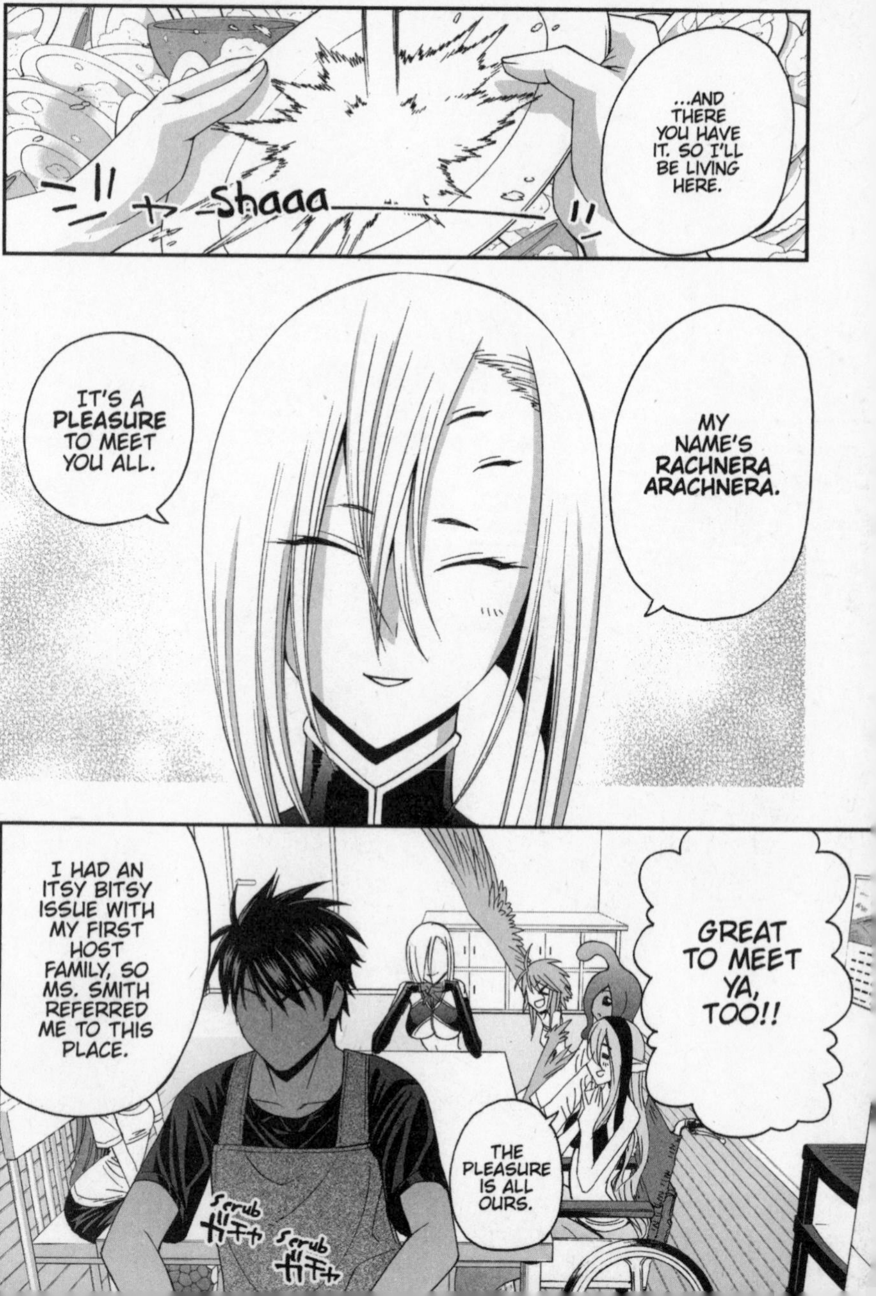
...AND THERE YOU HAVE IT. SO I'LL BE LIVING HERE.
Shaaa
MY NAME'S RACHNERA ARACHNERA.
IT'S A PLEASURE TO MEET YOU ALL.
I HAD AN ITSY BITSY ISSUE WITH MY FIRST HOST FAMILY, SO MS. SMITH REFERRED ME TO THIS PLACE.
GREAT TO MEET YA, TOO!!
THE PLEASURE IS ALL OURS.
Scrub
Scrub

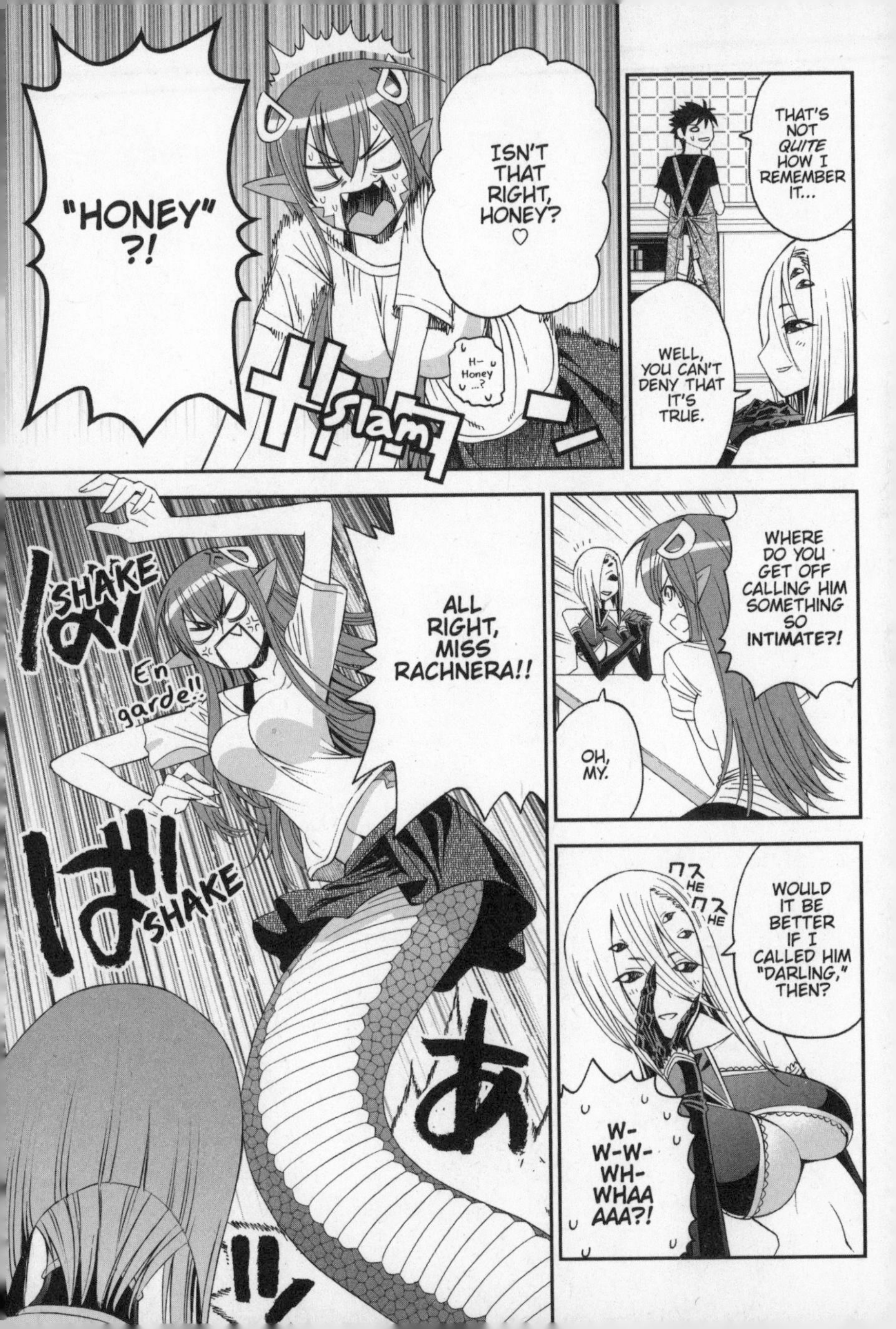
THAT'S NOT QUITE HOW I REMEMBER IT...
WELL, YOU CAN'T DENY THAT IT'S TRUE.
ISN'T THAT RIGHT, HONEY? ♡
"HONEY" ?!
H- Honey ...?
slam
WHERE DO YOU GET OFF CALLING HIM SOMETHING SO INTIMATE?!
OH, MY.
HE HE
WOULD IT BE BETTER IF I CALLED HIM "DARLING," THEN?
W-W-W-WH-WHAA AAA?!
ALL RIGHT, MISS RACHNERA!!
SHAKE
En garde!!
SHAKE

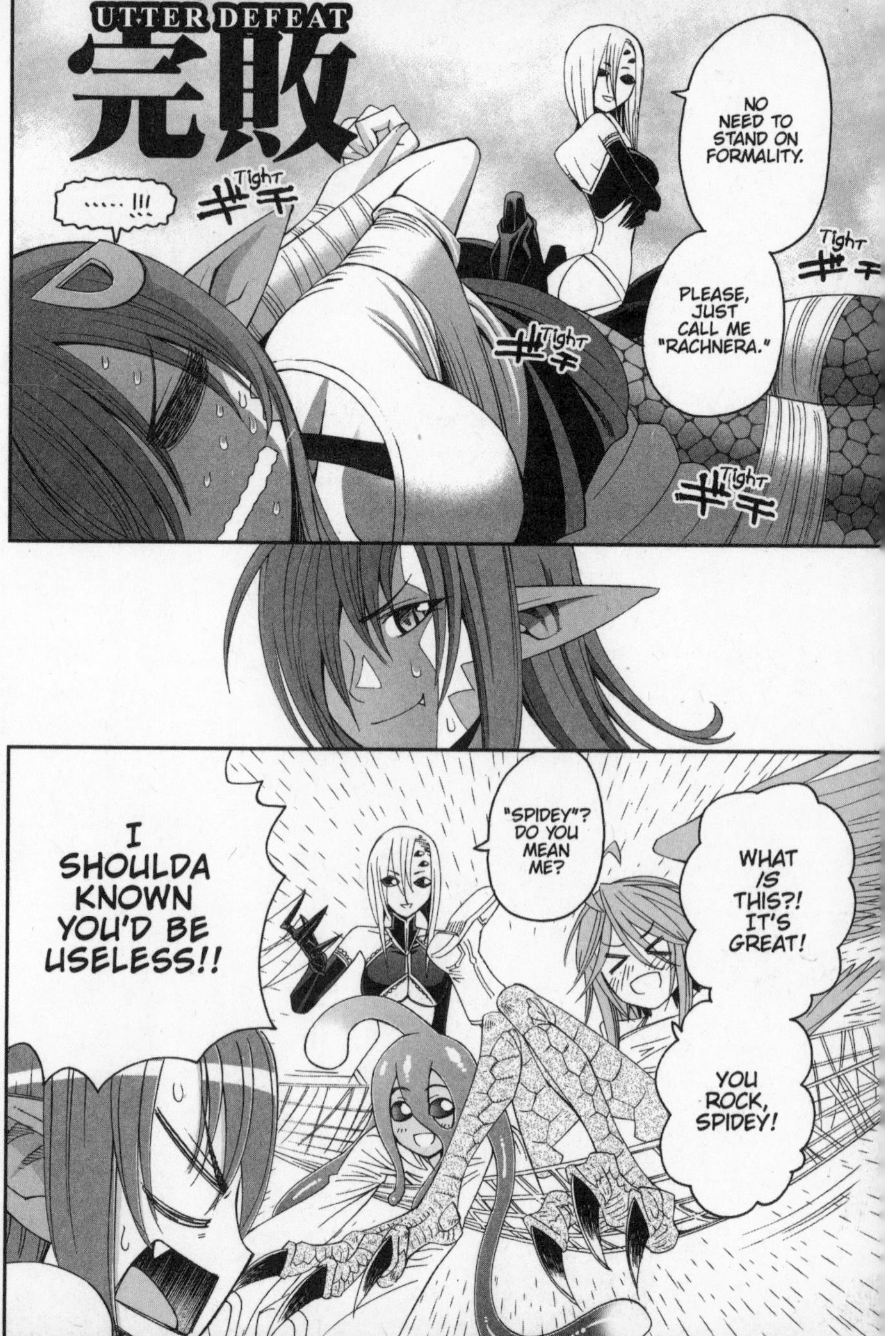
UTTER DEFEAT
完敗
NO NEED TO STAND ON FORMALITY.
PLEASE, JUST CALL ME "RACHNERA."
Tight
Tight
Tight
Tight
......!!!
WHAT IS THIS?! IT'S GREAT!
YOU ROCK, SPIDEY!
"SPIDEY"? DO YOU MEAN ME?
I SHOULDA KNOWN YOU'D BE USELESS!!

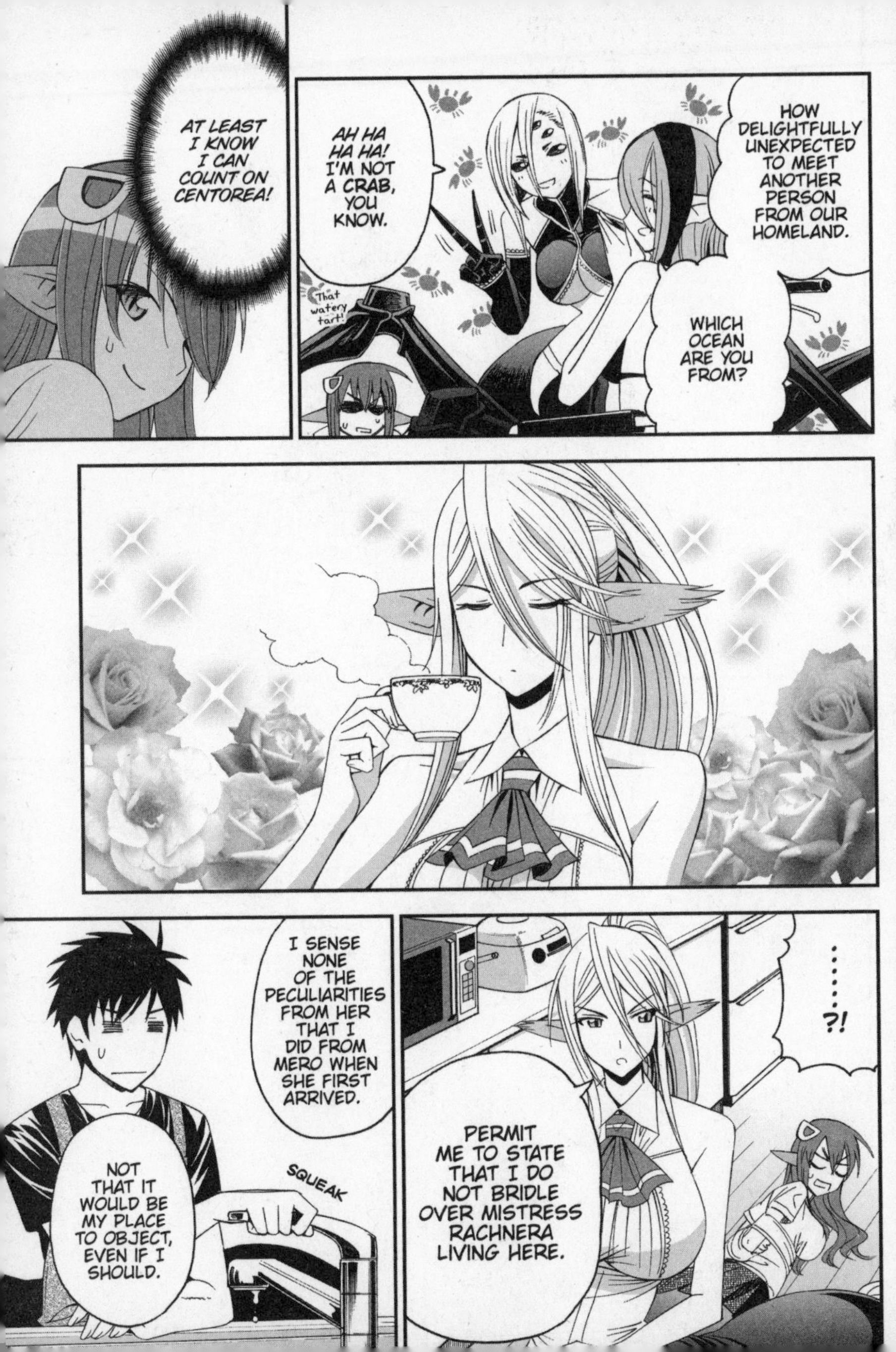
HOW DELIGHTFULLY UNEXPECTED TO MEET ANOTHER PERSON FROM OUR HOMELAND.
WHICH OCEAN ARE YOU FROM?
AH HA HA HA! I'M NOT A CRAB, YOU KNOW.
That watery tart!
AT LEAST I KNOW I CAN COUNT ON CENTOREA!
......?!
PERMIT ME TO STATE THAT I DO NOT BRIDLE OVER MISTRESS RACHNERA LIVING HERE.
I SENSE NONE OF THE PECULIARITIES FROM HER THAT I DID FROM MERO WHEN SHE FIRST ARRIVED.
NOT THAT IT WOULD BE MY PLACE TO OBJECT, EVEN IF I SHOULD.
SQUEAK

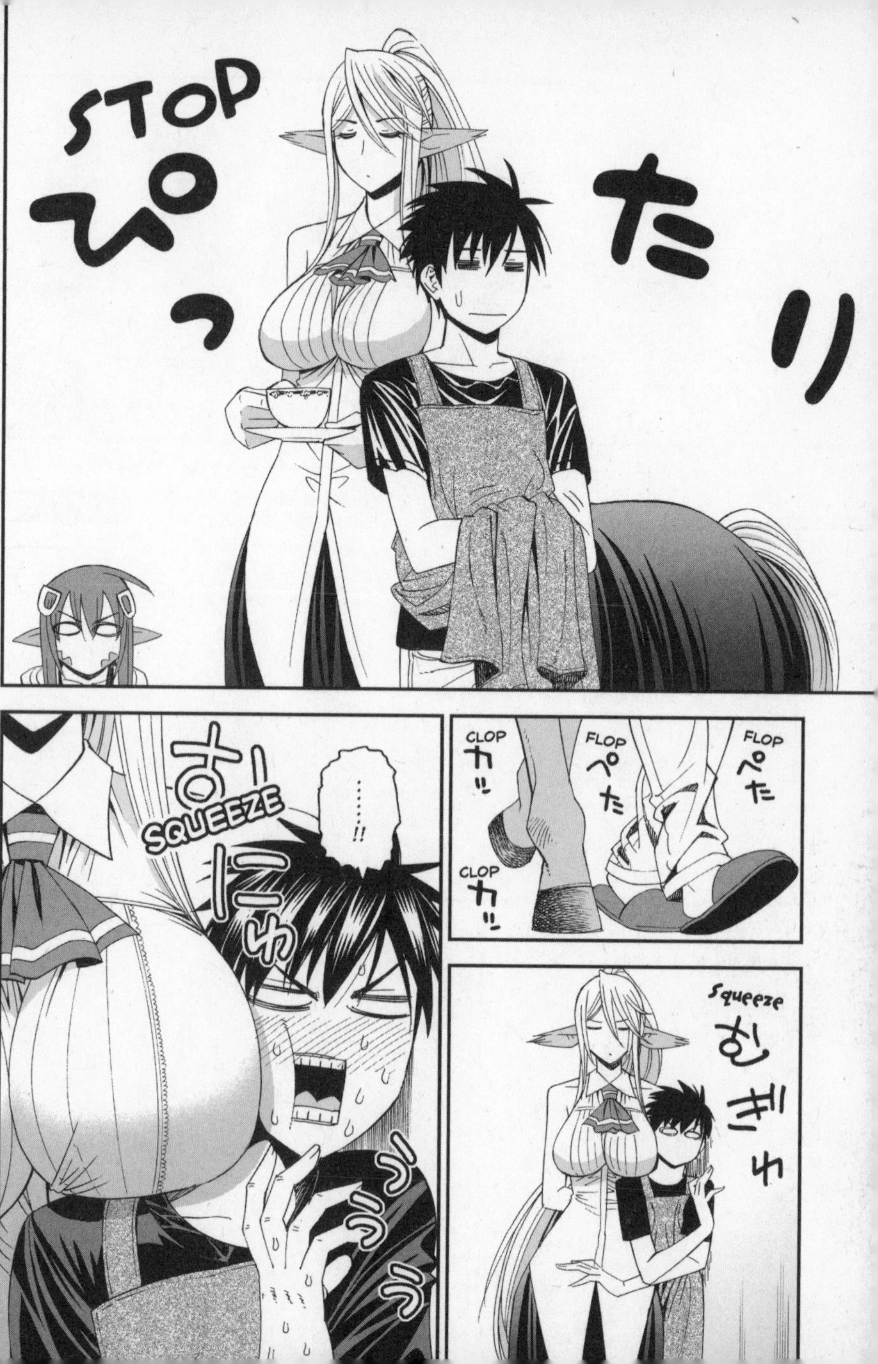
STOP
ぴったり
FLOP
ぺた
FLOP
ぺた
CLOP
カッ
CLOP
カッ
Squeeze
むぎゅ
……!!
SQUEEZE
むにゅー
ううう

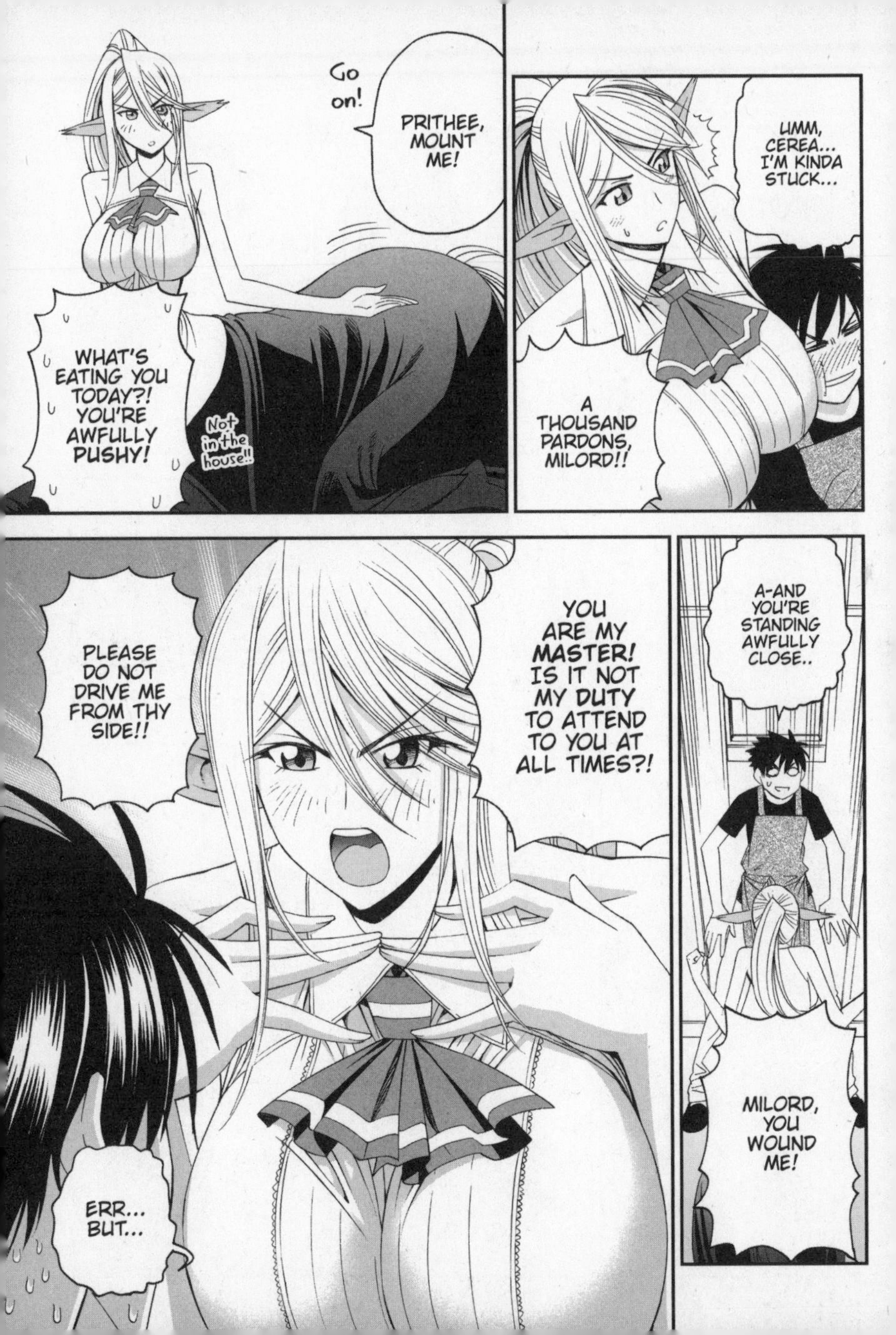
UMM, CEREA... I'M KINDA STUCK...
A THOUSAND PARDONS, MILORD!!
PRITHEE, MOUNT ME!
Go on!
WHAT'S EATING YOU TODAY?! YOU'RE AWFULLY PUSHY!
Not in the house!!
A-AND YOU'RE STANDING AWFULLY CLOSE..
MILORD, YOU WOUND ME!
YOU ARE MY MASTER! IS IT NOT MY DUTY TO ATTEND TO YOU AT ALL TIMES?!
PLEASE DO NOT DRIVE ME FROM THY SIDE!!
ERR... BUT...

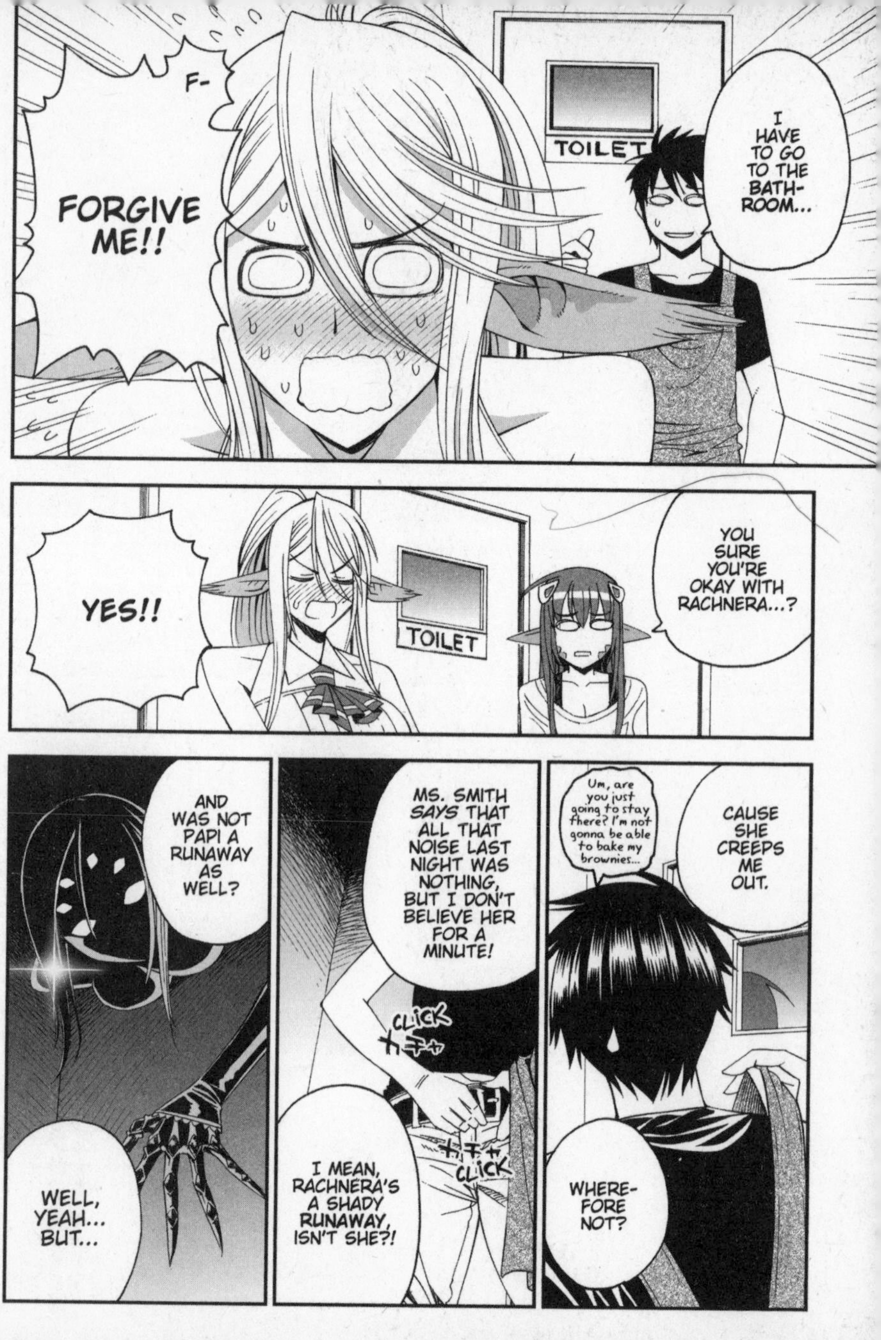
I HAVE TO GO TO THE BATH-ROOM...
F-
FORGIVE ME!!
YOU SURE YOU'RE OKAY WITH RACHNERA...?
YES!!
CAUSE SHE CREEPS ME OUT.
Um, are you just going to stay there? I'm not gonna be able to bake my brownies...
WHERE-FORE NOT?
MS. SMITH SAYS THAT ALL THAT NOISE LAST NIGHT WAS NOTHING, BUT I DON'T BELIEVE HER FOR A MINUTE!
CLICK
CLICK
I MEAN, RACHNERA'S A SHADY RUNAWAY, ISN'T SHE?!
AND WAS NOT PAPI A RUNAWAY AS WELL?
WELL, YEAH... BUT...

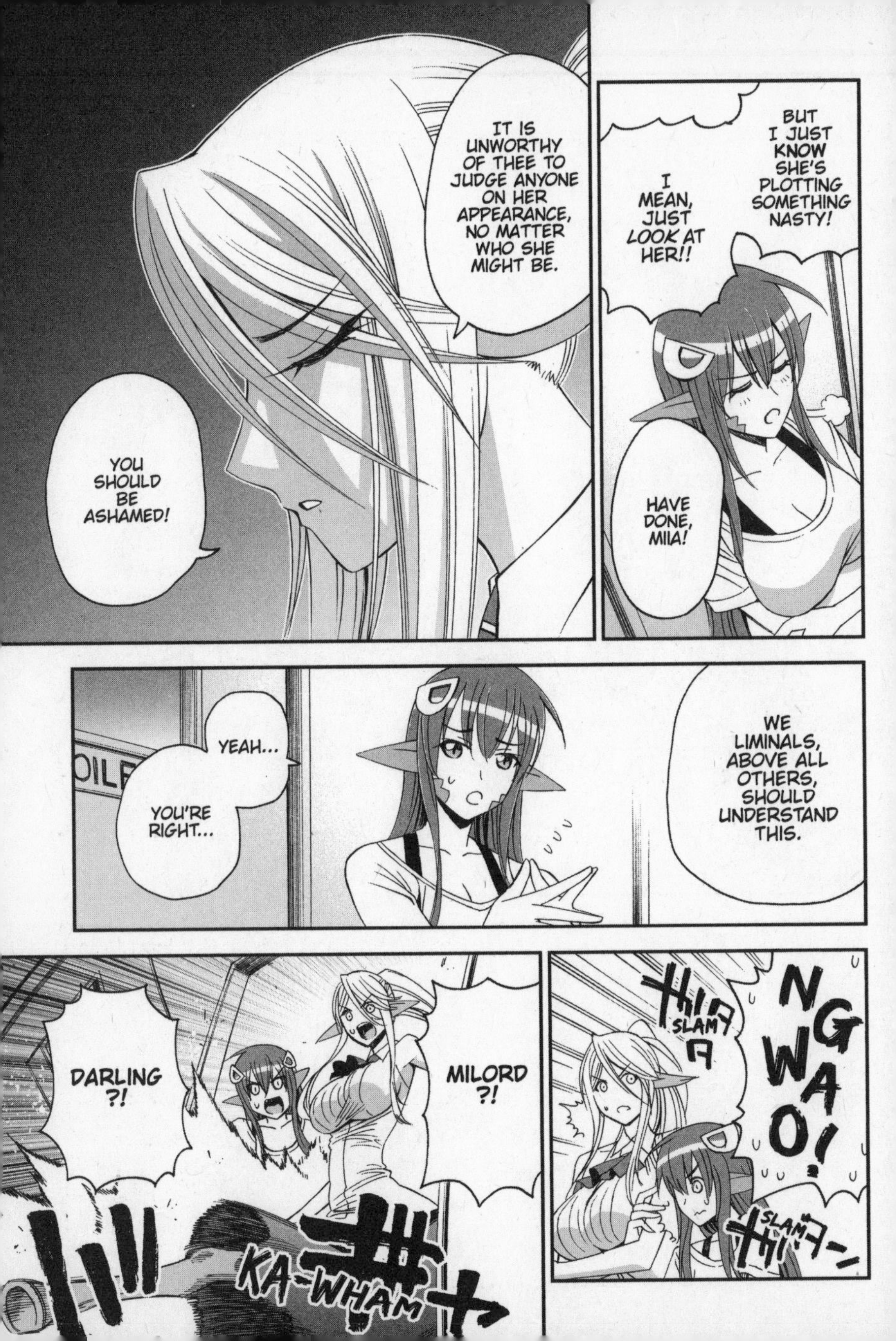
BUT I JUST KNOW SHE'S PLOTTING SOMETHING NASTY!
I MEAN, JUST LOOK AT HER!!
HAVE DONE, MIIA!
IT IS UNWORTHY OF THEE TO JUDGE ANYONE ON HER APPEARANCE, NO MATTER WHO SHE MIGHT BE.
YOU SHOULD BE ASHAMED!
WE LIMINALS, ABOVE ALL OTHERS, SHOULD UNDERSTAND THIS.
YEAH...
YOU'RE RIGHT...
NGWAO!
SLAM
SLAM
MILORD?!
DARLING?!
KA-WHAM

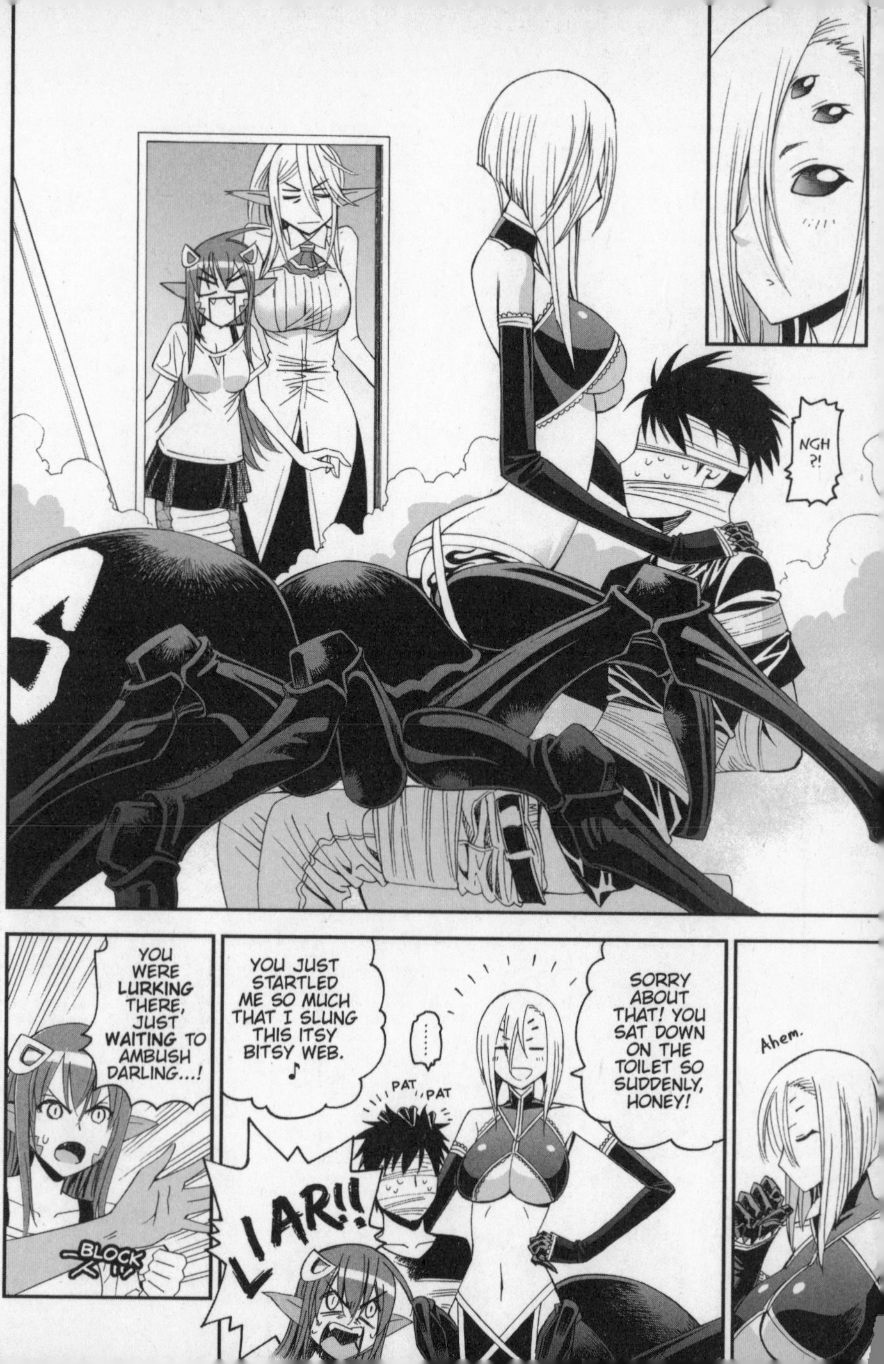
NGH ?!
Ahem.
SORRY ABOUT THAT! YOU SAT DOWN ON THE TOILET SO SUDDENLY, HONEY!
YOU JUST STARTLED ME SO MUCH THAT I SLUNG THIS ITSY BITSY WEB. ♪
......
PAT PAT
LIAR!!
YOU WERE LURKING THERE, JUST WAITING TO AMBUSH DARLING...!
BLOCK

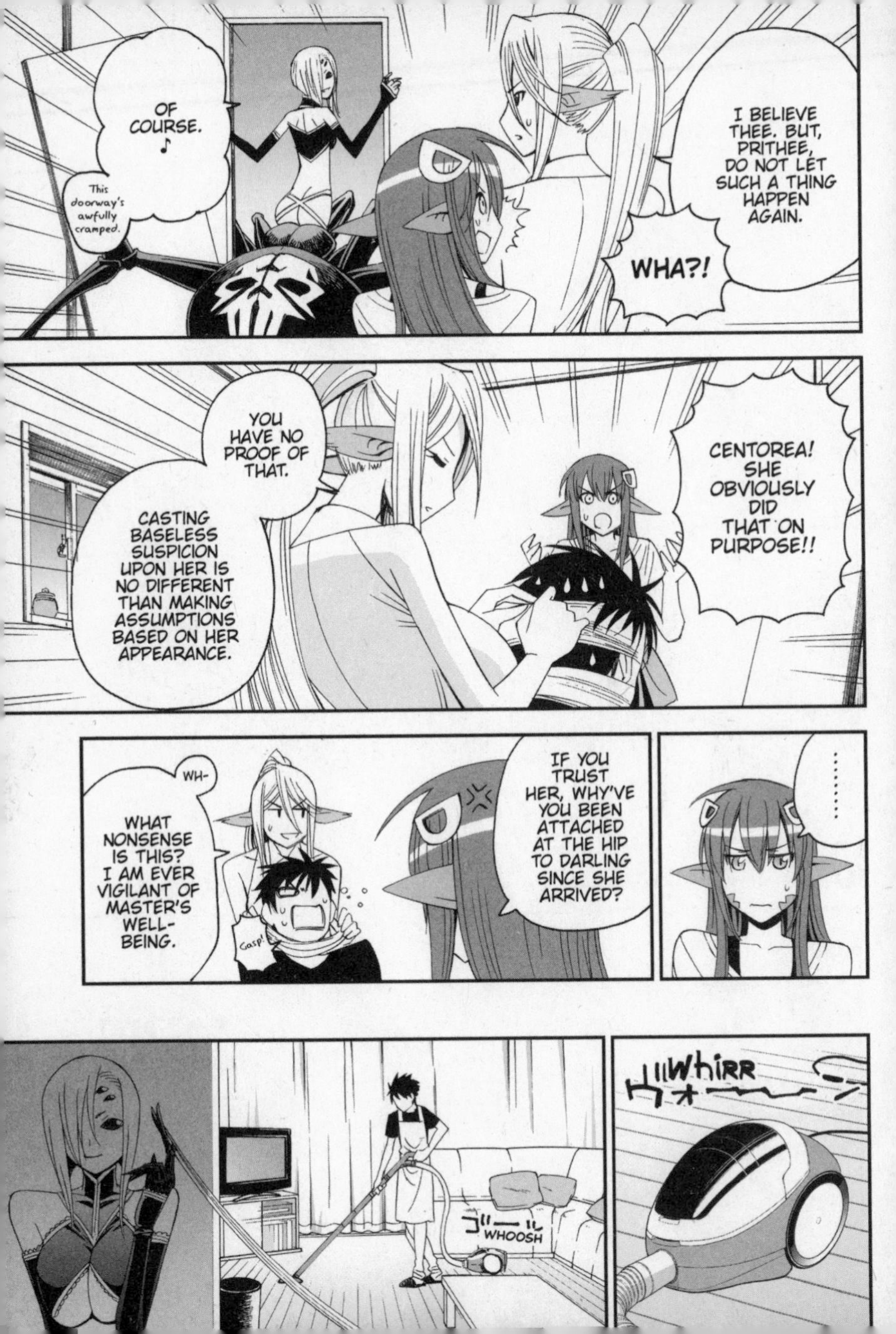
I BELIEVE THEE. BUT, PRITHEE, DO NOT LET SUCH A THING HAPPEN AGAIN.
WHA?!
OF COURSE. ♪
This doorway's awfully cramped.
CENTOREA! SHE OBVIOUSLY DID THAT ON PURPOSE!!
YOU HAVE NO PROOF OF THAT.
CASTING BASELESS SUSPICION UPON HER IS NO DIFFERENT THAN MAKING ASSUMPTIONS BASED ON HER APPEARANCE.
....
IF YOU TRUST HER, WHY'VE YOU BEEN ATTACHED AT THE HIP TO DARLING SINCE SHE ARRIVED?
WH-
WHAT NONSENSE IS THIS? I AM EVER VIGILANT OF MASTER'S WELL-BEING.
Gasp!
Whirr
WHOOSH

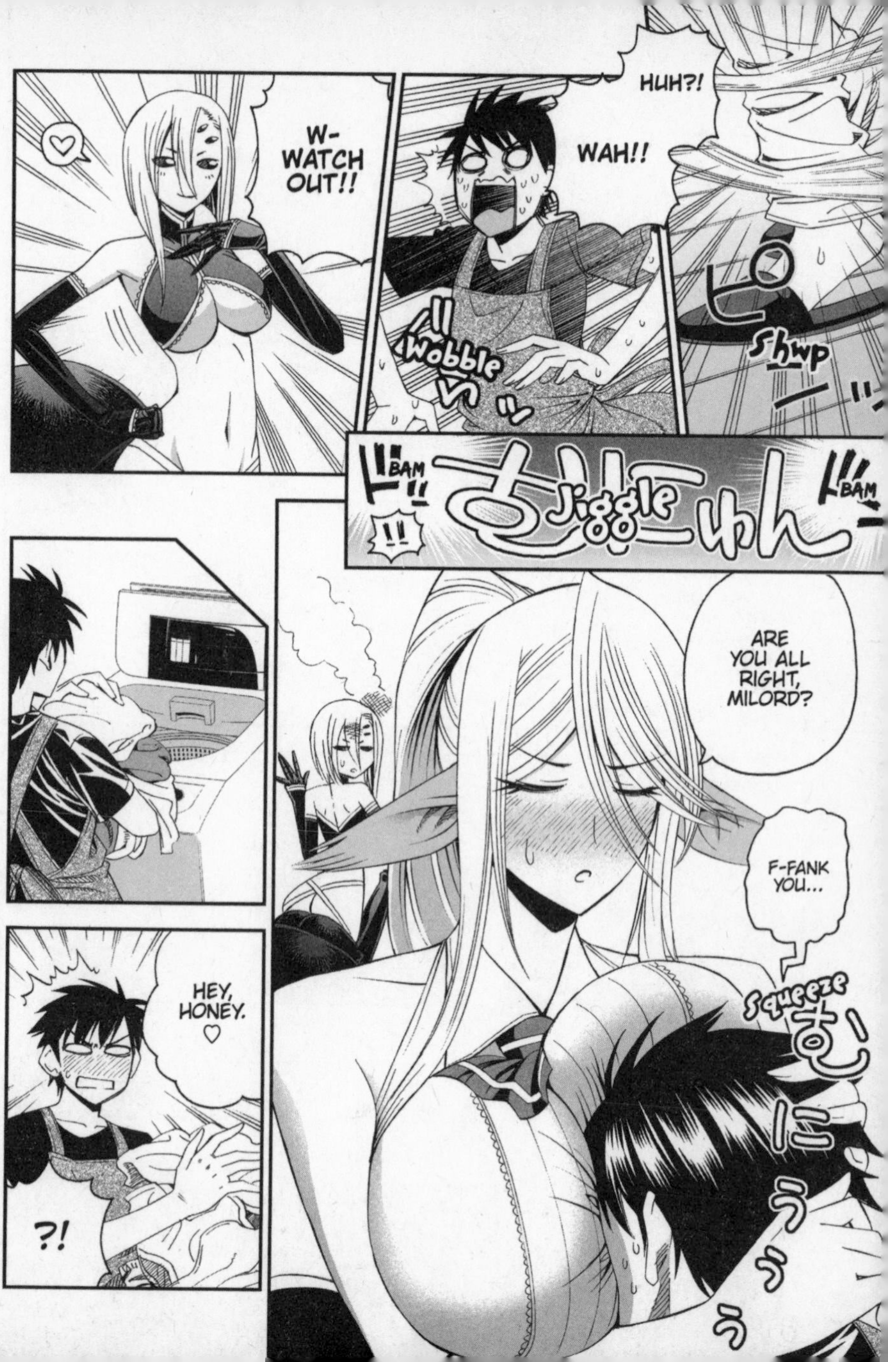
HUH?!
shwp
WAH!!
wobble
W-WATCH OUT!!
♡
BAM!!
!!
jiggle
BAM
ARE YOU ALL RIGHT, MILORD?
F-FANK YOU...
squeeze
HEY, HONEY. ♡
?!

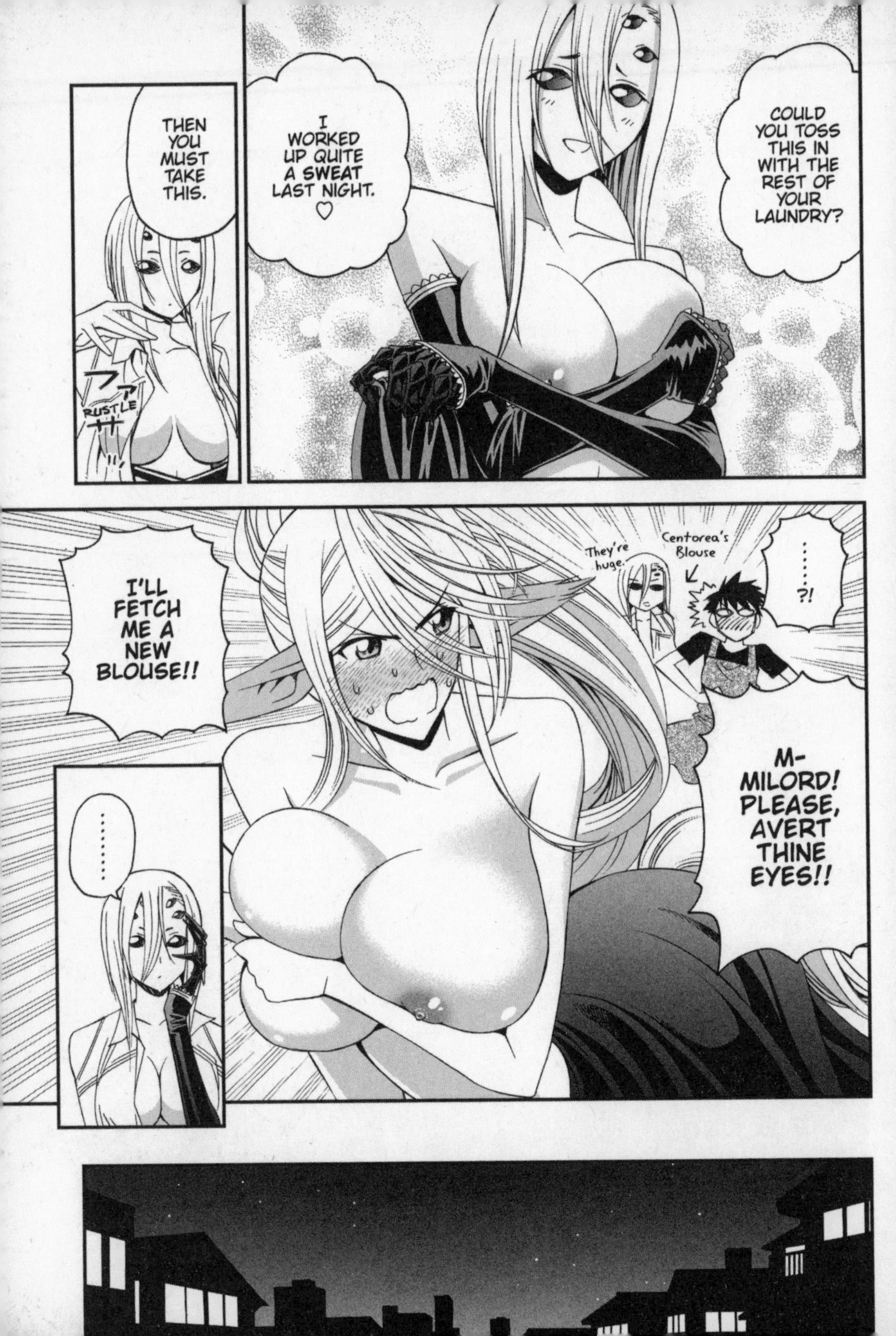
COULD YOU TOSS THIS IN WITH THE REST OF YOUR LAUNDRY?
I WORKED UP QUITE A SWEAT LAST NIGHT. ♡
THEN YOU MUST TAKE THIS.
RUSTLE
......?!
Centorea's Blouse
They're huge.
I'LL FETCH ME A NEW BLOUSE!!
M-MILORD! PLEASE, AVERT THINE EYES!!
......

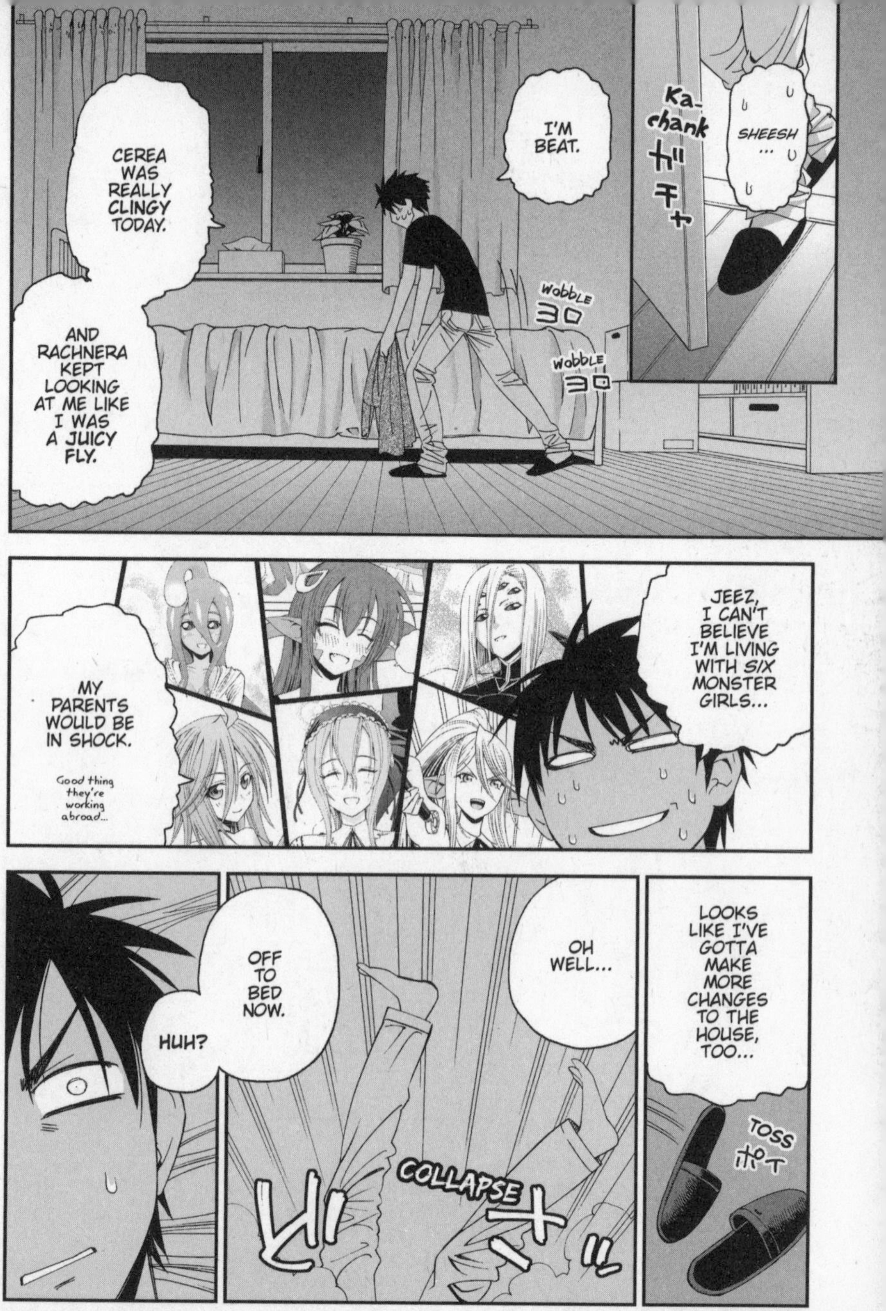
Ka-chank ガチャ
SHEESH ...
I'M BEAT.
wobble ヨロ
wobble ヨロ
CEREA WAS REALLY CLINGY TODAY.
AND RACHNERA KEPT LOOKING AT ME LIKE I WAS A JUICY FLY.
JEEZ, I CAN'T BELIEVE I'M LIVING WITH SIX MONSTER GIRLS...
MY PARENTS WOULD BE IN SHOCK.
Good thing they're working abroad...
LOOKS LIKE I'VE GOTTA MAKE MORE CHANGES TO THE HOUSE, TOO...
TOSS ポイ
OH WELL...
OFF TO BED NOW.
COLLAPSE
HUH?

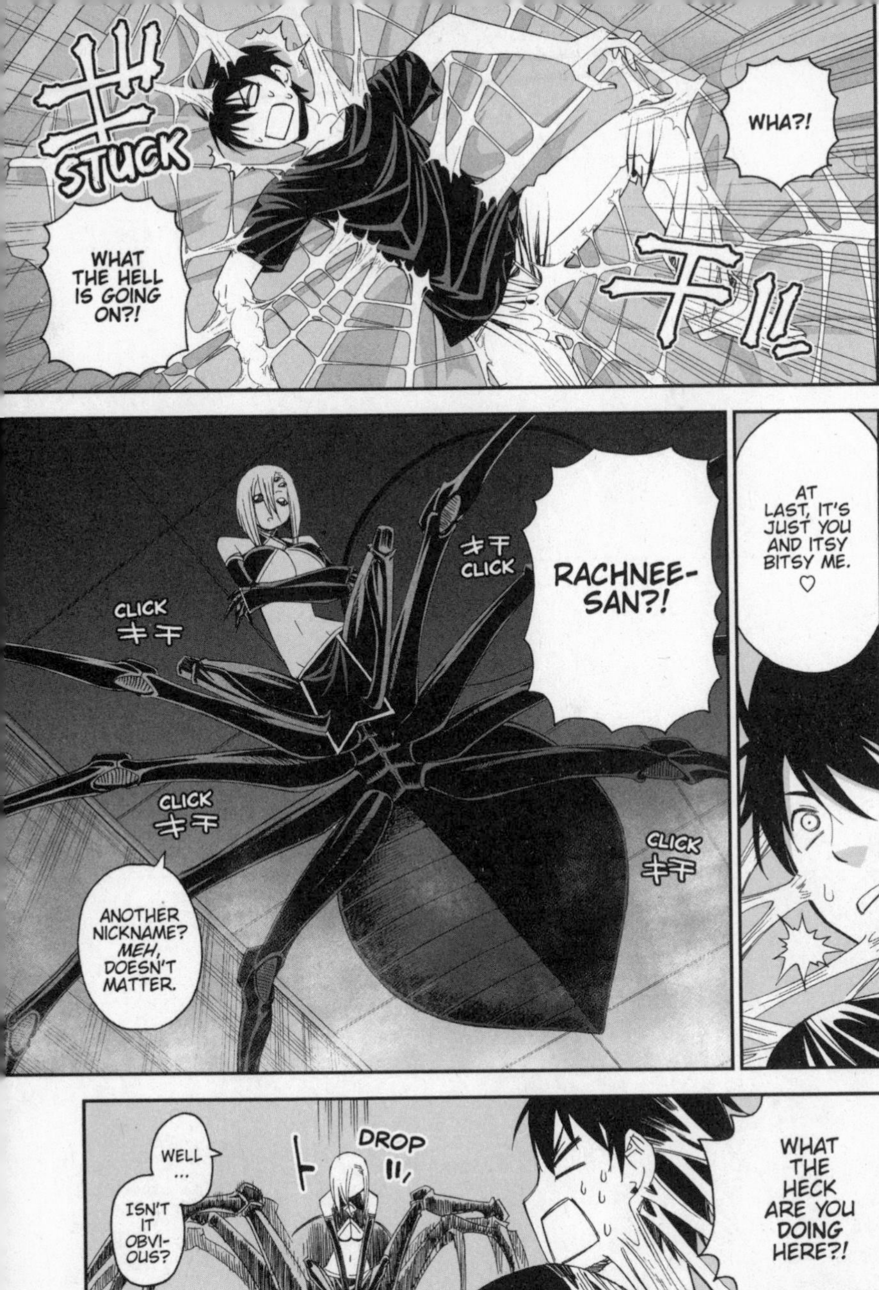
WHA?!
STUCK
WHAT THE HELL IS GOING ON?!
AT LAST, IT'S JUST YOU AND ITSY BITSY ME. ♡
RACHNEE-SAN?!
CLICK
CLICK
CLICK
CLICK
ANOTHER NICKNAME? MEH, DOESN'T MATTER.
WHAT THE HECK ARE YOU DOING HERE?!
DROP
WELL... ISN'T IT OBVI-OUS?

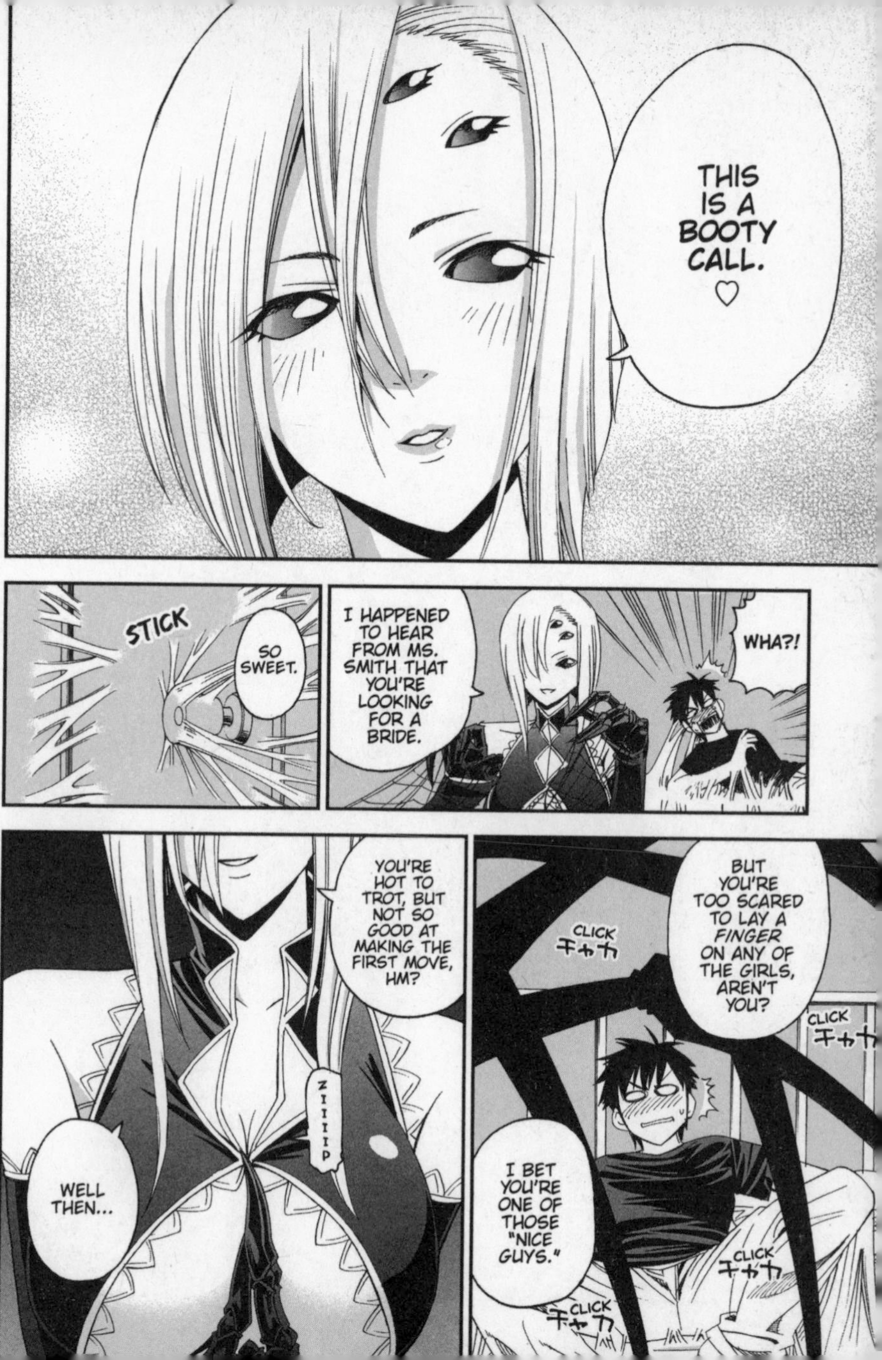
THIS IS A BOOTY CALL. ♡
WHA?!
I HAPPENED TO HEAR FROM MS. SMITH THAT YOU'RE LOOKING FOR A BRIDE.
STICK
SO SWEET.
BUT YOU'RE TOO SCARED TO LAY A *FINGER* ON ANY OF THE GIRLS, AREN'T YOU?
CLICK
CLICK
I BET YOU'RE ONE OF THOSE "NICE GUYS."
CLICK
CLICK
YOU'RE HOT TO TROT, BUT NOT SO GOOD AT MAKING THE FIRST MOVE, HM?
ZIIIIP
WELL THEN...

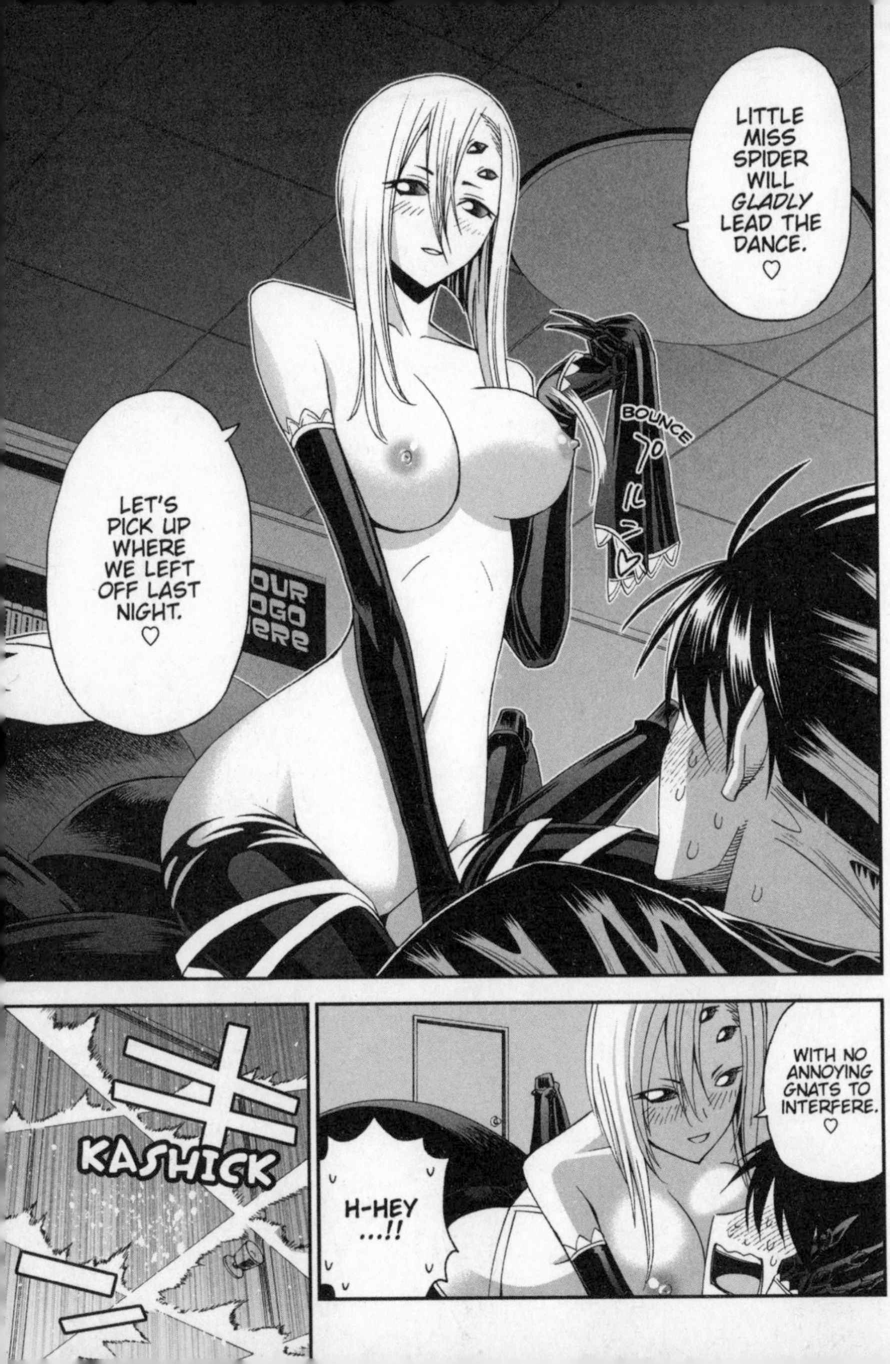
LITTLE MISS SPIDER WILL GLADLY LEAD THE DANCE. ♡
BOUNCE
LET'S PICK UP WHERE WE LEFT OFF LAST NIGHT. ♡
WITH NO ANNOYING GNATS TO INTERFERE. ♡
H-HEY ...!!
KASHICK

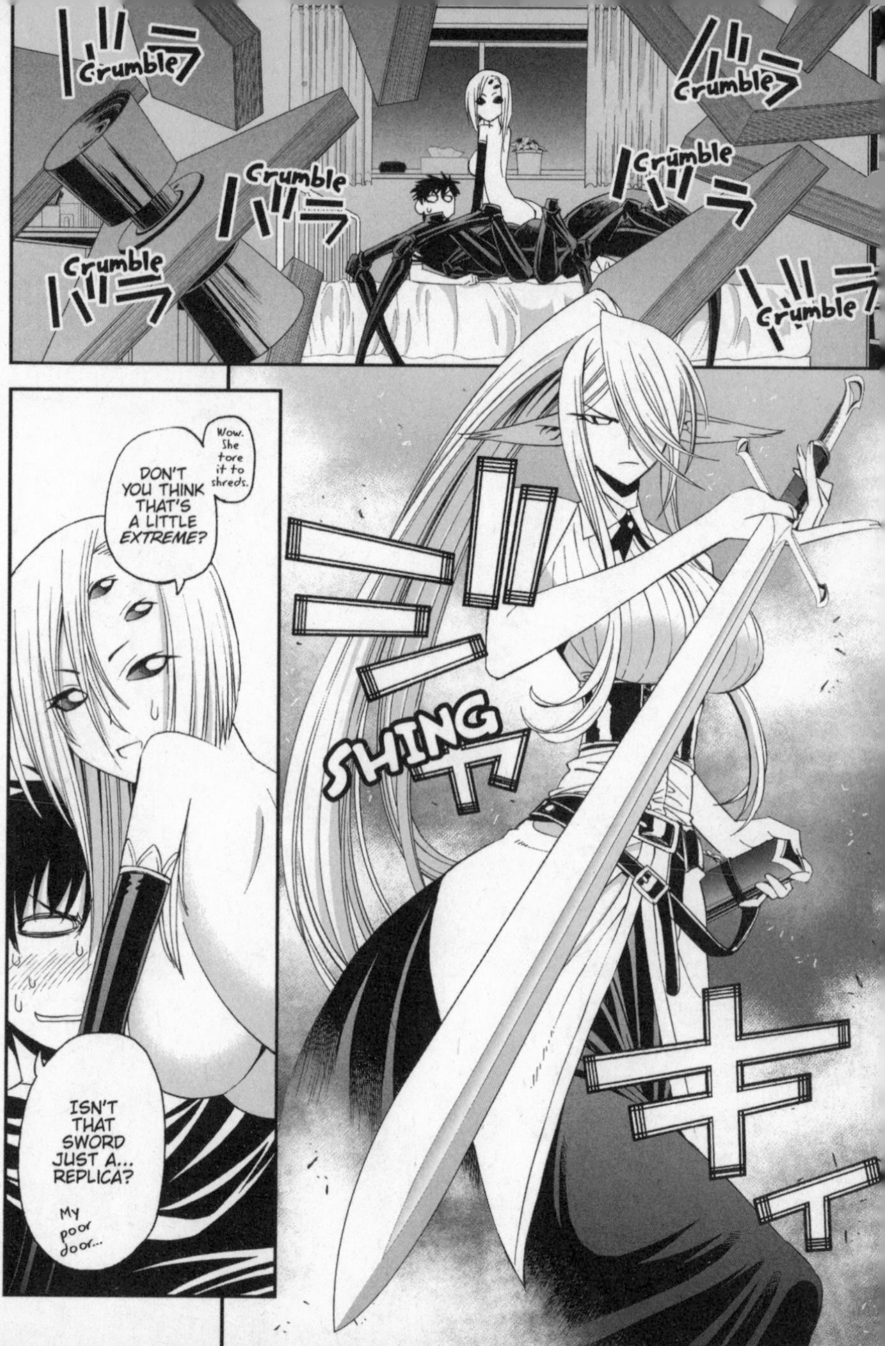
Crumble
Crumble
Crumble
Crumble
Crumble
SHING
Wow. She tore it to shreds.
DON'T YOU THINK THAT'S A LITTLE EXTREME?
ISN'T THAT SWORD JUST A... REPLICA?
My poor door...

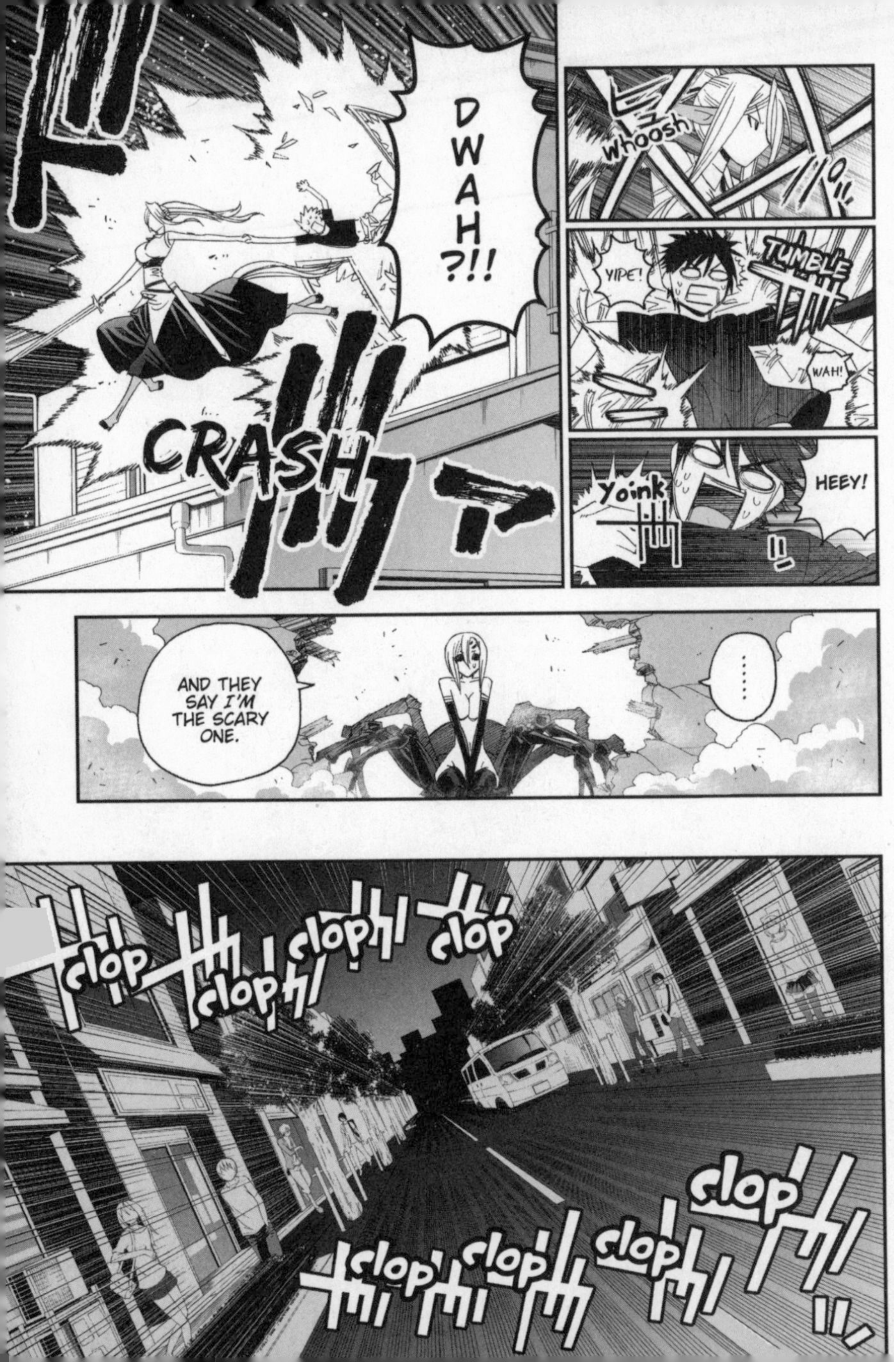
whoosh
YIPE!
TUMBLE
WAH!
HEEY!
yoink
DWAH?!!
CRASH
......
AND THEY SAY I'M THE SCARY ONE.
clop
clop
clop
clop
clop
clop
clop
clop

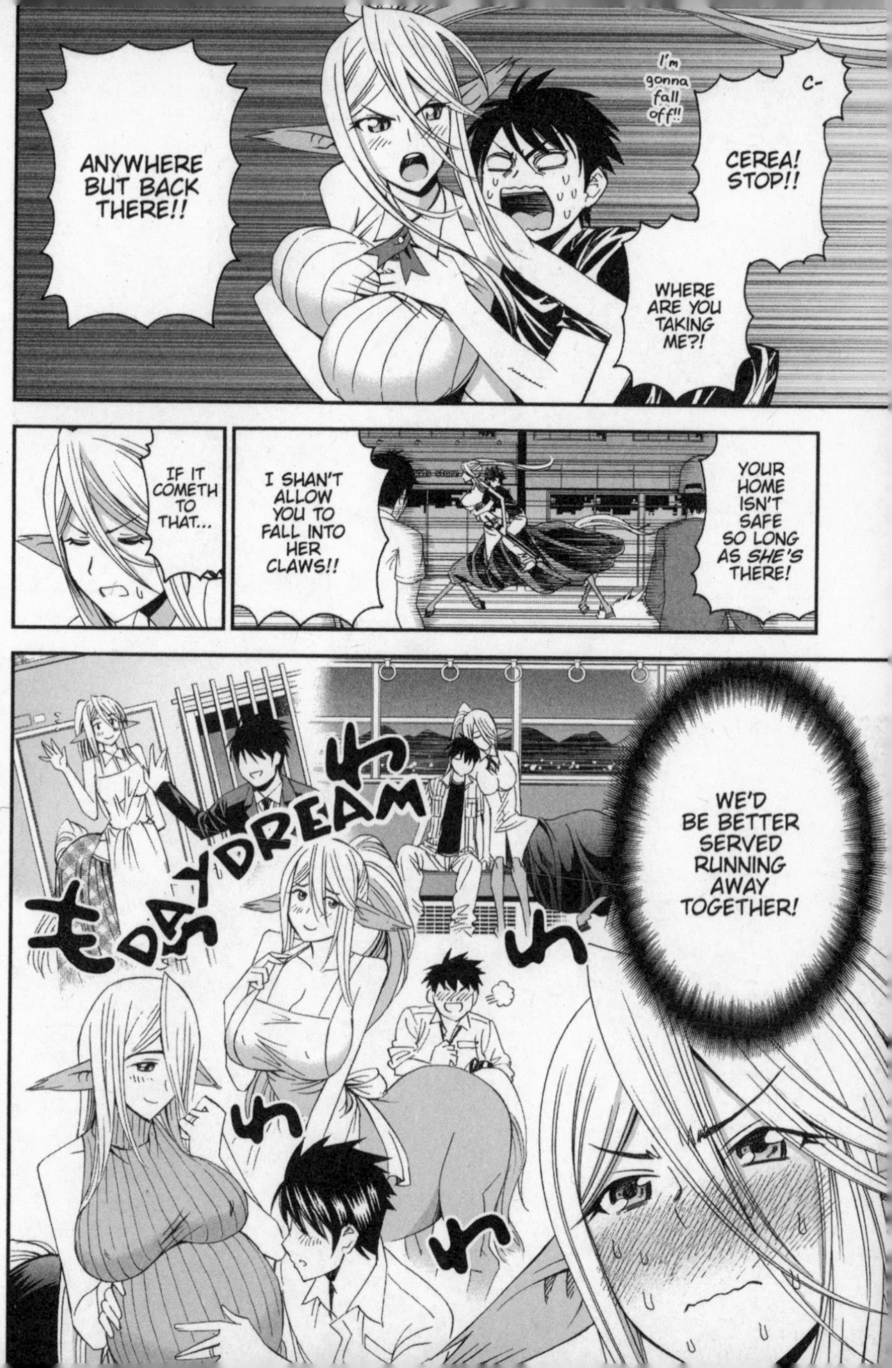
C-
CEREA! STOP!!
I'm gonna fall off!!
WHERE ARE YOU TAKING ME?!
ANYWHERE BUT BACK THERE!!
YOUR HOME ISN'T SAFE SO LONG AS SHE'S THERE!
I SHAN'T ALLOW YOU TO FALL INTO HER CLAWS!!
IF IT COMETH TO THAT...
WE'D BE BETTER SERVED RUNNING AWAY TOGETHER!
DAYDREAM

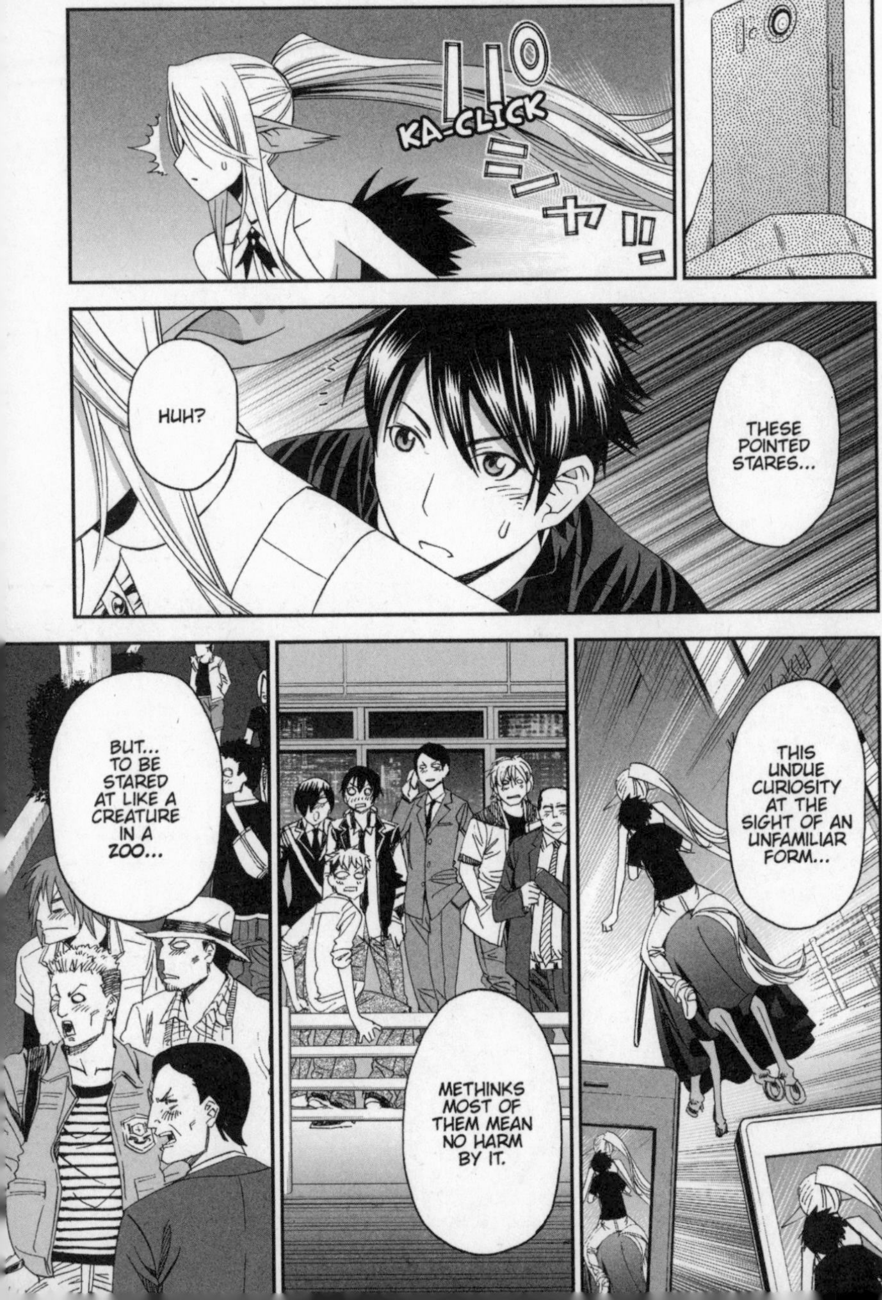
KA-CLICK
THESE POINTED STARES...
HUH?
THIS UNDUE CURIOSITY AT THE SIGHT OF AN UNFAMILIAR FORM...
METHINKS MOST OF THEM MEAN NO HARM BY IT.
BUT... TO BE STARED AT LIKE A CREATURE IN A ZOO...

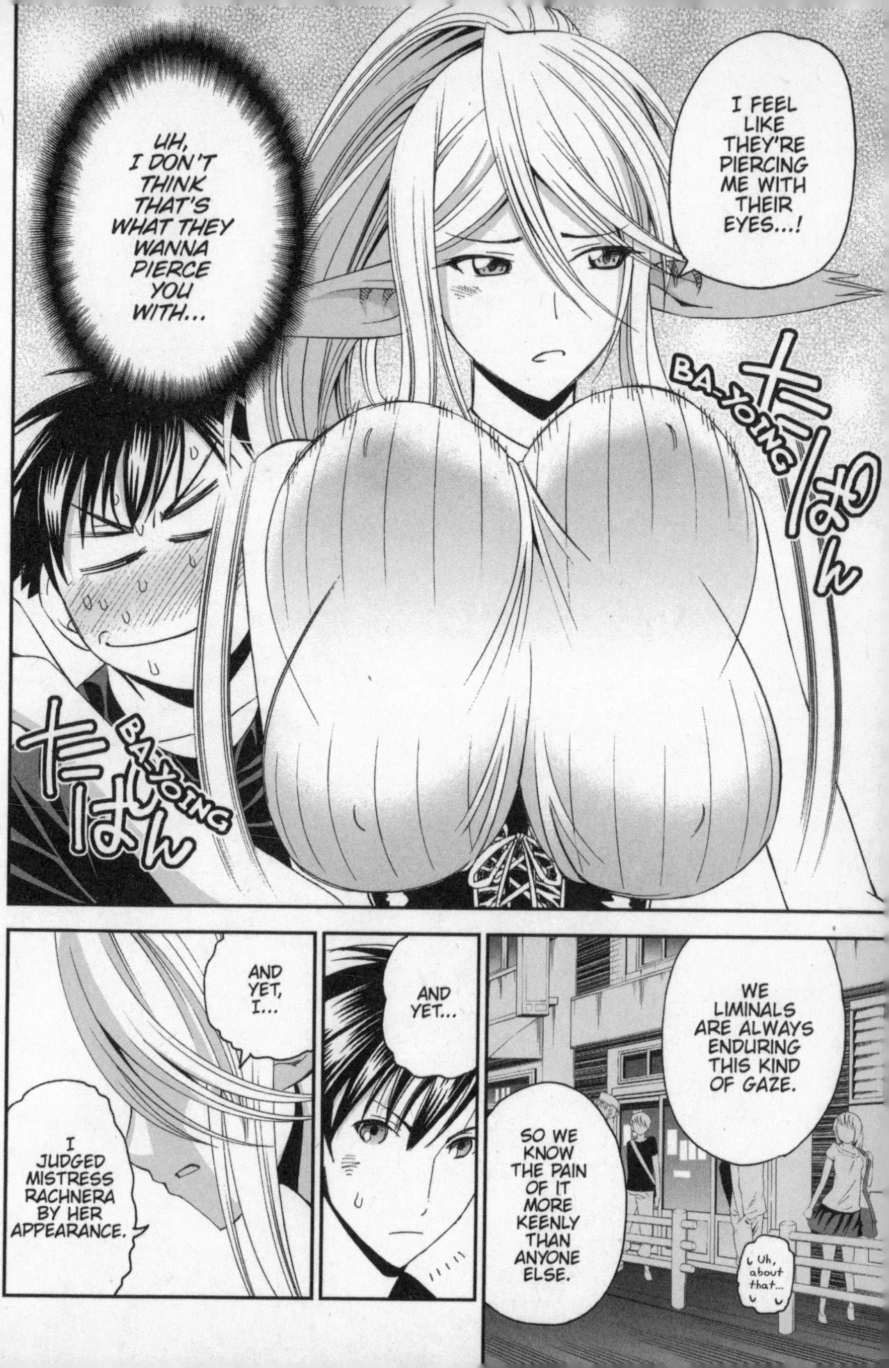
I FEEL LIKE THEY'RE PIERCING ME WITH THEIR EYES...!
BA-YOING
UH, I DON'T THINK THAT'S WHAT THEY WANNA PIERCE YOU WITH...
BA-YOING
WE LIMINALS ARE ALWAYS ENDURING THIS KIND OF GAZE.
SO WE KNOW THE PAIN OF IT MORE KEENLY THAN ANYONE ELSE.
Uh, about that...
AND YET...
AND YET, I...
I JUDGED MISTRESS RACHNERA BY HER APPEARANCE.

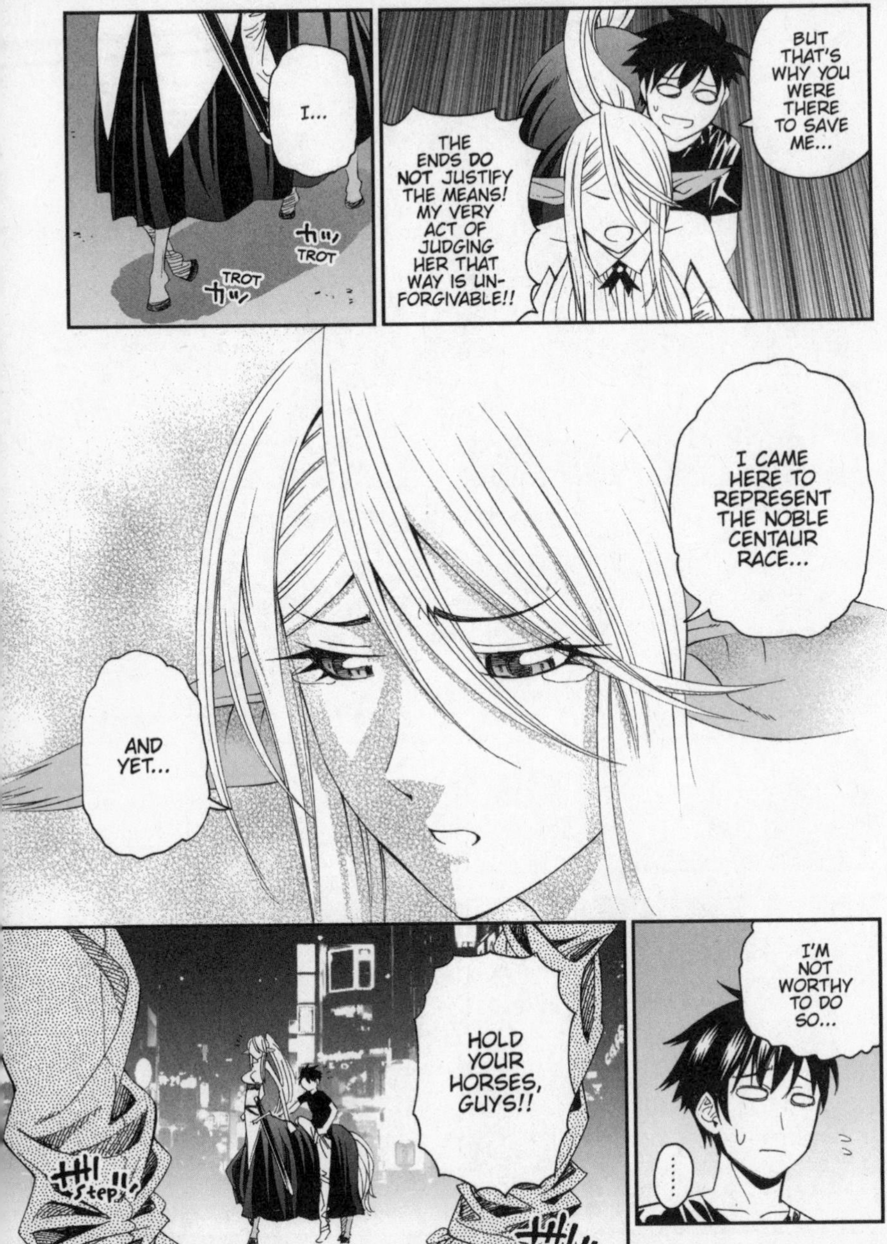
BUT THAT'S WHY YOU WERE THERE TO SAVE ME...
THE ENDS DO NOT JUSTIFY THE MEANS! MY VERY ACT OF JUDGING HER THAT WAY IS UN-FORGIVABLE!!
I...
TROT
TROT
I CAME HERE TO REPRESENT THE NOBLE CENTAUR RACE...
AND YET...
I'M NOT WORTHY TO DO SO...
......
HOLD YOUR HORSES, GUYS!!
Step
Step

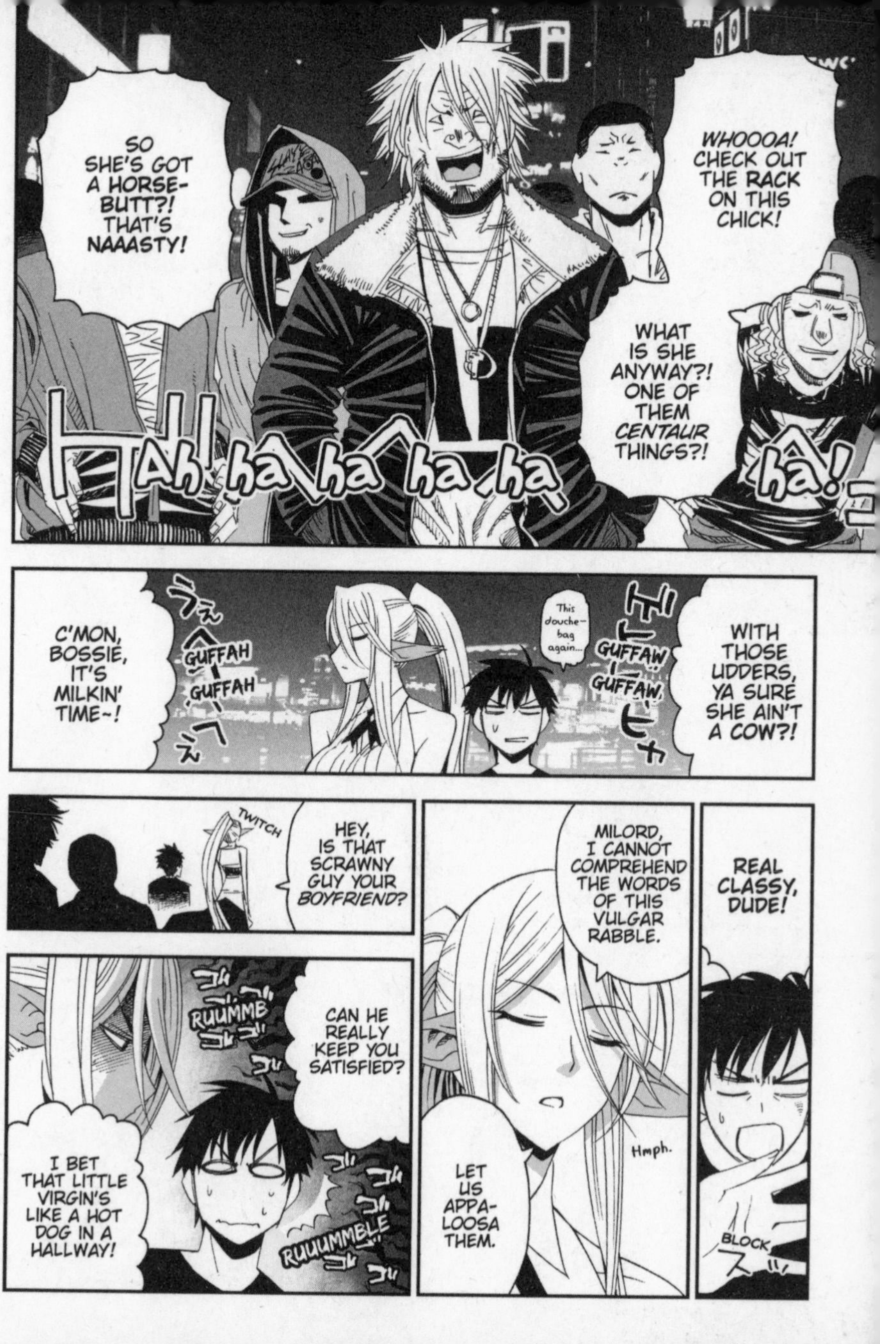
WHOOOA! CHECK OUT THE RACK ON THIS CHICK!
WHAT IS SHE ANYWAY?! ONE OF THEM CENTAUR THINGS?!
SO SHE'S GOT A HORSE-BUTT?! THAT'S NAAASTY!
HAh! ha ha ha ha ha!
WITH THOSE UDDERS, YA SURE SHE AIN'T A COW?!
GUFFAW GUFFAW
This douche-bag again...
GUFFAH GUFFAH
C'MON, BOSSIE, IT'S MILKIN' TIME~!
REAL CLASSY, DUDE!
BLOCK
MILORD, I CANNOT COMPREHEND THE WORDS OF THIS VULGAR RABBLE.
Hmph.
LET US APPA-LOOSA THEM.
TWITCH
HEY, IS THAT SCRAWNY GUY YOUR BOYFRIEND?
CAN HE REALLY KEEP YOU SATISFIED?
RUUUMMB
I BET THAT LITTLE VIRGIN'S LIKE A HOT DOG IN A HALLWAY!
RUUUMMBLE

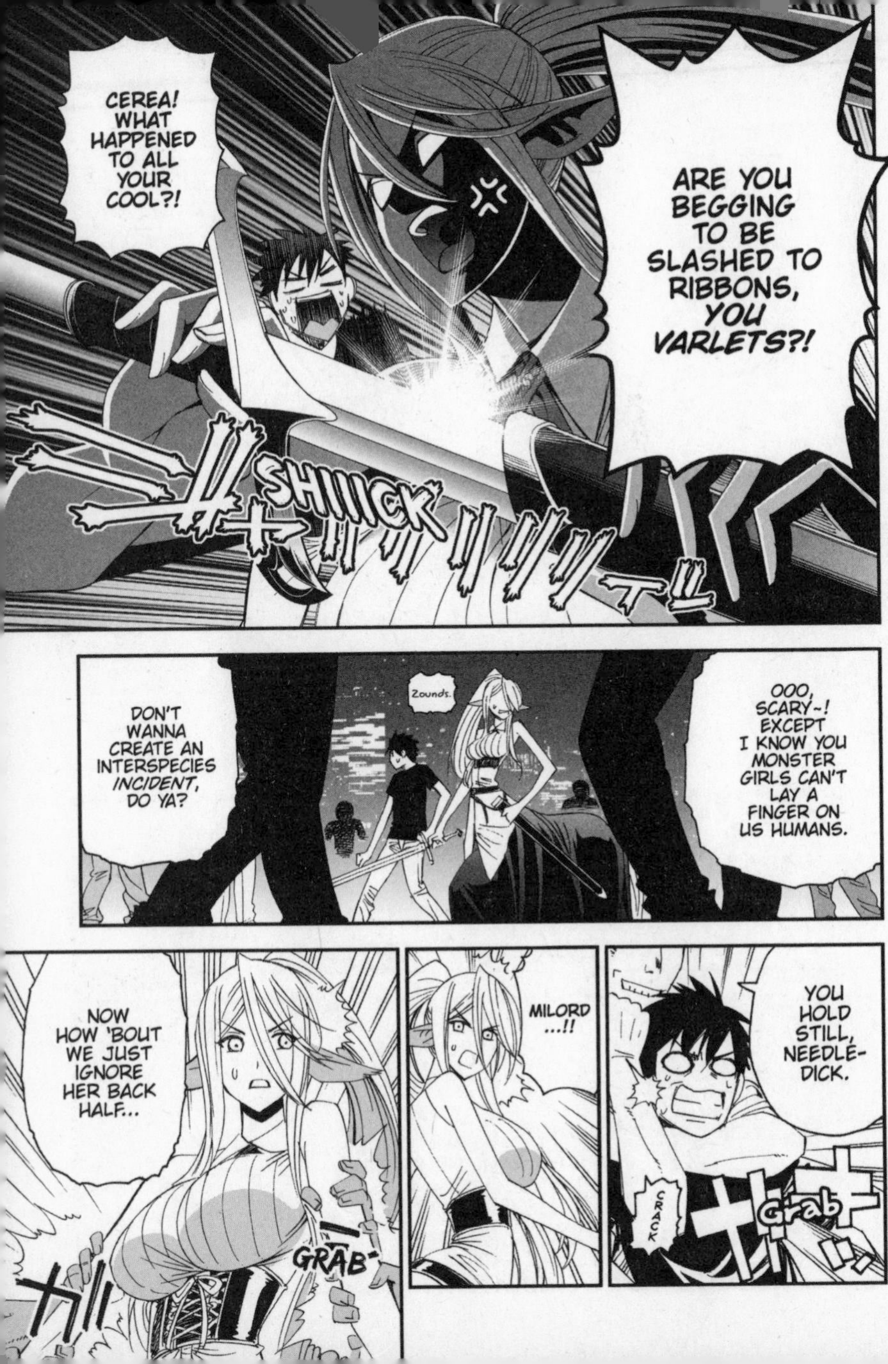
ARE YOU BEGGING TO BE SLASHED TO RIBBONS, YOU VARLETS?!
CEREA! WHAT HAPPENED TO ALL YOUR COOL?!
SHIIICK
OOO, SCARY~! EXCEPT I KNOW YOU MONSTER GIRLS CAN'T LAY A FINGER ON US HUMANS.
Zounds.
DON'T WANNA CREATE AN INTERSPECIES INCIDENT, DO YA?
YOU HOLD STILL, NEEDLE-DICK.
Grab
CRACK
MILORD ...!!
NOW HOW 'BOUT WE JUST IGNORE HER BACK HALF...
GRAB

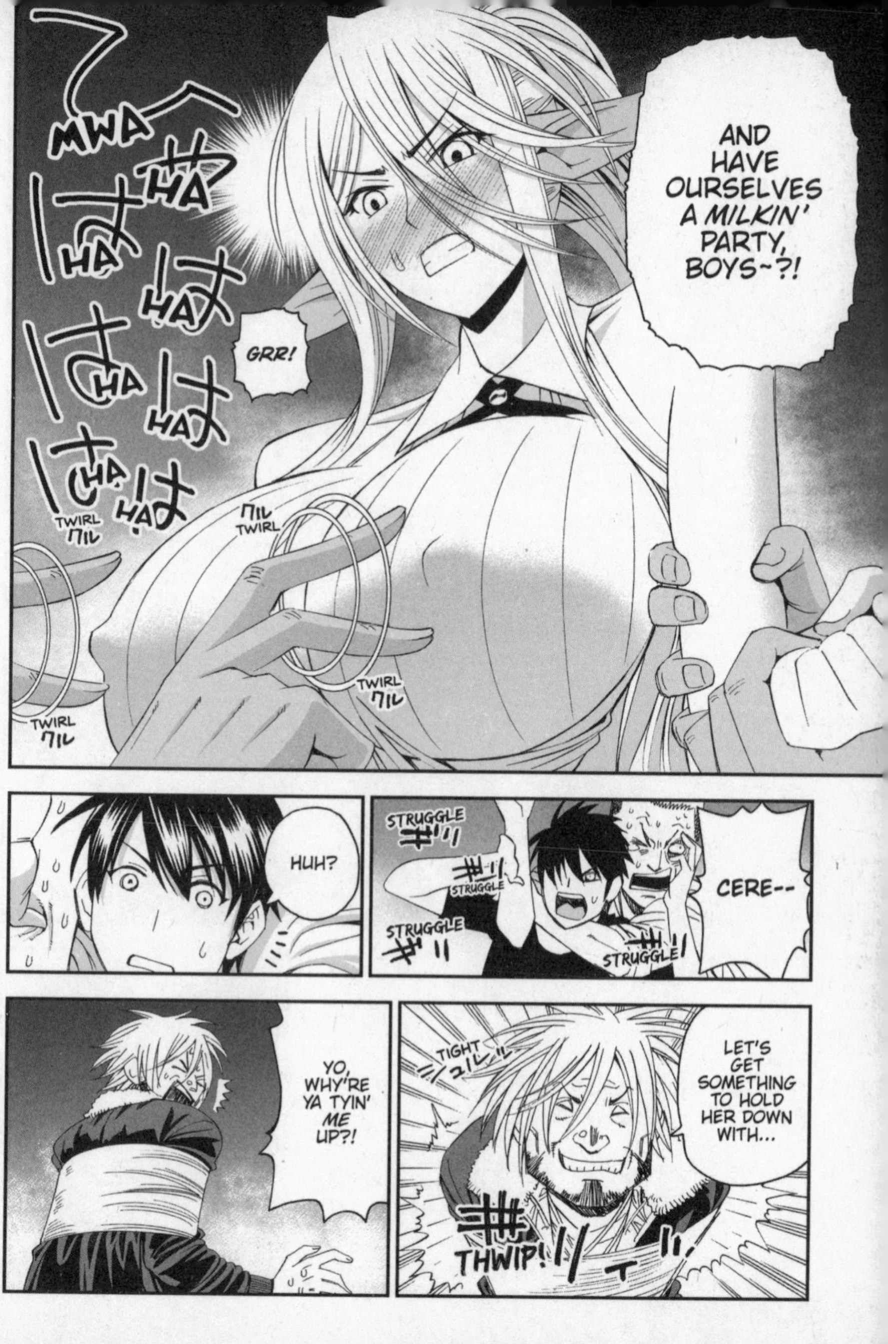
AND HAVE OURSELVES A MILKIN' PARTY, BOYS~?!
GRR!
MWA HA HA HA HA HA HA HA
TWIRL
TWIRL
TWIRL
TWIRL
CERE--
STRUGGLE
STRUGGLE
STRUGGLE
STRUGGLE
HUH?
TIGHT
LET'S GET SOMETHING TO HOLD HER DOWN WITH...
THWIP!
YO, WHY'RE YA TYIN' ME UP?!

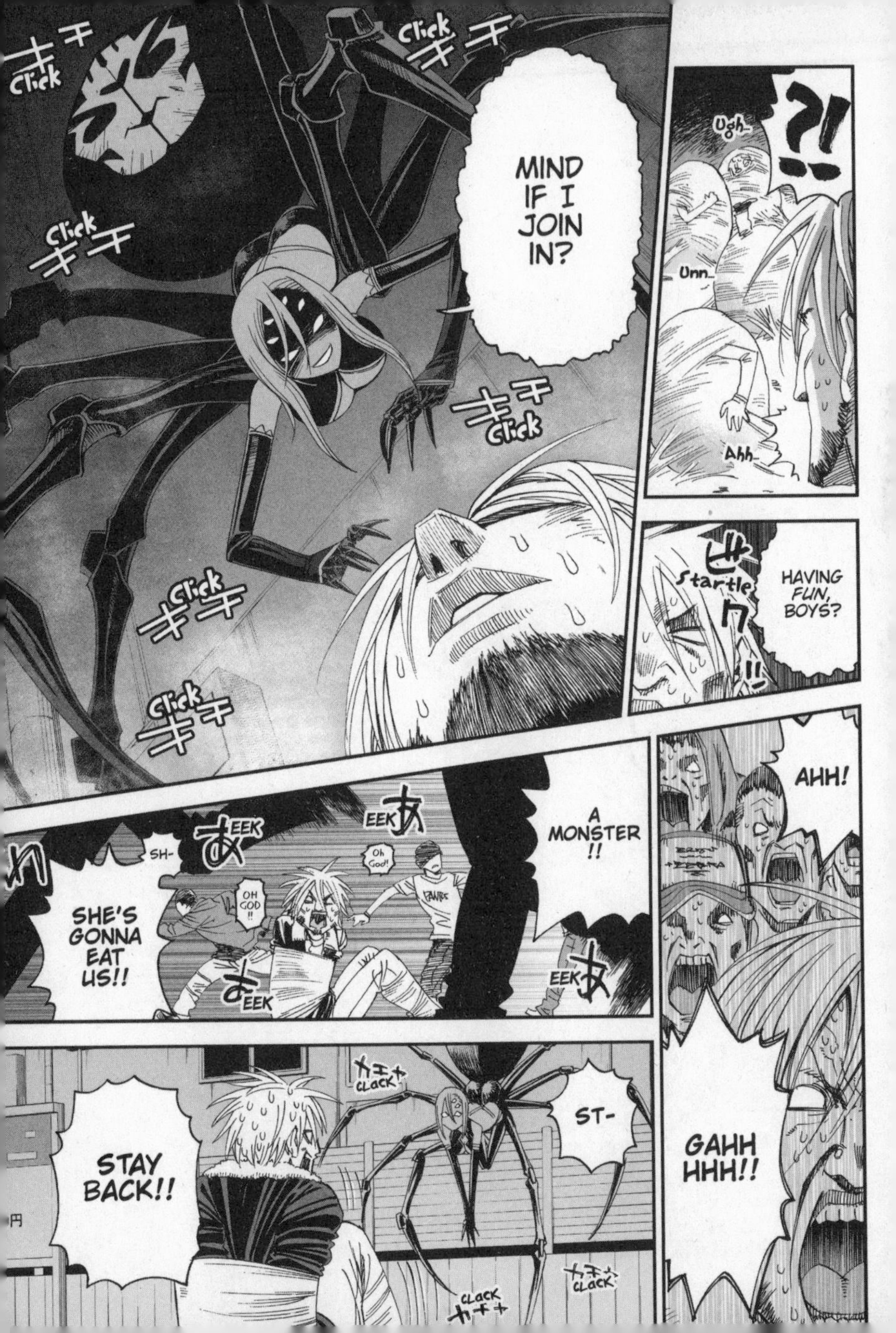
?!
Ugh...
Unn...
Ahh...
Startle
HAVING FUN, BOYS?
Click
Click
MIND IF I JOIN IN?
Click
Click
Click
Click
AHH!
GAHH HHH!!
A MONSTER!!
EEK
Oh God!
EEK
SH-
OH GOD!!
SHE'S GONNA EAT US!!
EEK
EEK
ST-
CLACK
STAY BACK!!
CLACK
CLACK

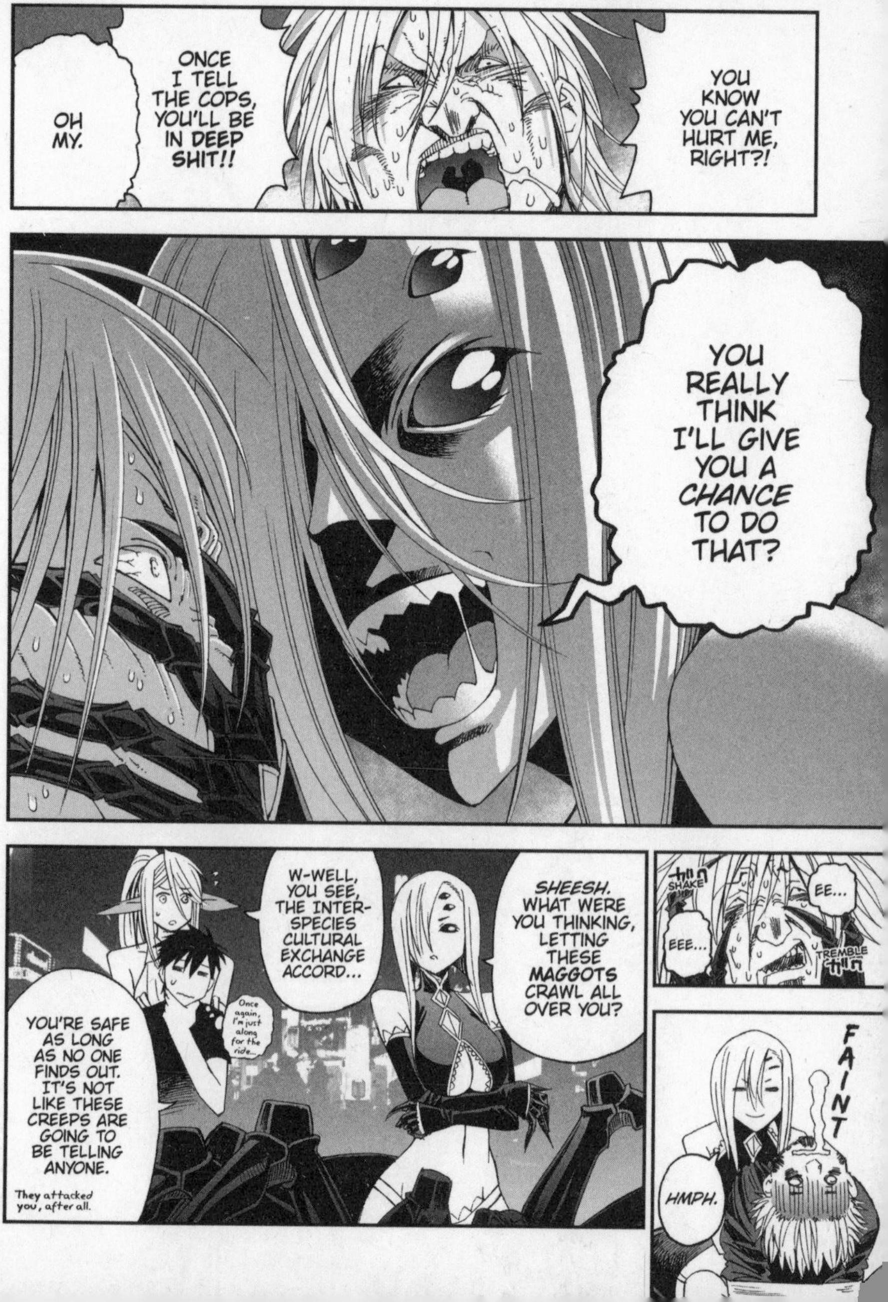
YOU KNOW YOU CAN'T HURT ME, RIGHT?!
ONCE I TELL THE COPS, YOU'LL BE IN DEEP SHIT!!
OH MY.
YOU REALLY THINK I'LL GIVE YOU A CHANCE TO DO THAT?
SHAKE
EE...
EEE...
TREMBLE
FAINT
HMPH.
SHEESH. WHAT WERE YOU THINKING, LETTING THESE MAGGOTS CRAWL ALL OVER YOU?
W-WELL, YOU SEE, THE INTER-SPECIES CULTURAL EXCHANGE ACCORD...
Once again, I'm just along for the ride...
YOU'RE SAFE AS LONG AS NO ONE FINDS OUT. IT'S NOT LIKE THESE CREEPS ARE GOING TO BE TELLING ANYONE.
They attacked you, after all.

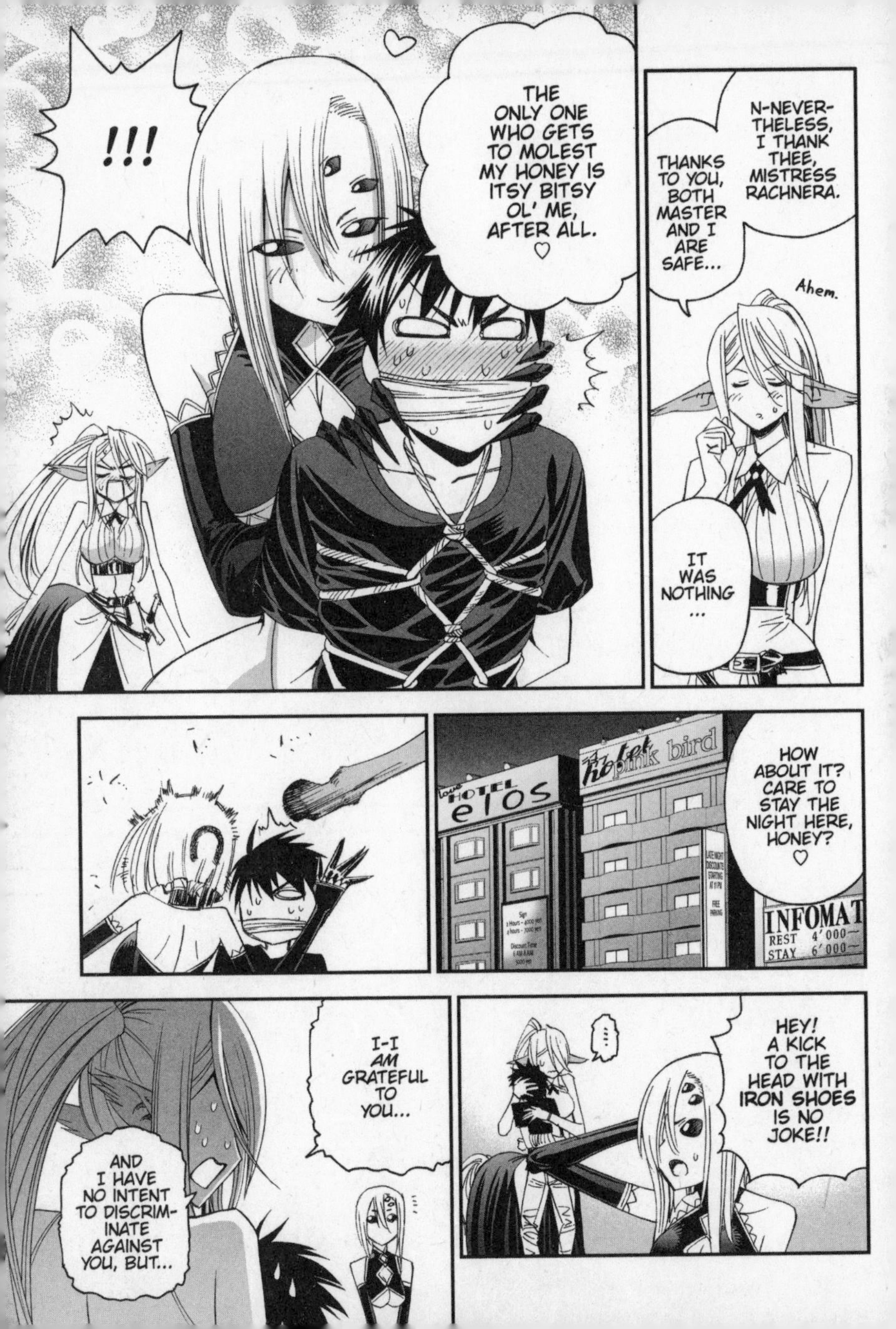
N-NEVERTHELESS, I THANK THEE, MISTRESS RACHNERA.
THANKS TO YOU, BOTH MASTER AND I ARE SAFE...
Ahem.
IT WAS NOTHING...
THE ONLY ONE WHO GETS TO MOLEST MY HONEY IS ITSY BITSY OL' ME, AFTER ALL. ♡
!!!
HOW ABOUT IT? CARE TO STAY THE NIGHT HERE, HONEY? ♡
pink bird
love HOTEL elos
INFOMAT
REST 4'000~
STAY 6'000~
HEY! A KICK TO THE HEAD WITH IRON SHOES IS NO JOKE!!
...
I-I AM GRATEFUL TO YOU...
AND I HAVE NO INTENT TO DISCRIMINATE AGAINST YOU, BUT...

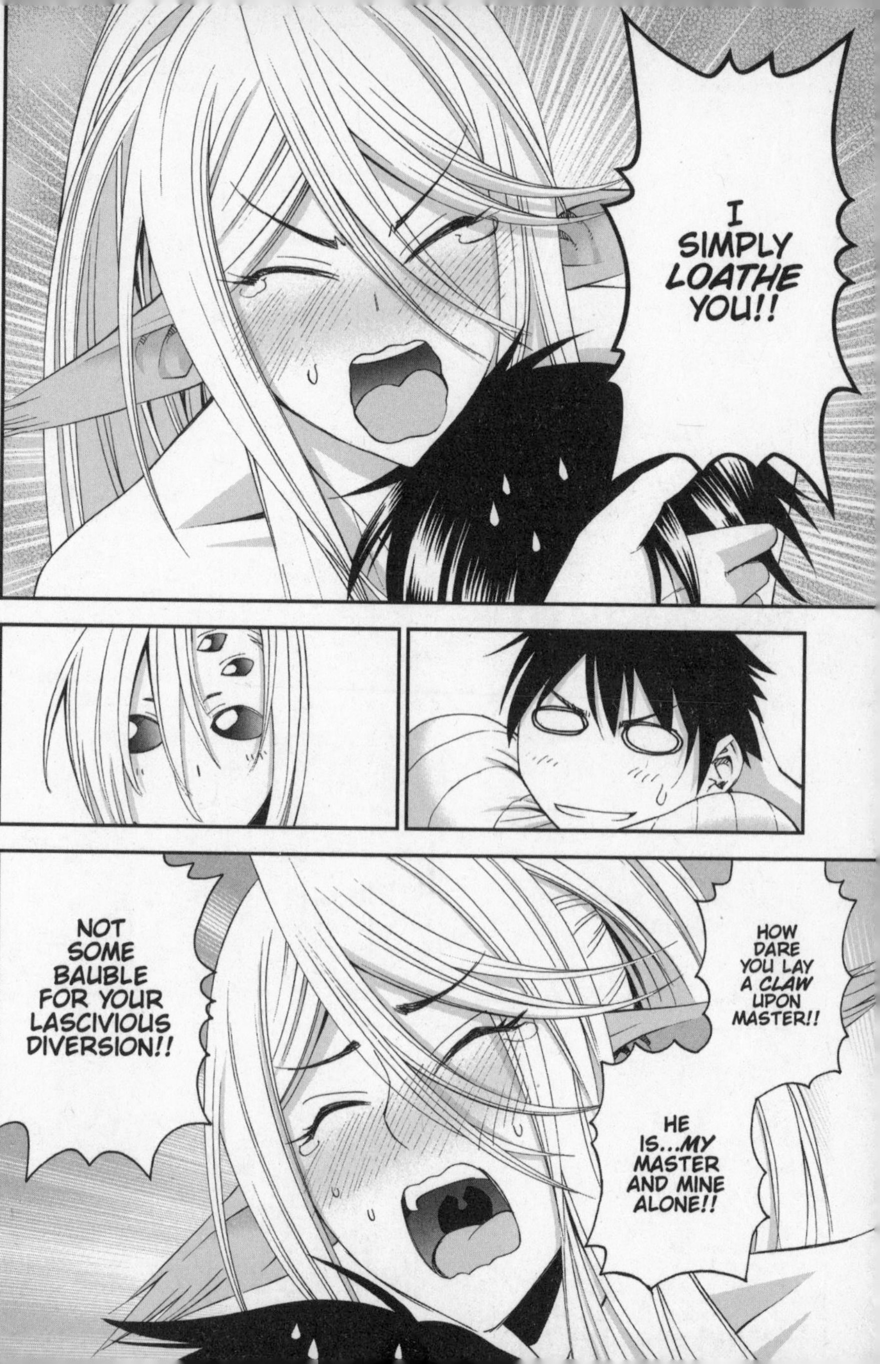
I SIMPLY *LOATHE* YOU!!
HOW DARE YOU LAY A *CLAW* UPON MASTER!!
HE IS...*MY* MASTER AND MINE ALONE!!
NOT SOME BAUBLE FOR YOUR LASCIVIOUS DIVERSION!!

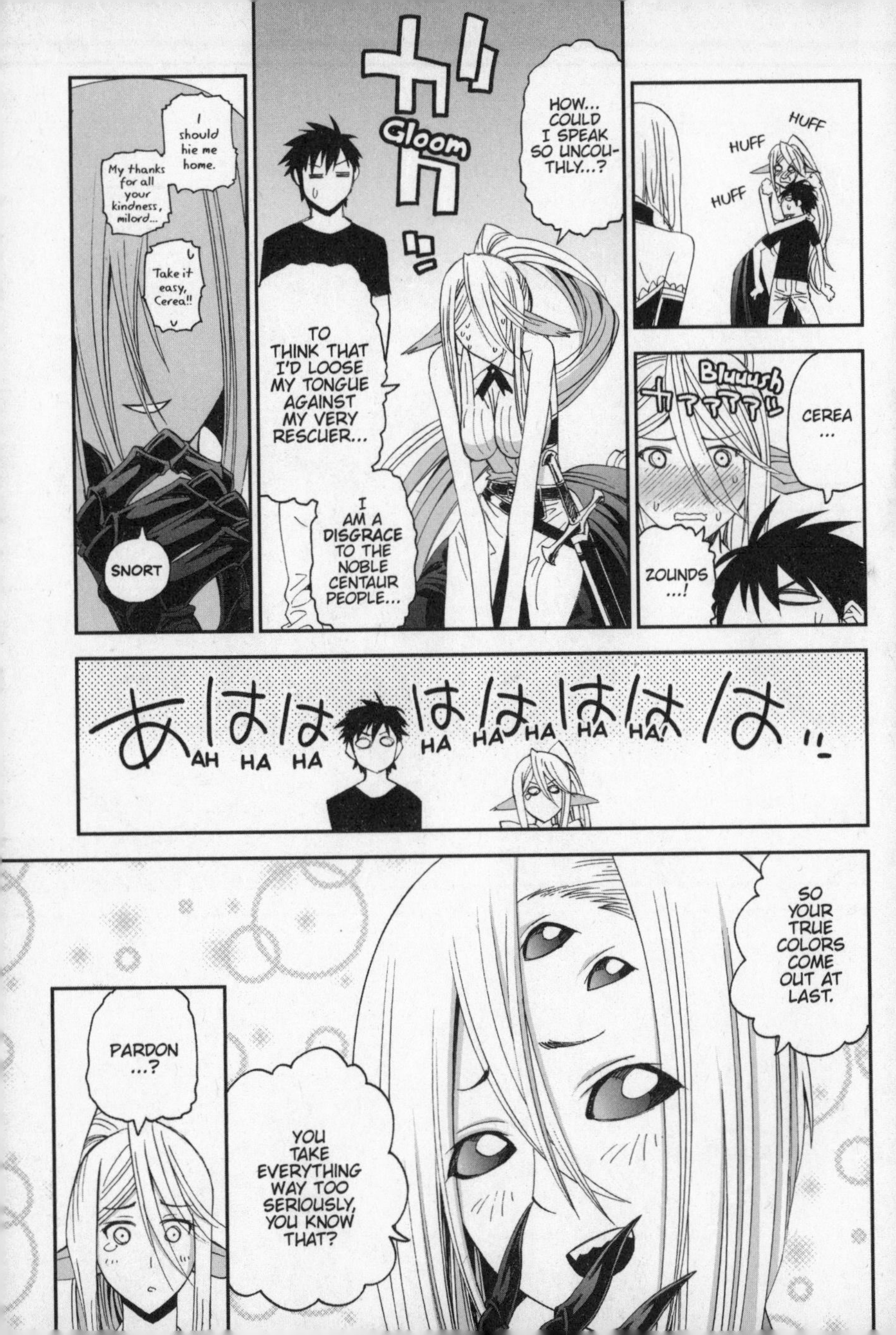
HUFF
HUFF
HUFF
Bluuush
カァァァァ!!
CEREA ...
ZOUNDS ...!
カク
Gloom
HOW... COULD I SPEAK SO UNCOUTHLY...?
TO THINK THAT I'D LOOSE MY TONGUE AGAINST MY VERY RESCUER...
I AM A DISGRACE TO THE NOBLE CENTAUR PEOPLE...
I should hie me home.
My thanks for all your kindness, milord...
Take it easy, Cerea!!
SNORT
あはははははははは!!
AH HA HA HA HA HA HA HA!
SO YOUR TRUE COLORS COME OUT AT LAST.
PARDON ...?
YOU TAKE EVERYTHING WAY TOO SERIOUSLY, YOU KNOW THAT?

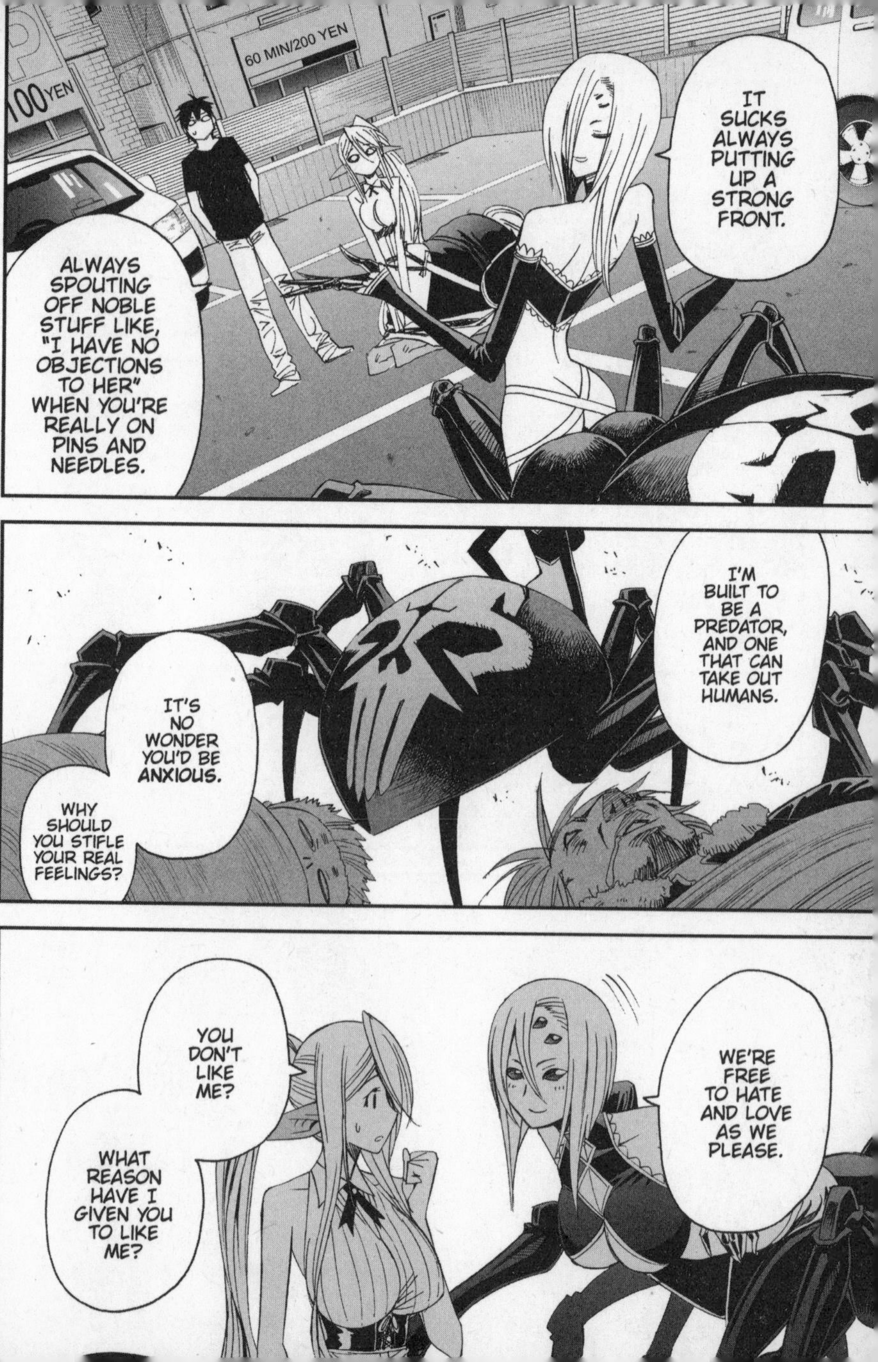
60 MIN/200 YEN
100YEN
IT SUCKS ALWAYS PUTTING UP A STRONG FRONT.
ALWAYS SPOUTING OFF NOBLE STUFF LIKE, "I HAVE NO OBJECTIONS TO HER" WHEN YOU'RE REALLY ON PINS AND NEEDLES.
I'M BUILT TO BE A PREDATOR, AND ONE THAT CAN TAKE OUT HUMANS.
IT'S NO WONDER YOU'D BE ANXIOUS.
WHY SHOULD YOU STIFLE YOUR REAL FEELINGS?
WE'RE FREE TO HATE AND LOVE AS WE PLEASE.
YOU DON'T LIKE ME?
WHAT REASON HAVE I GIVEN YOU TO LIKE ME?

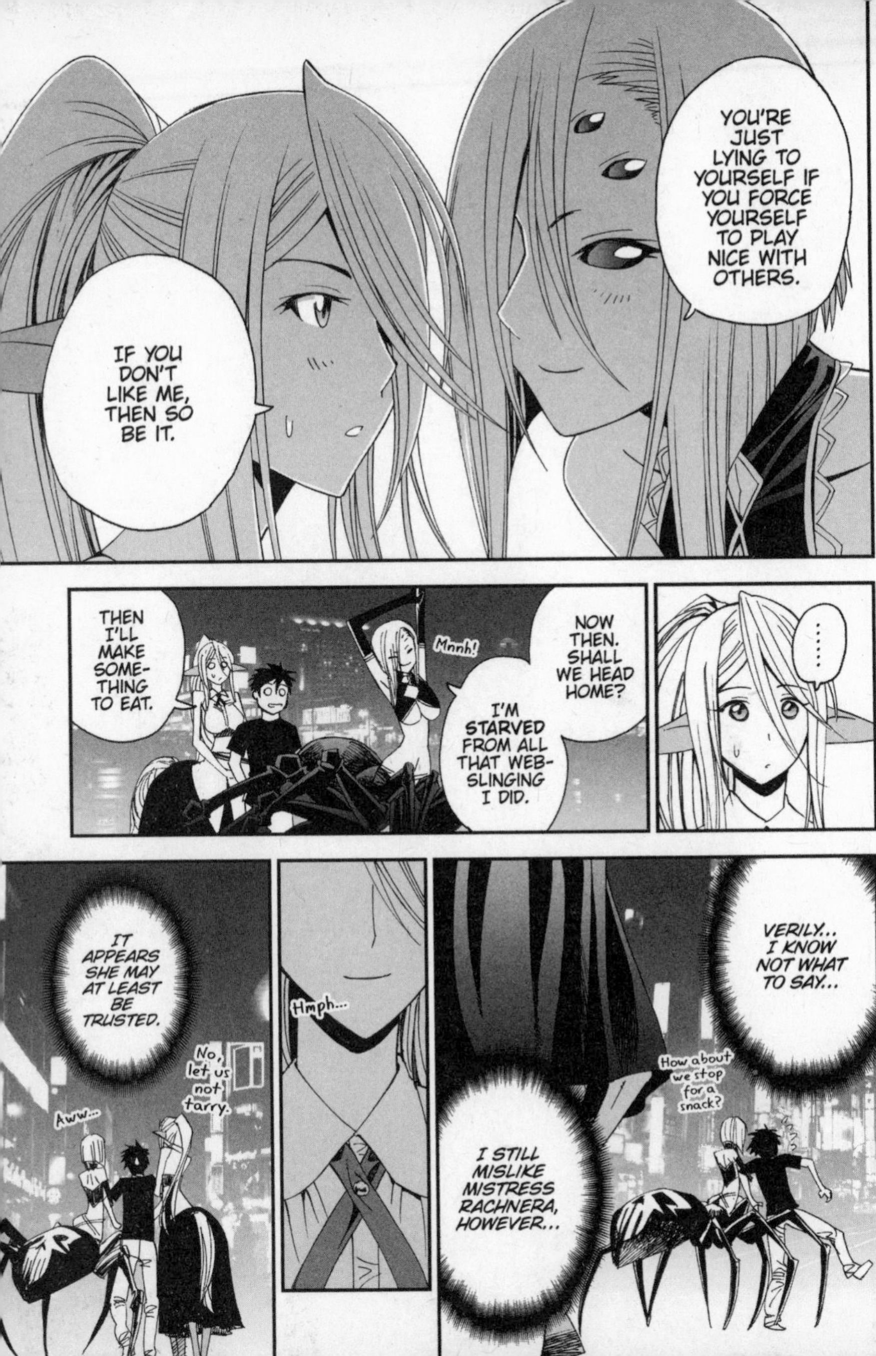
YOU'RE JUST LYING TO YOURSELF IF YOU FORCE YOURSELF TO PLAY NICE WITH OTHERS.
IF YOU DON'T LIKE ME, THEN SO BE IT.
......
NOW THEN. SHALL WE HEAD HOME?
I'M STARVED FROM ALL THAT WEB-SLINGING I DID.
Mnnh!
THEN I'LL MAKE SOME-THING TO EAT.
VERILY... I KNOW NOT WHAT TO SAY...
How about we stop for a snack?
I STILL MISLIKE MISTRESS RACHNERA, HOWEVER...
Hmph...
IT APPEARS SHE MAY AT LEAST BE TRUSTED.
No, let us not tarry.
Aww...

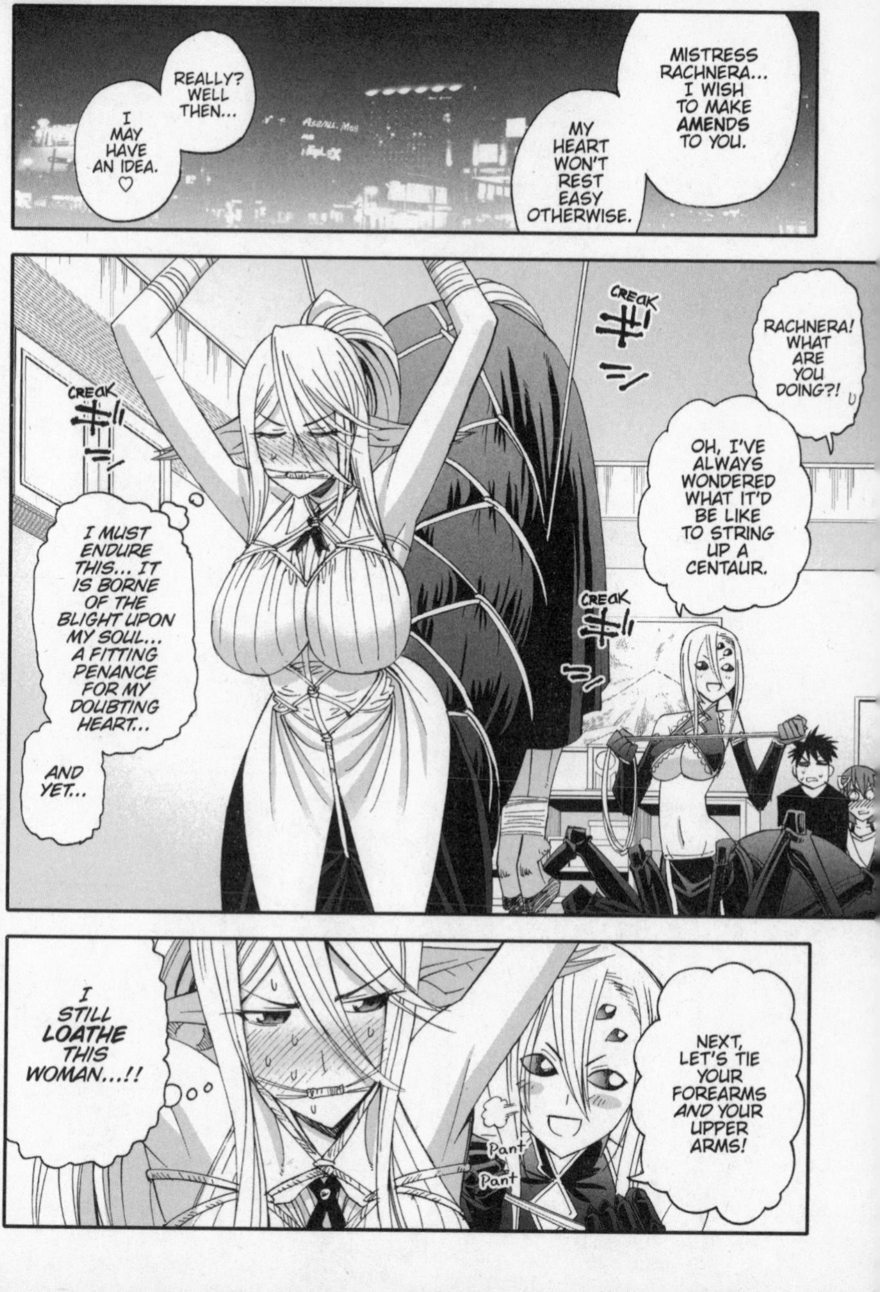

MISTRESS RACHNERA... I WISH TO MAKE AMENDS TO YOU.
MY HEART WON'T REST EASY OTHERWISE.
REALLY? WELL THEN...
I MAY HAVE AN IDEA. ♡
CREAK
RACHNERA! WHAT ARE YOU DOING?!
CREAK
OH, I'VE ALWAYS WONDERED WHAT IT'D BE LIKE TO STRING UP A CENTAUR.
CREAK
I MUST ENDURE THIS... IT IS BORNE OF THE BLIGHT UPON MY SOUL... A FITTING PENANCE FOR MY DOUBTING HEART...
AND YET...
NEXT, LET'S TIE YOUR FOREARMS AND YOUR UPPER ARMS!
Pant
Pant
I STILL LOATHE THIS WOMAN...!!

Monster Musume
Everyday Life with Monster Girls

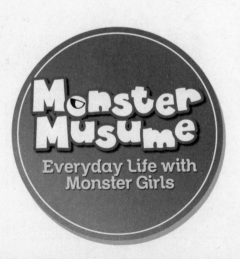

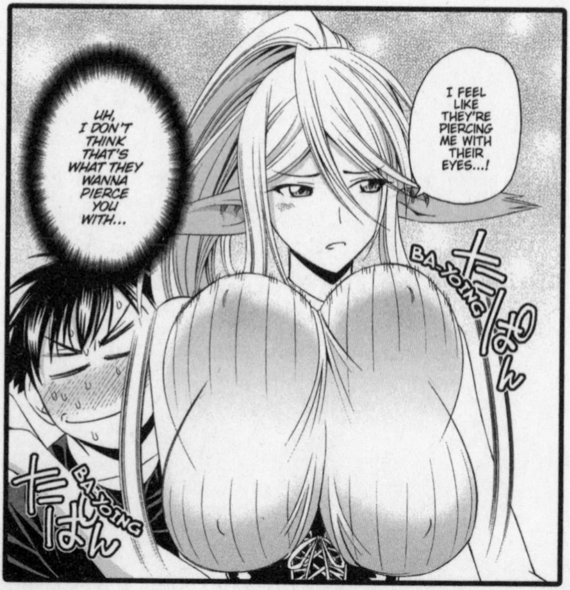
I FEEL LIKE THEY'RE PIERCING ME WITH THEIR EYES...!
BA-YOING
UH, I DON'T THINK THAT'S WHAT THEY WANNA PIERCE YOU WITH...
BA-YOING

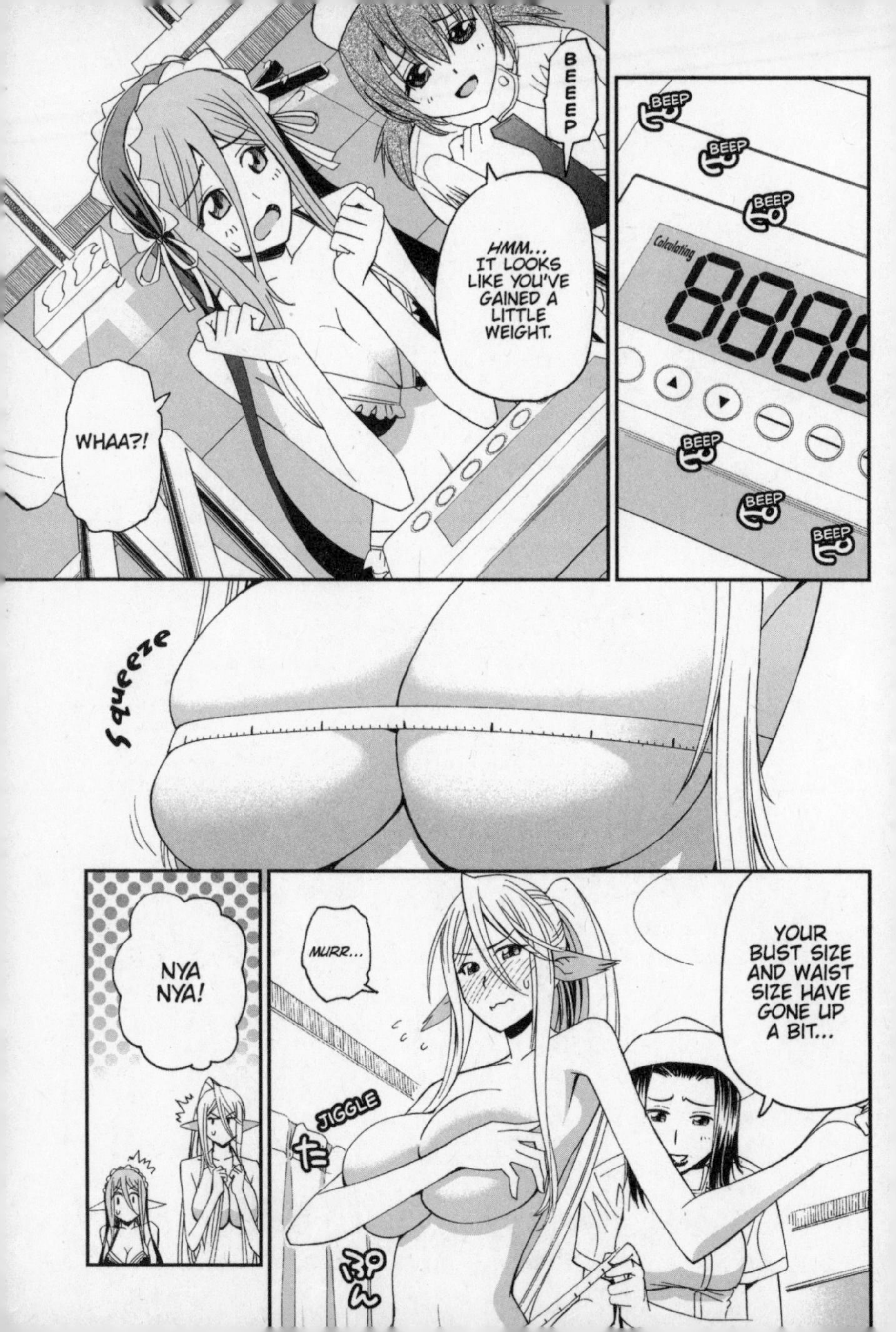
BEEP
BEEP
BEEP
Calculating
8888
BEEP
BEEP
BEEP
BEEEP
HMM... IT LOOKS LIKE YOU'VE GAINED A LITTLE WEIGHT.
WHAA?!
squeeze
YOUR BUST SIZE AND WAIST SIZE HAVE GONE UP A BIT...
MURR...
JIGGLE
NYA NYA!

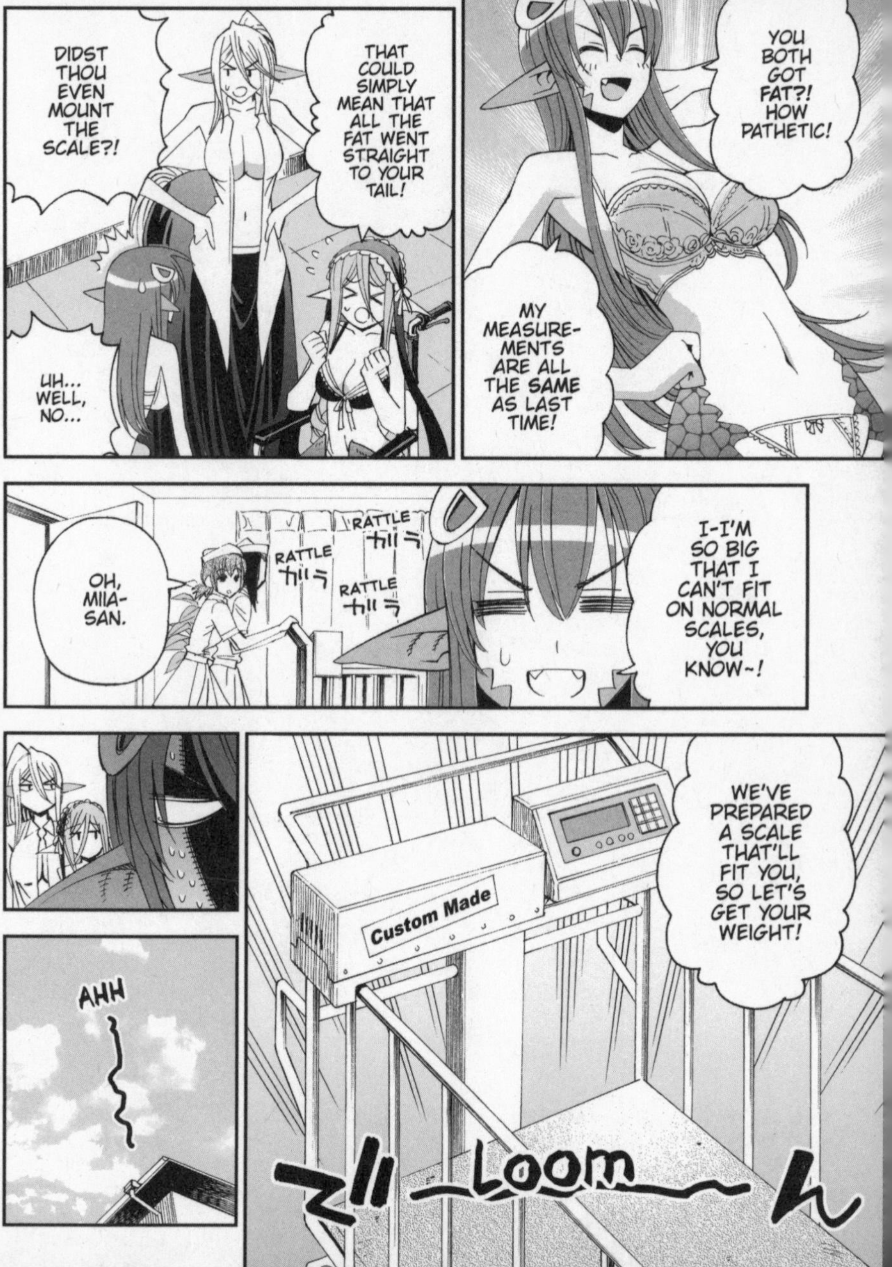
YOU BOTH GOT FAT?! HOW PATHETIC!
MY MEASUREMENTS ARE ALL THE SAME AS LAST TIME!
THAT COULD SIMPLY MEAN THAT ALL THE FAT WENT STRAIGHT TO YOUR TAIL!
DIDST THOU EVEN MOUNT THE SCALE?!
UH... WELL, NO...
I-I'M SO BIG THAT I CAN'T FIT ON NORMAL SCALES, YOU KNOW~!
RATTLE
ガラ
RATTLE
ガラ
RATTLE
ガラ
OH, MIIA-SAN.
WE'VE PREPARED A SCALE THAT'LL FIT YOU, SO LET'S GET YOUR WEIGHT!
Custom Made
LOOM
AHH

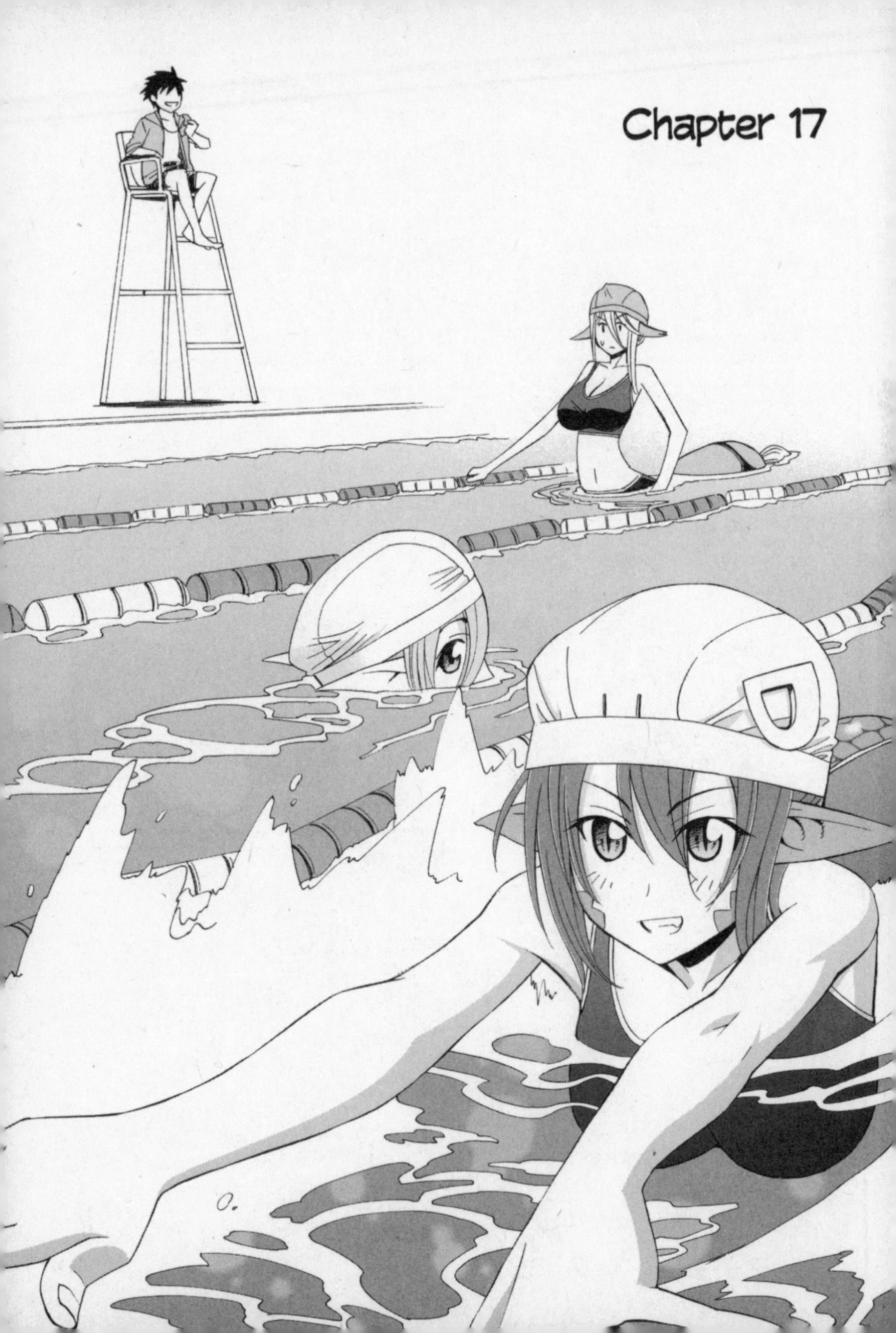
Chapter 17

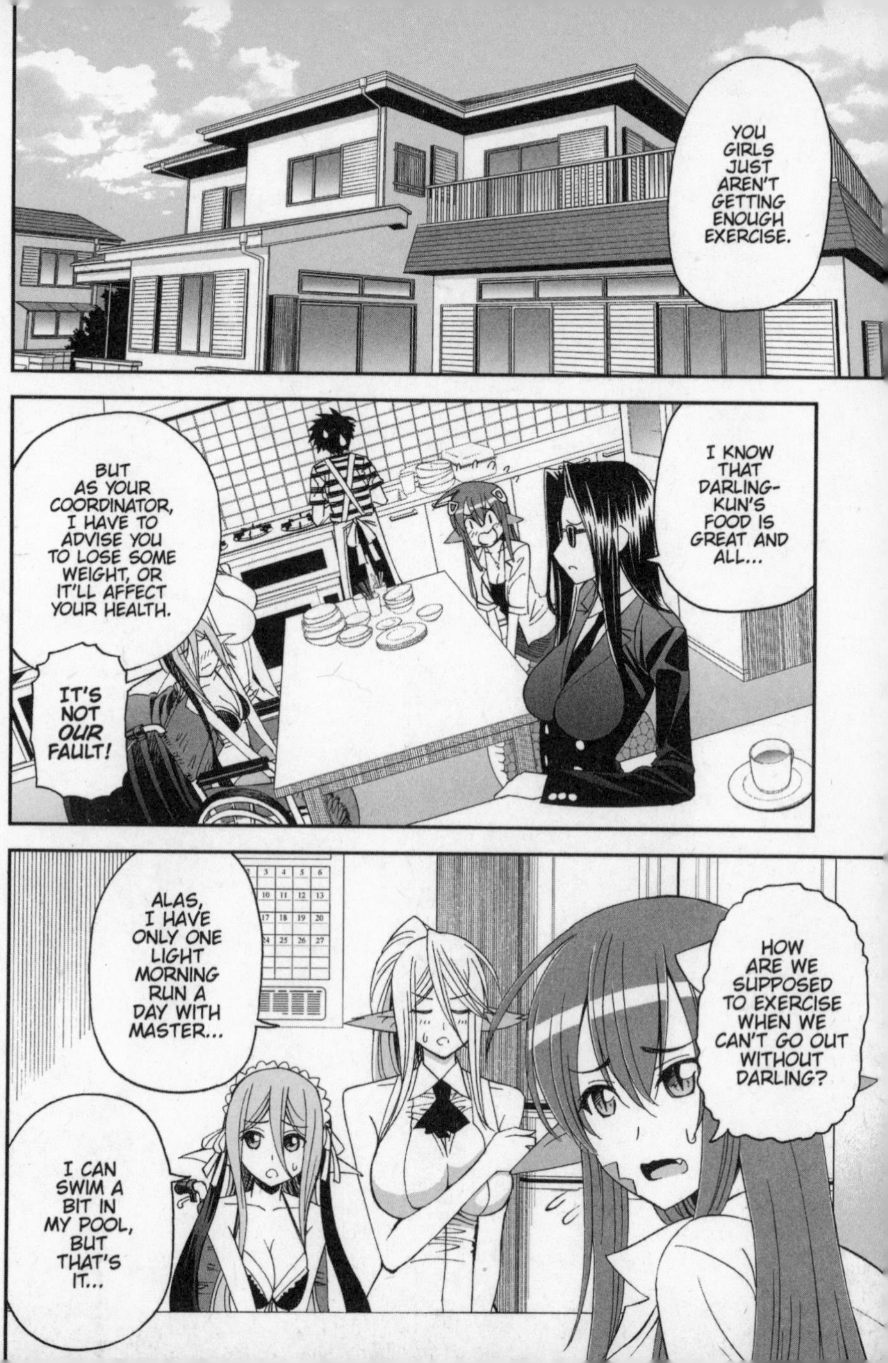
YOU GIRLS JUST AREN'T GETTING ENOUGH EXERCISE.
I KNOW THAT DARLING-KUN'S FOOD IS GREAT AND ALL...
BUT AS YOUR COORDINATOR, I HAVE TO ADVISE YOU TO LOSE SOME WEIGHT, OR IT'LL AFFECT YOUR HEALTH.
IT'S NOT *OUR* FAULT!
HOW ARE WE SUPPOSED TO EXERCISE WHEN WE CAN'T GO OUT WITHOUT DARLING?
ALAS, I HAVE ONLY ONE LIGHT MORNING RUN A DAY WITH MASTER...
I CAN SWIM A BIT IN MY POOL, BUT THAT'S IT...

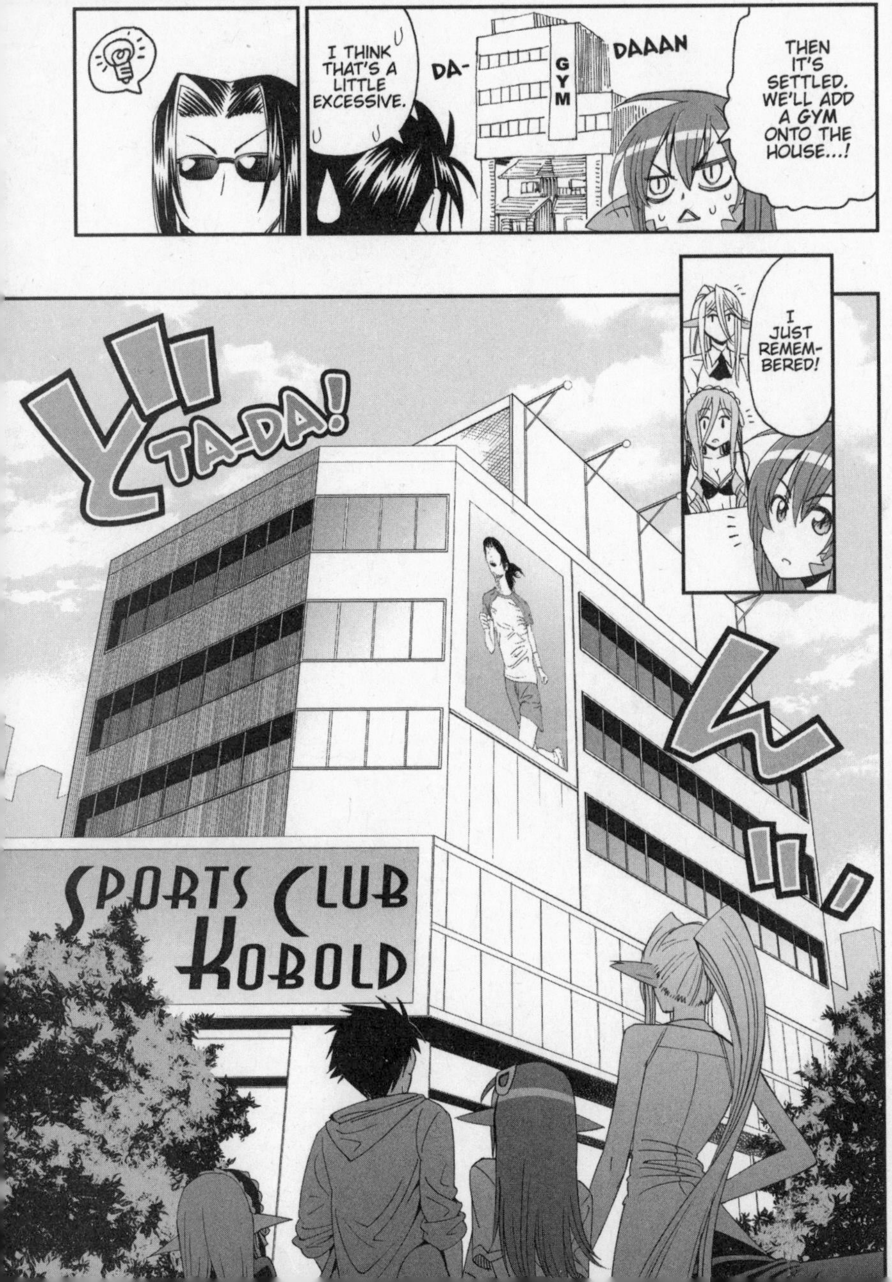
THEN IT'S SETTLED. WE'LL ADD A GYM ONTO THE HOUSE...!
DA- DAAAN
GYM
I THINK THAT'S A LITTLE EXCESSIVE.
I JUST REMEM-BERED!
TA-DA!
SPORTS CLUB KOBOLD

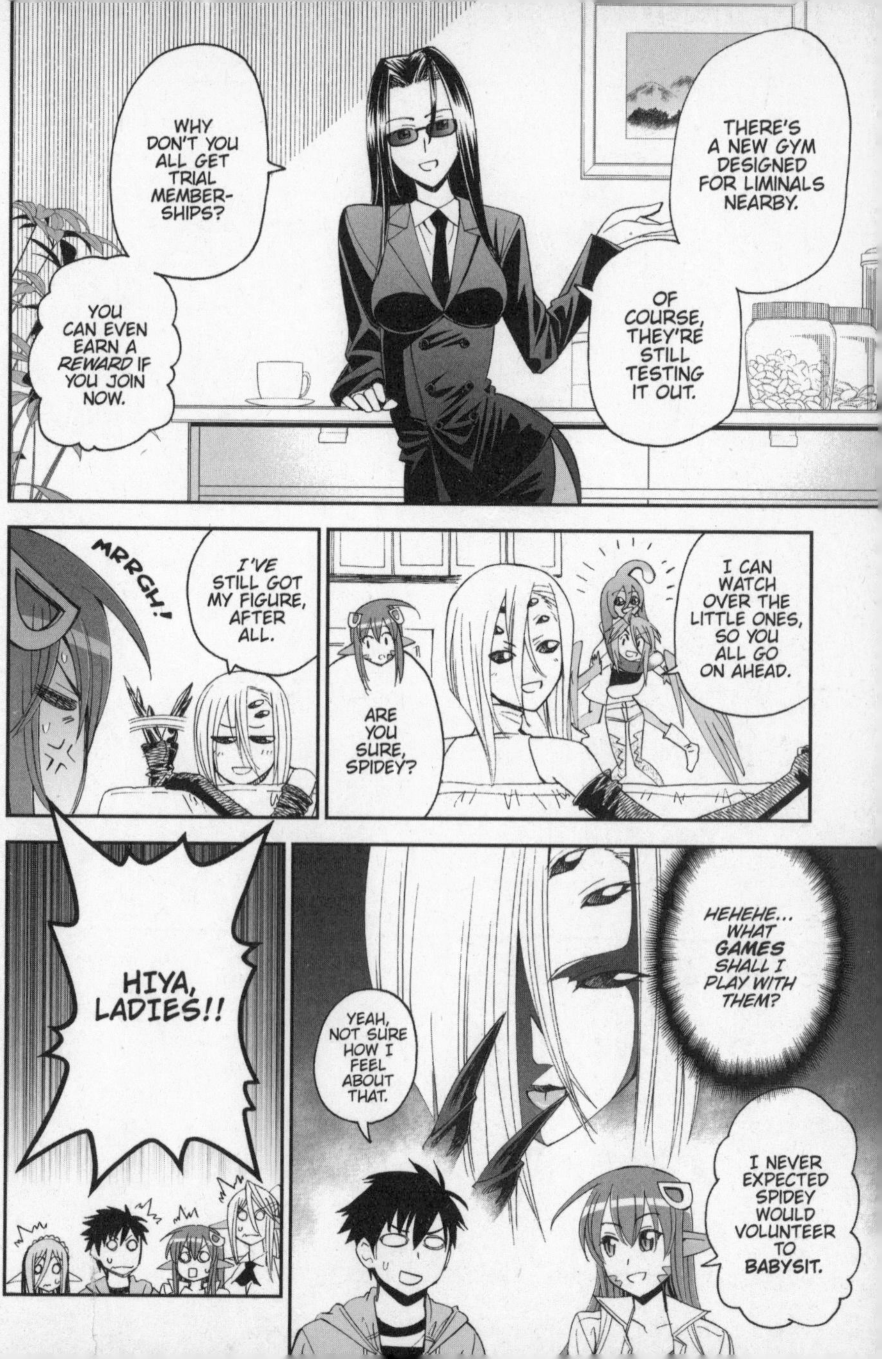
THERE'S A NEW GYM DESIGNED FOR LIMINALS NEARBY.
OF COURSE, THEY'RE STILL TESTING IT OUT.
WHY DON'T YOU ALL GET TRIAL MEMBERSHIPS?
YOU CAN EVEN EARN A *REWARD* IF YOU JOIN NOW.
I CAN WATCH OVER THE LITTLE ONES, SO YOU ALL GO ON AHEAD.
ARE YOU SURE, SPIDEY?
I'VE STILL GOT MY FIGURE, AFTER ALL.
MRRGH!
HEHEHE... WHAT **GAMES** *SHALL I PLAY WITH THEM?*
I NEVER EXPECTED SPIDEY WOULD VOLUNTEER TO BABYSIT.
YEAH, NOT SURE HOW I FEEL ABOUT THAT.
HIYA, LADIES!!

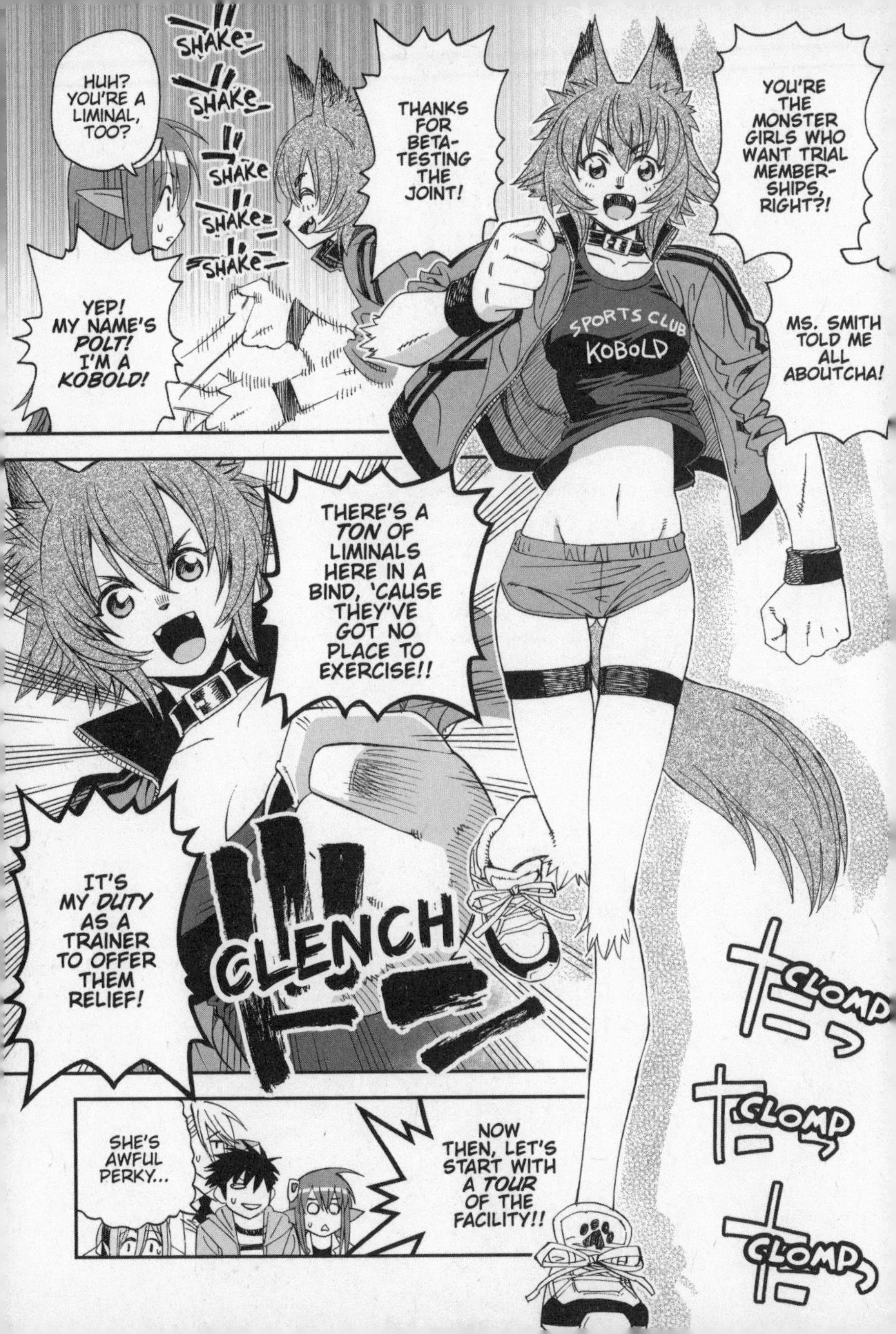
YOU'RE THE MONSTER GIRLS WHO WANT TRIAL MEMBER-SHIPS, RIGHT?!
MS. SMITH TOLD ME ALL ABOUTCHA!
SPORTS CLUB KOBOLD
CLOMP
CLOMP
CLOMP
THANKS FOR BETA-TESTING THE JOINT!
SHAKE
SHAKE
SHAKE
SHAKE
SHAKE
HUH? YOU'RE A LIMINAL, TOO?
YEP! MY NAME'S *POLT*! I'M A *KOBOLD*!
THERE'S A *TON* OF LIMINALS HERE IN A BIND, 'CAUSE THEY'VE GOT NO PLACE TO EXERCISE!!
IT'S MY *DUTY* AS A TRAINER TO OFFER THEM RELIEF!
CLENCH
NOW THEN, LET'S START WITH A *TOUR* OF THE FACILITY!!
SHE'S AWFUL PERKY...

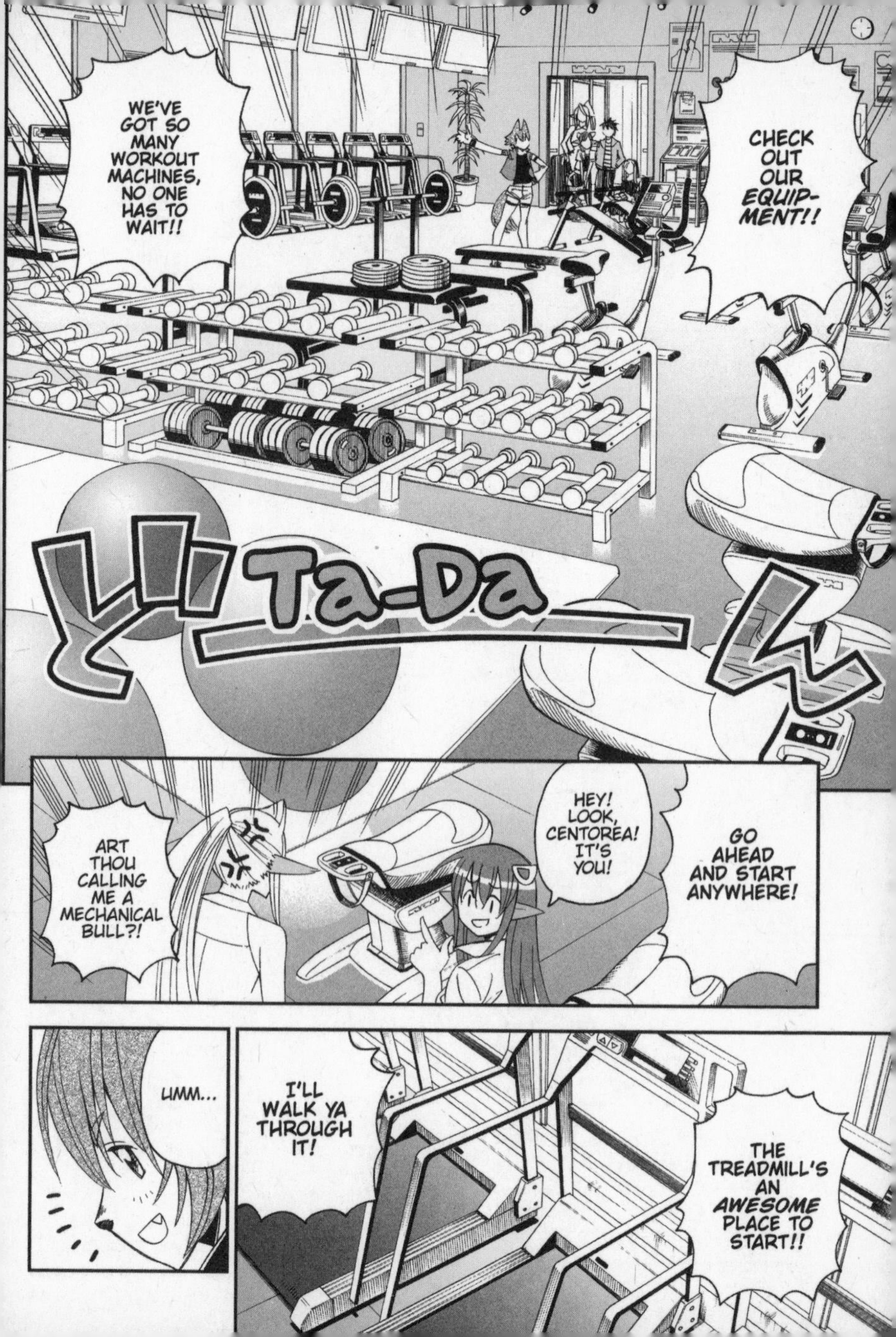
CHECK OUT OUR EQUIPMENT!!
WE'VE GOT SO MANY WORKOUT MACHINES, NO ONE HAS TO WAIT!!
Ta-Da
GO AHEAD AND START ANYWHERE!
HEY! LOOK, CENTOREA! IT'S YOU!
ART THOU CALLING ME A MECHANICAL BULL?!
THE TREADMILL'S AN AWESOME PLACE TO START!!
I'LL WALK YA THROUGH IT!
UMM...

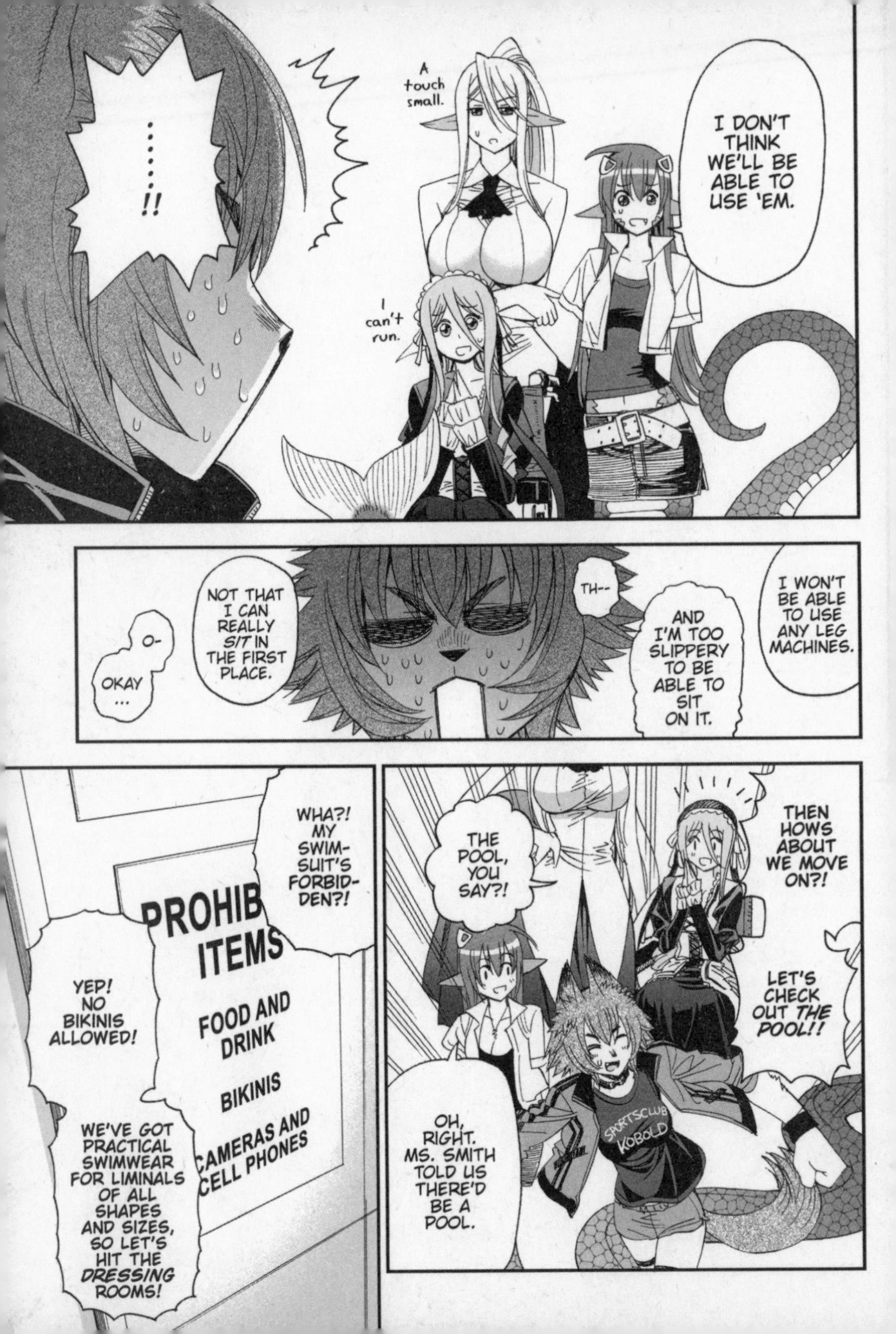
I DON'T THINK WE'LL BE ABLE TO USE 'EM.
A touch small.
I can't run.
......!!
I WON'T BE ABLE TO USE ANY LEG MACHINES.
AND I'M TOO SLIPPERY TO BE ABLE TO SIT ON IT.
TH--
NOT THAT I CAN REALLY *SIT* IN THE FIRST PLACE.
O- OKAY ...
THEN HOWS ABOUT WE MOVE ON?!
THE POOL, YOU SAY?!
LET'S CHECK OUT *THE POOL!!*
OH, RIGHT. MS. SMITH TOLD US THERE'D BE A POOL.
SPORTSCLUB KOBOLD
WHA?! MY SWIM-SUIT'S FORBID-DEN?!
PROHIB ITEMS
FOOD AND DRINK
BIKINIS
CAMERAS AND CELL PHONES
YEP! NO BIKINIS ALLOWED!
WE'VE GOT PRACTICAL SWIMWEAR FOR LIMINALS OF ALL SHAPES AND SIZES, SO LET'S HIT THE *DRESSING* ROOMS!

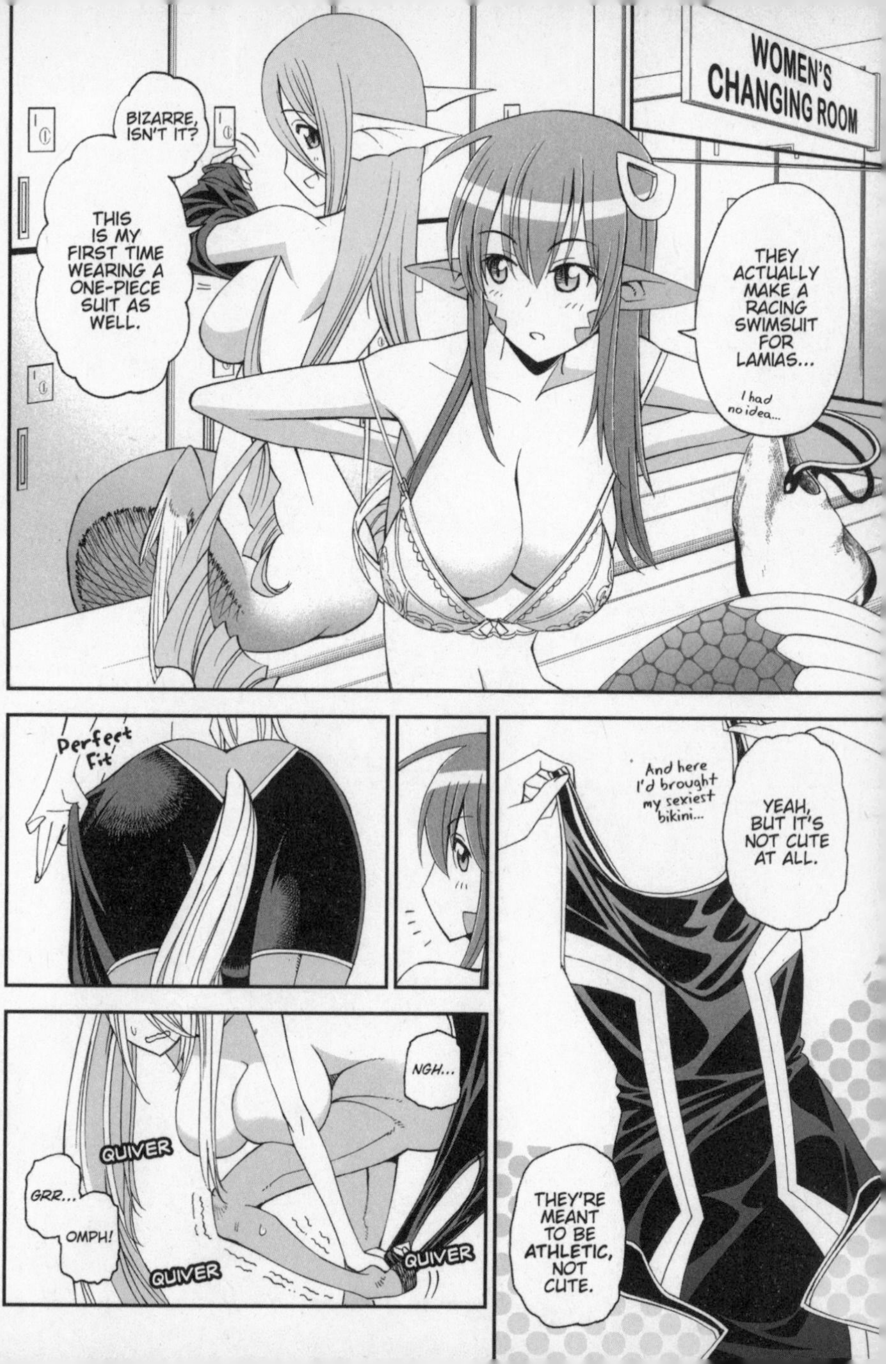
WOMEN'S CHANGING ROOM
THEY ACTUALLY MAKE A RACING SWIMSUIT FOR LAMIAS...
I had no idea...
BIZARRE, ISN'T IT?
THIS IS MY FIRST TIME WEARING A ONE-PIECE SUIT AS WELL.
YEAH, BUT IT'S NOT CUTE AT ALL.
And here I'd brought my sexiest bikini...
THEY'RE MEANT TO BE ATHLETIC, NOT CUTE.
Perfect Fit
NGH...
QUIVER
GRR...
OMPH!
QUIVER
QUIVER

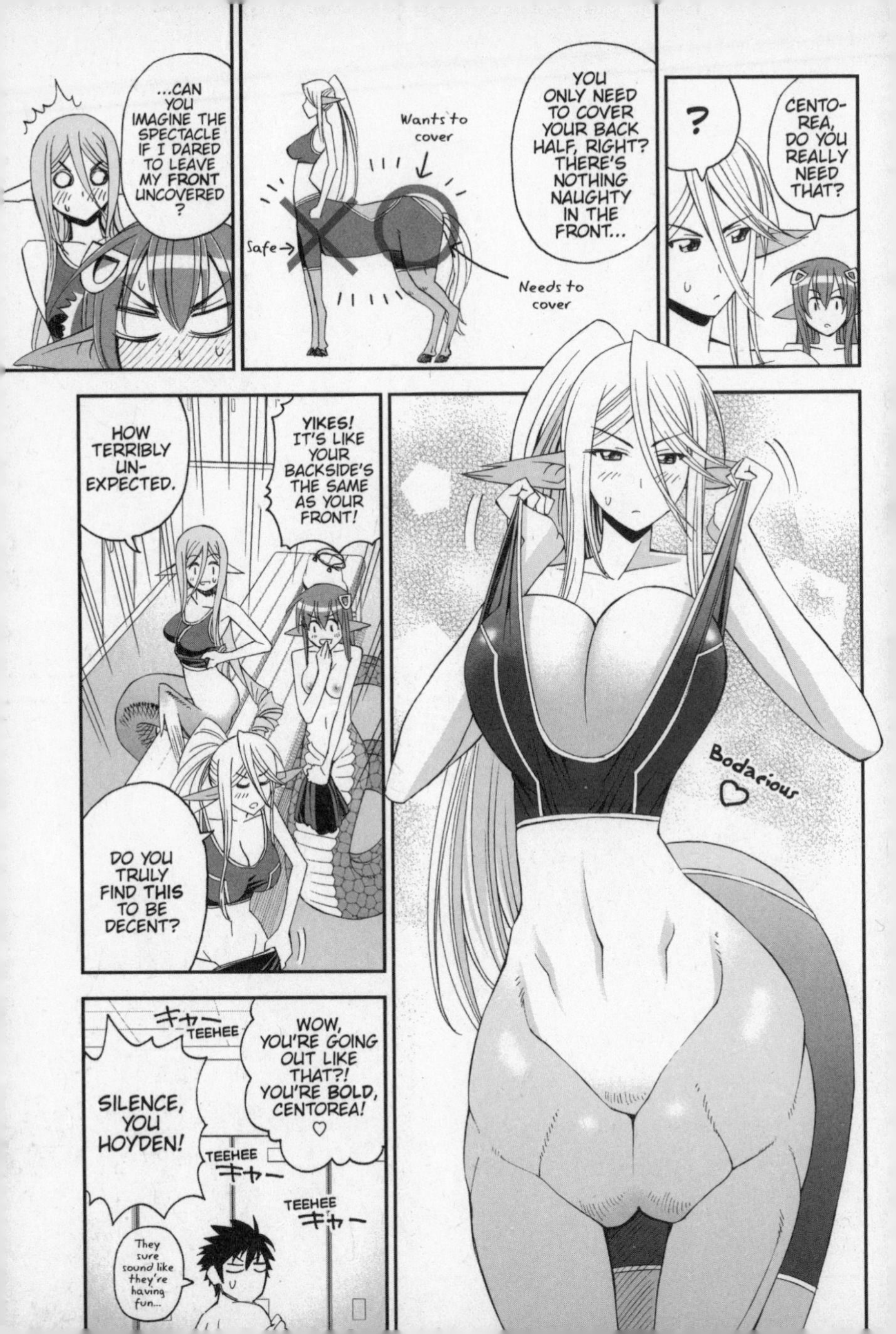
CENTO-REA, DO YOU REALLY NEED THAT?
?
YOU ONLY NEED TO COVER YOUR BACK HALF, RIGHT? THERE'S NOTHING NAUGHTY IN THE FRONT...
Wants to cover
Safe→
Needs to cover
...CAN YOU IMAGINE THE SPECTACLE IF I DARED TO LEAVE MY FRONT UNCOVERED?
Bodacious ♡
YIKES! IT'S LIKE YOUR BACKSIDE'S THE SAME AS YOUR FRONT!
HOW TERRIBLY UN-EXPECTED.
DO YOU TRULY FIND THIS TO BE DECENT?
WOW, YOU'RE GOING OUT LIKE THAT?! YOU'RE BOLD, CENTOREA! ♡
キャー TEEHEE
SILENCE, YOU HOYDEN!
TEEHEE キャー
TEEHEE キャー
They sure sound like they're having fun...

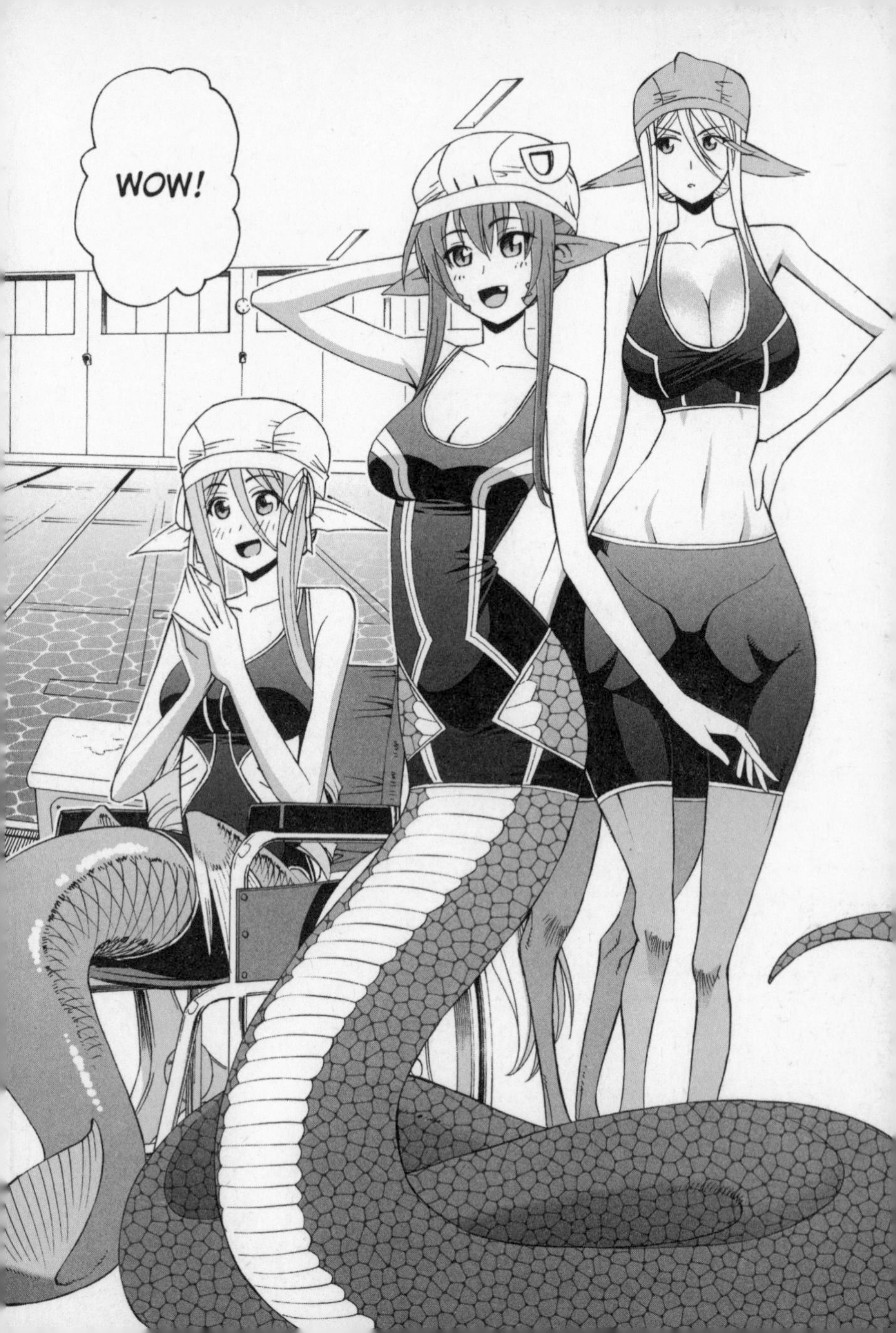
WOW!

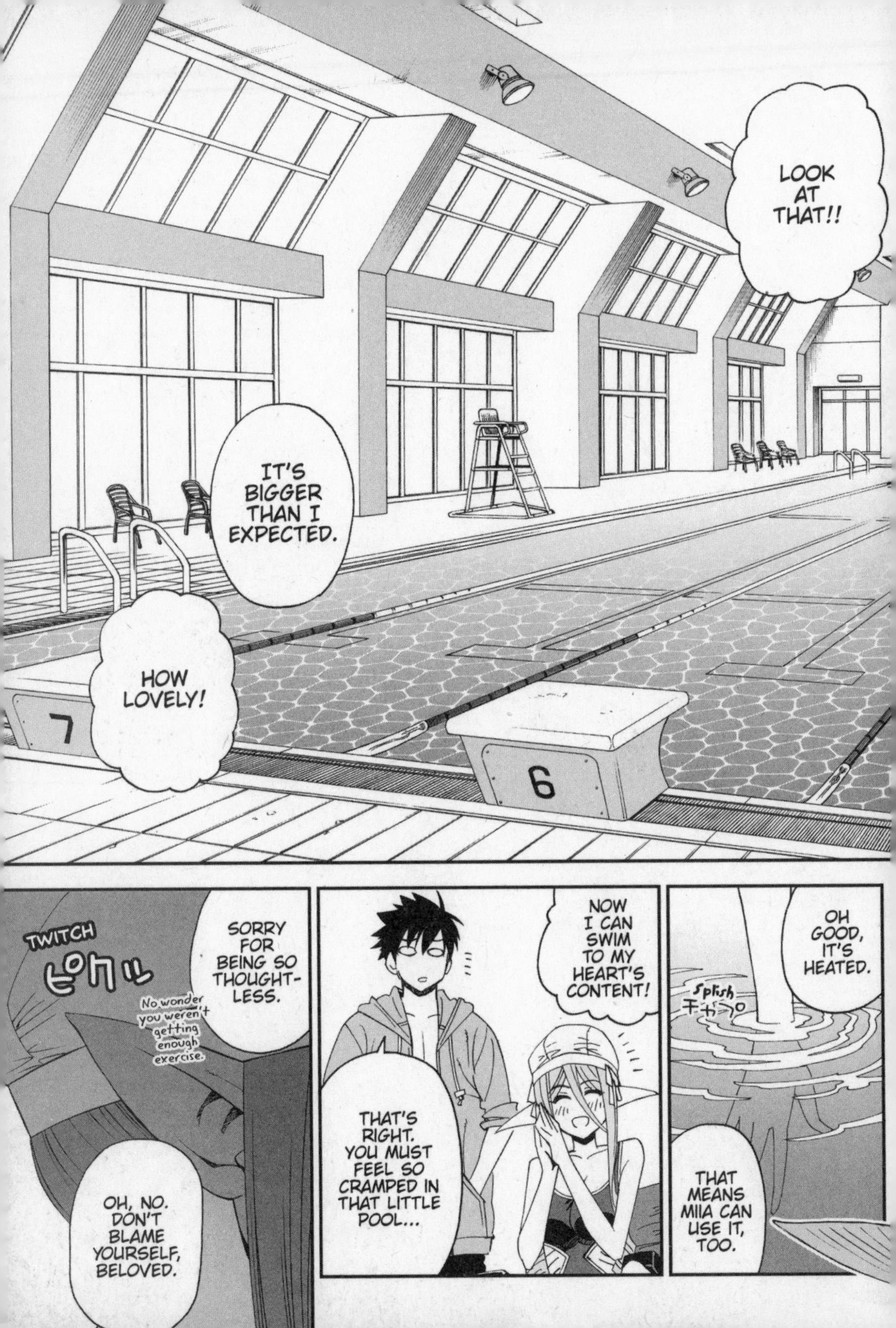
LOOK AT THAT!!
IT'S BIGGER THAN I EXPECTED.
HOW LOVELY!
OH GOOD, IT'S HEATED.
Splish
THAT MEANS MIIA CAN USE IT, TOO.
NOW I CAN SWIM TO MY HEART'S CONTENT!
THAT'S RIGHT. YOU MUST FEEL SO CRAMPED IN THAT LITTLE POOL...
SORRY FOR BEING SO THOUGHTLESS.
TWITCH
No wonder you weren't getting enough exercise.
OH, NO. DON'T BLAME YOURSELF, BELOVED.

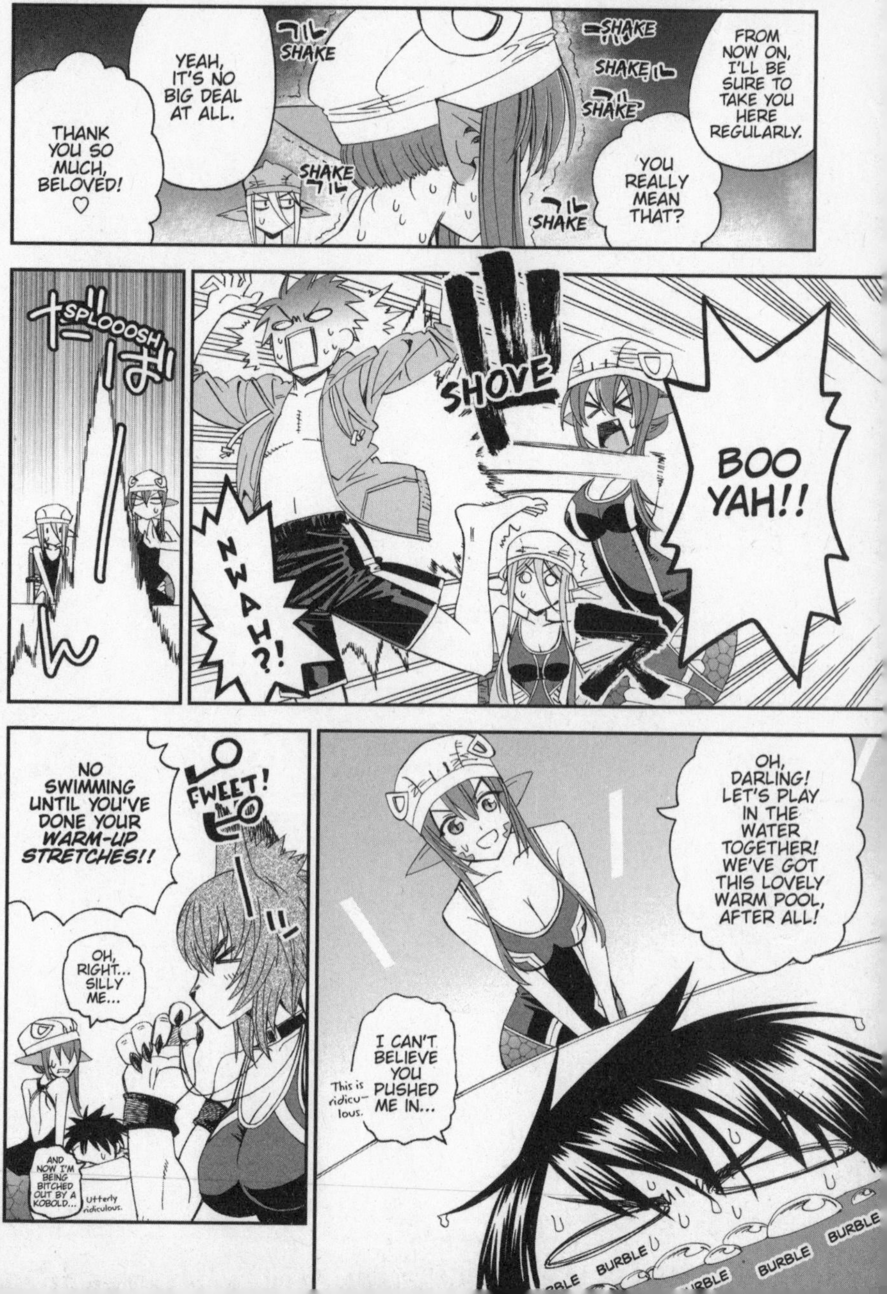
FROM NOW ON, I'LL BE SURE TO TAKE YOU HERE REGULARLY.
SHAKE
SHAKE
SHAKE
YOU REALLY MEAN THAT?
SHAKE
SHAKE
SHAKE
YEAH, IT'S NO BIG DEAL AT ALL.
THANK YOU SO MUCH, BELOVED! ♡
BOO YAH!!
SHOVE
NWAH?!
SPLOOOSH
OH, DARLING! LET'S PLAY IN THE WATER TOGETHER! WE'VE GOT THIS LOVELY WARM POOL, AFTER ALL!
I CAN'T BELIEVE YOU PUSHED ME IN...
This is ridiculous.
BURBLE BURBLE BURBLE BURBLE BURBLE
FWEET!
NO SWIMMING UNTIL YOU'VE DONE YOUR WARM-UP STRETCHES!!
OH, RIGHT... SILLY ME...
AND NOW I'M BEING BITCHED OUT BY A KOBOLD...
Utterly ridiculous.

BOING

?

Okay, on your feet now!!

I can't!

BOING

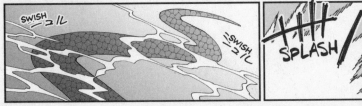

SWISH

SWISH

SPLASH

♪

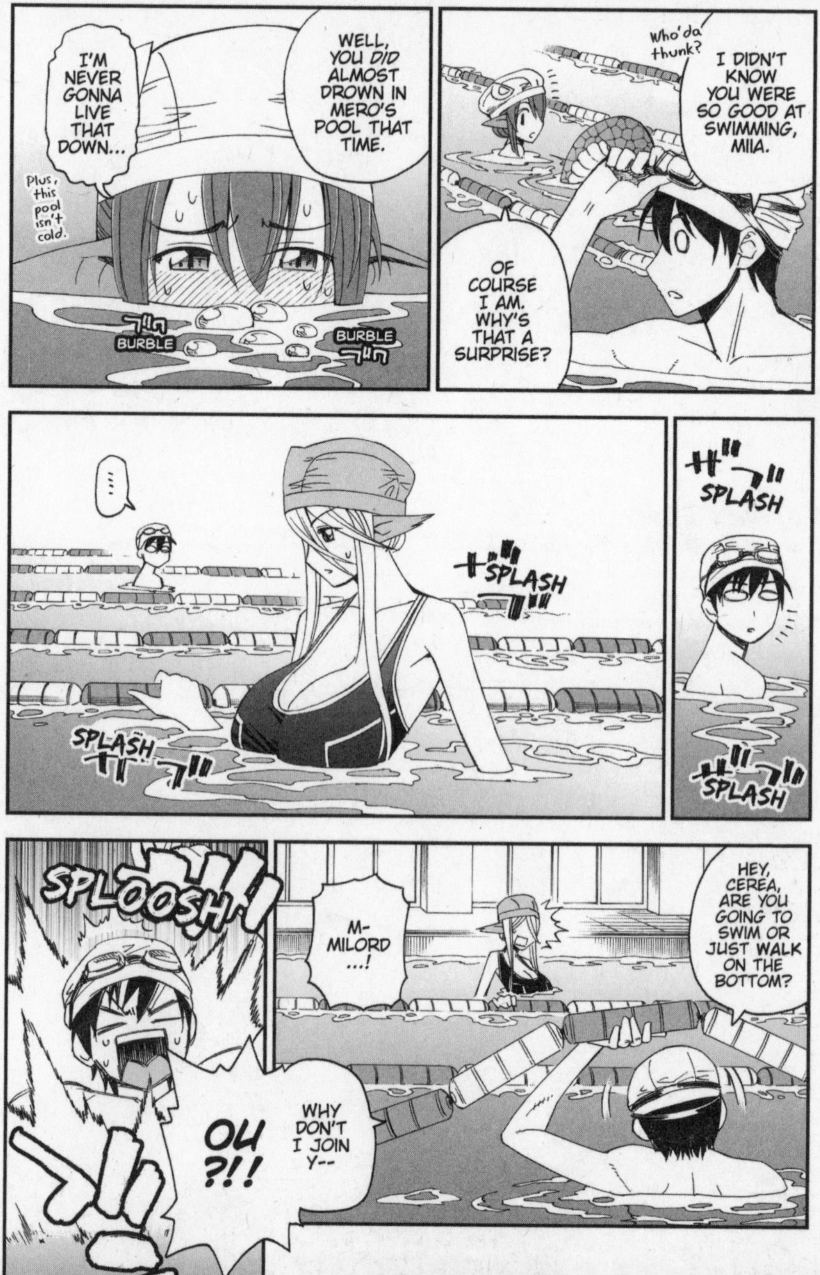
Who'da thunk?
I DIDN'T KNOW YOU WERE SO GOOD AT SWIMMING, MIIA.
OF COURSE I AM. WHY'S THAT A SURPRISE?
WELL, YOU DID ALMOST DROWN IN MERO'S POOL THAT TIME.
I'M NEVER GONNA LIVE THAT DOWN...
Plus, this pool isn't cold.
BURBLE
BURBLE
SPLASH
SPLASH
...
SPLASH
SPLASH
HEY, CEREA, ARE YOU GOING TO SWIM OR JUST WALK ON THE BOTTOM?
M-MILORD ...!
WHY DON'T I JOIN Y--
SPLOOSH!!
OU ?!!

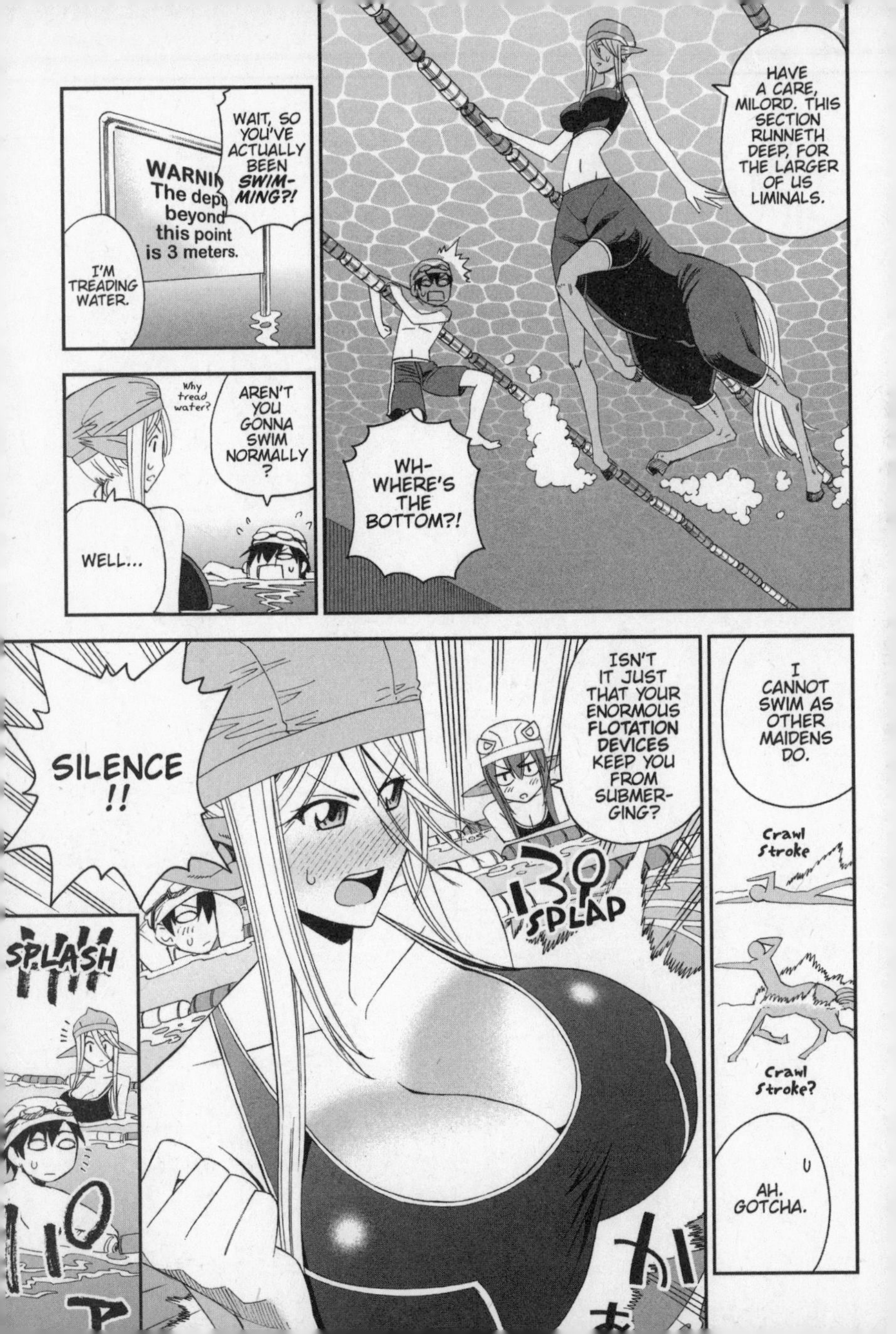
HAVE A CARE, MILORD. THIS SECTION RUNNETH DEEP, FOR THE LARGER OF US LIMINALS.
WH-WHERE'S THE BOTTOM?!
WAIT, SO YOU'VE ACTUALLY BEEN SWIMMING?!
WARNIN
The dept
beyond
this point
is 3 meters.
I'M TREADING WATER.
AREN'T YOU GONNA SWIM NORMALLY?
Why tread water?
WELL...
I CANNOT SWIM AS OTHER MAIDENS DO.
Crawl Stroke
Crawl Stroke?
AH. GOTCHA.
ISN'T IT JUST THAT YOUR ENORMOUS FLOTATION DEVICES KEEP YOU FROM SUBMERGING?
SPLAP
SILENCE!!
SPLASH

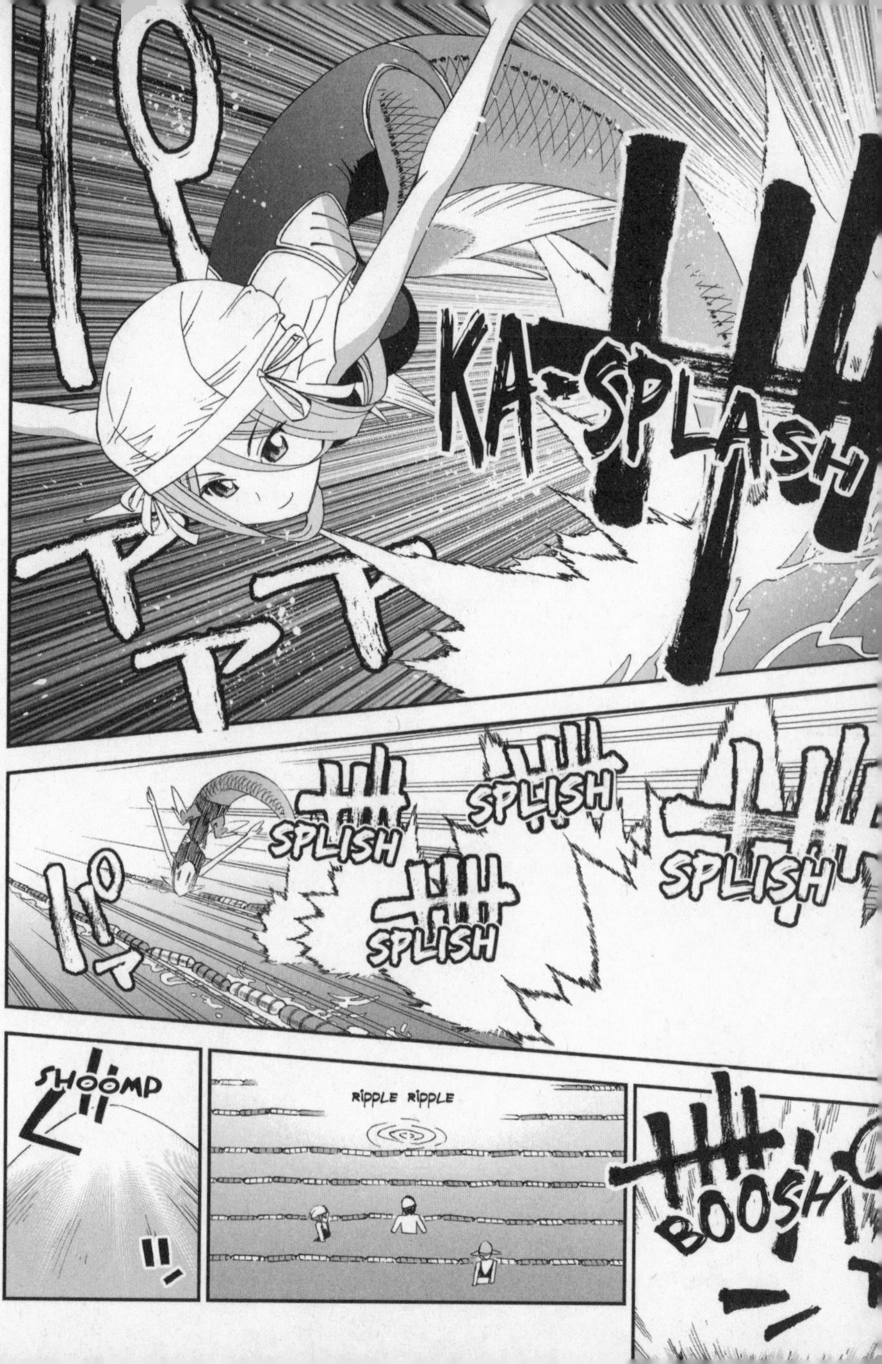
KA-SPLASH
SPLISH
SPLISH
SPLISH
SPLISH
BOOSH
RIPPLE RIPPLE
SHOOMP

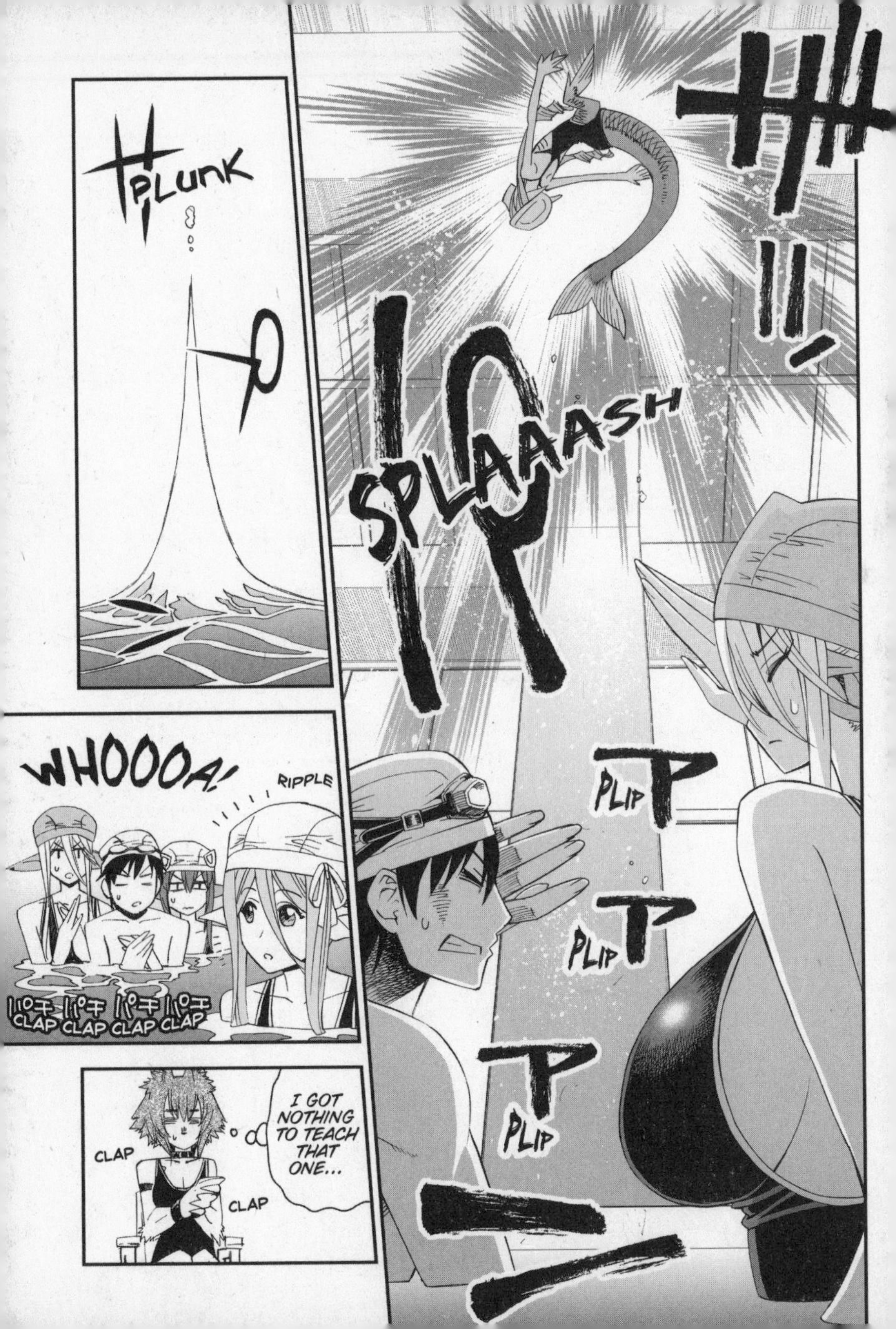
SPLAAASH
PLIP
PLIP
PLIP
PLUNK
WHOOOA!
RIPPLE
パチ パチ パチ パチ
CLAP CLAP CLAP CLAP
I GOT NOTHING TO TEACH THAT ONE...
CLAP
CLAP

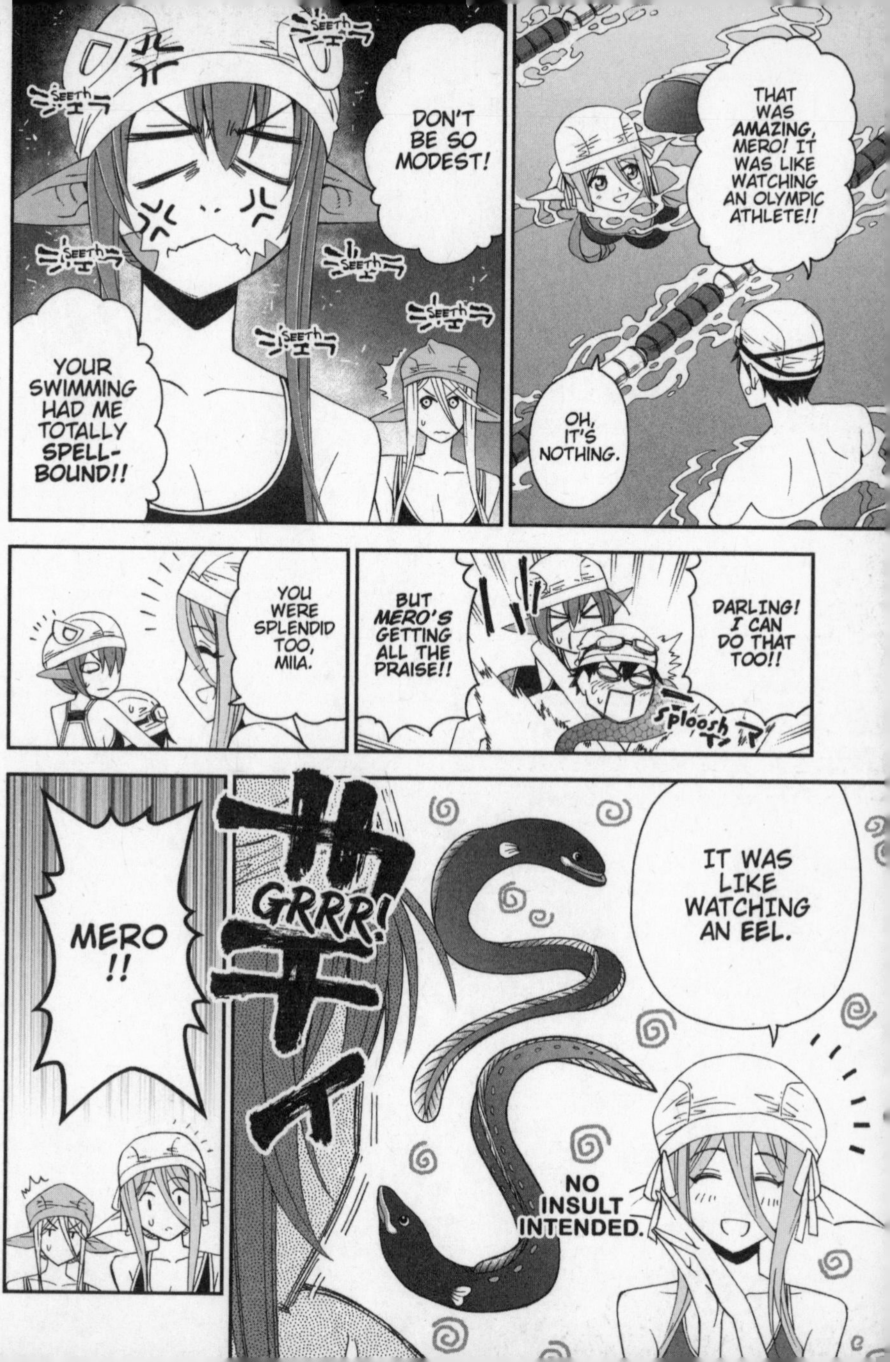
THAT WAS AMAZING, MERO! IT WAS LIKE WATCHING AN OLYMPIC ATHLETE!!
OH, IT'S NOTHING.
DON'T BE SO MODEST!
SEETH
SEETH
YOUR SWIMMING HAD ME TOTALLY SPELL-BOUND!!
SEETH
SEETH
SEETH
SEETH
DARLING! I CAN DO THAT TOO!!
BUT MERO'S GETTING ALL THE PRAISE!!
Sploosh
YOU WERE SPLENDID TOO, MIIA.
IT WAS LIKE WATCHING AN EEL.
NO INSULT INTENDED.
GRRR!
MERO !!

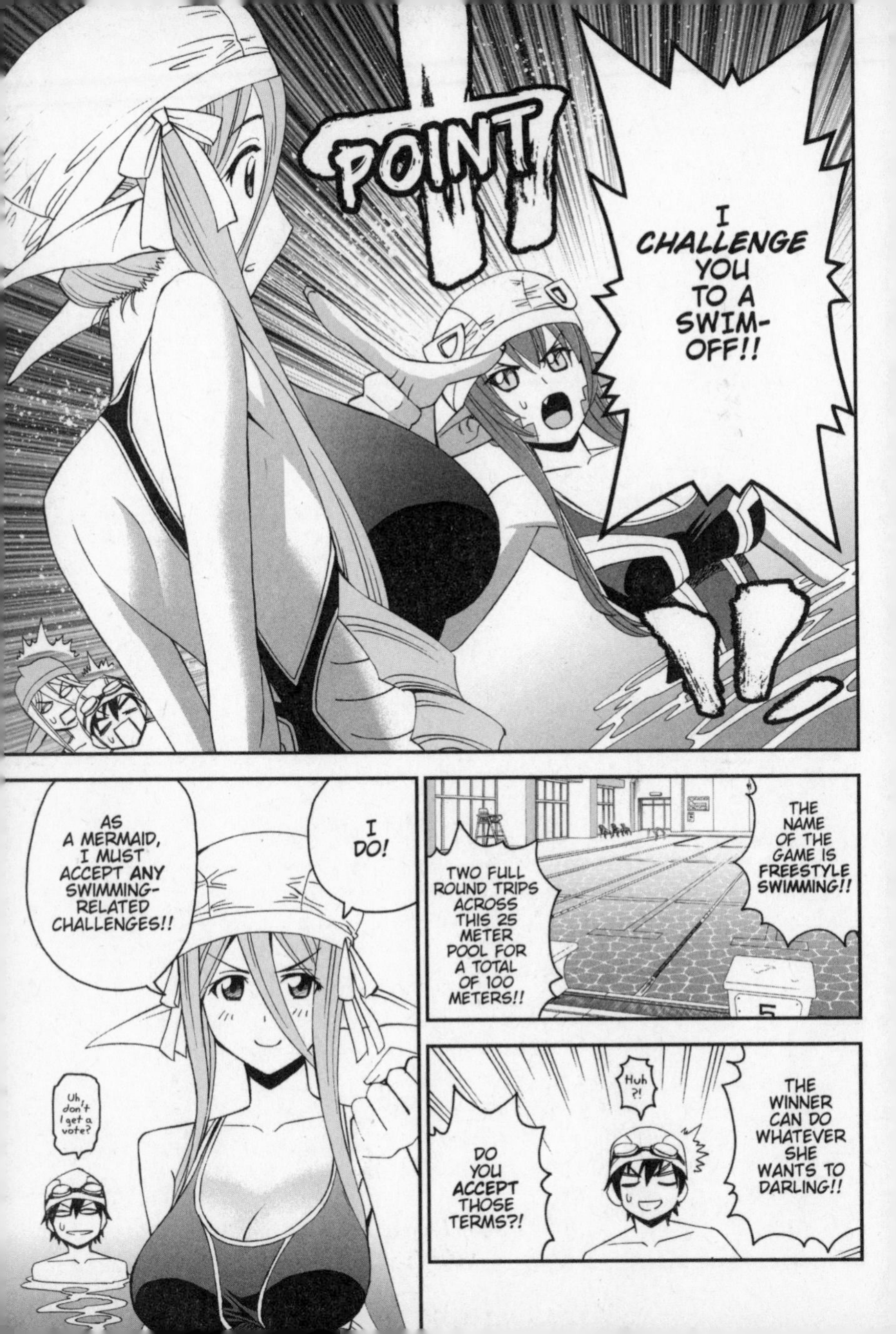
POINT
I CHALLENGE YOU TO A SWIM-OFF!!
THE NAME OF THE GAME IS FREESTYLE SWIMMING!!
TWO FULL ROUND TRIPS ACROSS THIS 25 METER POOL FOR A TOTAL OF 100 METERS!!
THE WINNER CAN DO WHATEVER SHE WANTS TO DARLING!!
Huh ?!
DO YOU ACCEPT THOSE TERMS?!
I DO!
AS A MERMAID, I MUST ACCEPT ANY SWIMMING-RELATED CHALLENGES!!
Uh, don't I get a vote?

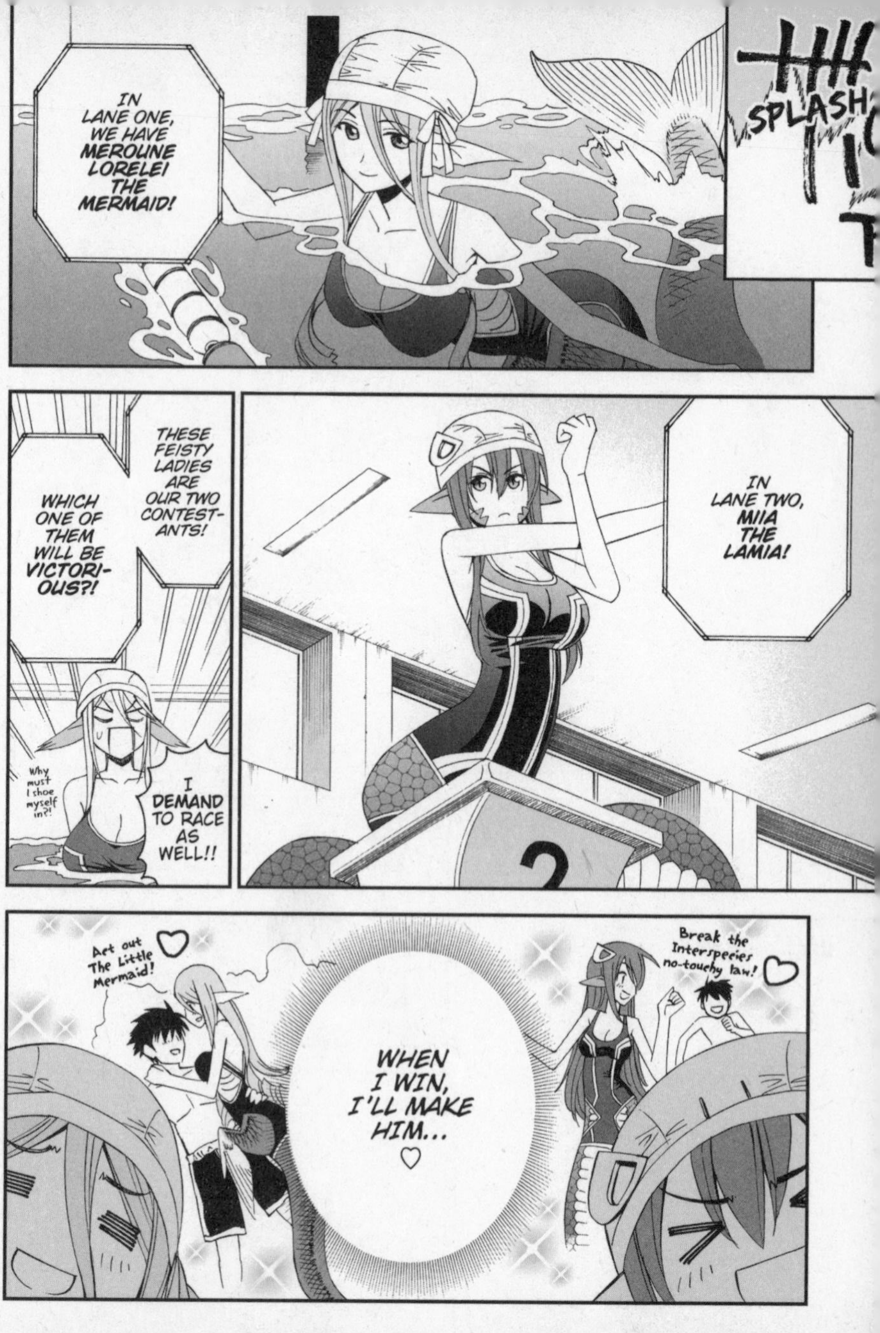
SPLASH
IN LANE ONE, WE HAVE MEROUNE LORELEI THE MERMAID!
IN LANE TWO, MIIA THE LAMIA!
THESE FEISTY LADIES ARE OUR TWO CONTEST-ANTS!
WHICH ONE OF THEM WILL BE VICTORI-OUS?!
I DEMAND TO RACE AS WELL!!
Why must I shoe myself in?!
Break the Interspecies no-touchy law!
WHEN I WIN, I'LL MAKE HIM...
Act out The Little Mermaid!

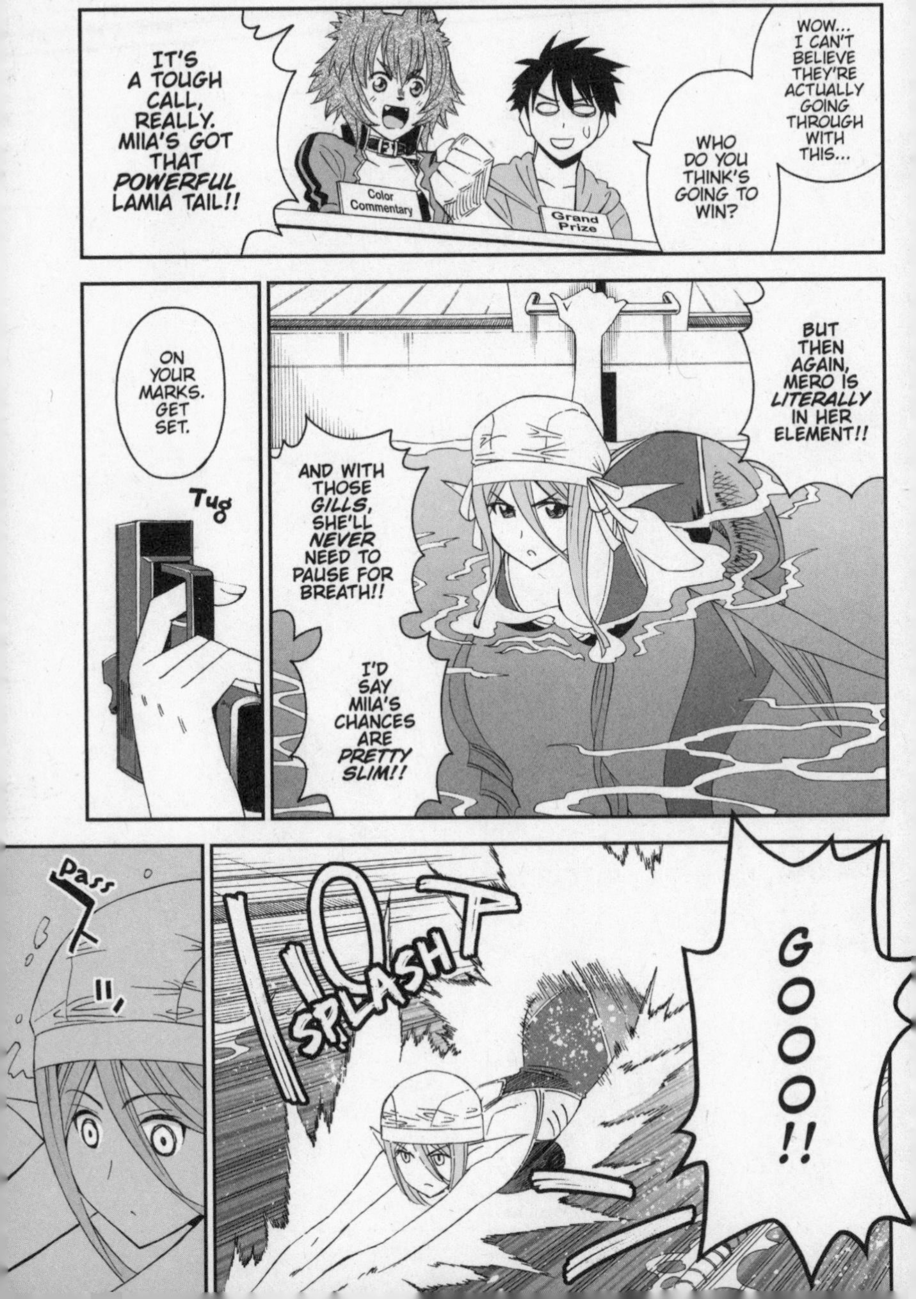
WOW... I CAN'T BELIEVE THEY'RE ACTUALLY GOING THROUGH WITH THIS...
WHO DO YOU THINK'S GOING TO WIN?
Grand Prize
Color Commentary
IT'S A TOUGH CALL, REALLY. MIIA'S GOT THAT POWERFUL LAMIA TAIL!!
BUT THEN AGAIN, MERO IS LITERALLY IN HER ELEMENT!!
AND WITH THOSE GILLS, SHE'LL NEVER NEED TO PAUSE FOR BREATH!!
I'D SAY MIIA'S CHANCES ARE PRETTY SLIM!!
ON YOUR MARKS. GET SET.
Tug
GOOOO!!
SPLASH
Pass

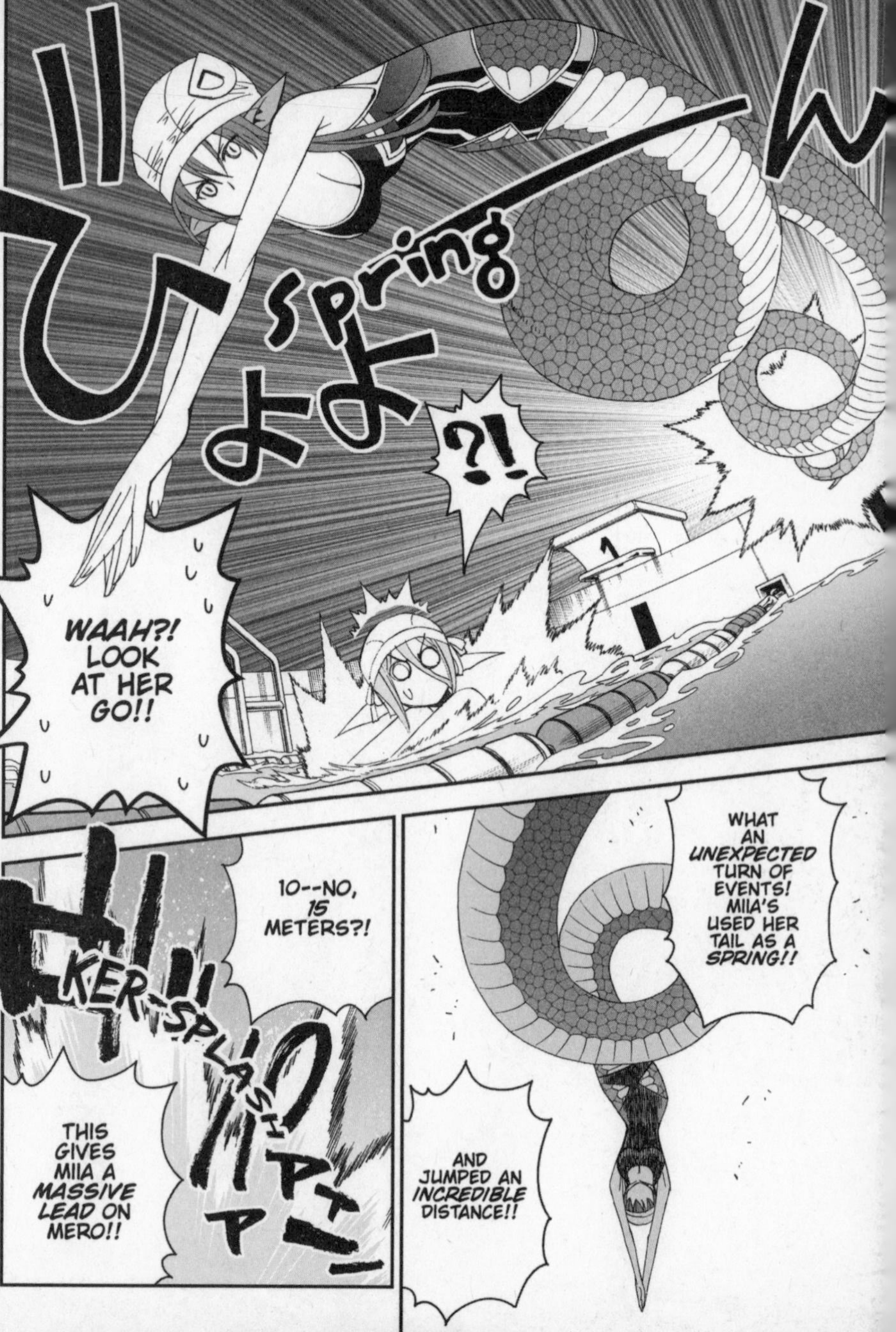
spring
?!
WAAH?! LOOK AT HER GO!!
WHAT AN UNEXPECTED TURN OF EVENTS! MIIA'S USED HER TAIL AS A SPRING!!
AND JUMPED AN INCREDIBLE DISTANCE!!
10--NO, 15 METERS?!
KER-SPLASH
THIS GIVES MIIA A MASSIVE LEAD ON MERO!!

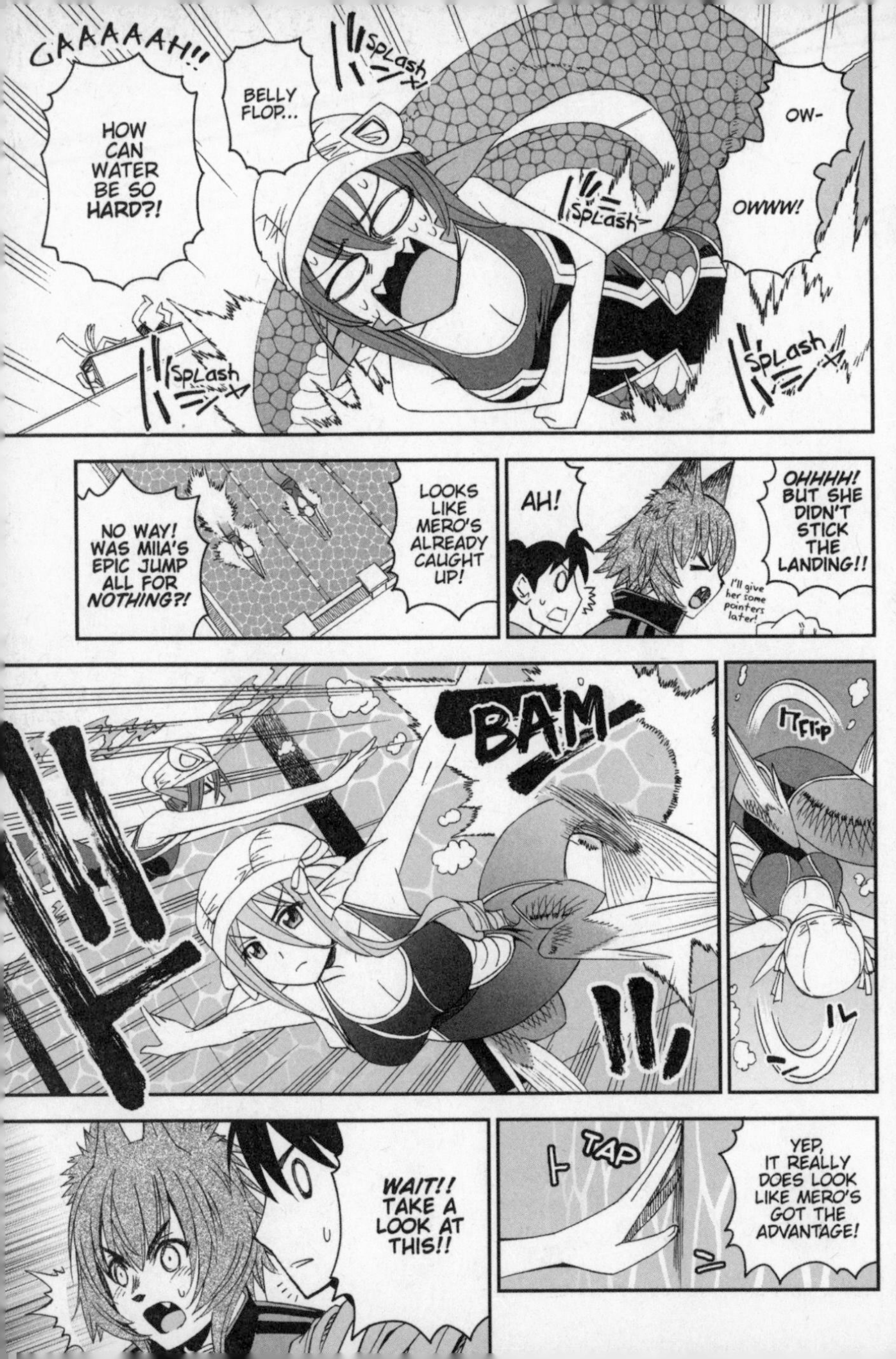
OW-
OWWW!
SPLASH
SPLASH
BELLY FLOP...
SPLASH
GAAAAAH!!
HOW CAN WATER BE SO HARD?!
SPLASH
OHHHH! BUT SHE DIDN'T STICK THE LANDING!!
I'll give her some pointers later!
AH!
LOOKS LIKE MERO'S ALREADY CAUGHT UP!
NO WAY! WAS MIIA'S EPIC JUMP ALL FOR NOTHING?!
FLIP
BAM
YEP, IT REALLY DOES LOOK LIKE MERO'S GOT THE ADVANTAGE!
TAP
WAIT!! TAKE A LOOK AT THIS!!

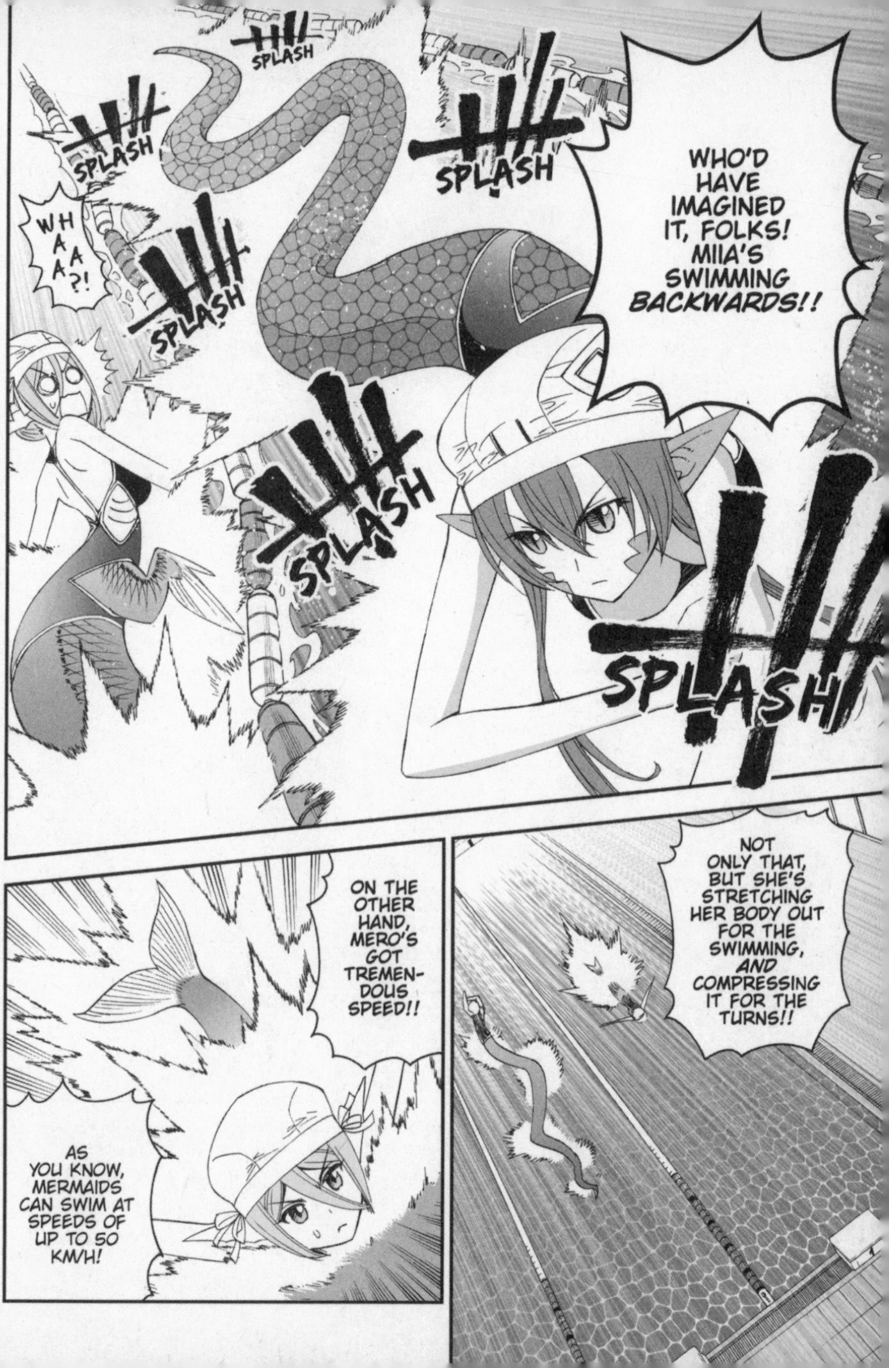
WHO'D HAVE IMAGINED IT, FOLKS! MIIA'S SWIMMING *BACKWARDS!!*
SPLASH
SPLASH
SPLASH
SPLASH
WHAAAA?!
SPLASH
SPLASH
SPLASH
NOT ONLY THAT, BUT SHE'S STRETCHING HER BODY OUT FOR THE SWIMMING, *AND* COMPRESSING IT FOR THE TURNS!!
ON THE OTHER HAND, MERO'S GOT TREMEN-DOUS SPEED!!
AS YOU KNOW, MERMAIDS CAN SWIM AT SPEEDS OF UP TO 50 KM/H!

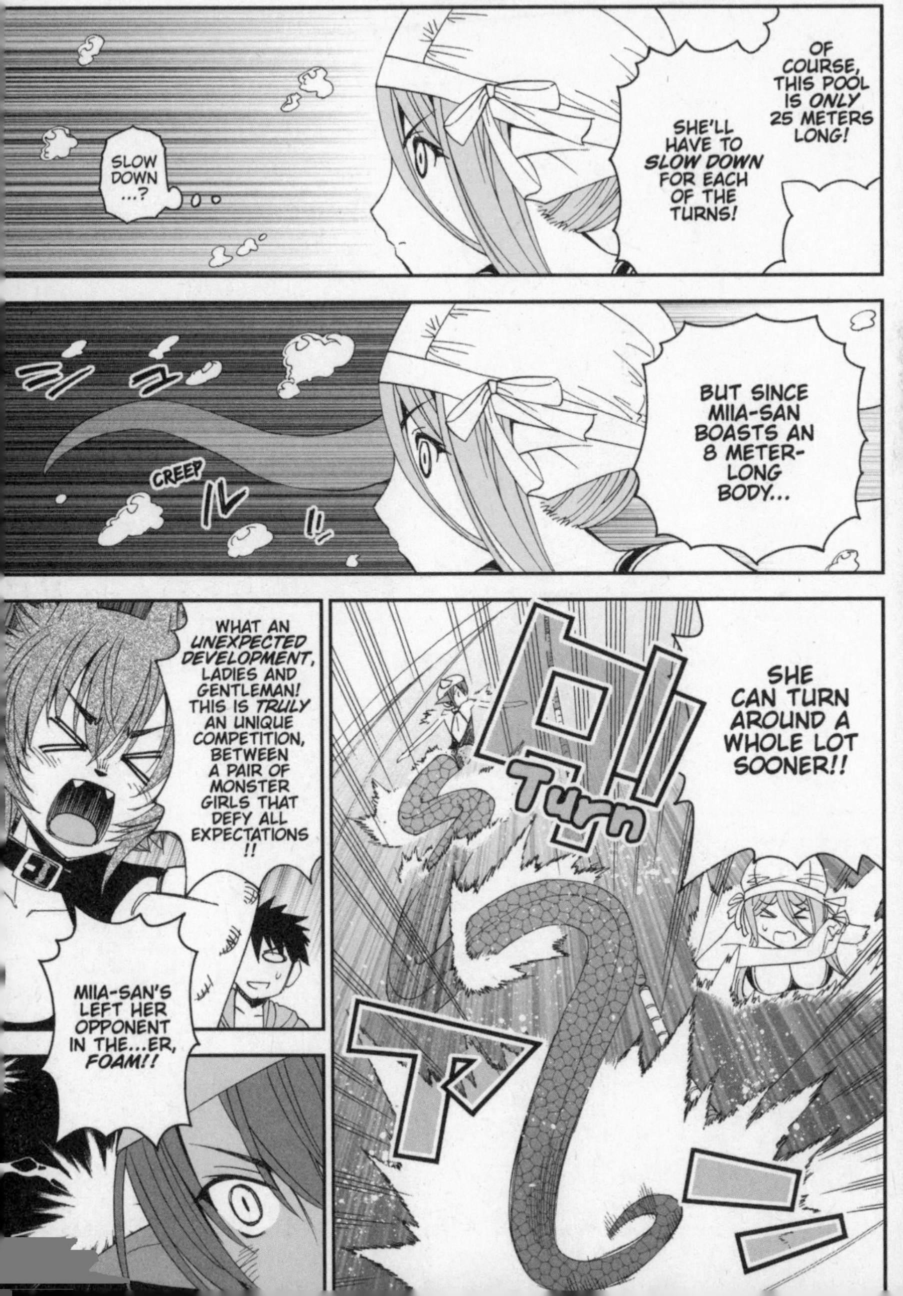
OF COURSE, THIS POOL IS *ONLY* 25 METERS LONG!
SHE'LL HAVE TO *SLOW DOWN* FOR EACH OF THE TURNS!
SLOW DOWN ...?
BUT SINCE MIIA-SAN BOASTS AN 8 METER-LONG BODY...
CREEP
SHE CAN TURN AROUND A WHOLE LOT SOONER!!
Turn
WHAT AN *UNEXPECTED DEVELOPMENT*, LADIES AND GENTLEMAN! THIS IS *TRULY* AN UNIQUE COMPETITION, BETWEEN A PAIR OF MONSTER GIRLS THAT DEFY ALL EXPECTATIONS !!
MIIA-SAN'S LEFT HER OPPONENT IN THE...ER, *FOAM!!*

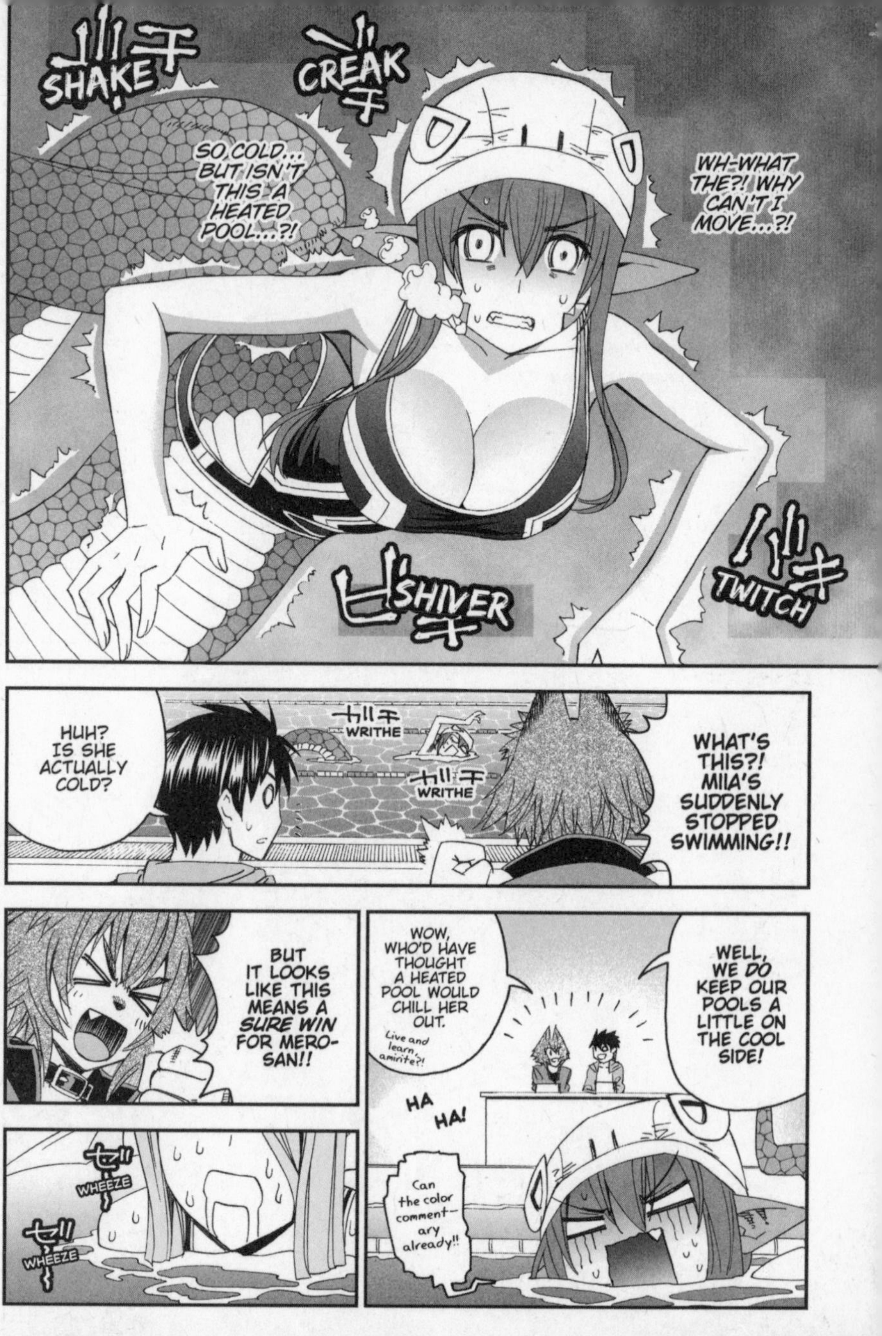
WH-WHAT THE?! WHY CAN'T I MOVE...?!
CREAK
SO COLD... BUT ISN'T THIS A HEATED POOL...?!
SHAKE
TWITCH
SHIVER
WHAT'S THIS?! MIIA'S SUDDENLY STOPPED SWIMMING!!
WRITHE
WRITHE
HUH? IS SHE ACTUALLY COLD?
WELL, WE *DO* KEEP OUR POOLS A LITTLE ON THE COOL SIDE!
WOW, WHO'D HAVE THOUGHT A HEATED POOL WOULD CHILL HER OUT.
Live and learn, amirite?!
BUT IT LOOKS LIKE THIS MEANS A *SURE WIN* FOR MERO-SAN!!
HA HA!
Can the color comment-ary already!!
WHEEZE
WHEEZE

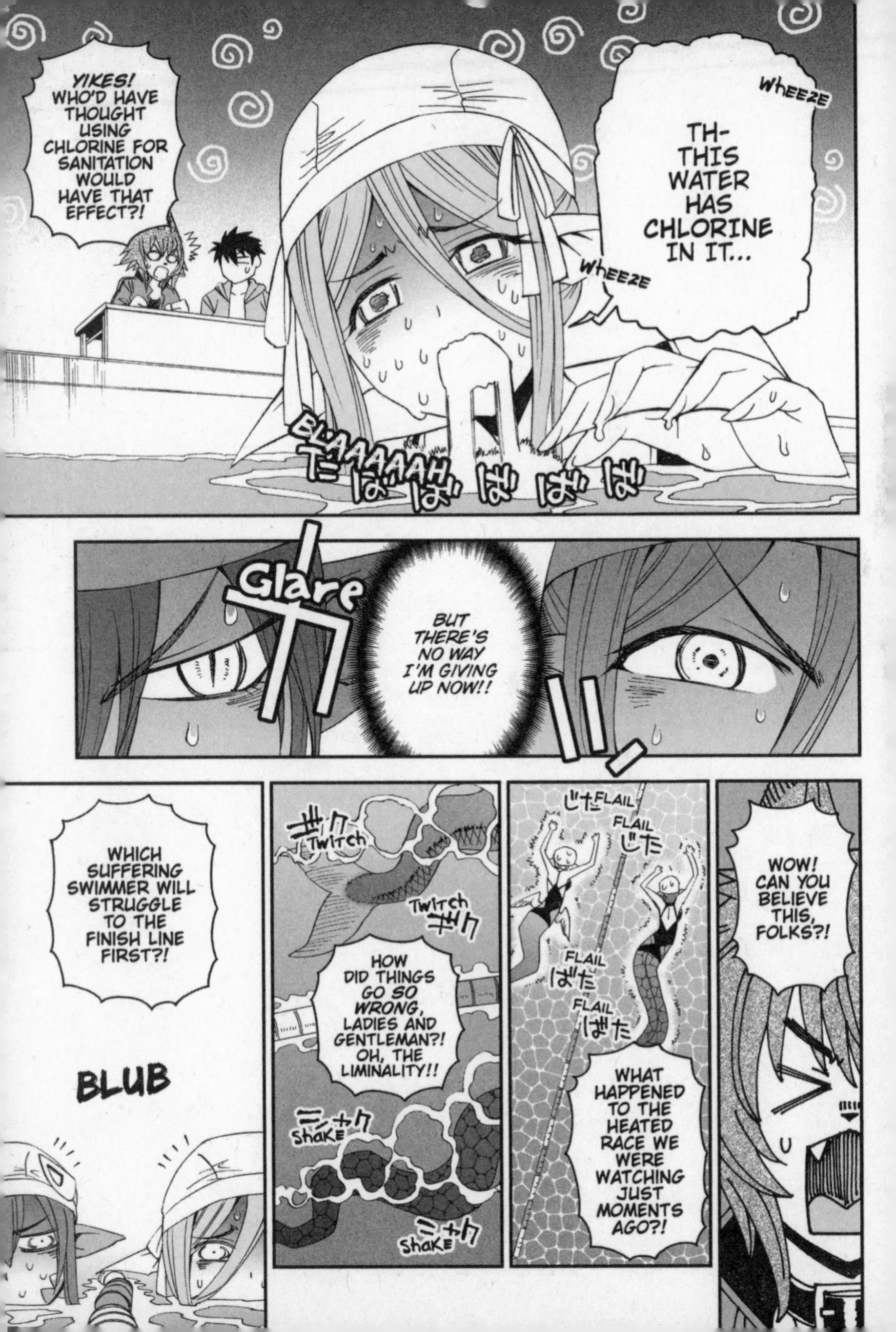
TH-THIS WATER HAS CHLORINE IN IT...
Wheeze
Wheeze
YIKES! WHO'D HAVE THOUGHT USING CHLORINE FOR SANITATION WOULD HAVE THAT EFFECT?!
BLAAAAAAH
Glare
BUT THERE'S NO WAY I'M GIVING UP NOW!!
WOW! CAN YOU BELIEVE THIS, FOLKS?!
FLAIL
FLAIL
FLAIL
FLAIL
WHAT HAPPENED TO THE HEATED RACE WE WERE WATCHING JUST MOMENTS AGO?!
Twitch
Twitch
HOW DID THINGS GO SO WRONG, LADIES AND GENTLEMAN?! OH, THE LIMINALITY!!
Shake
Shake
WHICH SUFFERING SWIMMER WILL STRUGGLE TO THE FINISH LINE FIRST?!
BLUB

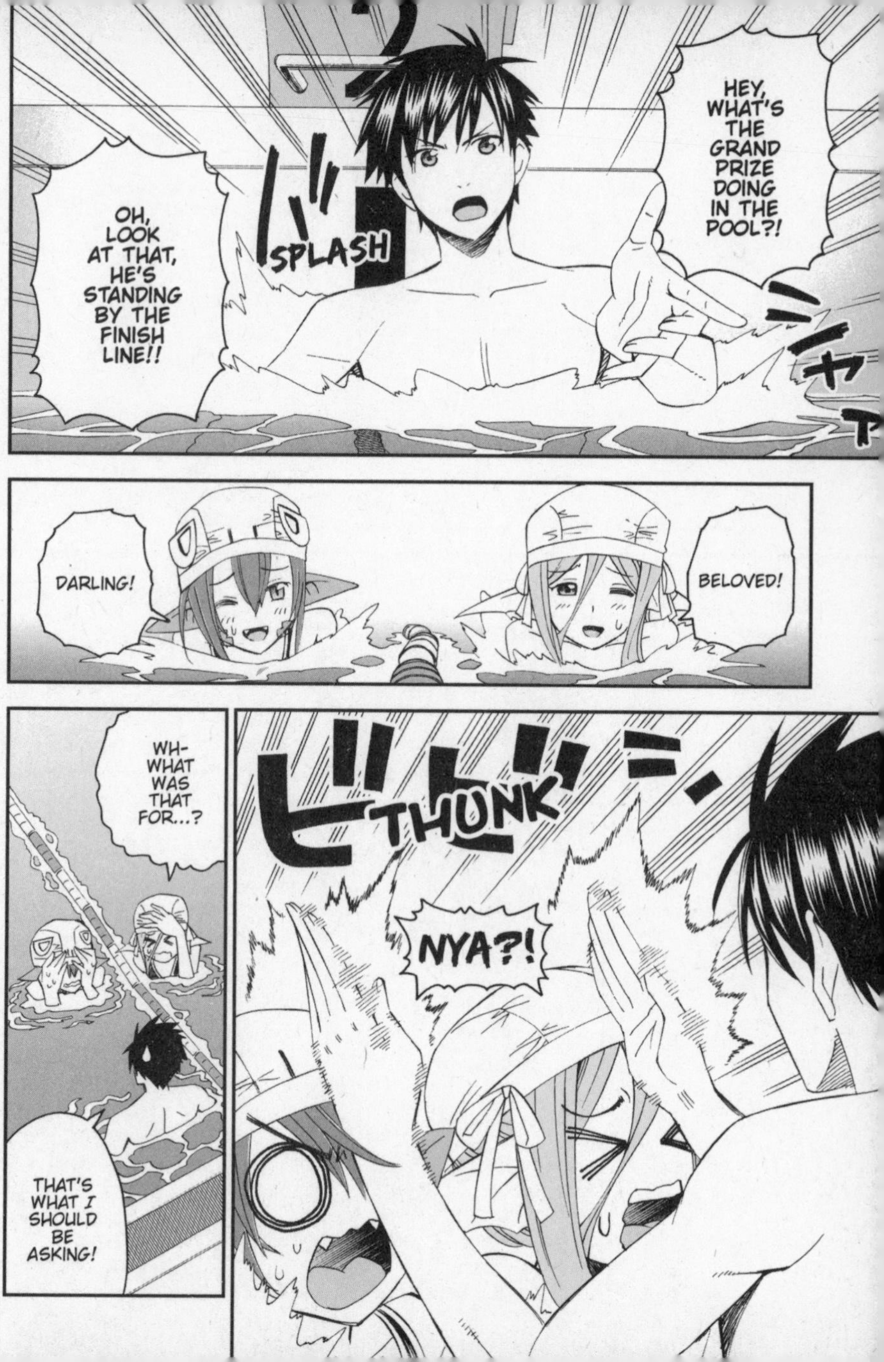
HEY, WHAT'S THE GRAND PRIZE DOING IN THE POOL?!
SPLASH
OH, LOOK AT THAT, HE'S STANDING BY THE FINISH LINE!!
BELOVED!
DARLING!
THUNK
NYA?!
WH-WHAT WAS THAT FOR...?
THAT'S WHAT I SHOULD BE ASKING!

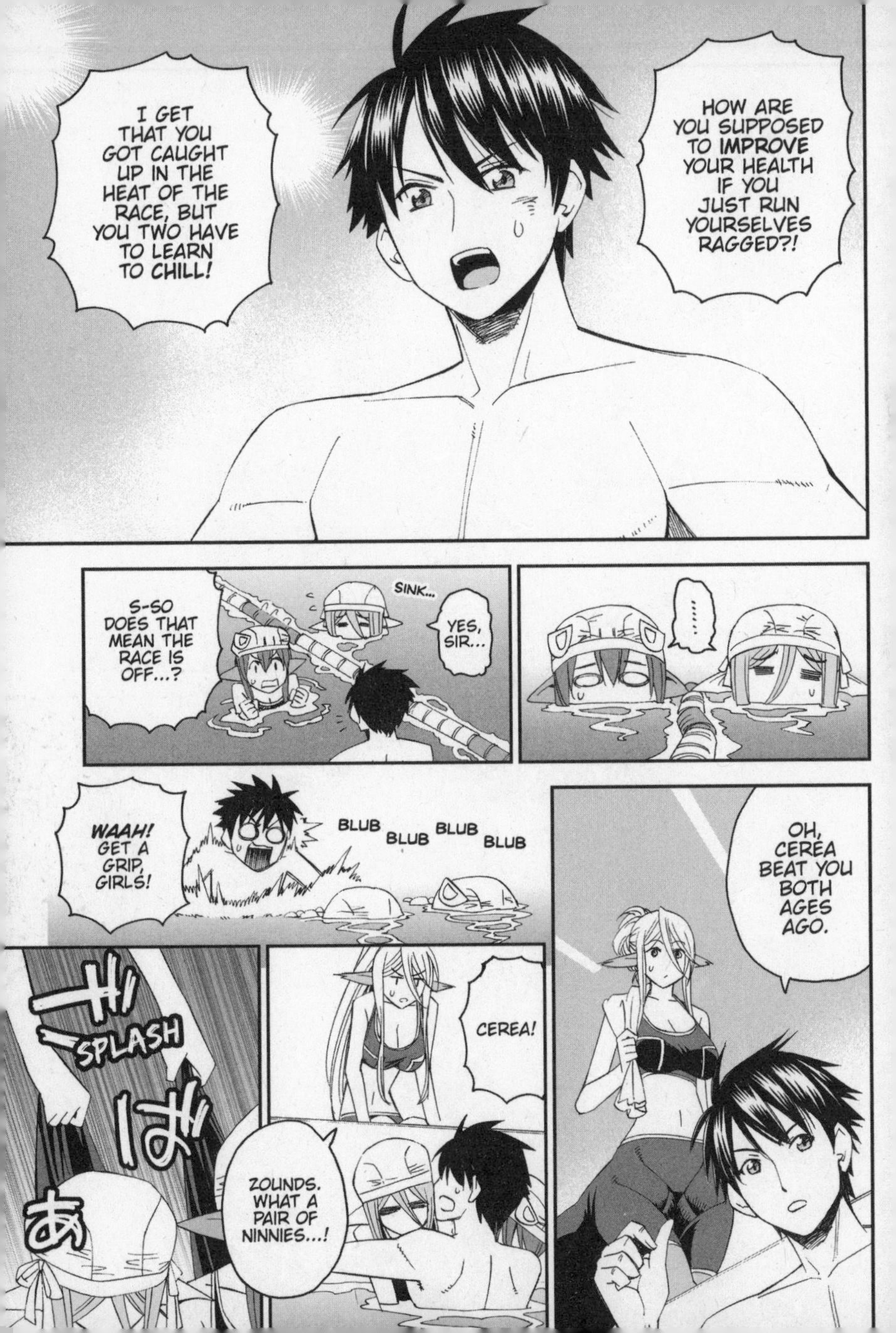
HOW ARE YOU SUPPOSED TO IMPROVE YOUR HEALTH IF YOU JUST RUN YOURSELVES RAGGED?!
I GET THAT YOU GOT CAUGHT UP IN THE HEAT OF THE RACE, BUT YOU TWO HAVE TO LEARN TO CHILL!
......
SINK...
YES, SIR...
S-SO DOES THAT MEAN THE RACE IS OFF...?
OH, CEREA BEAT YOU BOTH AGES AGO.
BLUB BLUB BLUB BLUB
WAAH! GET A GRIP, GIRLS!
CEREA!
ZOUNDS. WHAT A PAIR OF NINNIES...!
SPLASH

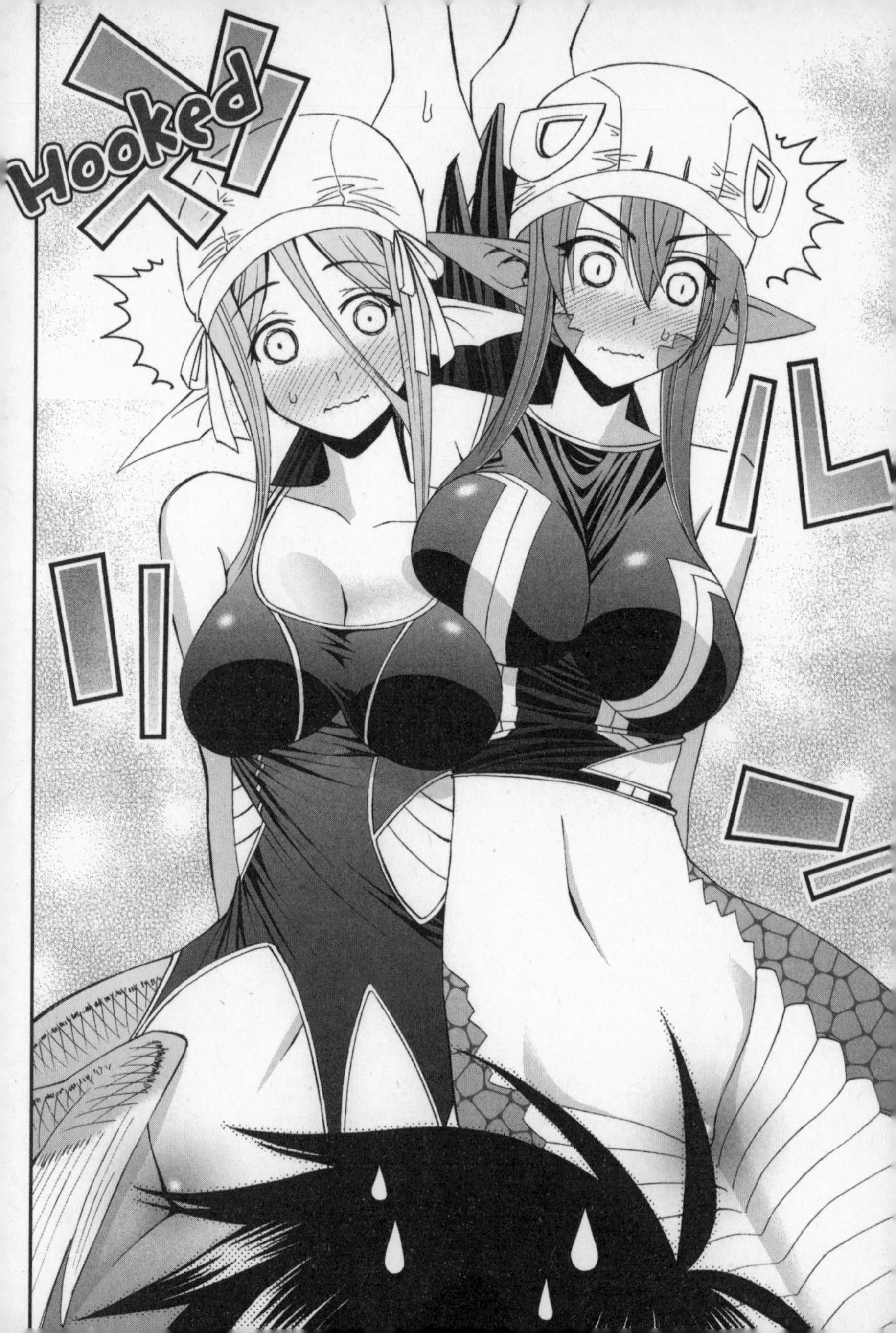
Hooked

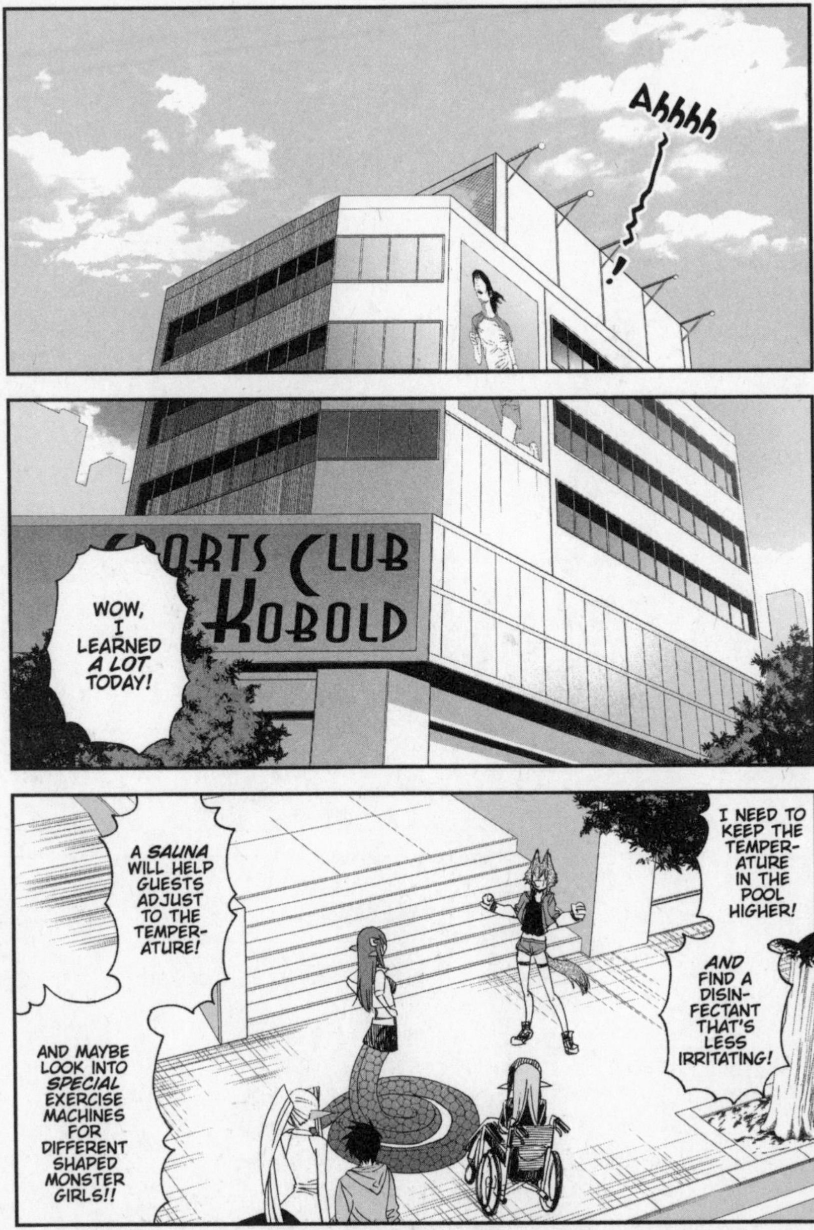
Ahhhh—!
PORTS CLUB
KOBOLD
WOW, I LEARNED *A LOT* TODAY!
I NEED TO KEEP THE TEMPER-ATURE IN THE POOL HIGHER!
AND FIND A DISIN-FECTANT THAT'S LESS IRRITATING!
A *SAUNA* WILL HELP GUESTS ADJUST TO THE TEMPER-ATURE!
AND MAYBE LOOK INTO *SPECIAL* EXERCISE MACHINES FOR DIFFERENT SHAPED MONSTER GIRLS!!

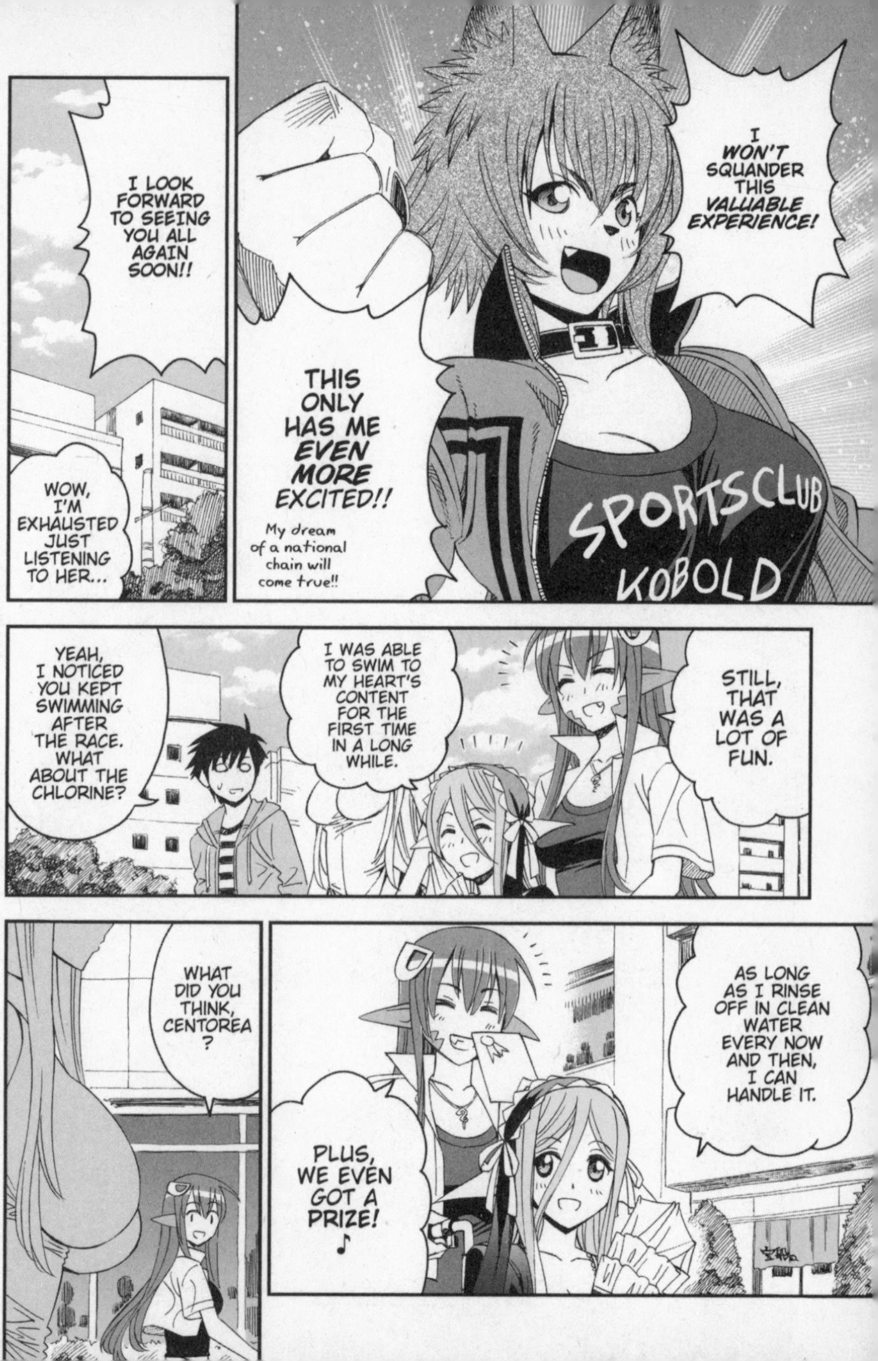
I WON'T SQUANDER THIS VALUABLE EXPERIENCE!
THIS ONLY HAS ME EVEN MORE EXCITED!!
My dream of a national chain will come true!!
SPORTSCLUB KOBOLD
I LOOK FORWARD TO SEEING YOU ALL AGAIN SOON!!
WOW, I'M EXHAUSTED JUST LISTENING TO HER...
STILL, THAT WAS A LOT OF FUN.
I WAS ABLE TO SWIM TO MY HEART'S CONTENT FOR THE FIRST TIME IN A LONG WHILE.
YEAH, I NOTICED YOU KEPT SWIMMING AFTER THE RACE. WHAT ABOUT THE CHLORINE?
AS LONG AS I RINSE OFF IN CLEAN WATER EVERY NOW AND THEN, I CAN HANDLE IT.
PLUS, WE EVEN GOT A PRIZE! ♪
WHAT DID YOU THINK, CENTOREA?

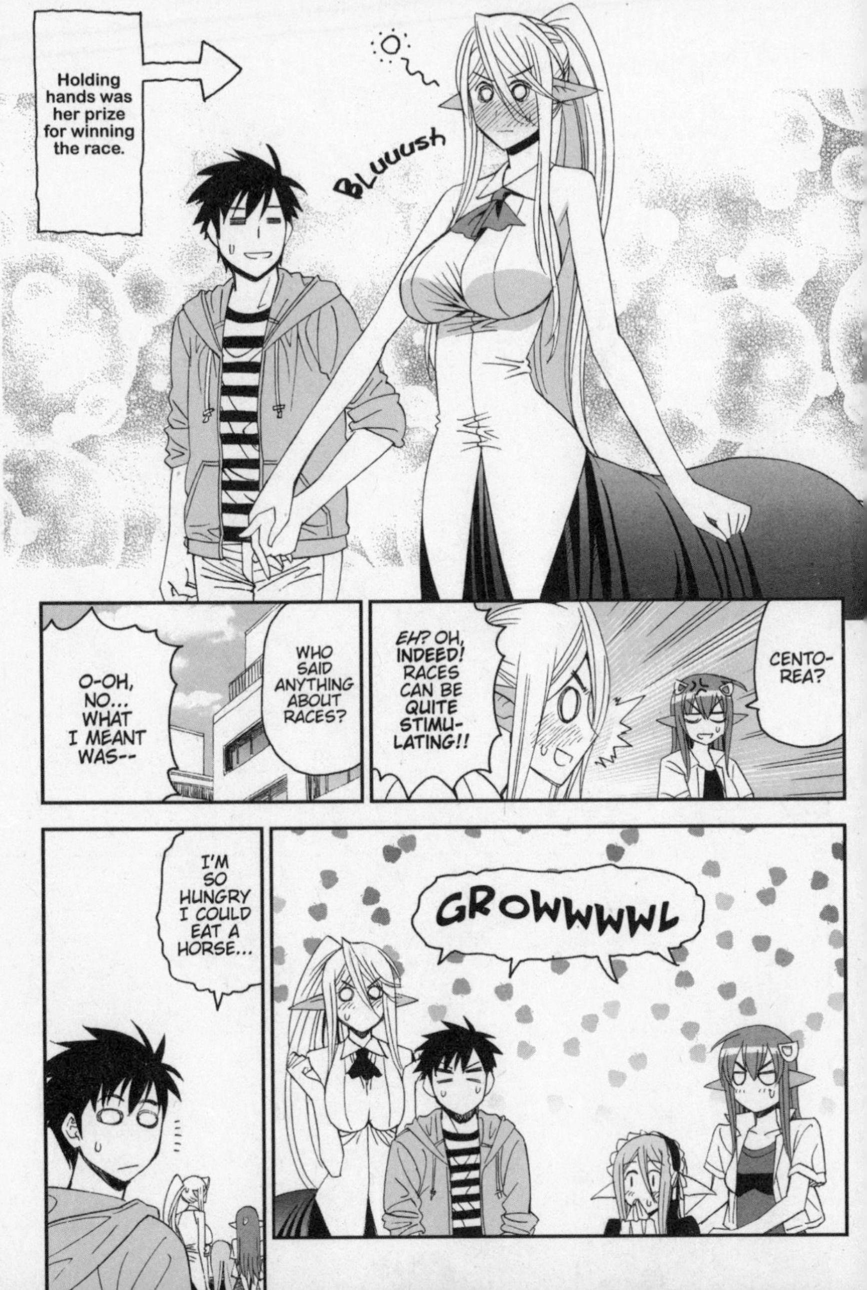
Holding hands was her prize for winning the race.
Bluuush
CENTO-REA?
EH? OH, INDEED! RACES CAN BE QUITE STIMULATING!!
WHO SAID ANYTHING ABOUT RACES?
O-OH, NO... WHAT I MEANT WAS--
GROWWWWL
I'M SO HUNGRY I COULD EAT A HORSE...

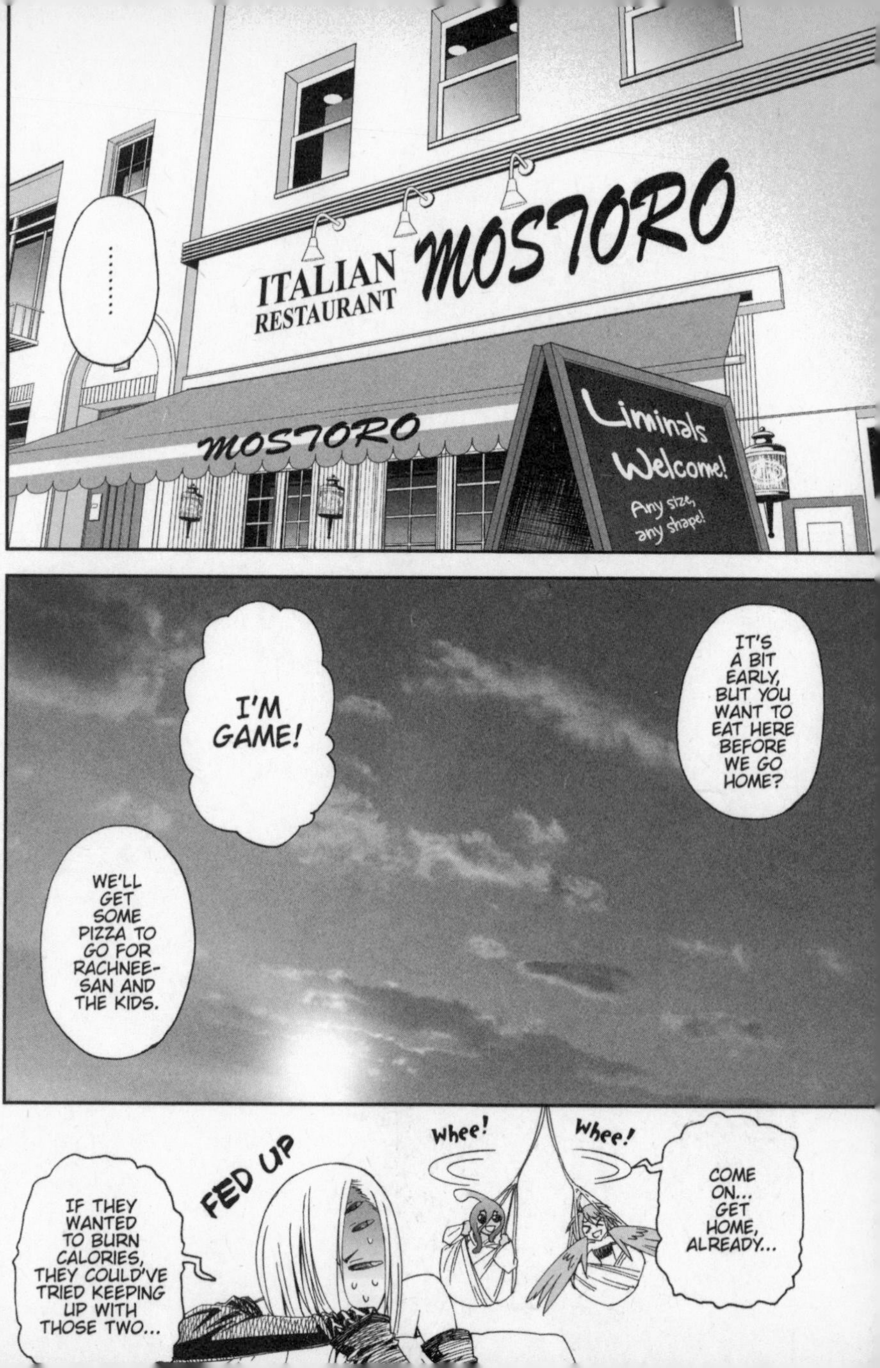
ITALIAN RESTAURANT MOSTORO
MOSTORO
Liminals Welcome!
Any size, any shape!
......
IT'S A BIT EARLY, BUT YOU WANT TO EAT HERE BEFORE WE GO HOME?
I'M GAME!
WE'LL GET SOME PIZZA TO GO FOR RACHNEE-SAN AND THE KIDS.
Whee!
Whee!
COME ON... GET HOME, ALREADY...
FED UP
IF THEY WANTED TO BURN CALORIES, THEY COULD'VE TRIED KEEPING UP WITH THOSE TWO...

Monster Musume

Everyday Life with Monster Girls

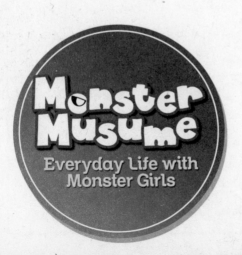

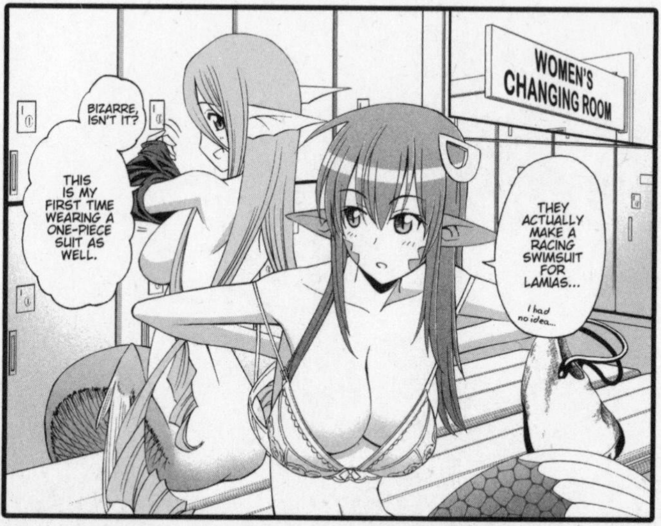
WOMEN'S CHANGING ROOM
THEY ACTUALLY MAKE A RACING SWIMSUIT FOR LAMIAS...
I had no idea...
BIZARRE, ISN'T IT?
THIS IS MY FIRST TIME WEARING A ONE-PIECE SUIT AS WELL.

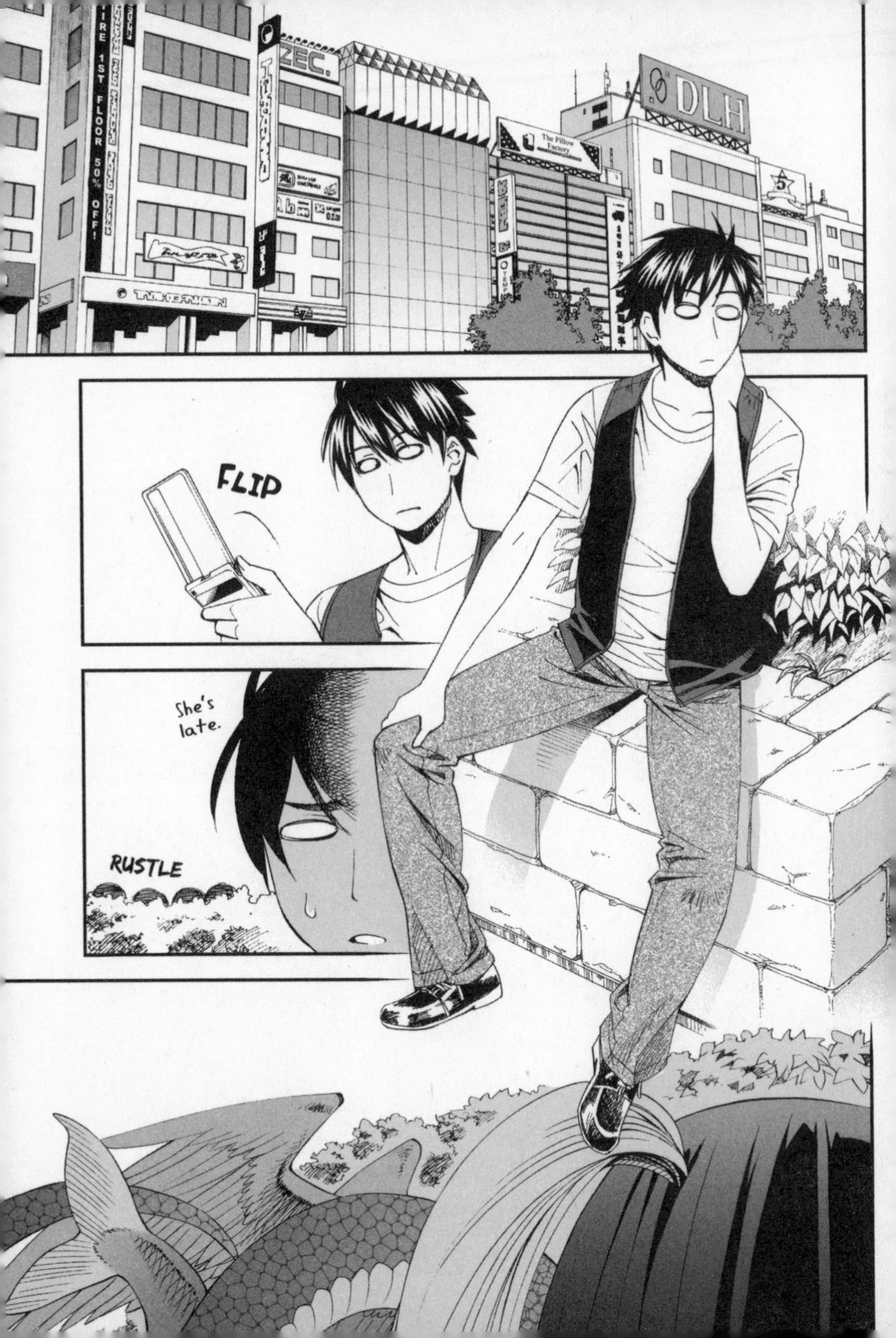
DLH
The Pillow Factory
ZEC.
IRE 1ST FLOOR 50% OFF!
FLIP
She's late.
RUSTLE

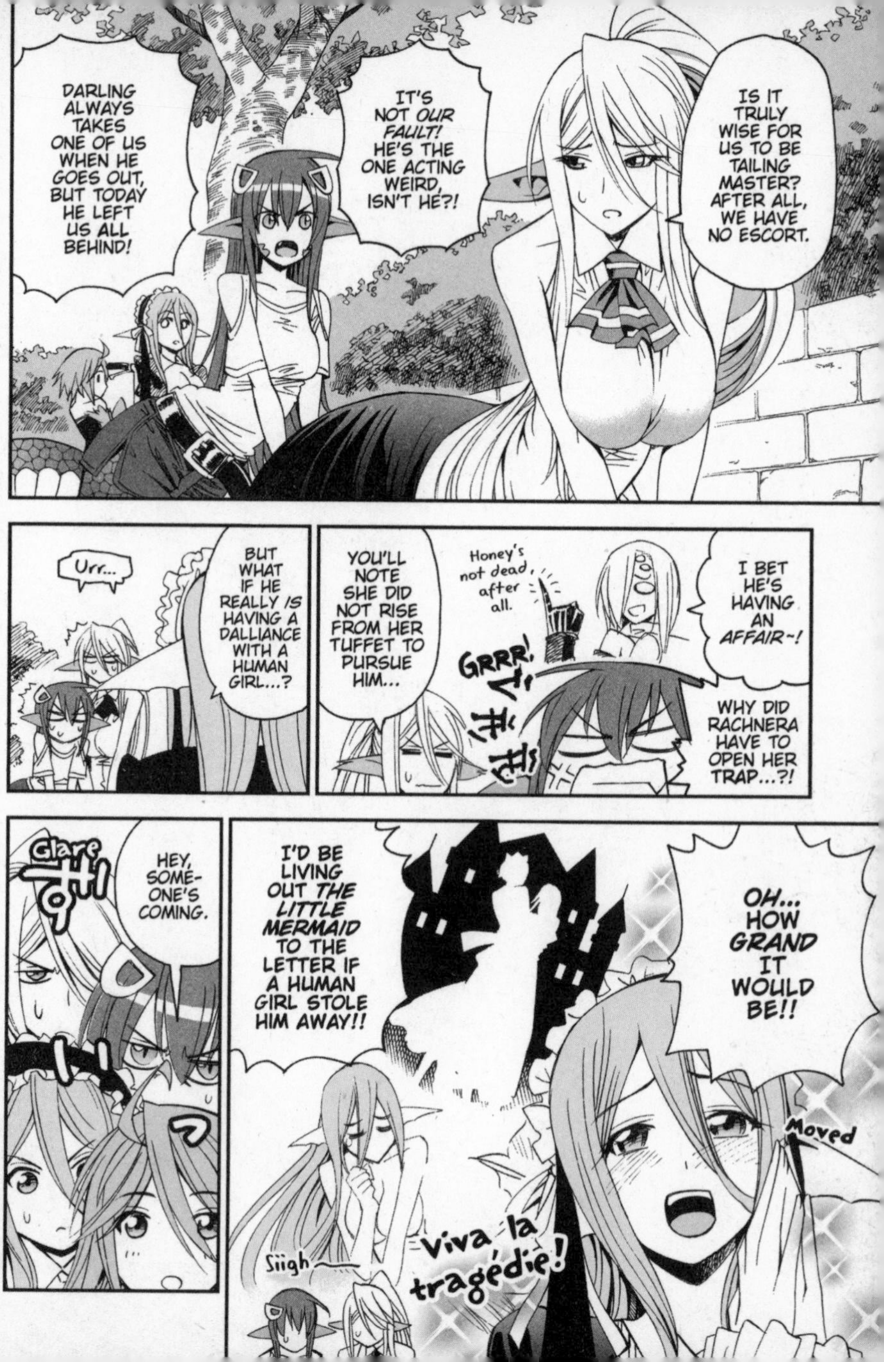
IS IT TRULY WISE FOR US TO BE TAILING MASTER? AFTER ALL, WE HAVE NO ESCORT.
IT'S NOT OUR FAULT! HE'S THE ONE ACTING WEIRD, ISN'T HE?!
DARLING ALWAYS TAKES ONE OF US WHEN HE GOES OUT, BUT TODAY HE LEFT US ALL BEHIND!
I BET HE'S HAVING AN AFFAIR~!
Honey's not dead after all.
GRRR
WHY DID RACHNERA HAVE TO OPEN HER TRAP...?!
YOU'LL NOTE SHE DID NOT RISE FROM HER TUFFET TO PURSUE HIM...
BUT WHAT IF HE REALLY IS HAVING A DALLIANCE WITH A HUMAN GIRL...?
Urr...
OH... HOW GRAND IT WOULD BE!!
I'D BE LIVING OUT THE LITTLE MERMAID TO THE LETTER IF A HUMAN GIRL STOLE HIM AWAY!!
Moved
Viva la tragédie!
Siigh~
HEY, SOME-ONE'S COMING.
Glare

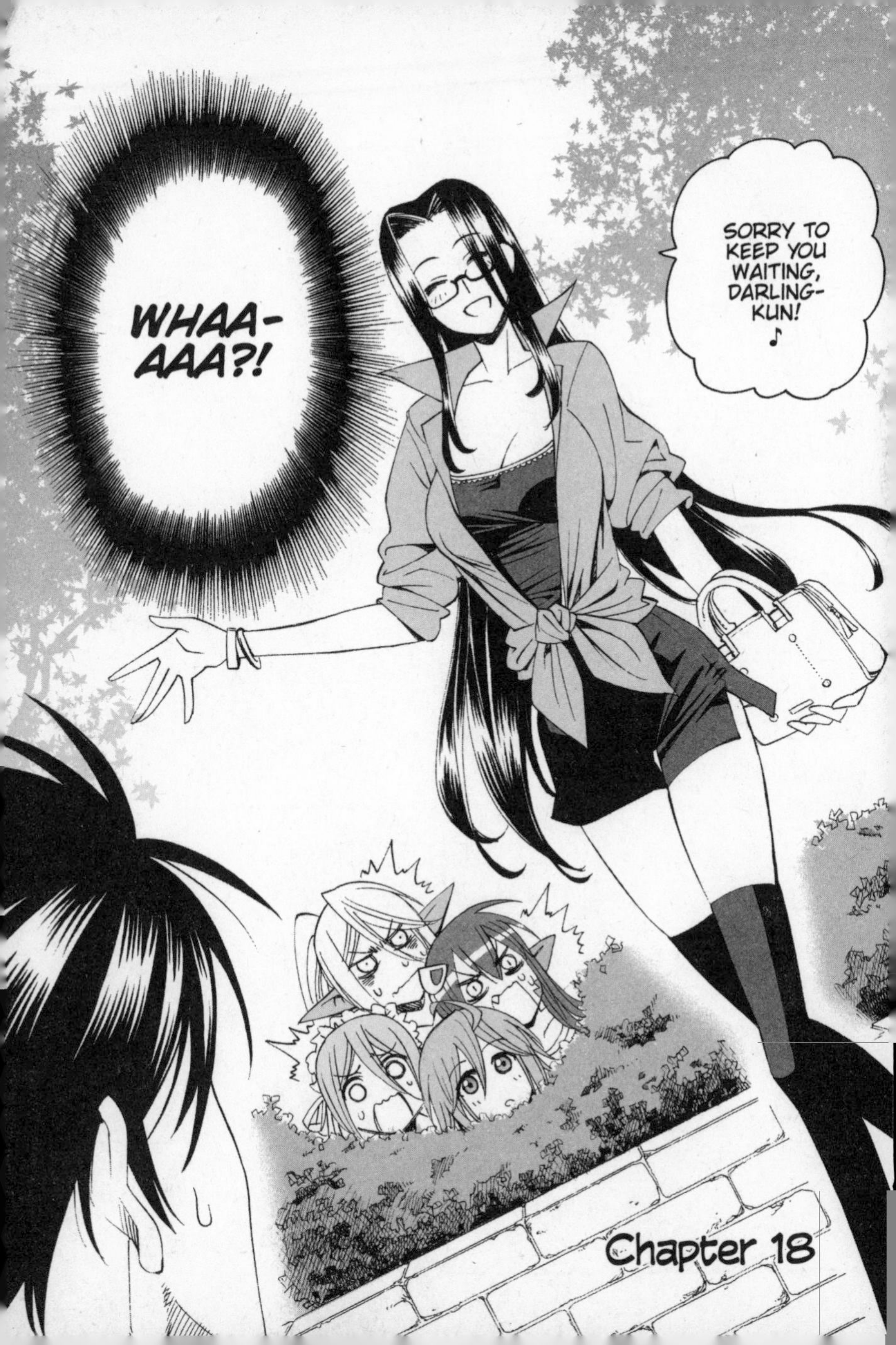
SORRY TO KEEP YOU WAITING, DARLING-KUN! ♪
WHAA-AAA?!
Chapter 18

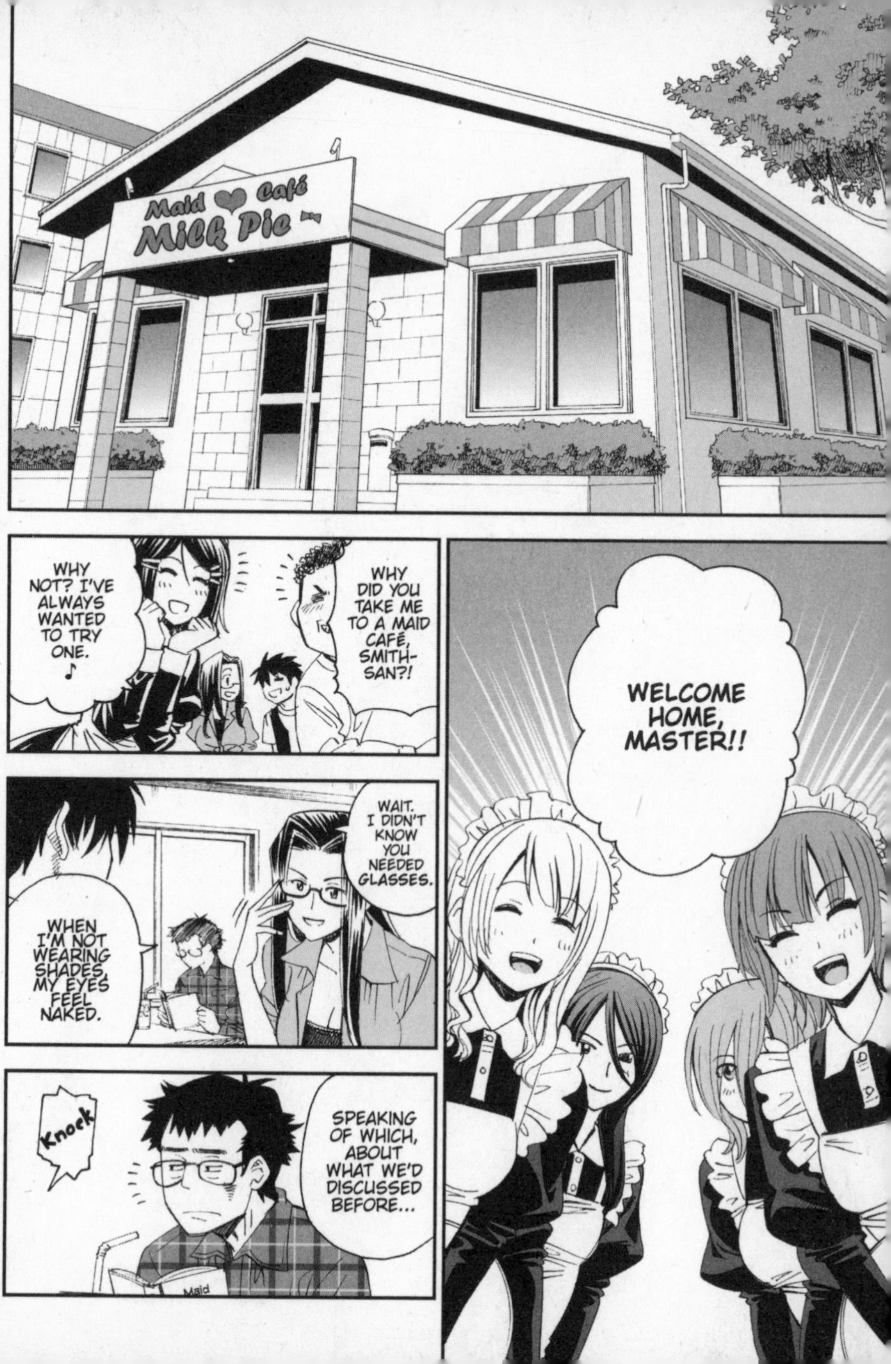
Maid Café
Milk Pie
WELCOME HOME, MASTER!!
WHY DID YOU TAKE ME TO A MAID CAFÉ, SMITH-SAN?!
WHY NOT? I'VE ALWAYS WANTED TO TRY ONE. ♪
WAIT. I DIDN'T KNOW YOU NEEDED GLASSES.
WHEN I'M NOT WEARING SHADES, MY EYES FEEL NAKED.
SPEAKING OF WHICH, ABOUT WHAT WE'D DISCUSSED BEFORE...
Knock
Maid

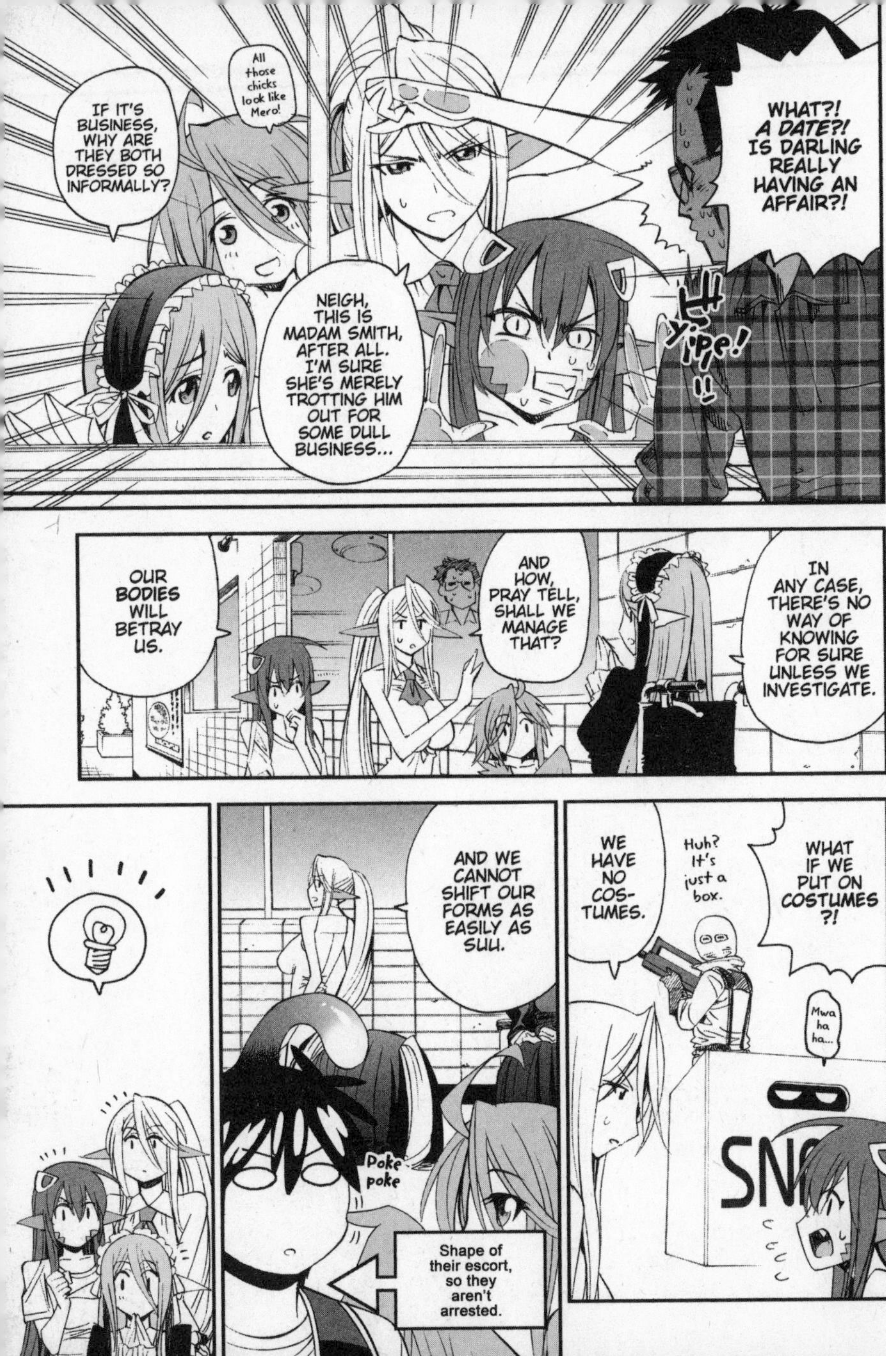
WHAT?! A DATE?! IS DARLING REALLY HAVING AN AFFAIR?!
All those chicks look like Mero!
IF IT'S BUSINESS, WHY ARE THEY BOTH DRESSED SO INFORMALLY?
Yipe!!
NEIGH, THIS IS MADAM SMITH, AFTER ALL. I'M SURE SHE'S MERELY TROTTING HIM OUT FOR SOME DULL BUSINESS...
IN ANY CASE, THERE'S NO WAY OF KNOWING FOR SURE UNLESS WE INVESTIGATE.
AND HOW, PRAY TELL, SHALL WE MANAGE THAT?
OUR BODIES WILL BETRAY US.
WHAT IF WE PUT ON COSTUMES?!
Huh? It's just a box.
WE HAVE NO COSTUMES.
Mwa ha ha...
AND WE CANNOT SHIFT OUR FORMS AS EASILY AS SUU.
Poke poke
Shape of their escort, so they aren't arrested.

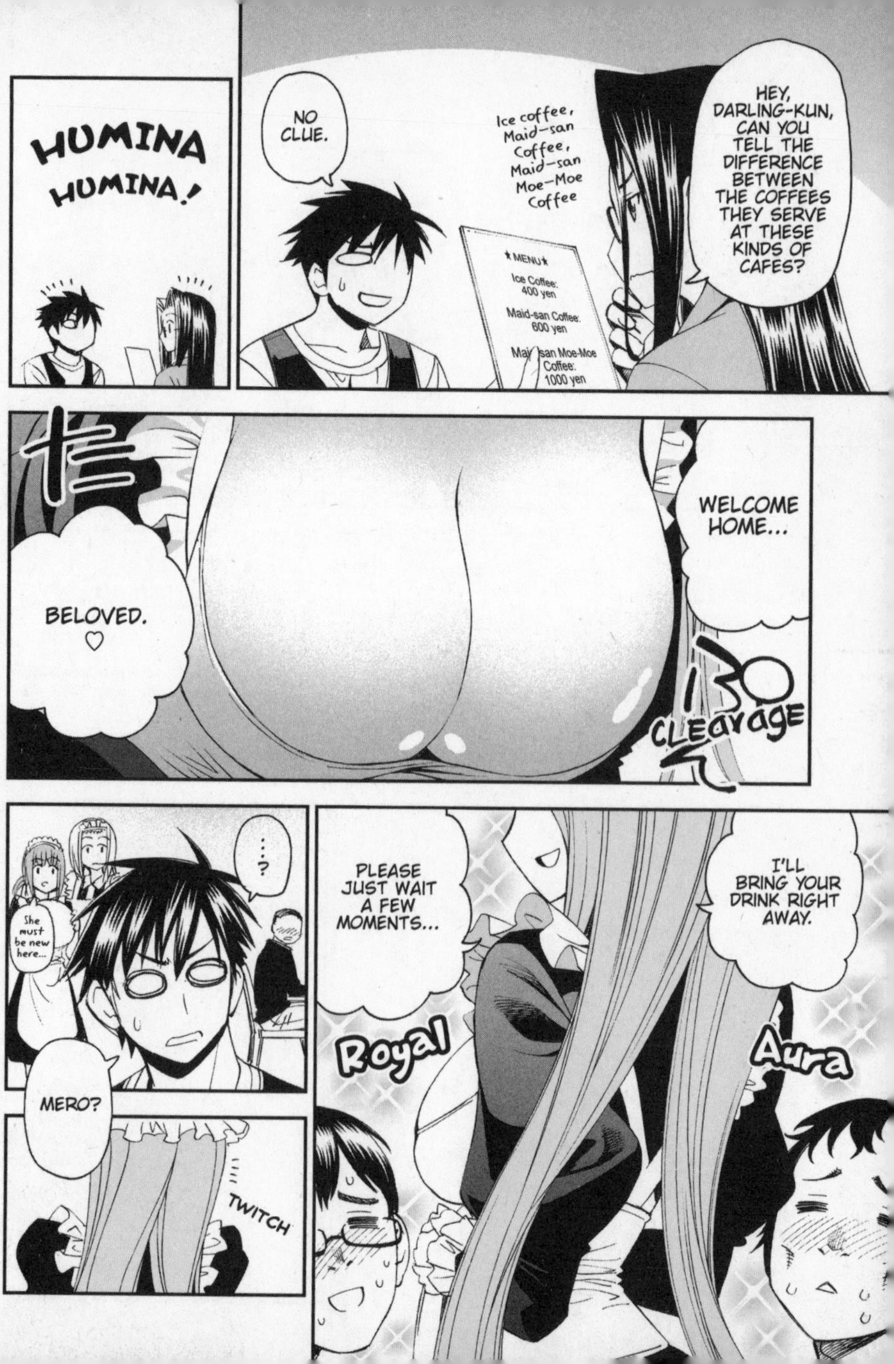
HEY, DARLING-KUN, CAN YOU TELL THE DIFFERENCE BETWEEN THE COFFEES THEY SERVE AT THESE KINDS OF CAFES?
Ice coffee, Maid-san Coffee, Maid-san Moe-Moe Coffee
★MENU★
Ice Coffee: 400 yen
Maid-san Coffee: 600 yen
Mai san Moe-Moe Coffee: 1000 yen
NO CLUE.
HUMINA HUMINA!
WELCOME HOME...
BELOVED. ♡
CLEAVAGE
I'LL BRING YOUR DRINK RIGHT AWAY.
PLEASE JUST WAIT A FEW MOMENTS...
Royal Aura
...?
She must be new here...
MERO?
TWITCH

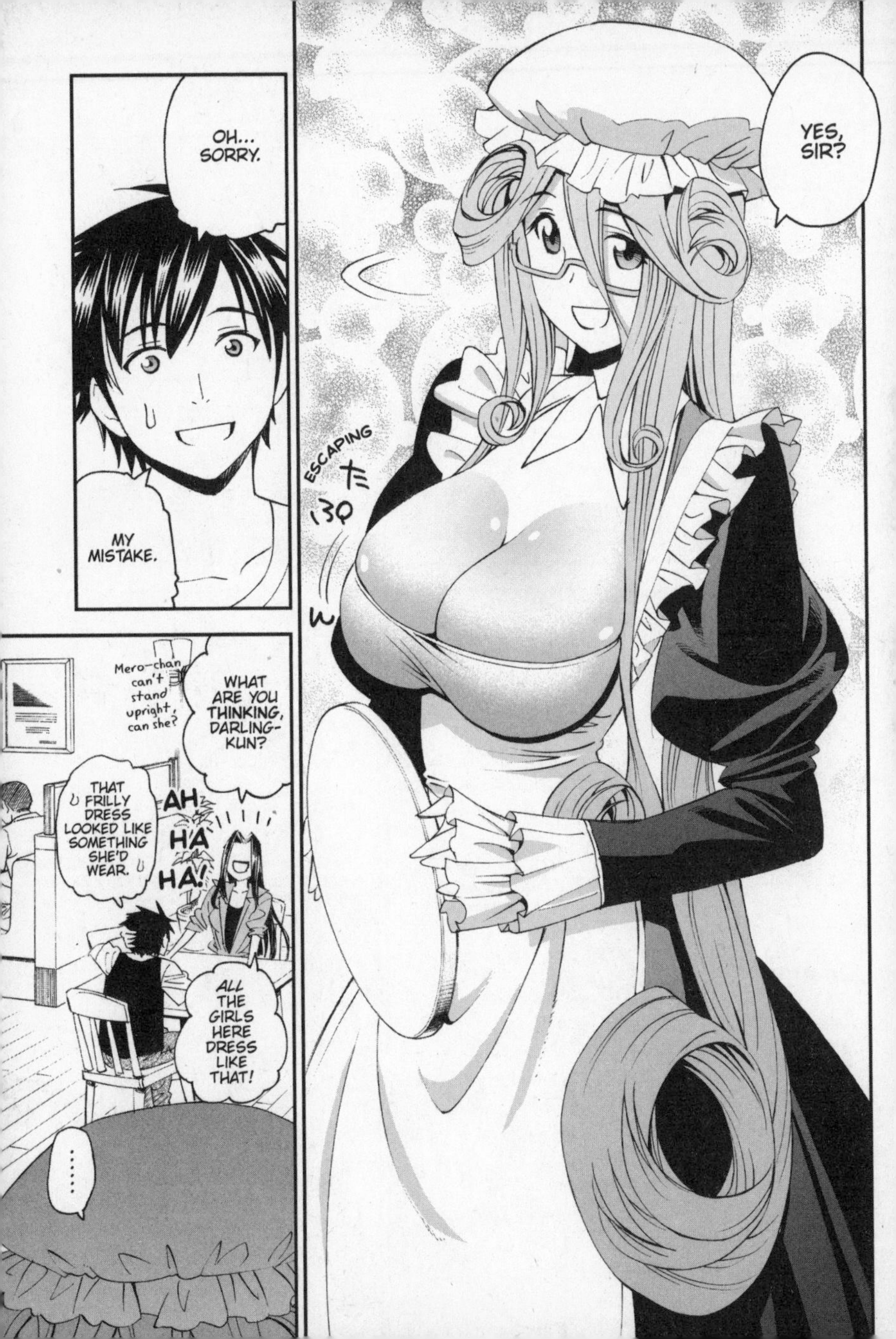
YES, SIR?
ESCAPING
OH... SORRY.
MY MISTAKE.
WHAT ARE YOU THINKING, DARLING-KUN?
Mero-chan can't stand upright, can she?
AH HA HA!
THAT FRILLY DRESS LOOKED LIKE SOMETHING SHE'D WEAR.
ALL THE GIRLS HERE DRESS LIKE THAT!
......

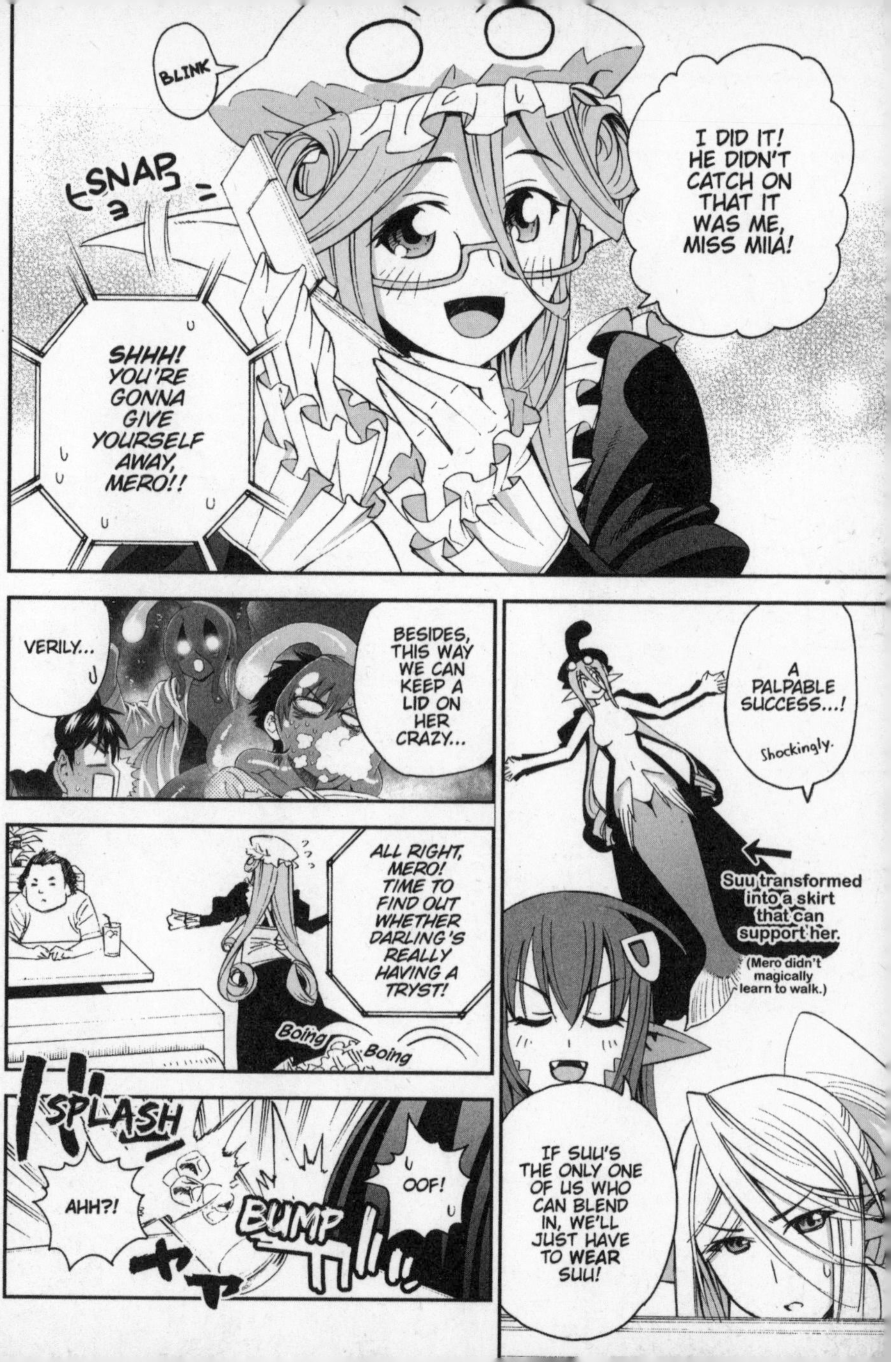
I DID IT! HE DIDN'T CATCH ON THAT IT WAS ME, MISS MIIA!
BLINK
SNAP
SHHH! YOU'RE GONNA GIVE YOURSELF AWAY, MERO!!
A PALPABLE SUCCESS...!
Shockingly.
Suu transformed into a skirt that can support her.
(Mero didn't magically learn to walk.)
IF SUU'S THE ONLY ONE OF US WHO CAN BLEND IN, WE'LL JUST HAVE TO WEAR SUU!
BESIDES, THIS WAY WE CAN KEEP A LID ON HER CRAZY...
VERILY...
ALL RIGHT, MERO! TIME TO FIND OUT WHETHER DARLING'S REALLY HAVING A TRYST!
Boing Boing
SPLASH
OOF!
BUMP
AHH?!

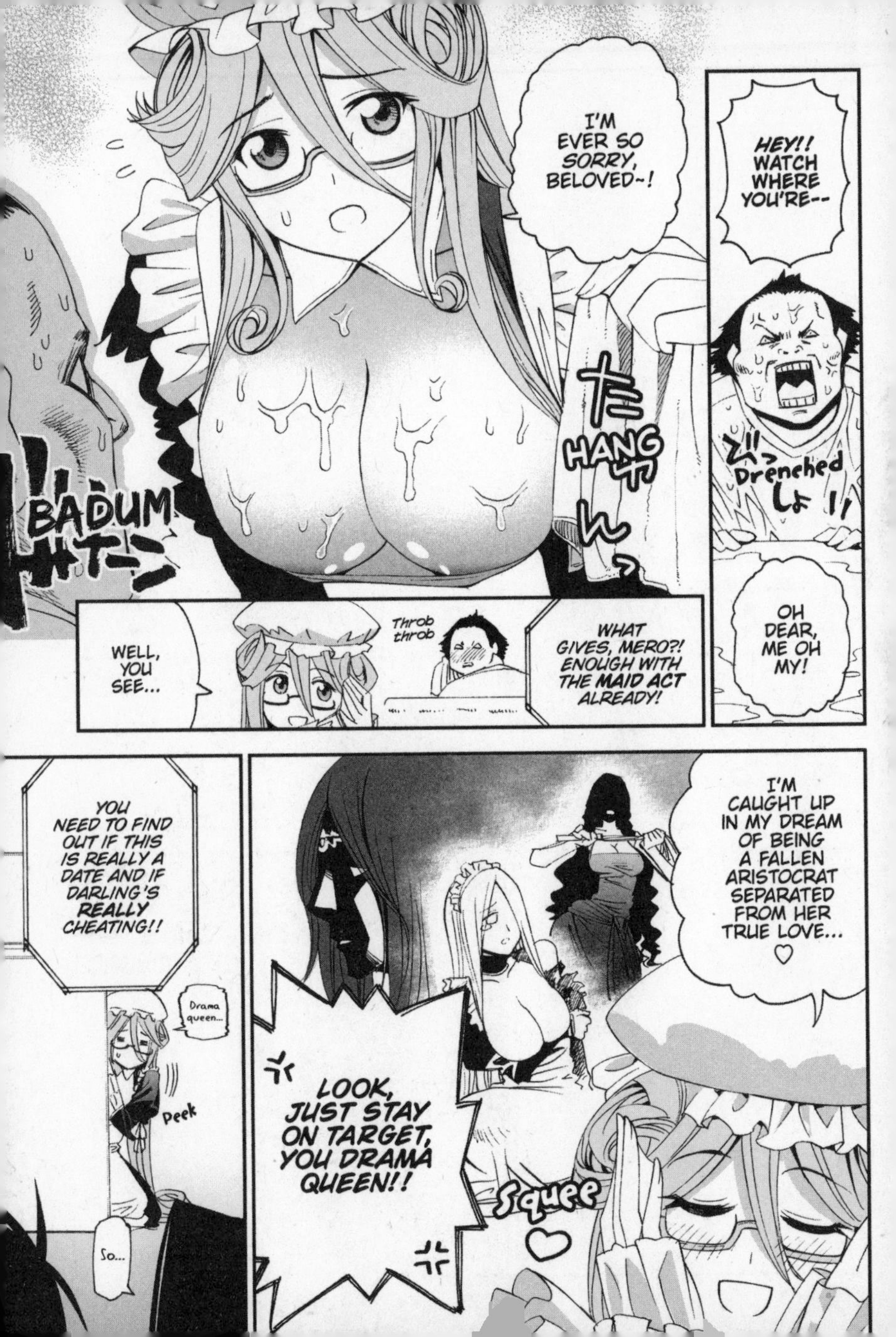
HEY!! WATCH WHERE YOU'RE--
Drenched
I'M EVER SO SORRY, BELOVED~!
HANG
BADUM
OH DEAR, ME OH MY!
WHAT GIVES, MERO?! ENOUGH WITH THE MAID ACT ALREADY!
Throb throb
WELL, YOU SEE...
I'M CAUGHT UP IN MY DREAM OF BEING A FALLEN ARISTOCRAT SEPARATED FROM HER TRUE LOVE... ♡
Squee
LOOK, JUST STAY ON TARGET, YOU DRAMA QUEEN!!
YOU NEED TO FIND OUT IF THIS IS REALLY A DATE AND IF DARLING'S REALLY CHEATING!!
Drama queen...
Peek
So...

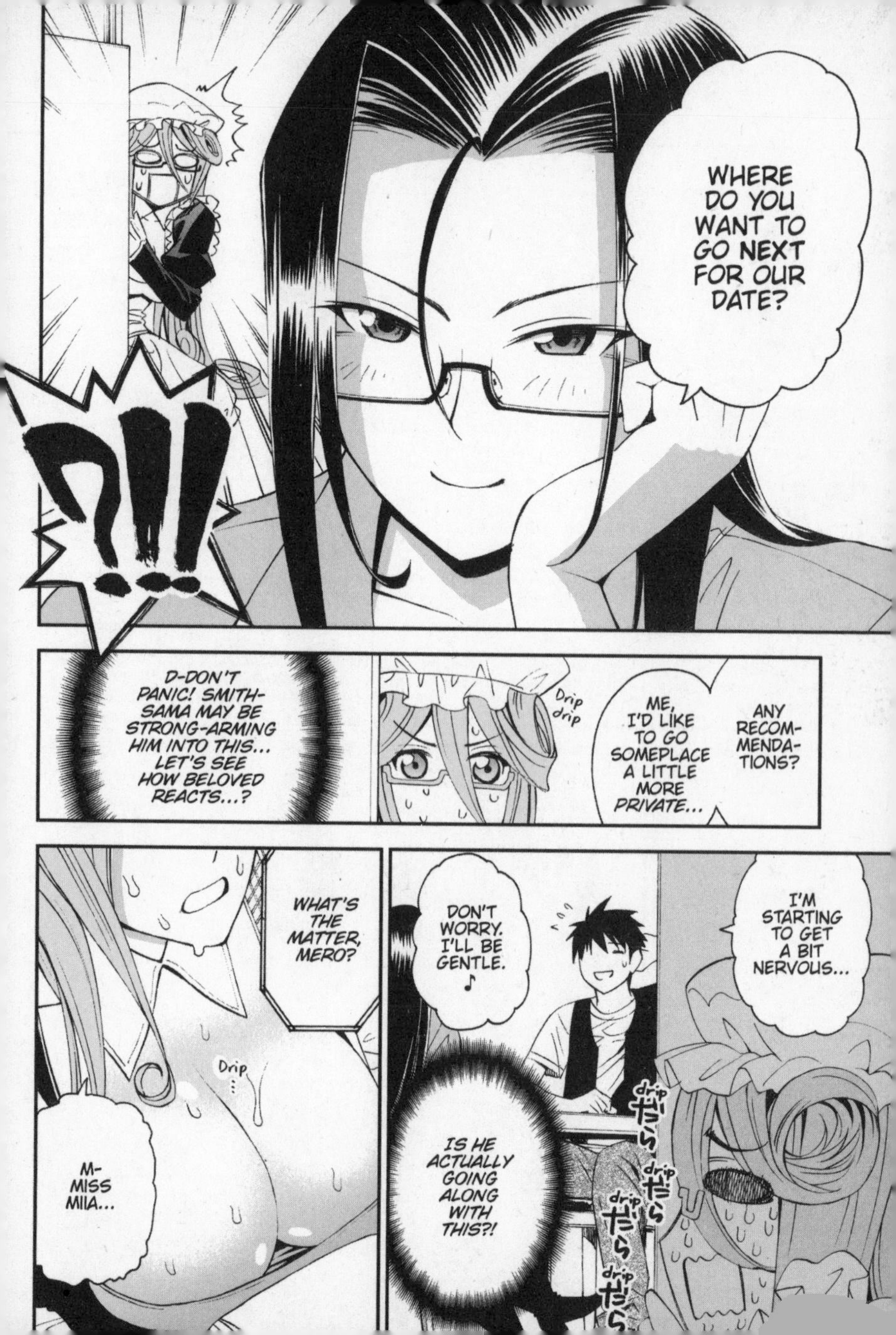
WHERE DO YOU WANT TO GO NEXT FOR OUR DATE?
?!!
ME, I'D LIKE TO GO SOMEPLACE A LITTLE MORE PRIVATE...
ANY RECOMMEN-DA-TIONS?
Drip drip
D-DON'T PANIC! SMITH-SAMA MAY BE STRONG-ARMING HIM INTO THIS... LET'S SEE HOW BELOVED REACTS...?
I'M STARTING TO GET A BIT NERVOUS...
drip だら
drip だら
drip だら
drip だら
DON'T WORRY. I'LL BE GENTLE. ♪
IS HE ACTUALLY GOING ALONG WITH THIS?!
WHAT'S THE MATTER, MERO?
Drip...
M-MISS MIIA...

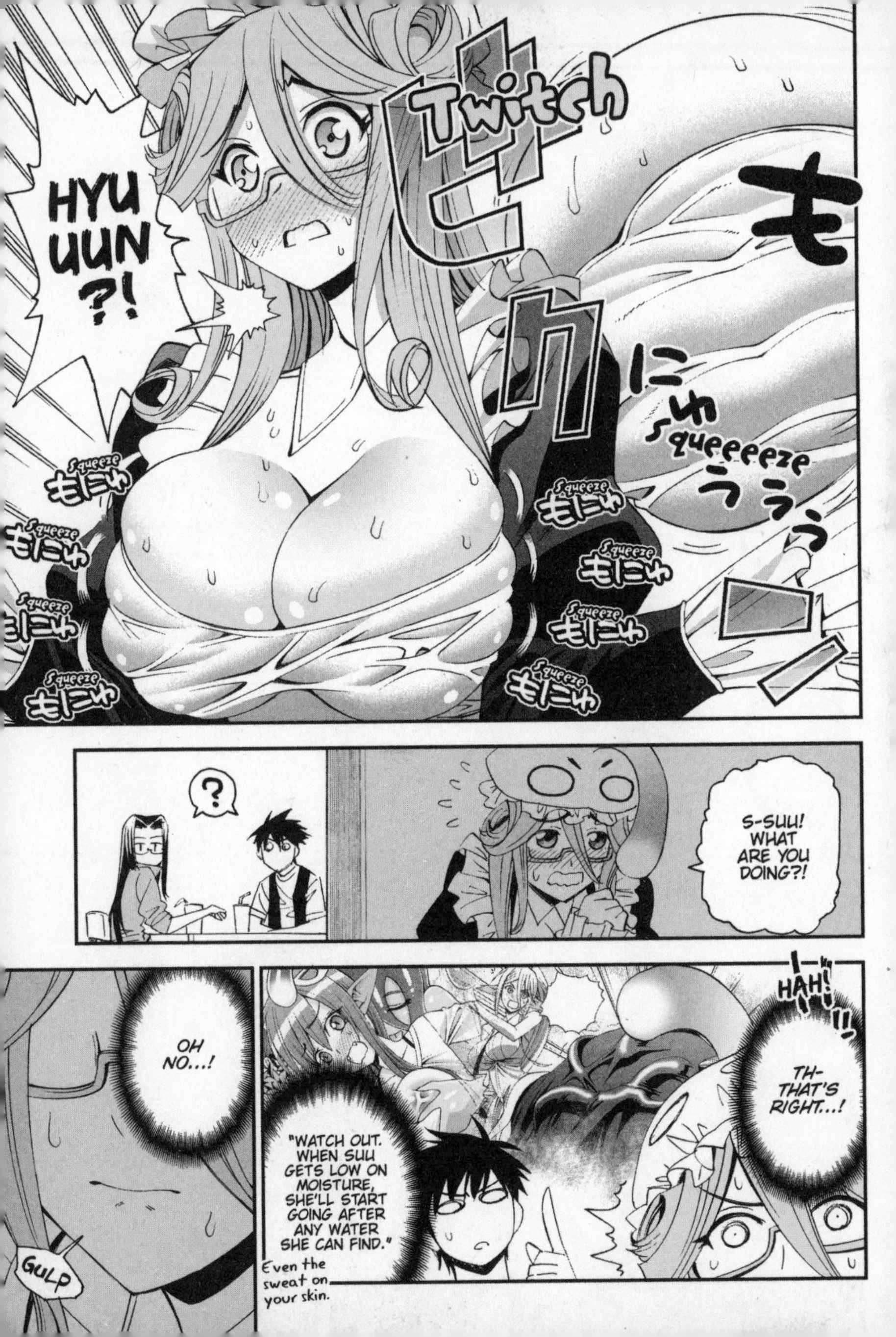
ビク
Twitch
もにゅうううう
Squeeeeeze
HYU UUN?!
Squeeze もにゅ
Squeeze もにゅ
Squeeze もにゅ
Squeeze もにゅ
Squeeze もにゅ
Squeeze もにゅ
Squeeze もにゅ
Squeeze もにゅ
S-SUU! WHAT ARE YOU DOING?!
?
I-HAH!!
TH-THAT'S RIGHT...!
"WATCH OUT. WHEN SUU GETS LOW ON MOISTURE, SHE'LL START GOING AFTER ANY WATER SHE CAN FIND."
Even the sweat on your skin.
OH NO...!
GULP

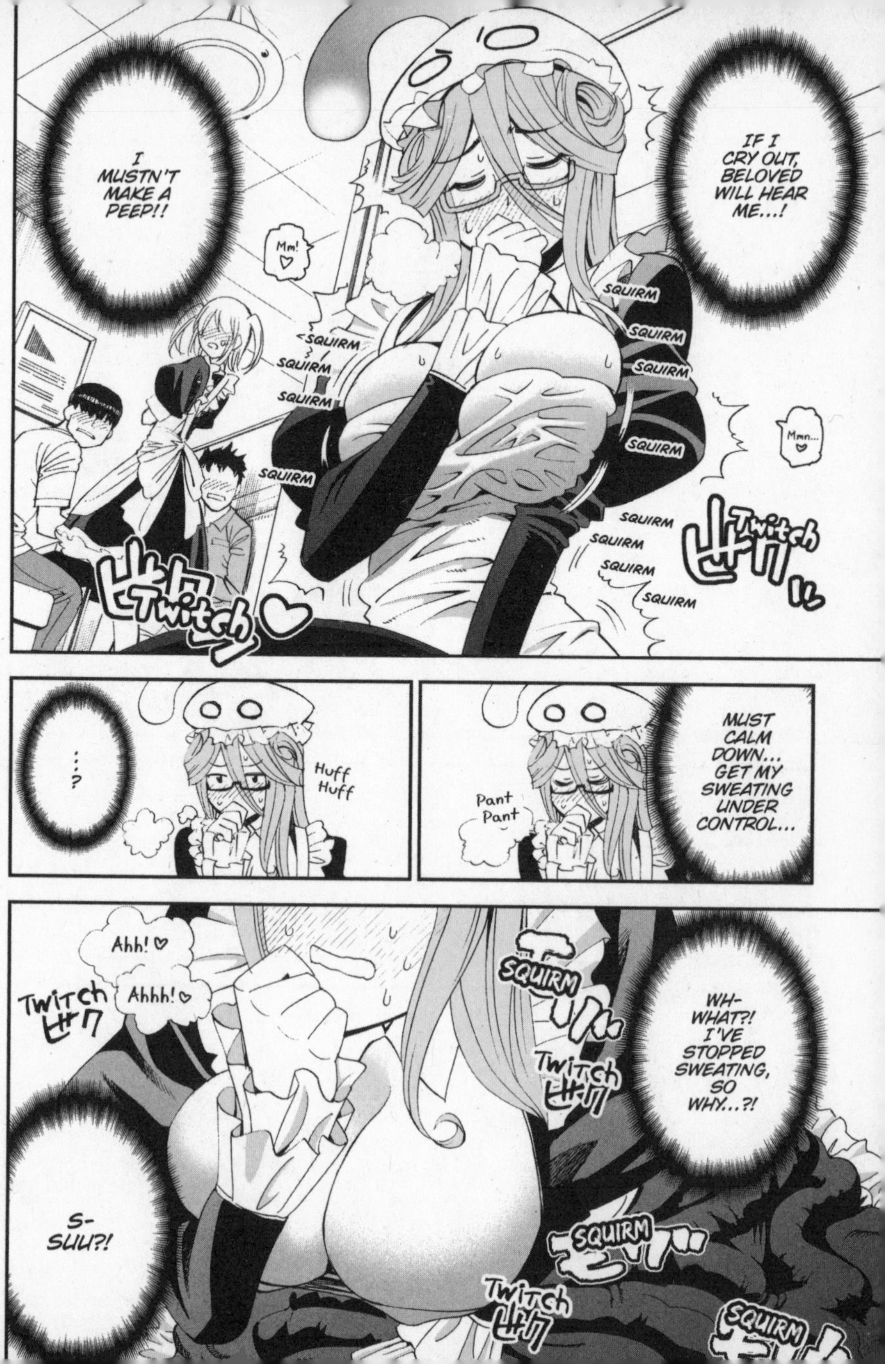
IF I CRY OUT, BELOVED WILL HEAR ME...!
Mmn... ♥
SQUIRM
SQUIRM
SQUIRM
SQUIRM
SQUIRM
SQUIRM
SQUIRM
SQUIRM
Twitch
Mm! ♥
I MUSTN'T MAKE A PEEP!!
SQUIRM
SQUIRM
SQUIRM
SQUIRM
Twitch ♥
MUST CALM DOWN... GET MY SWEATING UNDER CONTROL...
Pant Pant
Huff Huff
...?
WH-WHAT?! I'VE STOPPED SWEATING, SO WHY...?!
SQUIRM
Twitch
Ahh! ♥
Ahhh! ♥
Twitch
S-SUU?!
SQUIRM
Twitch
SQUIRM

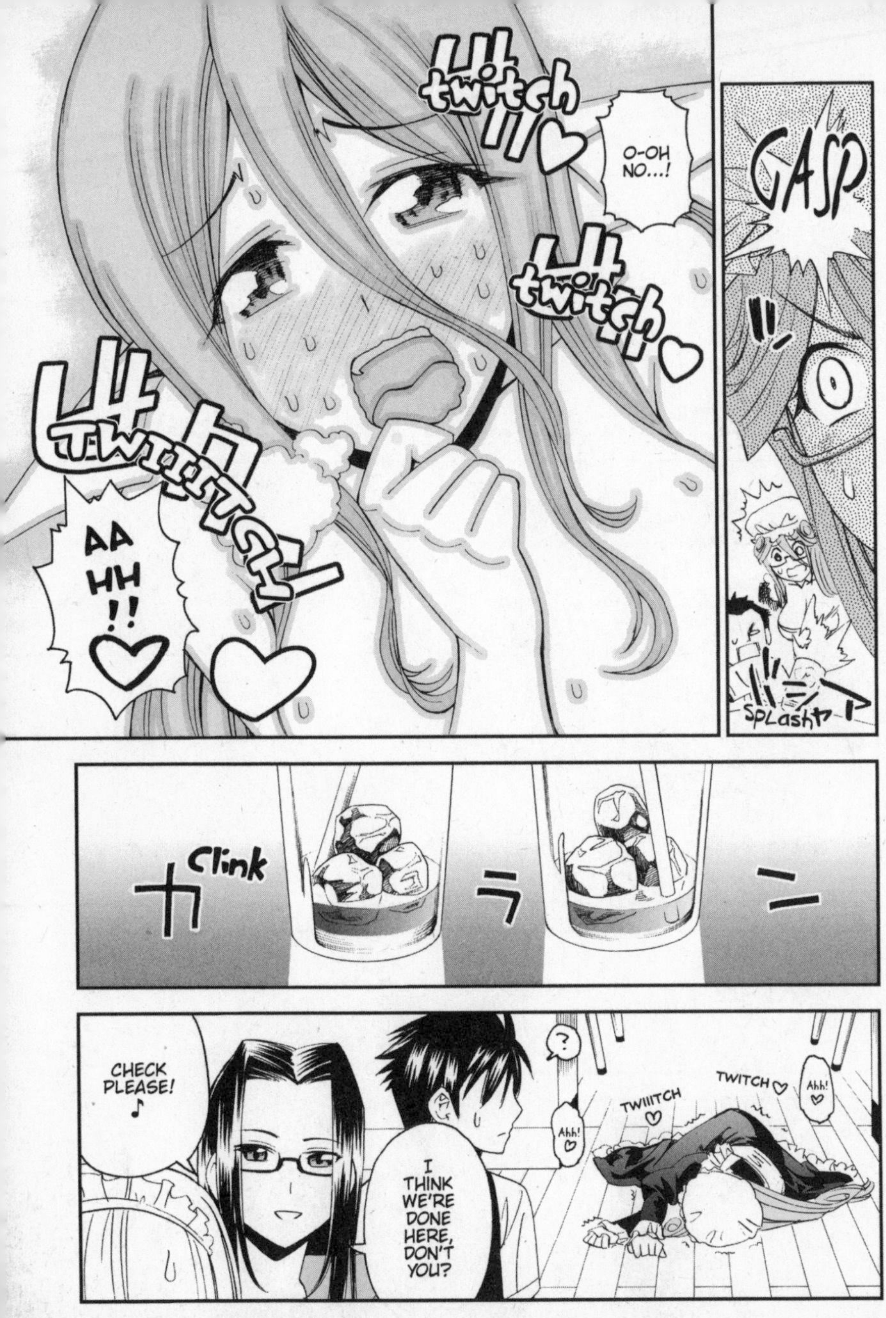
GASP
SPLASH
twitch
O-OH NO...!
twitch
TWIIITCH
AAHH!! ♥
Clink
Ahh! ♥
TWITCH ♥
?
TWIIITCH ♥
Ahh! ♥
I THINK WE'RE DONE HERE, DON'T YOU?
CHECK PLEASE! ♪

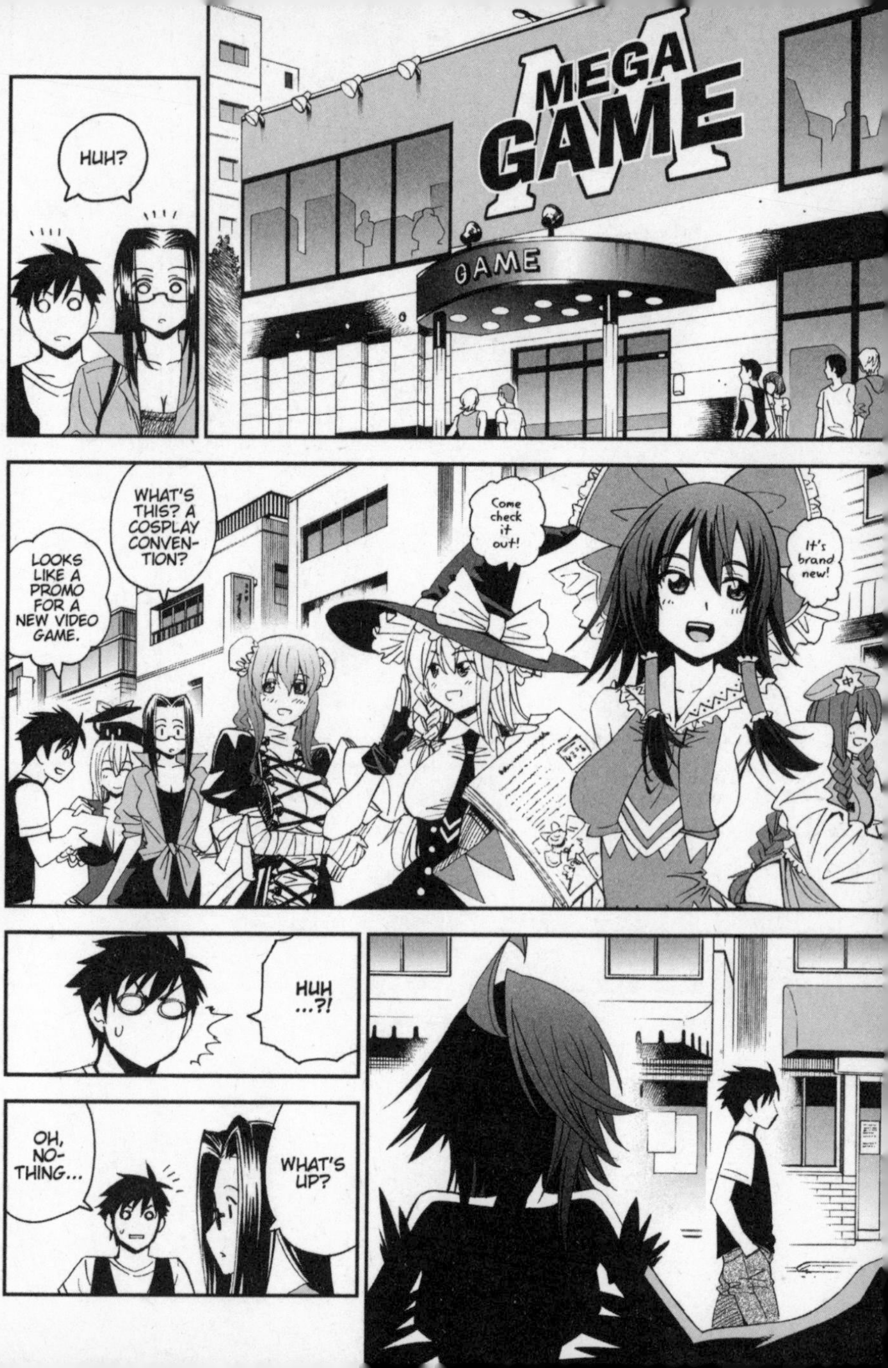
MEGA GAME
GAME
HUH?
It's brand new!
Come check it out!
WHAT'S THIS? A COSPLAY CONVENTION?
LOOKS LIKE A PROMO FOR A NEW VIDEO GAME.
HUH ...?!
WHAT'S UP?
OH, NOTHING...

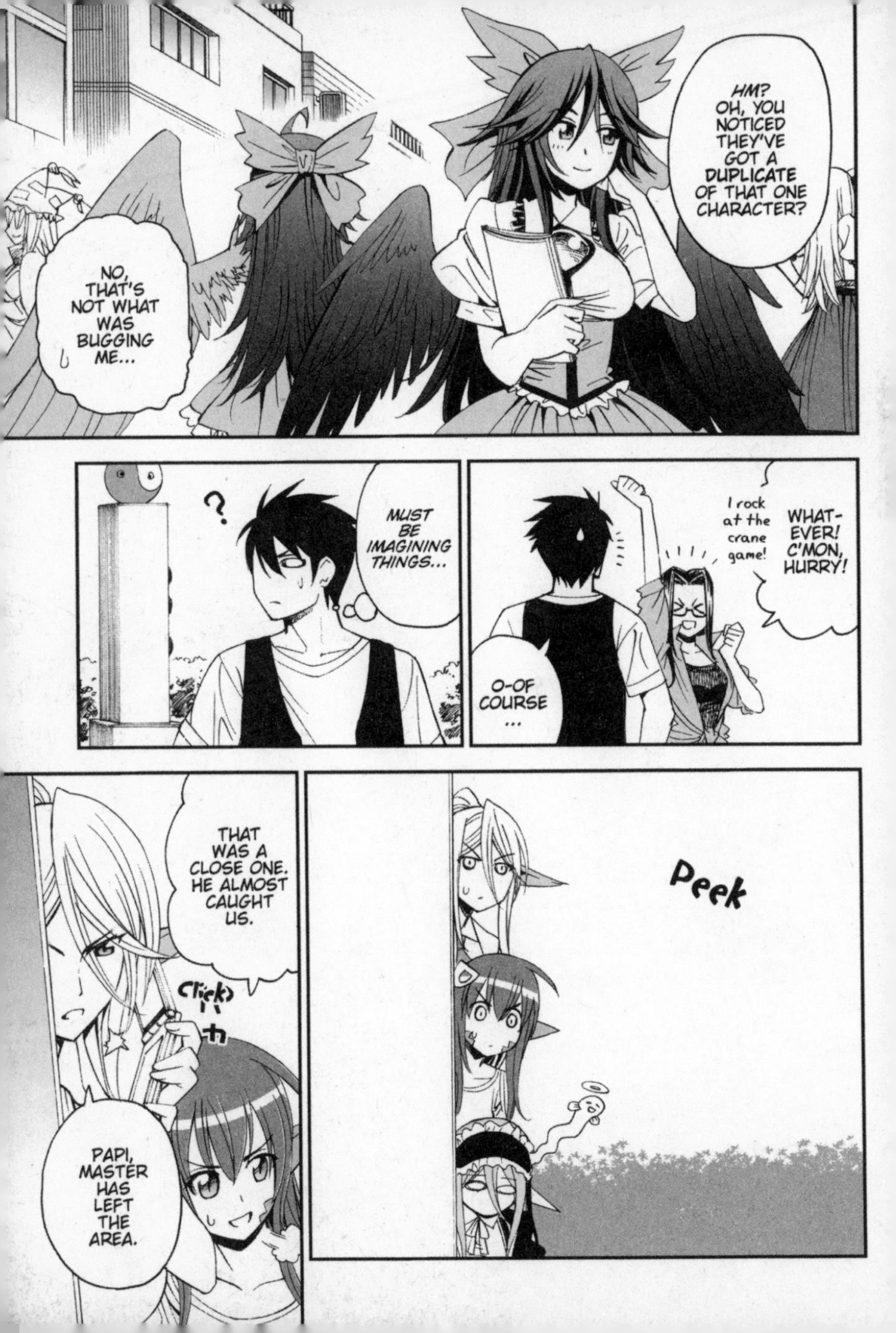
HM? OH, YOU NOTICED THEY'VE GOT A DUPLICATE OF THAT ONE CHARACTER?
NO, THAT'S NOT WHAT WAS BUGGING ME...
WHAT-EVER! C'MON, HURRY!
I rock at the crane game!
O-OF COURSE ...
MUST BE IMAGINING THINGS...
Peek
THAT WAS A CLOSE ONE. HE ALMOST CAUGHT US.
Click
PAPI, MASTER HAS LEFT THE AREA.

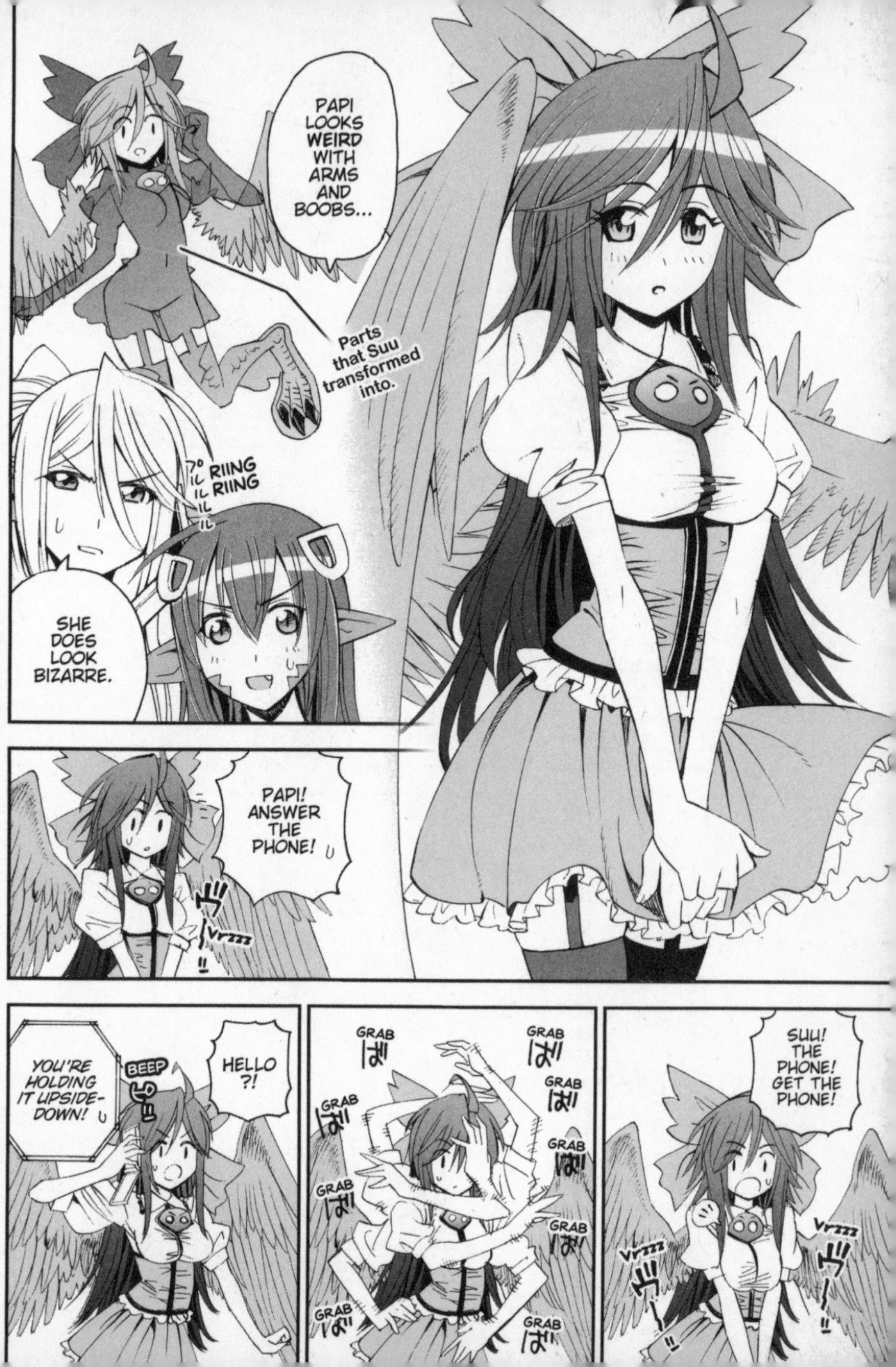
PAPI LOOKS WEIRD WITH ARMS AND BOOBS...
Parts that Suu transformed into.
RIING RIING
SHE DOES LOOK BIZARRE.
PAPI! ANSWER THE PHONE!
Vrzzz
SUU! THE PHONE! GET THE PHONE!
Vrzzz
Vrzzz
GRAB
GRAB
GRAB
GRAB
GRAB
GRAB
GRAB
GRAB
GRAB
HELLO ?!
BEEP
YOU'RE HOLDING IT UPSIDE-DOWN!

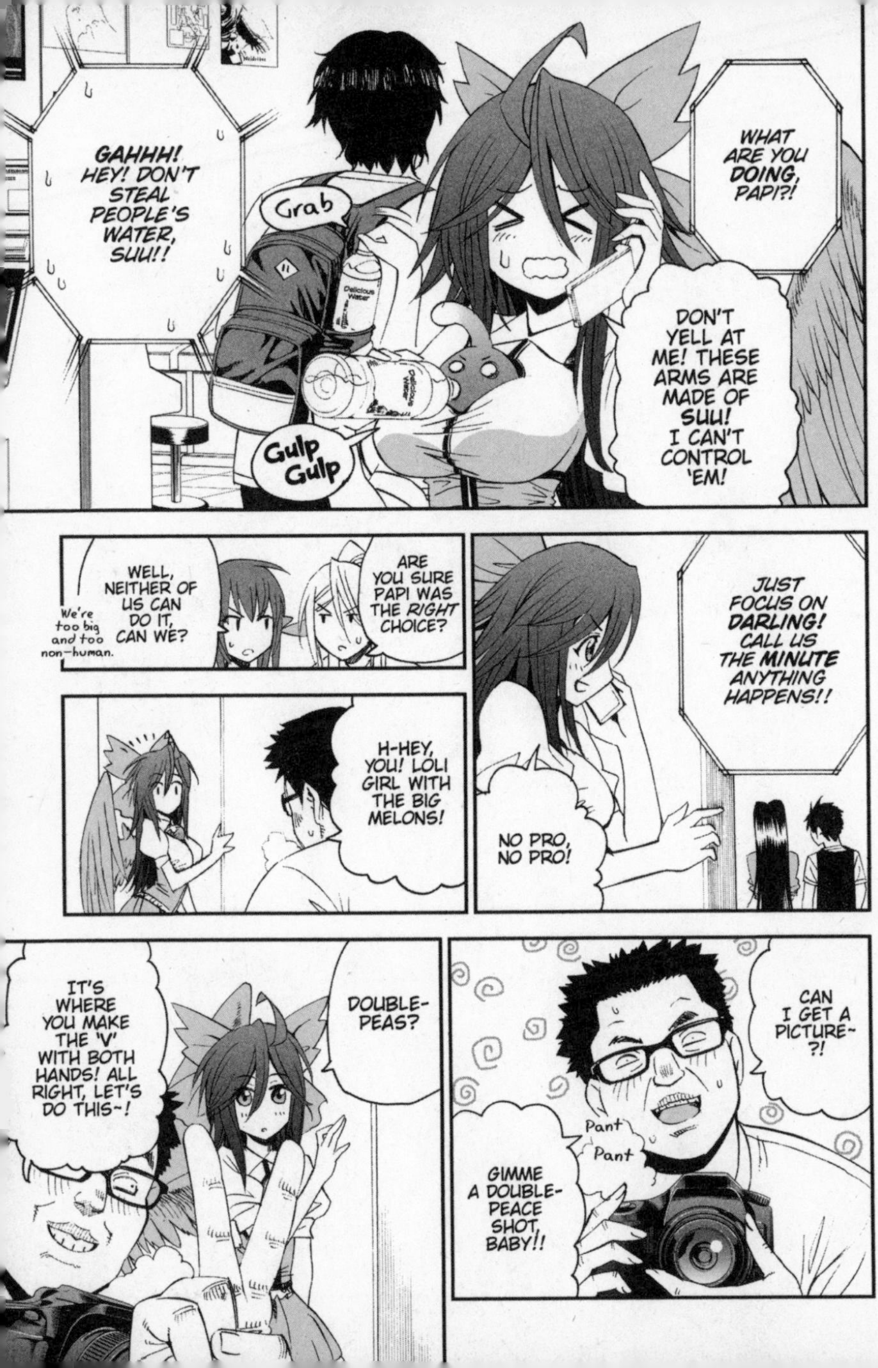
WHAT ARE YOU DOING, PAPI?!
DON'T YELL AT ME! THESE ARMS ARE MADE OF SUU! I CAN'T CONTROL 'EM!
GAHHH! HEY! DON'T STEAL PEOPLE'S WATER, SUU!!
Grab
Delicious Water
Delicious Water
Gulp Gulp
JUST FOCUS ON DARLING! CALL US THE MINUTE ANYTHING HAPPENS!!
NO PRO, NO PRO!
ARE YOU SURE PAPI WAS THE RIGHT CHOICE?
WELL, NEITHER OF US CAN DO IT, CAN WE?
We're too big and too non-human.
H-HEY, YOU! LOLI GIRL WITH THE BIG MELONS!
CAN I GET A PICTURE~?!
Pant Pant
GIMME A DOUBLE-PEACE SHOT, BABY!!
DOUBLE-PEAS?
IT'S WHERE YOU MAKE THE 'V' WITH BOTH HANDS! ALL RIGHT, LET'S DO THIS~!

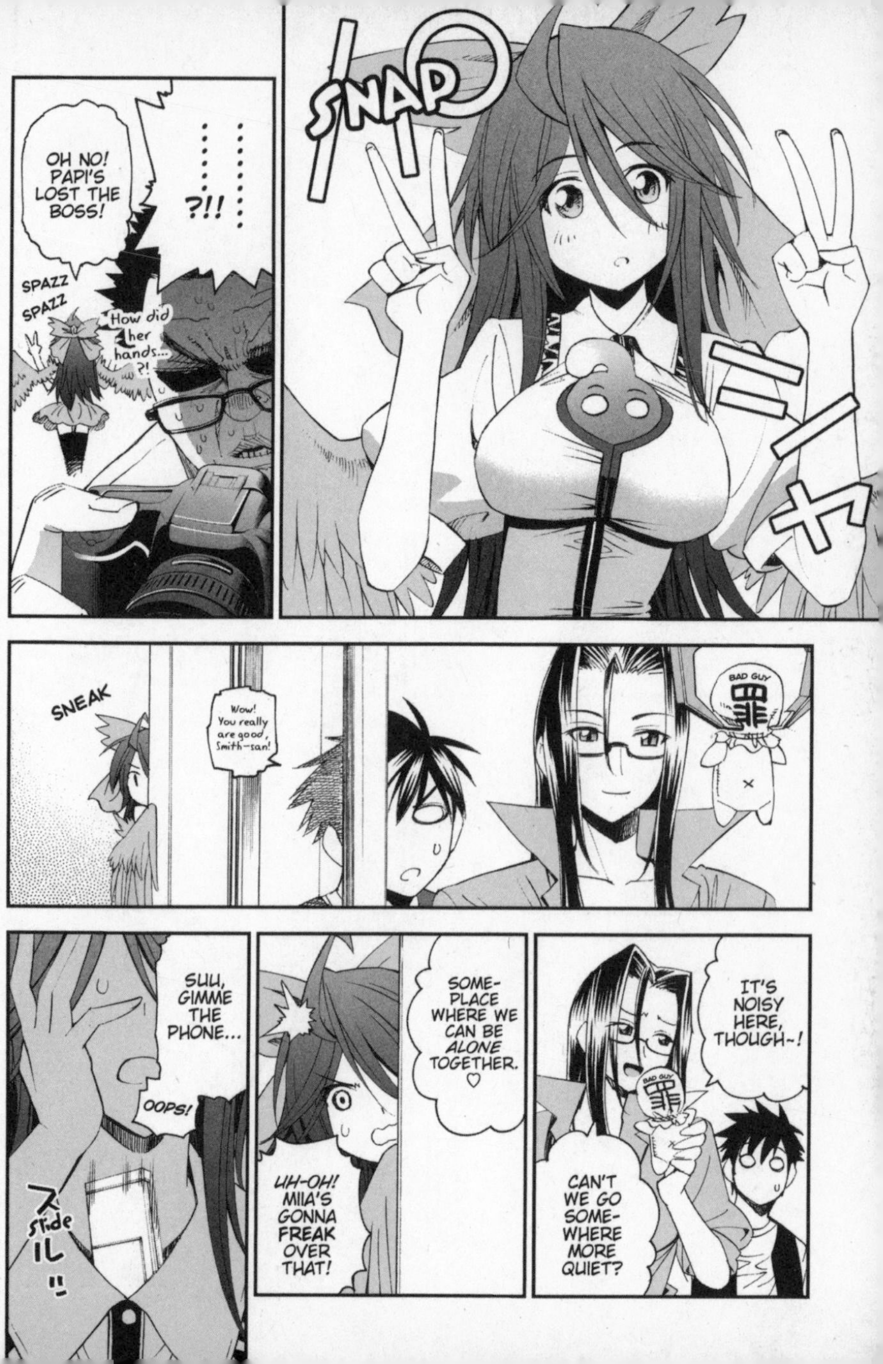
SNAP
?!!
OH NO! PAPI'S LOST THE BOSS!
SPAZZ SPAZZ
How did her hands... ?!
BAD GUY 罪
Wow! You really are good, Smith-san!
SNEAK
IT'S NOISY HERE, THOUGH~!
BAD GUY 罪
CAN'T WE GO SOME-WHERE MORE QUIET?
SOME-PLACE WHERE WE CAN BE *ALONE* TOGETHER. ♡
UH-OH! MIIA'S GONNA FREAK OVER THAT!
SUU, GIMME THE PHONE...
OOPS!
stride

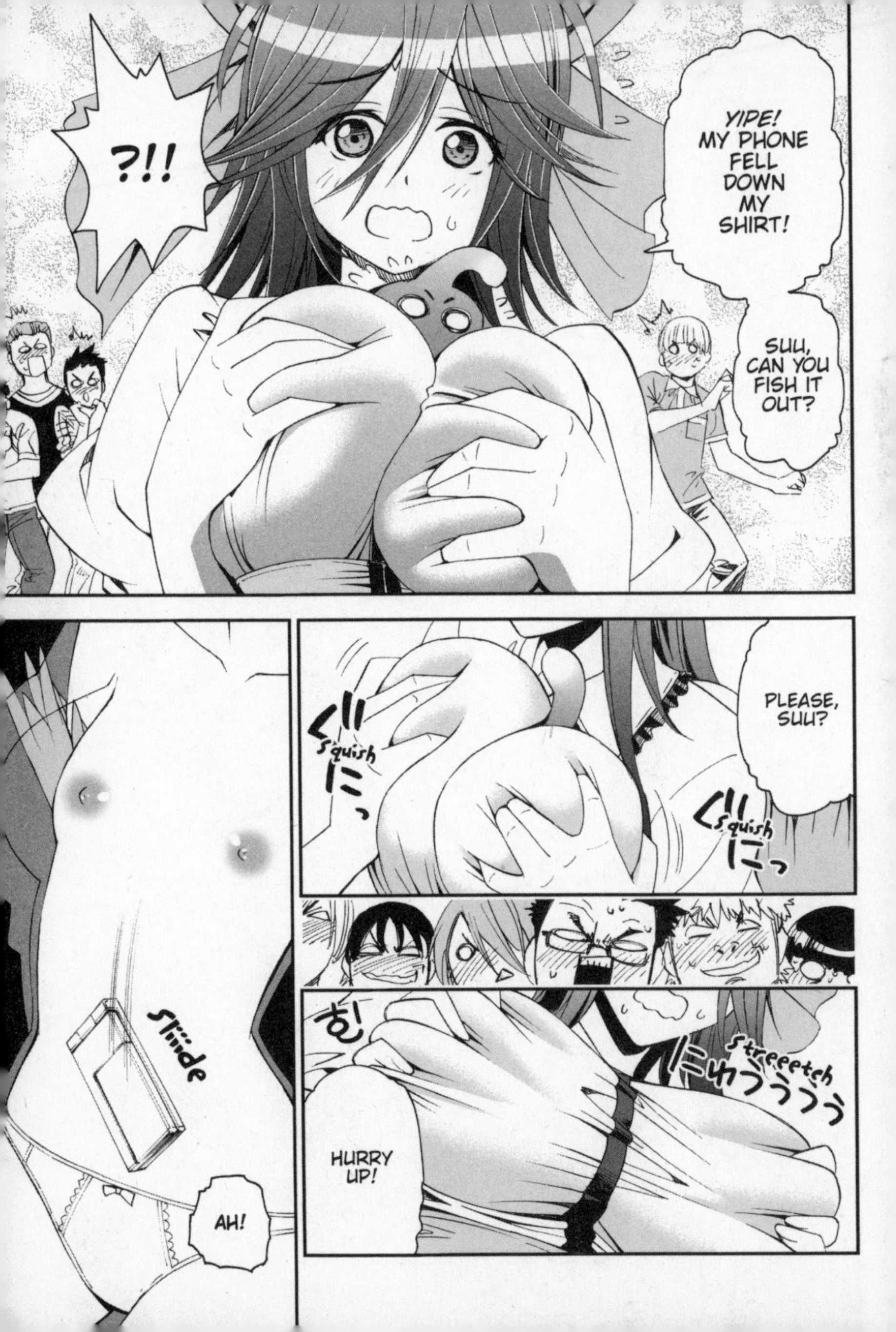
YIPE! MY PHONE FELL DOWN MY SHIRT!
?!!
SUU, CAN YOU FISH IT OUT?
PLEASE, SUU?
くにっ squish
くにっ squish
む!
にゅううう streeetch
HURRY UP!
Sliiide
AH!

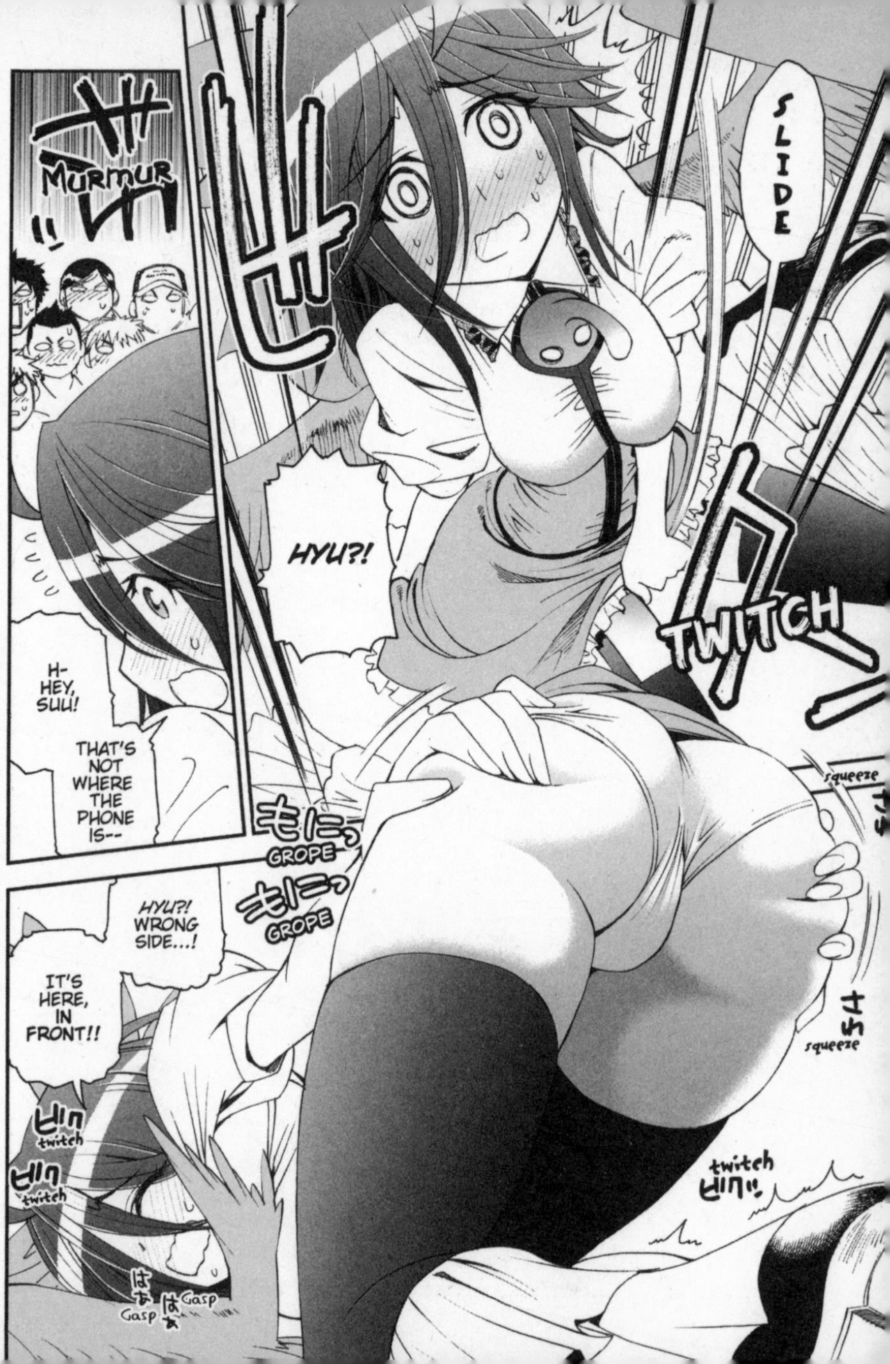
SLIDE
HYU?!
TWITCH
squeeze
squeeze
もにっ
GROPE
もにっ
GROPE
twitch
ビクッ!!
Murmur
H-HEY, SUU!
THAT'S NOT WHERE THE PHONE IS--
HYU?! WRONG SIDE...!
IT'S HERE, IN FRONT!!
ビクッ
twitch
ビクッ
twitch
はぁ
Gasp
はぁ
Gasp

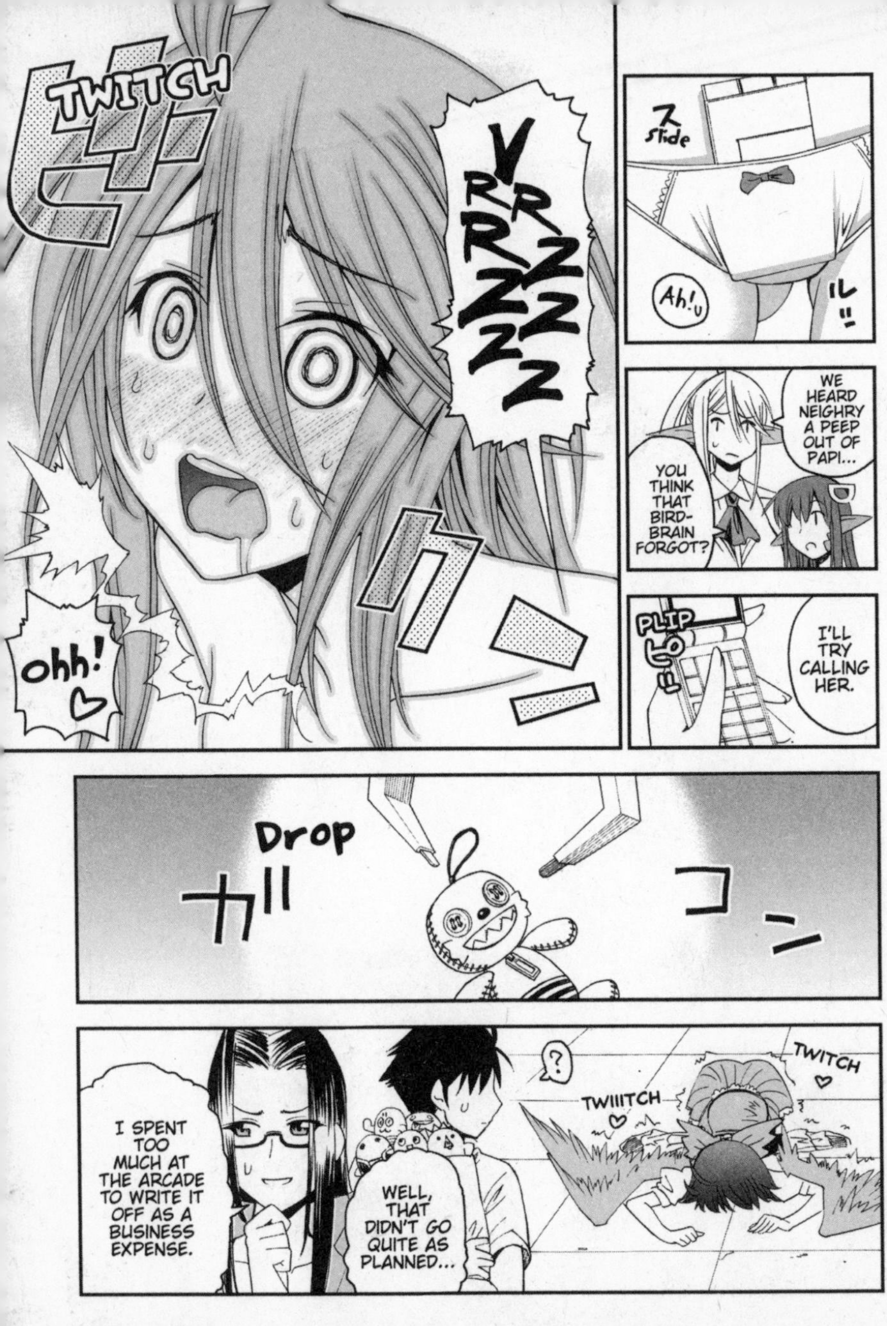
ス slide
Ah!
WE HEARD NEIGHRY A PEEP OUT OF PAPI...
YOU THINK THAT BIRD-BRAIN FORGOT?
PLIP
I'LL TRY CALLING HER.
TWITCH
VRRRRZZZZZ
ohh! ♥
Drop
TWITCH ♥
TWIIITCH ♥
?
WELL, THAT DIDN'T GO QUITE AS PLANNED...
I SPENT TOO MUCH AT THE ARCADE TO WRITE IT OFF AS A BUSINESS EXPENSE.

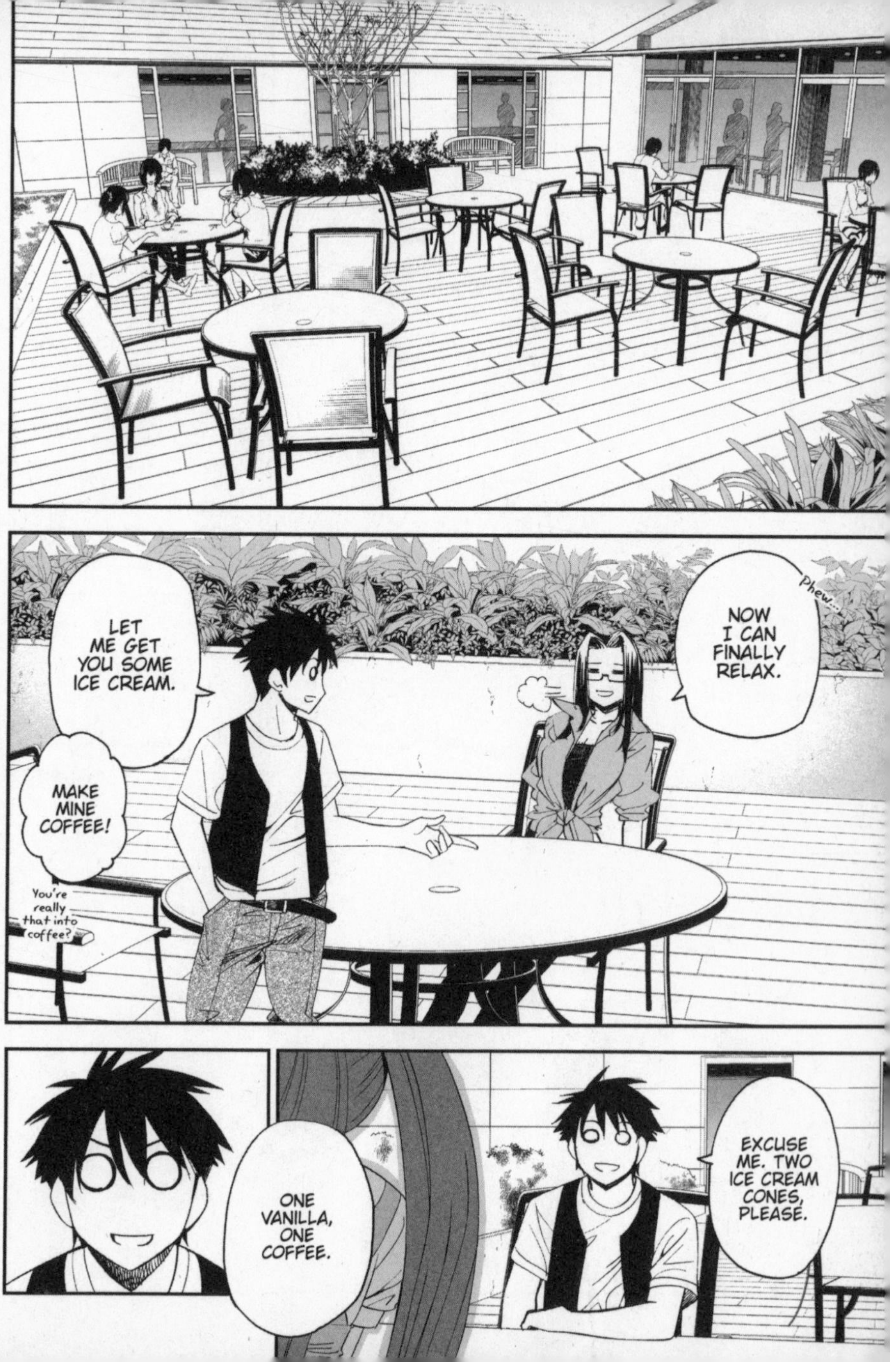
Phew...
NOW I CAN FINALLY RELAX.
LET ME GET YOU SOME ICE CREAM.
MAKE MINE COFFEE!
You're really that into coffee?
EXCUSE ME. TWO ICE CREAM CONES, PLEASE.
ONE VANILLA, ONE COFFEE.

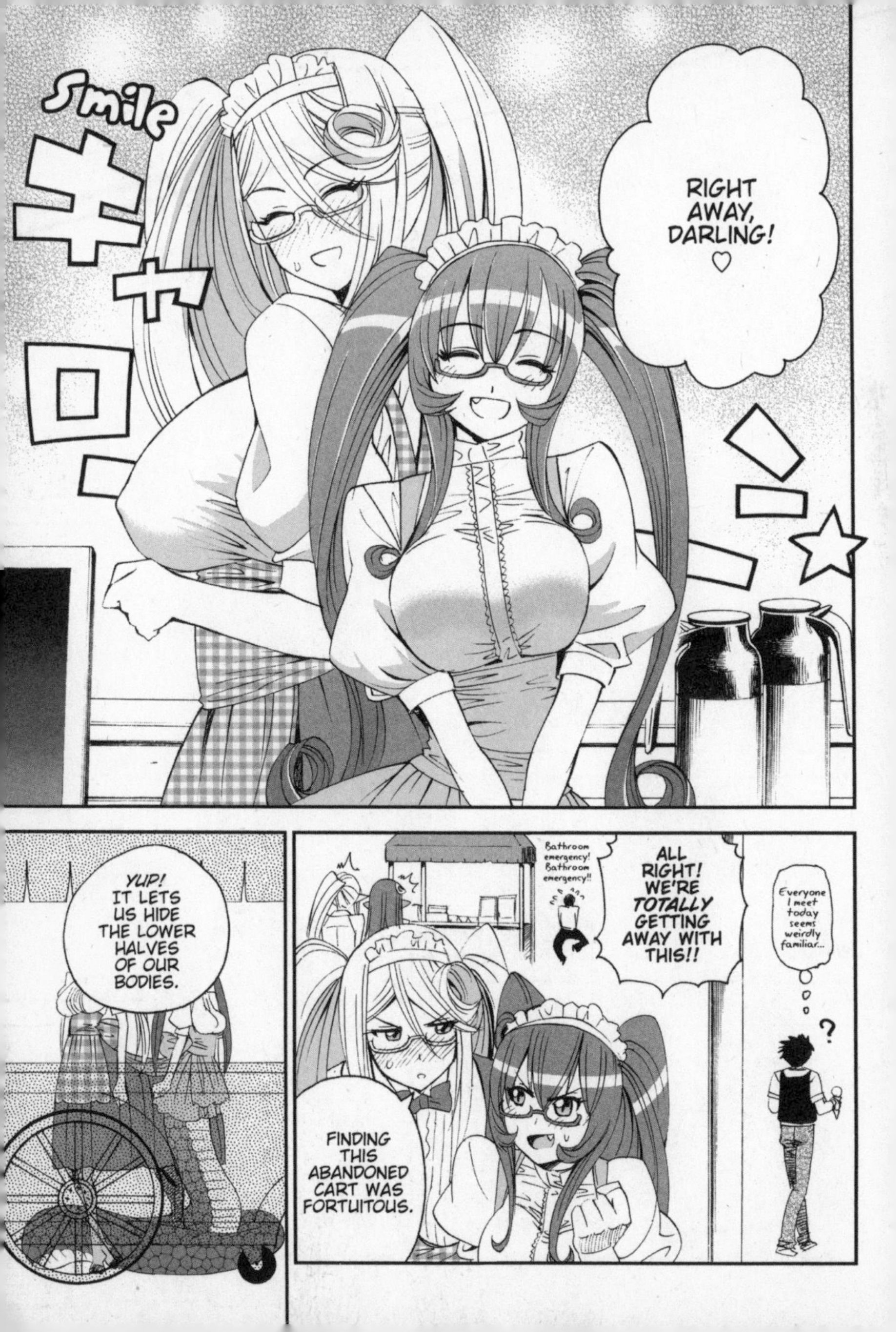

RIGHT AWAY, DARLING! ♡
Smile
Everyone I meet today seems weirdly familiar...
?
ALL RIGHT! WE'RE *TOTALLY* GETTING AWAY WITH THIS!!
Bathroom emergency! Bathroom emergency!!
FINDING THIS ABANDONED CART WAS FORTUITOUS.
YUP! IT LETS US HIDE THE LOWER HALVES OF OUR BODIES.

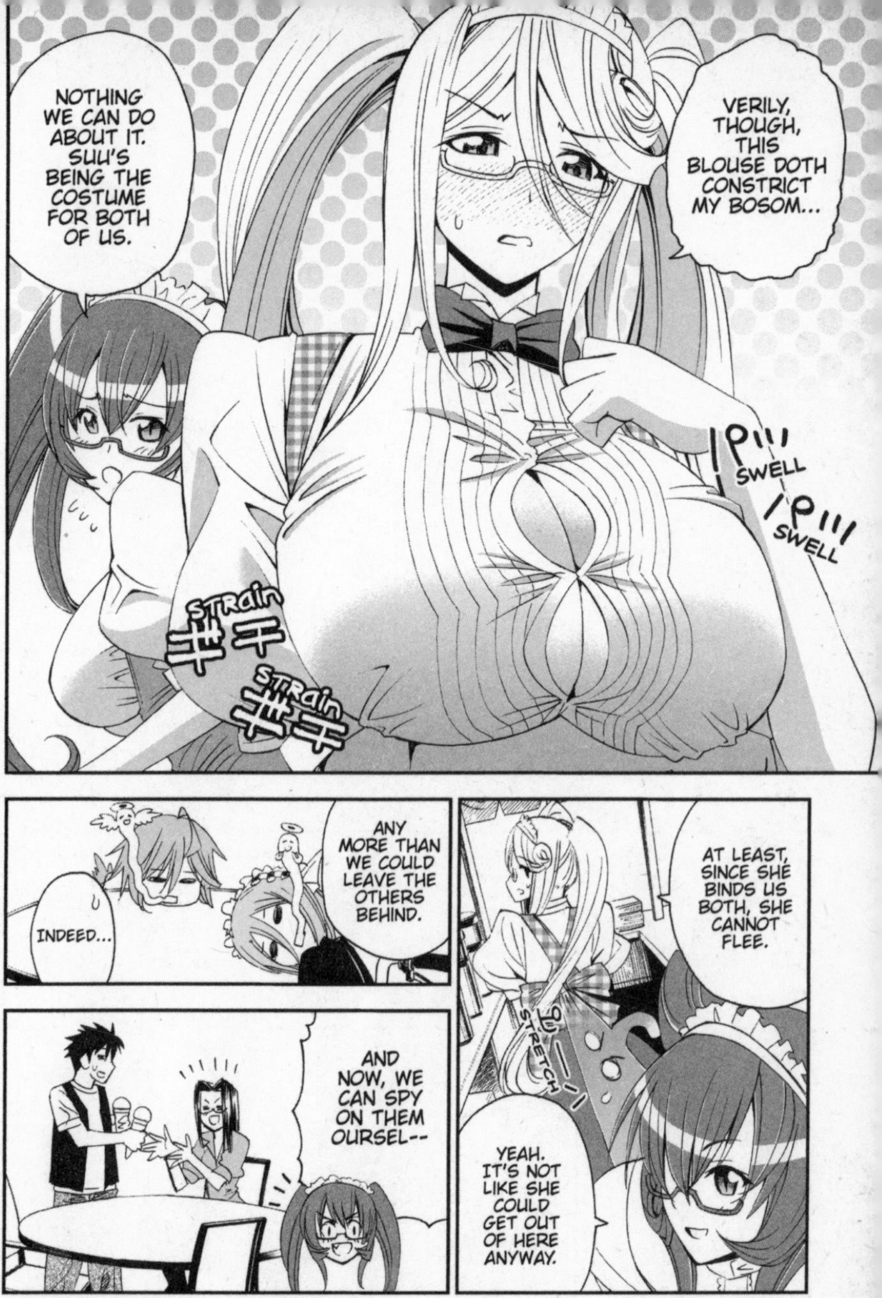
VERILY, THOUGH, THIS BLOUSE DOTH CONSTRICT MY BOSOM...
NOTHING WE CAN DO ABOUT IT. SUU'S BEING THE COSTUME FOR BOTH OF US.
SWELL
SWELL
STRAIN
STRAIN
AT LEAST, SINCE SHE BINDS US BOTH, SHE CANNOT FLEE.
STRETCH
YEAH. IT'S NOT LIKE SHE COULD GET OUT OF HERE ANYWAY.
ANY MORE THAN WE COULD LEAVE THE OTHERS BEHIND.
INDEED...
AND NOW, WE CAN SPY ON THEM OURSEL--

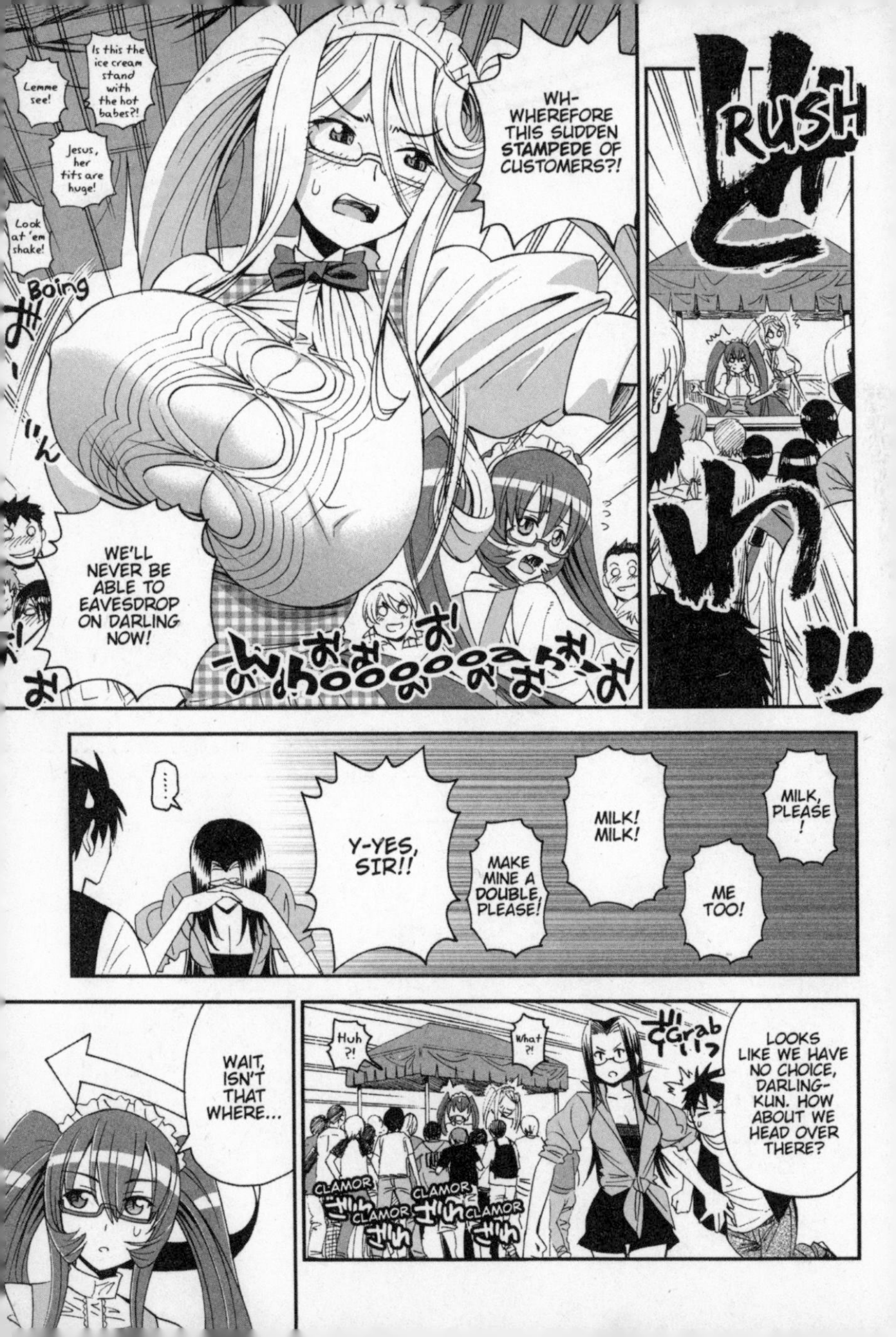
RUSH
WH-WHEREFORE THIS SUDDEN STAMPEDE OF CUSTOMERS?!
Is this the ice cream stand with the hot babes?!
Lemme see!
Jesus, her tits are huge!
Look at 'em shake!
Boing
WE'LL NEVER BE ABLE TO EAVESDROP ON DARLING NOW!
MILK, PLEASE!
ME TOO!
MILK! MILK!
MAKE MINE A DOUBLE, PLEASE!
Y-YES, SIR!!
.....
LOOKS LIKE WE HAVE NO CHOICE, DARLING-KUN. HOW ABOUT WE HEAD OVER THERE?
Grab
What?
Huh?!
CLAMOR
CLAMOR
CLAMOR
CLAMOR
WAIT, ISN'T THAT WHERE...

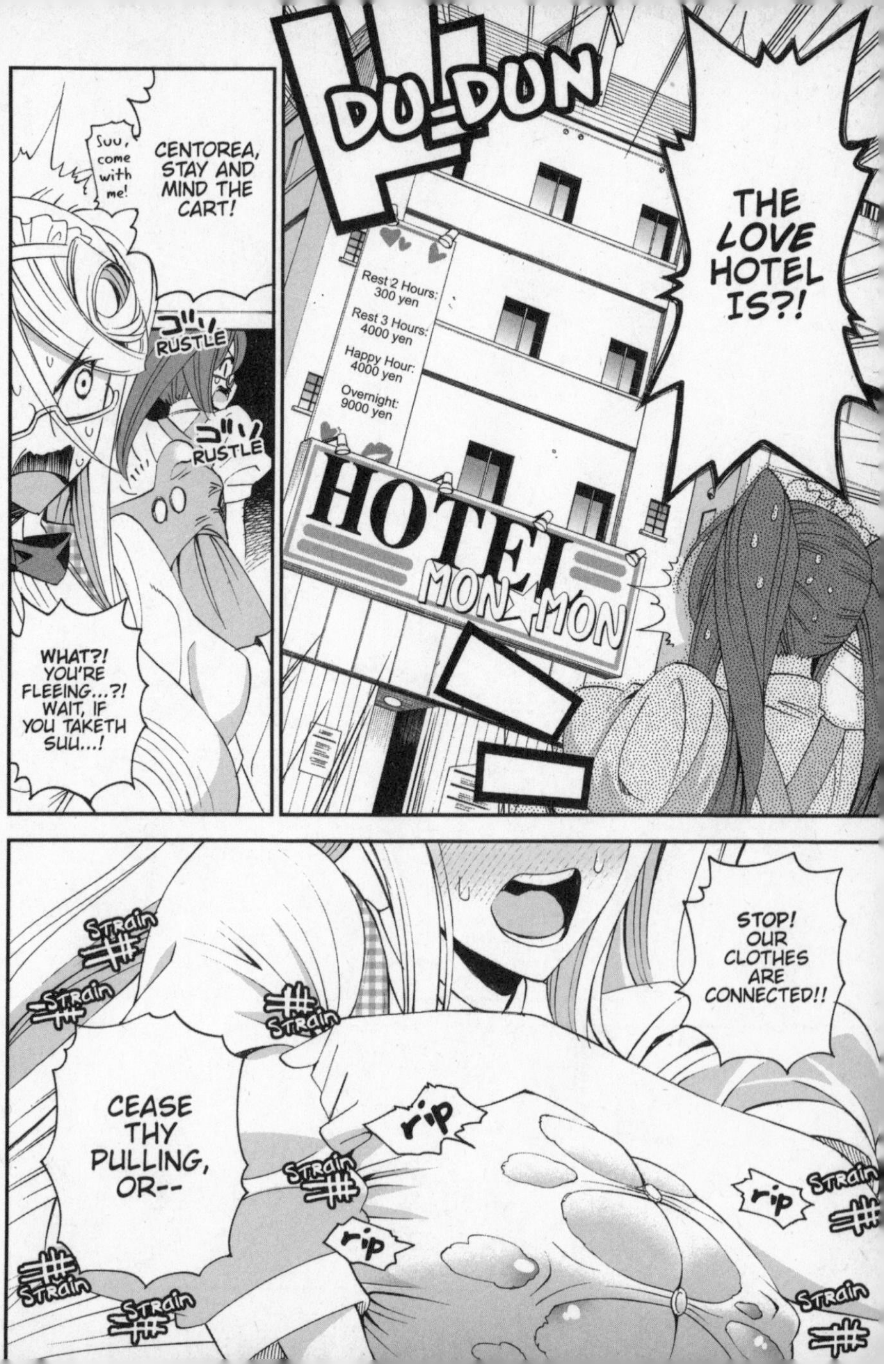
DU-DUN
THE LOVE HOTEL IS?!
Rest 2 Hours: 300 yen
Rest 3 Hours: 4000 yen
Happy Hour: 4000 yen
Overnight: 9000 yen
HOTEL
MON☆MON
CENTOREA, STAY AND MIND THE CART!
Suu, come with me!
RUSTLE
RUSTLE
WHAT?! YOU'RE FLEEING...?! WAIT, IF YOU TAKETH SUU...!
STOP! OUR CLOTHES ARE CONNECTED!!
STRAIN
STRAIN
STRAIN
CEASE THY PULLING, OR--
rip
STRAIN
rip
rip
STRAIN
STRAIN
STRAIN
STRAIN

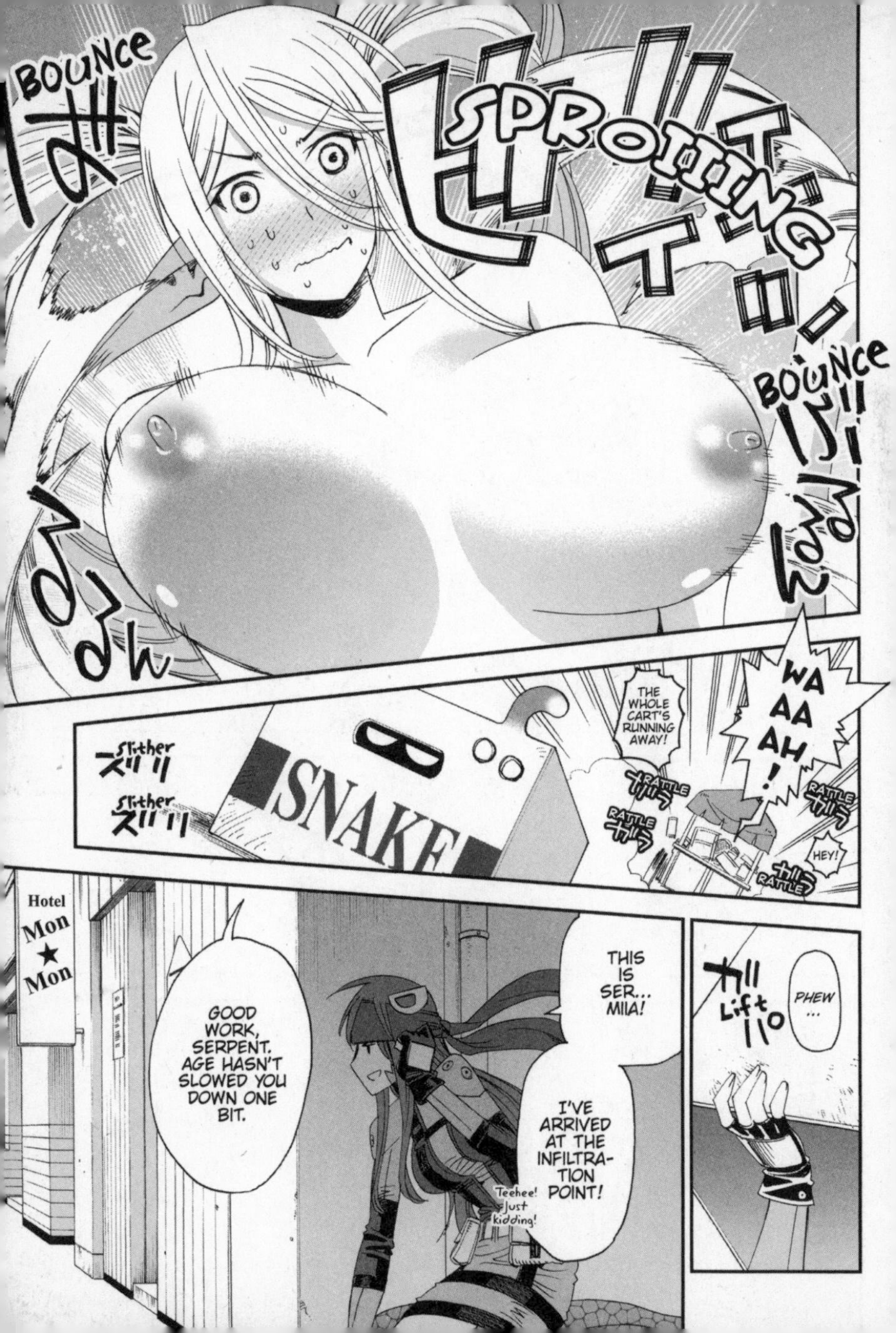
SPROIIING
BOUNCE
BOUNCE
WA AA AH!
THE WHOLE CART'S RUNNING AWAY!
RATTLE
HEY!
RATTLE
RATTLE
RATTLE
SNAKE
slither
slither
Lift
PHEW ...
THIS IS SER... MIIA!
I'VE ARRIVED AT THE INFILTRATION POINT!
Teehee! Just kidding!
GOOD WORK, SERPENT. AGE HASN'T SLOWED YOU DOWN ONE BIT.
Hotel Mon ★ Mon

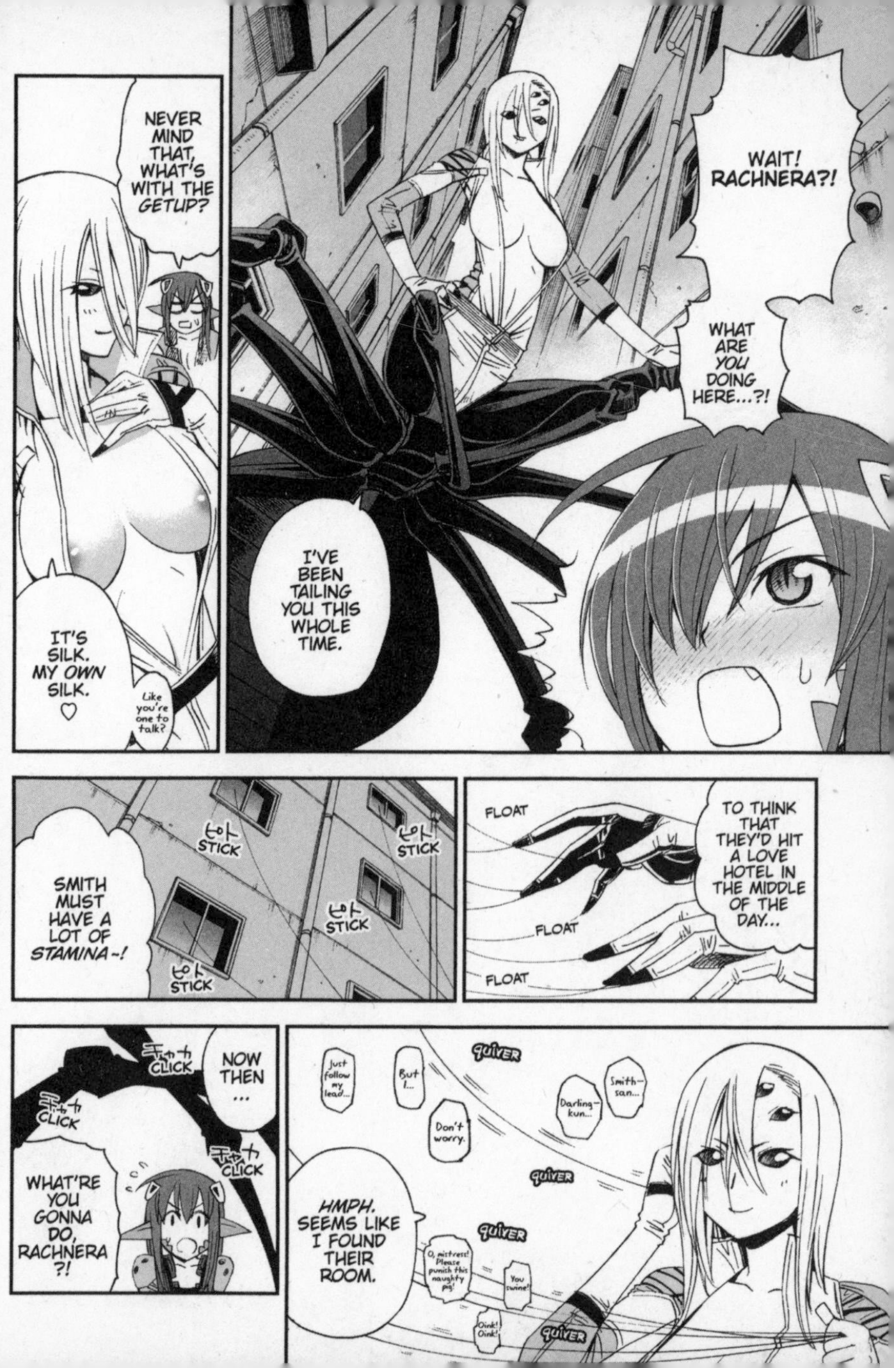
WAIT! RACHNERA?!
WHAT ARE *YOU* DOING HERE...?!
I'VE BEEN TAILING YOU THIS WHOLE TIME.
NEVER MIND THAT, WHAT'S WITH THE *GETUP*?
IT'S SILK. MY *OWN* SILK. ♡
Like you're one to talk?
FLOAT
TO THINK THAT THEY'D HIT A LOVE HOTEL IN THE MIDDLE OF THE DAY...
FLOAT
FLOAT
ピト STICK
ピト STICK
ピト STICK
SMITH MUST HAVE A LOT OF *STAMINA*~!
ピト STICK
quiver
Smith-san...
Darling-kun...
But I...
Just follow my lead...
Don't worry.
quiver
HMPH. SEEMS LIKE I FOUND THEIR ROOM.
quiver
You swine!
O, mistress! Please punish this naughty pig!
Oink! Oink!
quiver
NOW THEN ...
チャカ CLICK
チャカ CLICK
チャカ CLICK
WHAT'RE YOU GONNA DO, RACHNERA?!

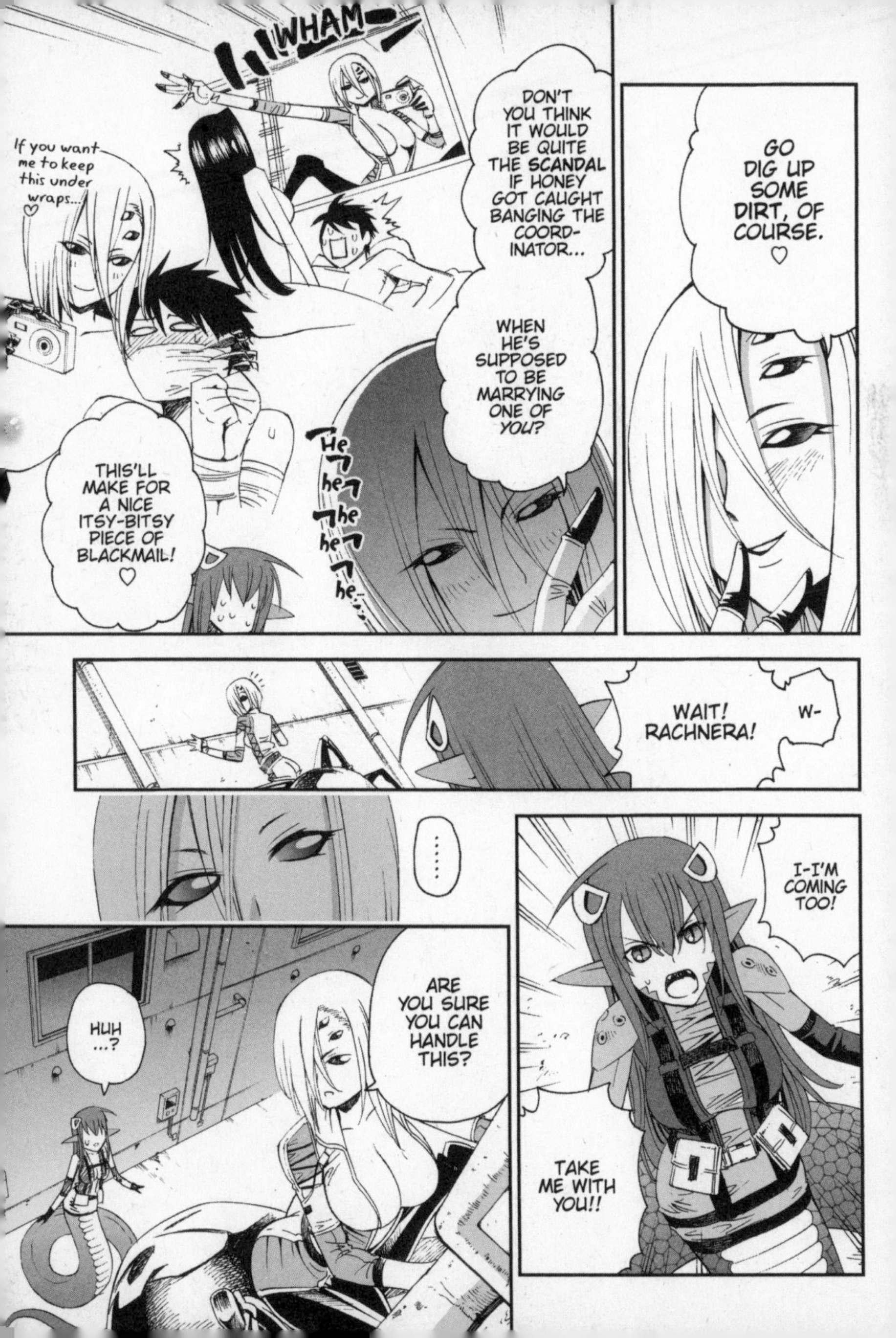
GO DIG UP SOME DIRT, OF COURSE. ♡
WHAM
DON'T YOU THINK IT WOULD BE QUITE THE SCANDAL IF HONEY GOT CAUGHT BANGING THE COORDINATOR...
If you want me to keep this under wraps... ♡
WHEN HE'S SUPPOSED TO BE MARRYING ONE OF YOU?
He he he he he...
THIS'LL MAKE FOR A NICE ITSY-BITSY PIECE OF BLACKMAIL! ♡
W- WAIT! RACHNERA!
I-I'M COMING TOO!
TAKE ME WITH YOU!!
......
ARE YOU SURE YOU CAN HANDLE THIS?
HUH ...?

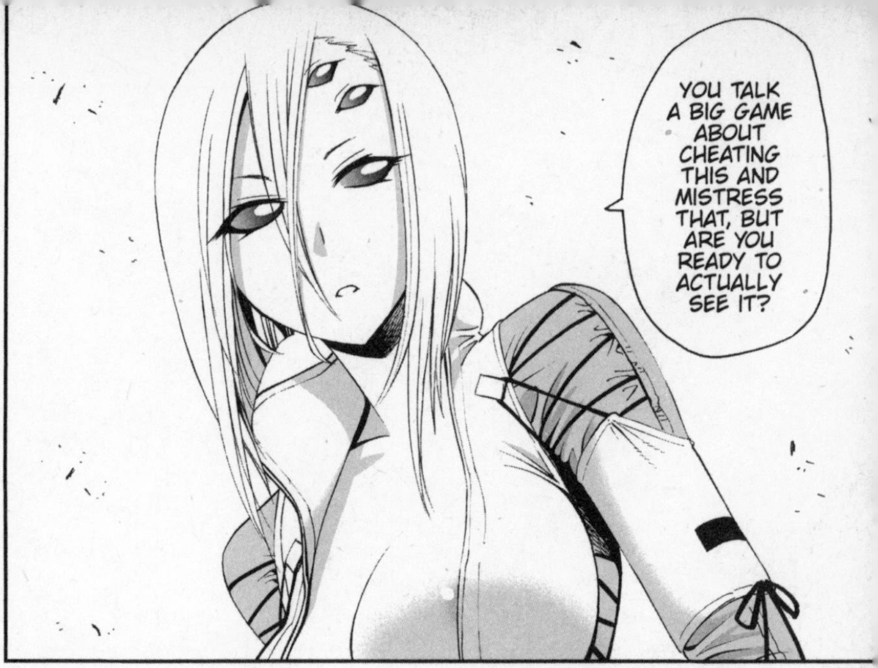
YOU TALK A BIG GAME ABOUT CHEATING THIS AND MISTRESS THAT, BUT ARE YOU READY TO ACTUALLY SEE IT?
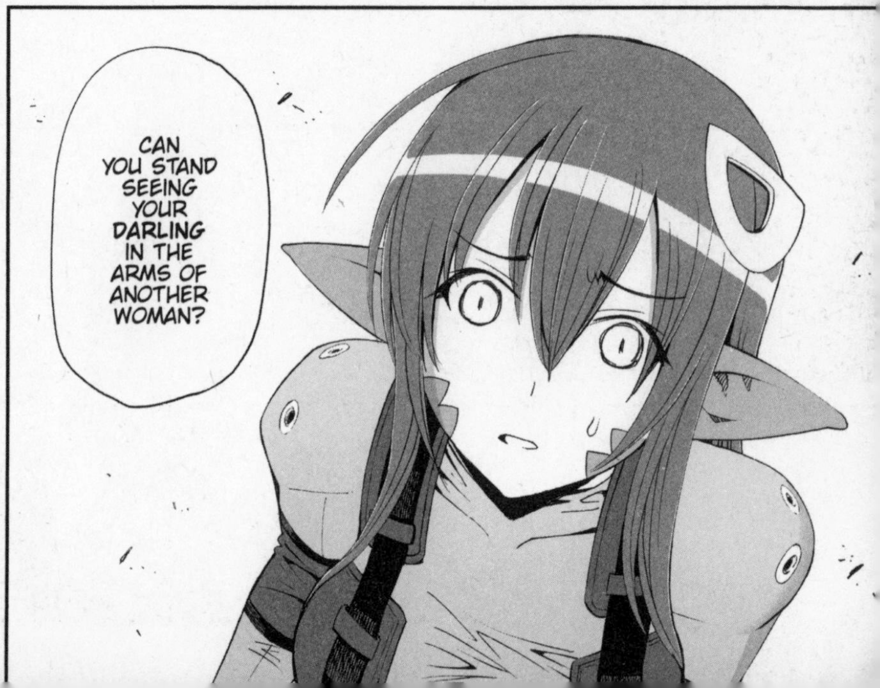
CAN YOU STAND SEEING YOUR DARLING IN THE ARMS OF ANOTHER WOMAN?

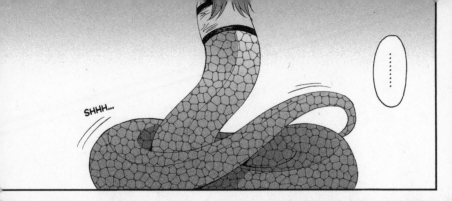

SHHH...

・・・・・・

STAY HERE. THERE'S NO SHAME IN IT.

?

whisper.

...ING.

・・・・・・

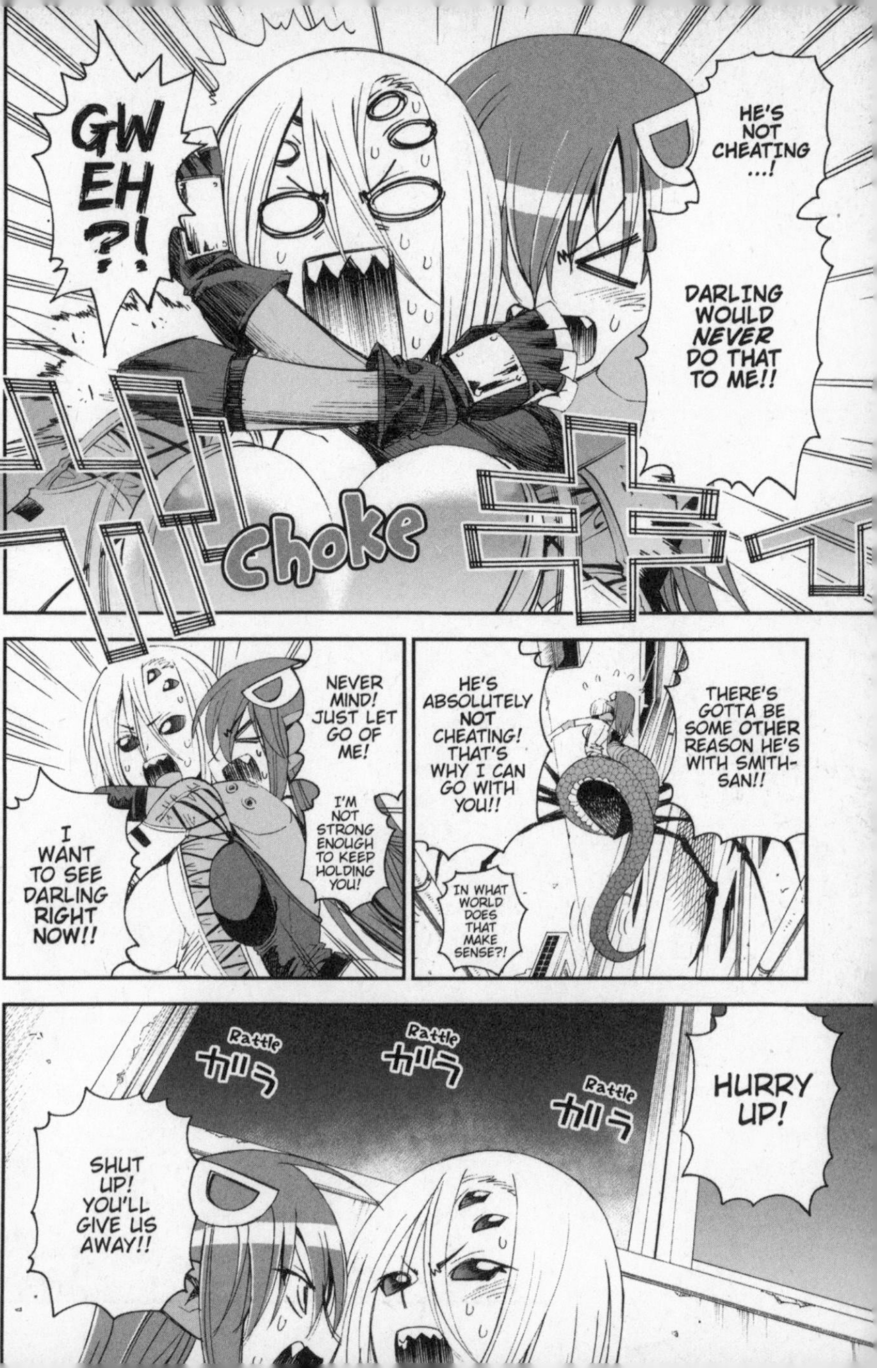
HE'S NOT CHEATING ...!
DARLING WOULD NEVER DO THAT TO ME!!
GWEH?!
Choke
THERE'S GOTTA BE SOME OTHER REASON HE'S WITH SMITH-SAN!!
HE'S ABSOLUTELY NOT CHEATING! THAT'S WHY I CAN GO WITH YOU!!
IN WHAT WORLD DOES THAT MAKE SENSE?!
NEVER MIND! JUST LET GO OF ME!
I'M NOT STRONG ENOUGH TO KEEP HOLDING YOU!
I WANT TO SEE DARLING RIGHT NOW!!
Rattle
Rattle
Rattle
HURRY UP!
SHUT UP! YOU'LL GIVE US AWAY!!

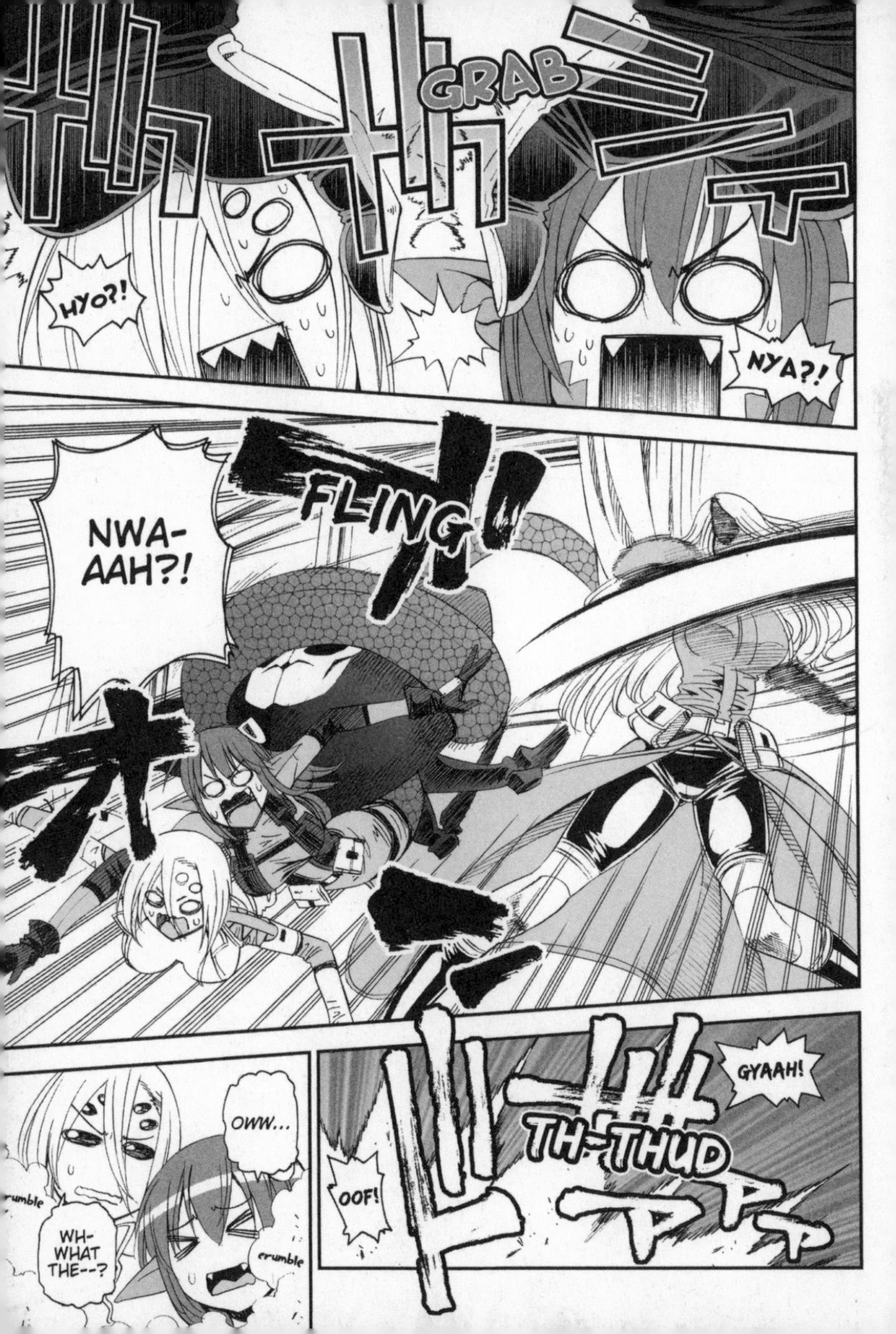
GRAB
NYA?!
HYO?!
FLING
NWA-AAH?!
GYAAH!
TH-THUD
OOF!
OWW...
crumble
WH-WHAT THE--?
crumble

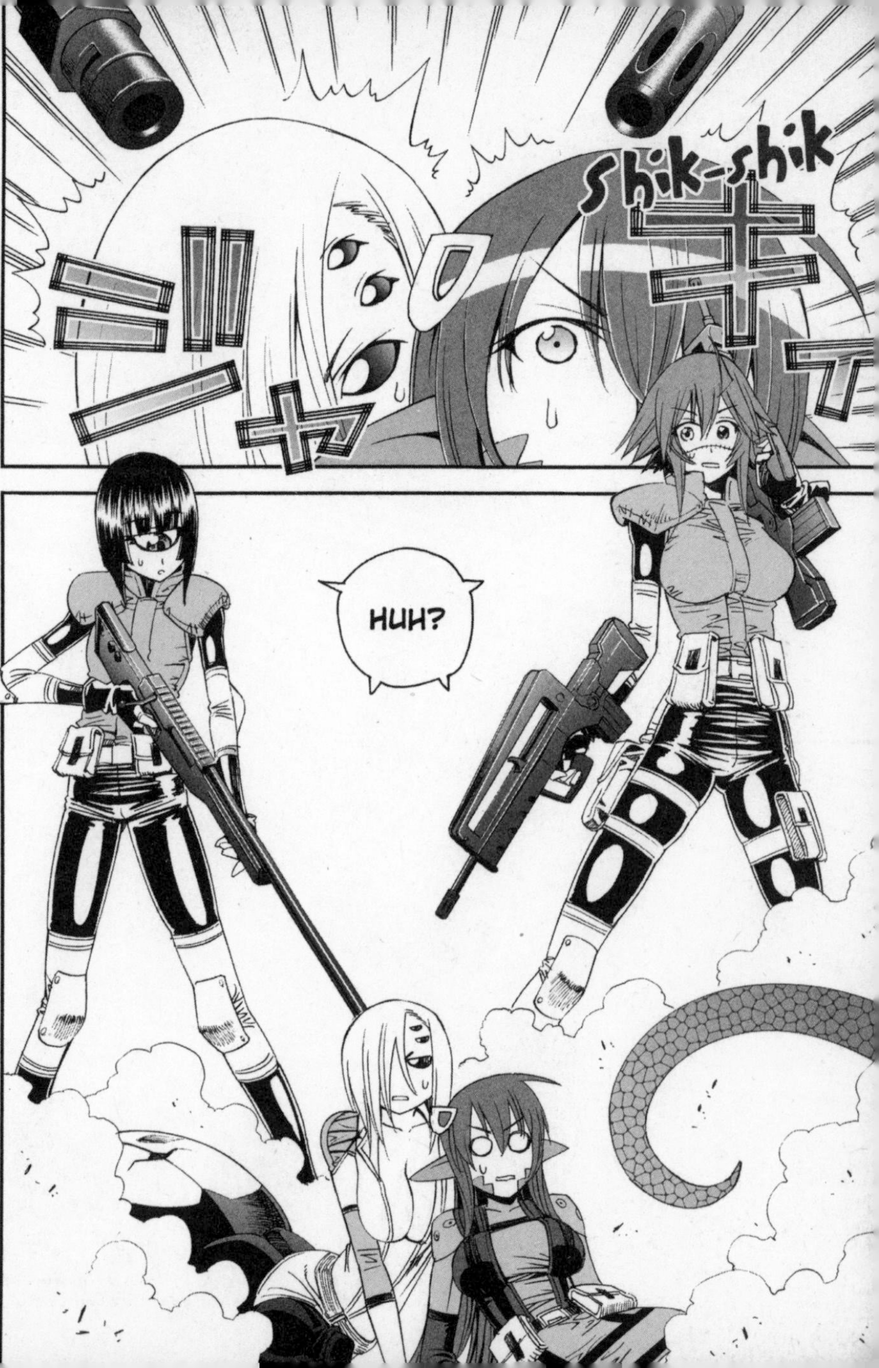
Shik-shik
HUH?

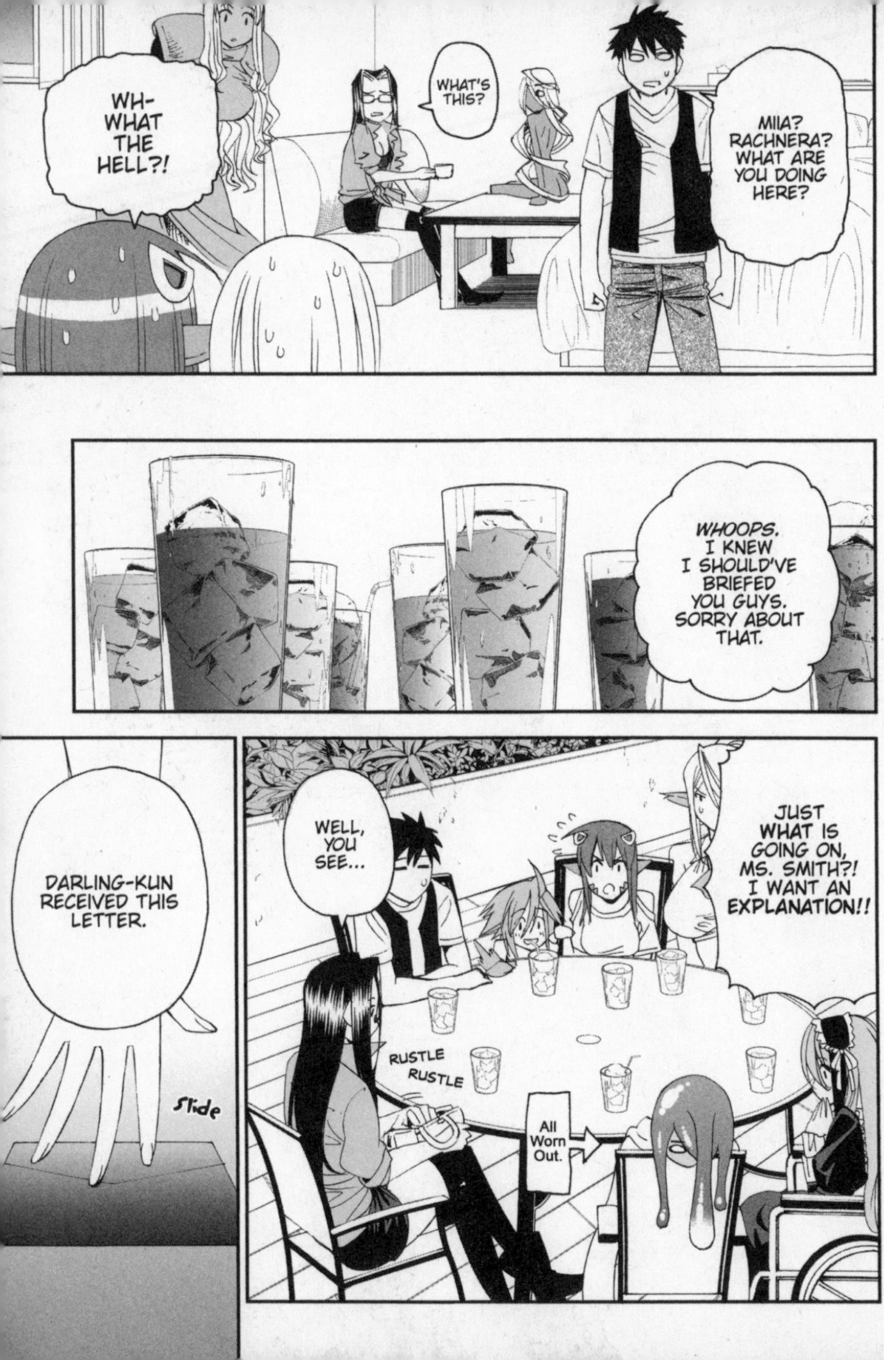
MIIA? RACHNERA? WHAT ARE YOU DOING HERE?
WHAT'S THIS?
WH- WHAT THE HELL?!
WHOOPS. I KNEW I SHOULD'VE BRIEFED YOU GUYS. SORRY ABOUT THAT.
JUST WHAT IS GOING ON, MS. SMITH?! I WANT AN EXPLANATION!!
WELL, YOU SEE...
RUSTLE RUSTLE
All Worn Out.
DARLING-KUN RECEIVED THIS LETTER.
Slide

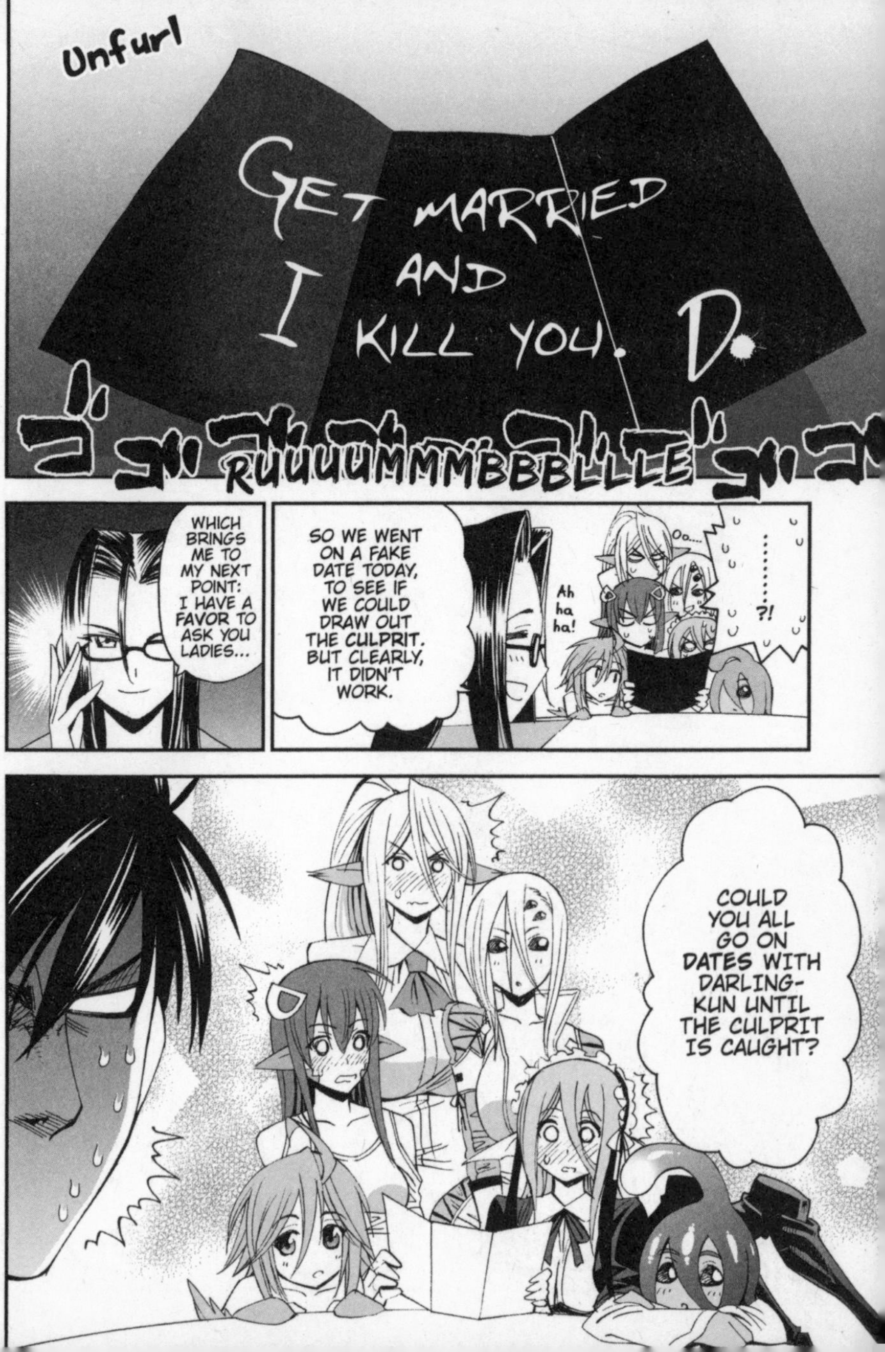
Unfurl
GET MARRIED AND I KILL YOU. D.
RUUUUMMMBBBLLLE
SO WE WENT ON A FAKE DATE TODAY, TO SEE IF WE COULD DRAW OUT THE CULPRIT. BUT CLEARLY, IT DIDN'T WORK.
Ah ha ha!
Oo....
......?!
WHICH BRINGS ME TO MY NEXT POINT: I HAVE A FAVOR TO ASK YOU LADIES...
COULD YOU ALL GO ON DATES WITH DARLING-KUN UNTIL THE CULPRIT IS CAUGHT?

Monster Musume

Everyday Life with Monster Girls

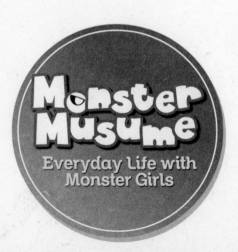

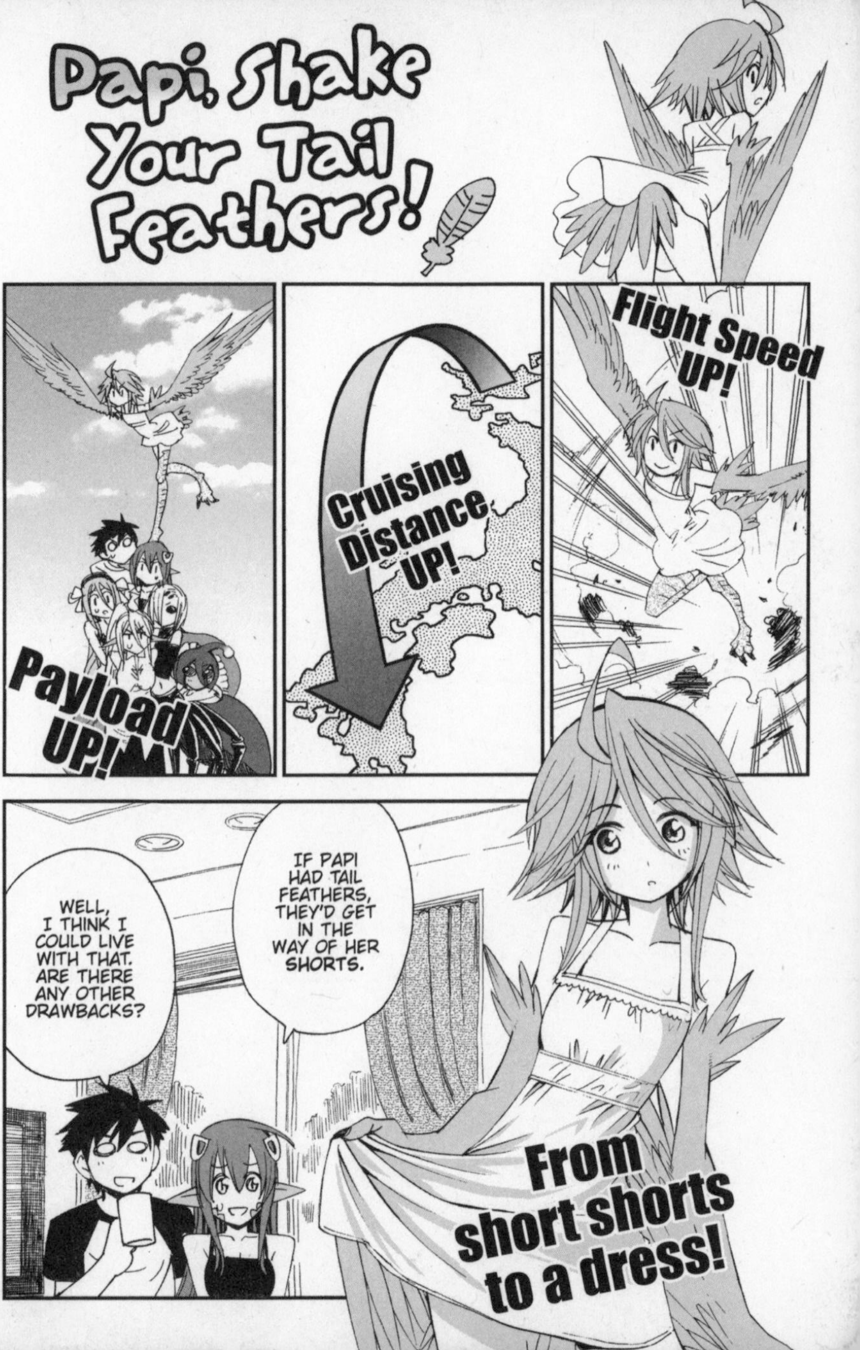
Papi, Shake Your Tail Feathers!
Flight Speed UP!
Cruising Distance UP!
Payload UP!
From short shorts to a dress!
IF PAPI HAD TAIL FEATHERS, THEY'D GET IN THE WAY OF HER SHORTS.
WELL, I THINK I COULD LIVE WITH THAT. ARE THERE ANY OTHER DRAWBACKS?

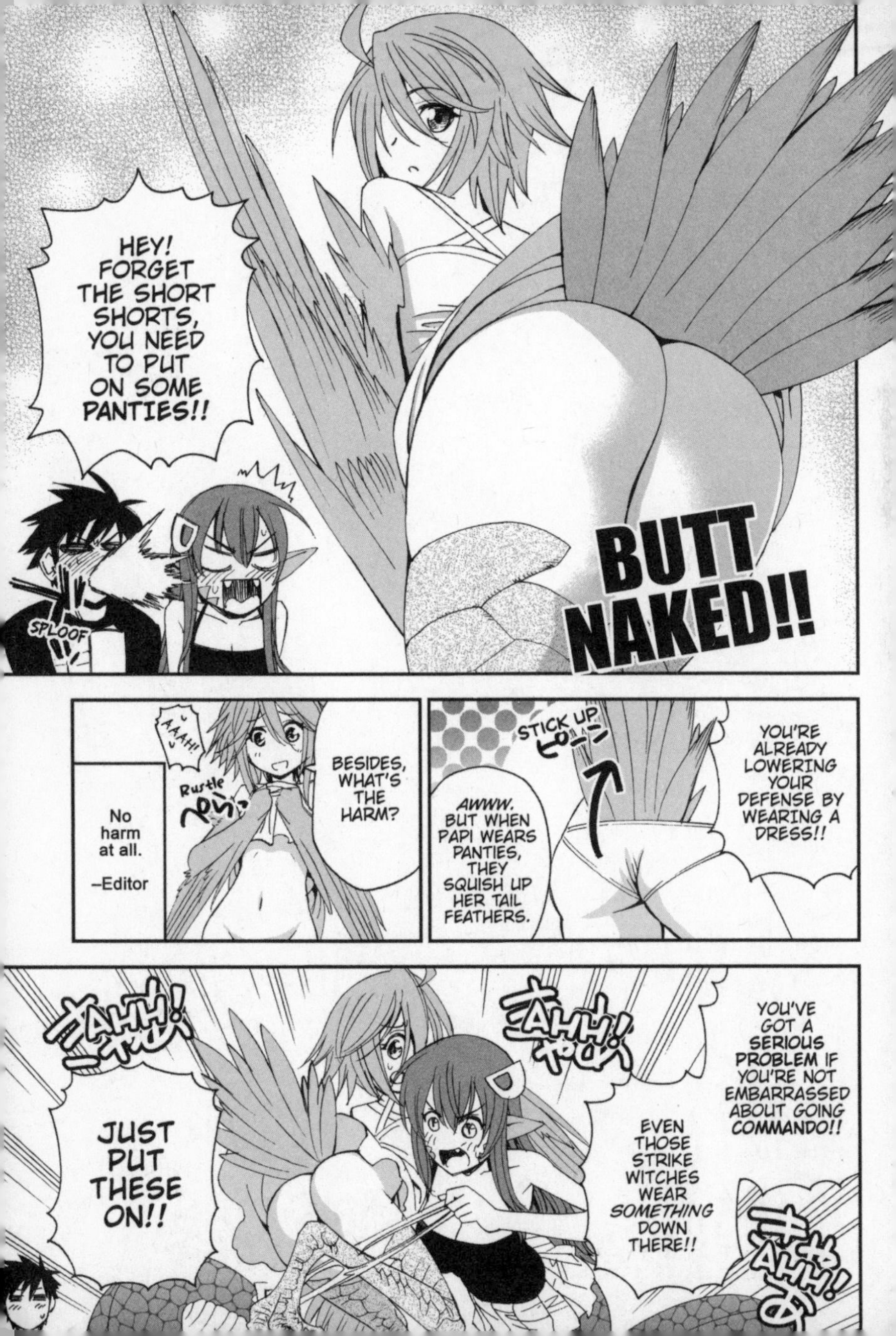
HEY! FORGET THE SHORT SHORTS, YOU NEED TO PUT ON SOME PANTIES!!
BUTT NAKED!!
SPLOOF
YOU'RE ALREADY LOWERING YOUR DEFENSE BY WEARING A DRESS!!
STICK UP ピーン
AWWW. BUT WHEN PAPI WEARS PANTIES, THEY SQUISH UP HER TAIL FEATHERS.
BESIDES, WHAT'S THE HARM?
AAAH!!
Rustle ぺらっ
No harm at all.
–Editor
YOU'VE GOT A SERIOUS PROBLEM IF YOU'RE NOT EMBARRASSED ABOUT GOING COMMANDO!!
AHH!
AHH!
EVEN THOSE STRIKE WITCHES WEAR SOMETHING DOWN THERE!!
AHH!
JUST PUT THESE ON!!

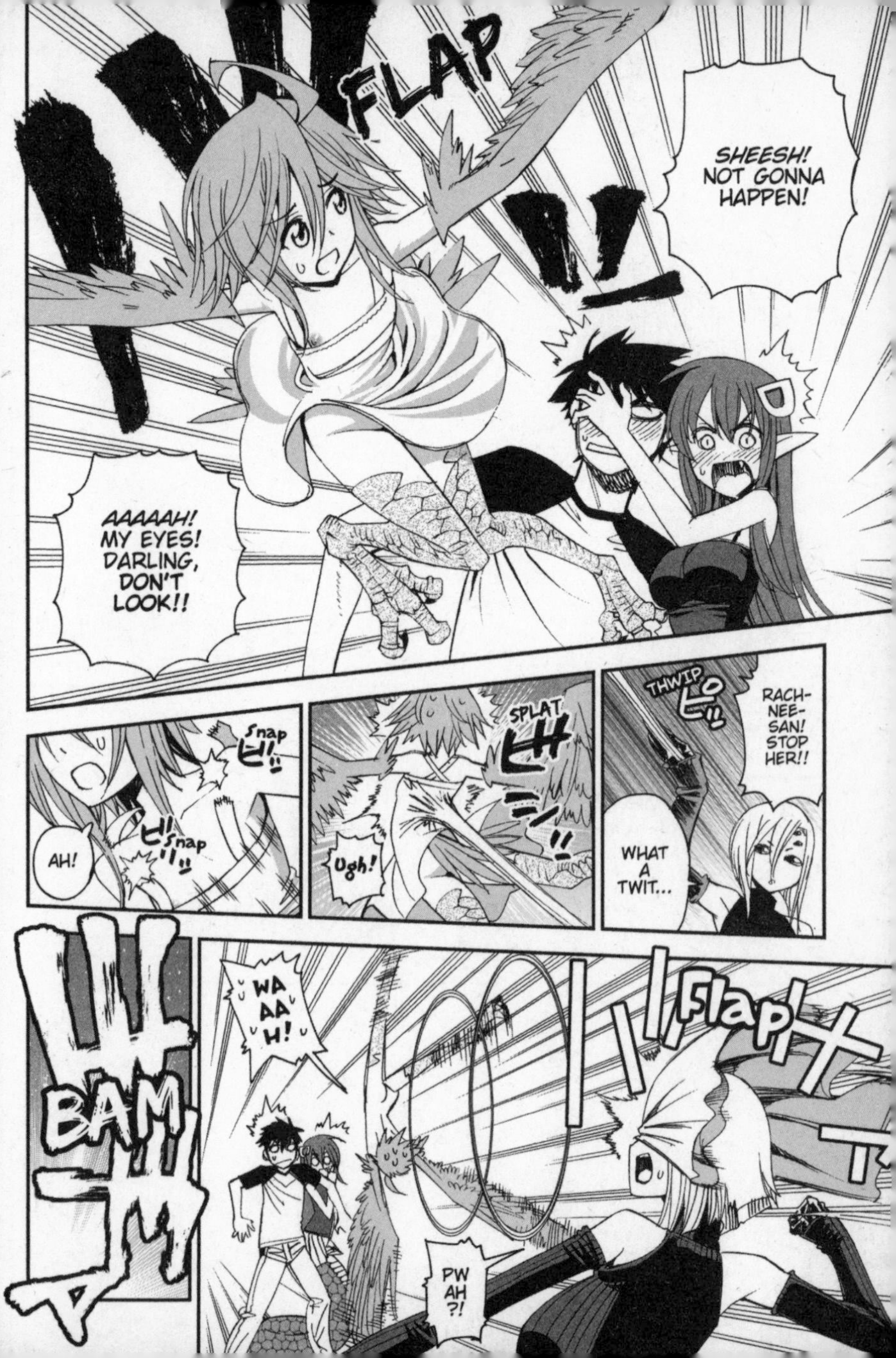
FLAP
SHEESH! NOT GONNA HAPPEN!
AAAAAH! MY EYES! DARLING, DON'T LOOK!!
THWIP
RACH-NEE-SAN! STOP HER!!
WHAT A TWIT...
SPLAT
Ugh!
Snap
Snap
AH!
Flap
WAAAH!
PWAH?!
BAM

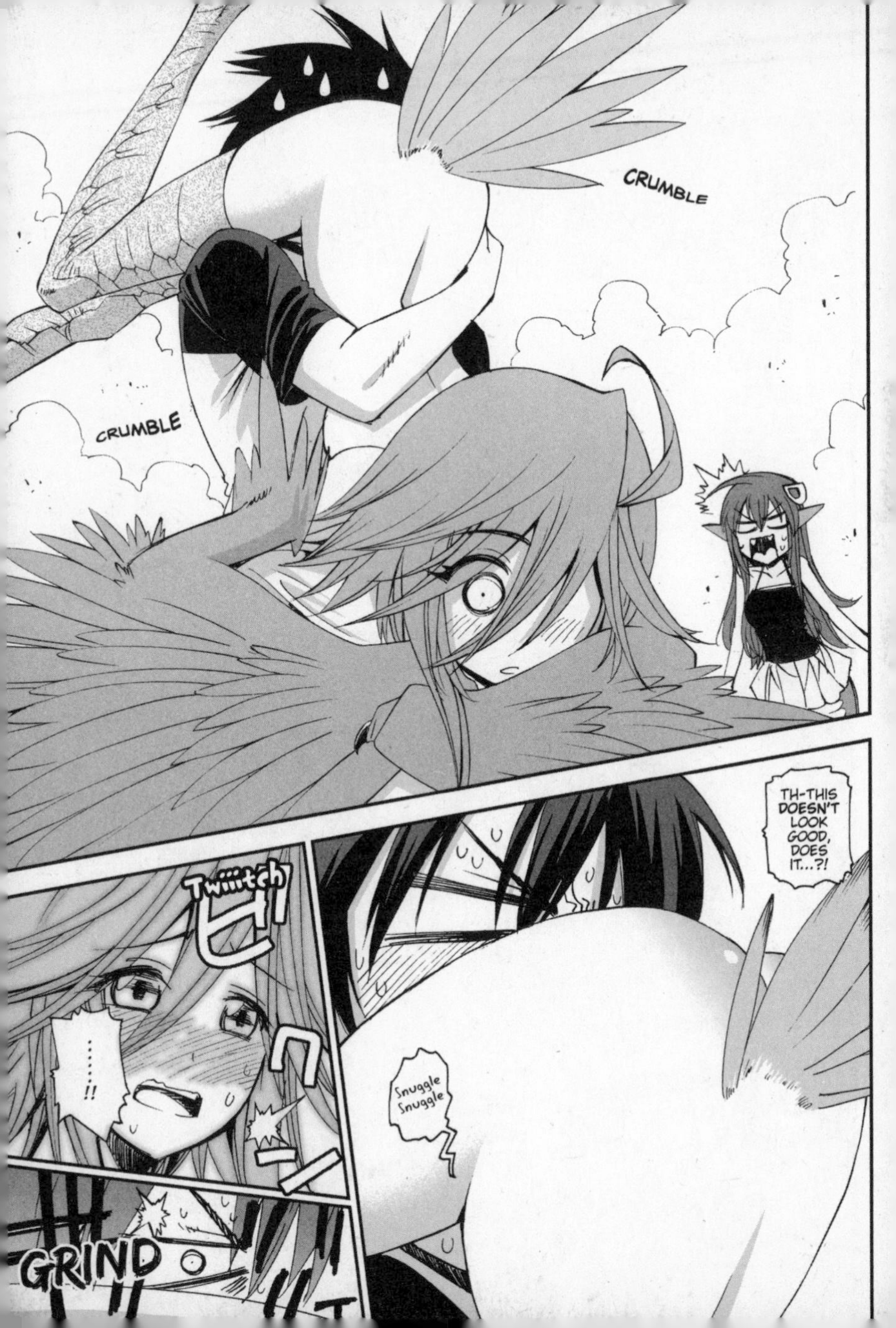
CRUMBLE
CRUMBLE
TH-THIS DOESN'T LOOK GOOD, DOES IT...?!
Snuggle Snuggle
Twiiitch
......!!
GRIND

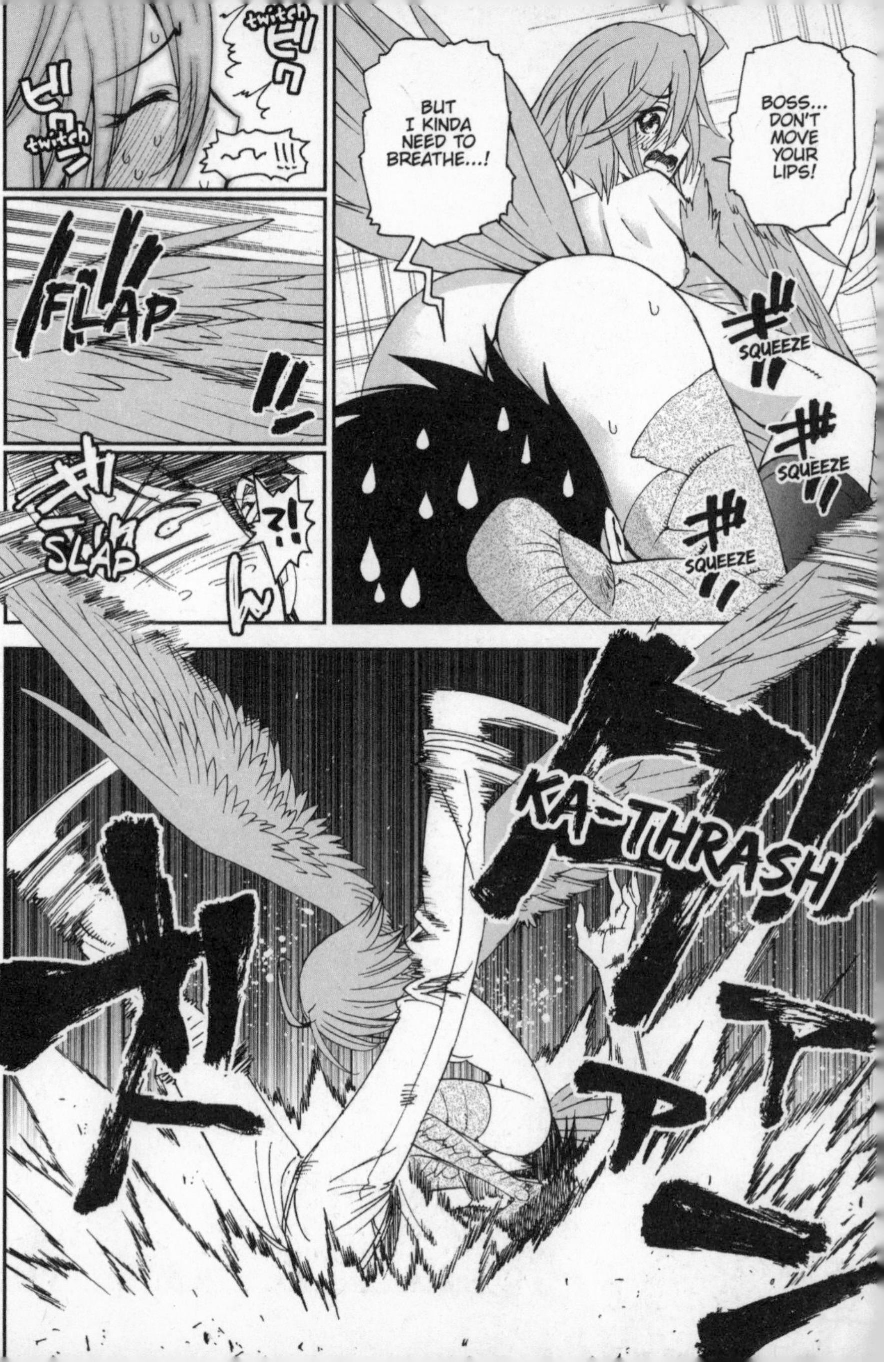
BOSS... DON'T MOVE YOUR LIPS!
BUT I KINDA NEED TO BREATHE...!
SQUEEZE
SQUEEZE
SQUEEZE
twitch
twitch
~~!!!
FLAP
SLAP
?!!
KA-THRASH

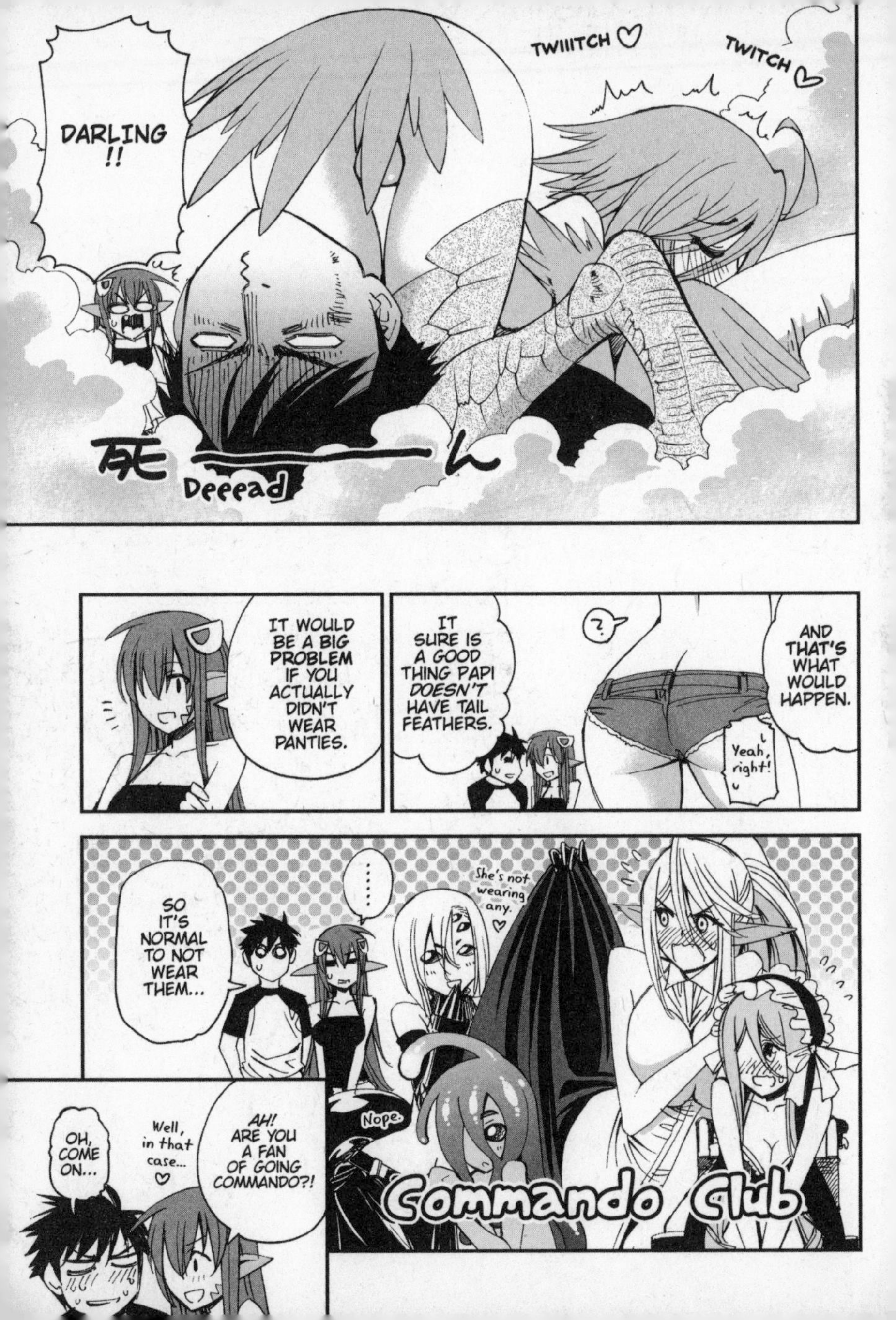
TWITCH ♡
TWIIITCH ♡
DARLING!!
Deeead
AND THAT'S WHAT WOULD HAPPEN.
Yeah, right!
?
IT SURE IS A GOOD THING PAPI DOESN'T HAVE TAIL FEATHERS.
IT WOULD BE A BIG PROBLEM IF YOU ACTUALLY DIDN'T WEAR PANTIES.
She's not wearing any. ♡
......
SO IT'S NORMAL TO NOT WEAR THEM...
Nope.
Commando Club
AH! ARE YOU A FAN OF GOING COMMANDO?!
Well, in that case... ♡
OH, COME ON...

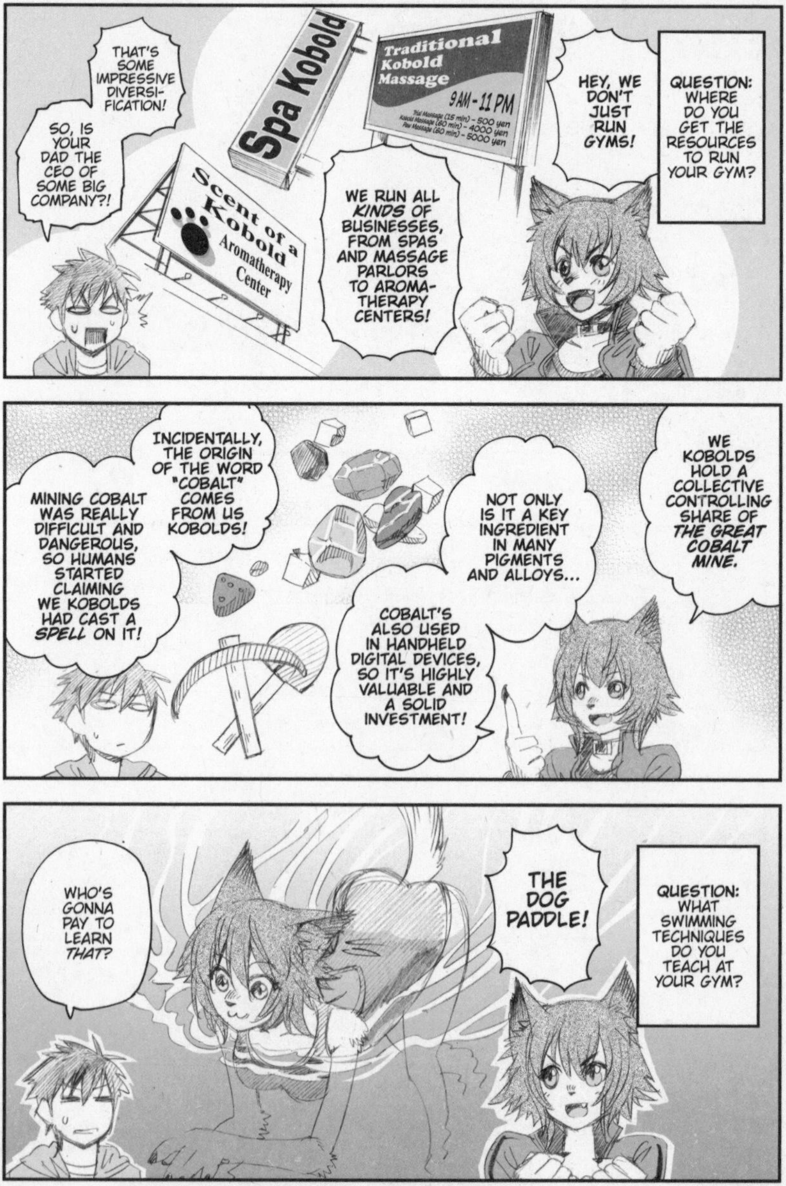
QUESTION: WHERE DO YOU GET THE RESOURCES TO RUN YOUR GYM?
HEY, WE DON'T JUST RUN GYMS!
Traditional Kobold Massage
9AM - 11 PM
Trial Massage (15 min) - 500 yen
Kobold Massage (60 min) - 4000 yen
Paw Massage (60 min) - 5000 yen
Spa Kobold
WE RUN ALL *KINDS* OF BUSINESSES, FROM SPAS AND MASSAGE PARLORS TO AROMA-THERAPY CENTERS!
Scent of a Kobold Aromatherapy Center
THAT'S SOME IMPRESSIVE DIVERSI-FICATION!
SO, IS YOUR DAD THE CEO OF SOME BIG COMPANY?!
WE KOBOLDS HOLD A COLLECTIVE CONTROLLING SHARE OF *THE GREAT COBALT MINE.*
NOT ONLY IS IT A KEY INGREDIENT IN MANY PIGMENTS AND ALLOYS...
COBALT'S ALSO USED IN HANDHELD DIGITAL DEVICES, SO IT'S HIGHLY VALUABLE AND A SOLID INVESTMENT!
INCIDENTALLY, THE ORIGIN OF THE WORD "COBALT" COMES FROM US KOBOLDS!
MINING COBALT WAS REALLY DIFFICULT AND DANGEROUS, SO HUMANS STARTED CLAIMING WE KOBOLDS HAD CAST A *SPELL* ON IT!
QUESTION: WHAT SWIMMING TECHNIQUES DO YOU TEACH AT YOUR GYM?
THE DOG PADDLE!
WHO'S GONNA PAY TO LEARN *THAT*?

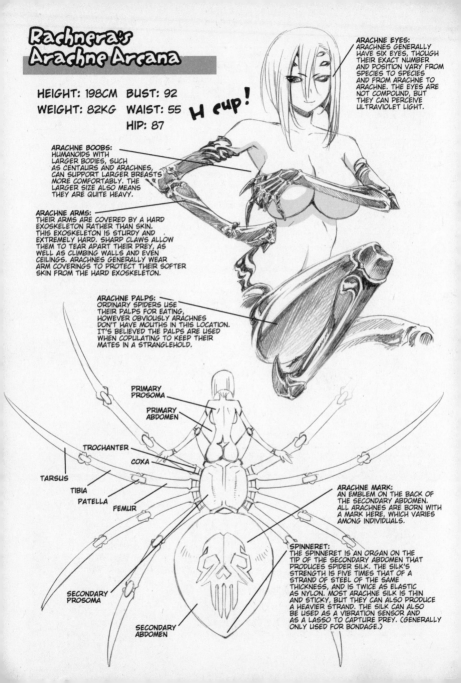

Rachnera's Arachne Arcana

HEIGHT: 198CM BUST: 92

WEIGHT: 82KG WAIST: 55

HIP: 87

H cup!

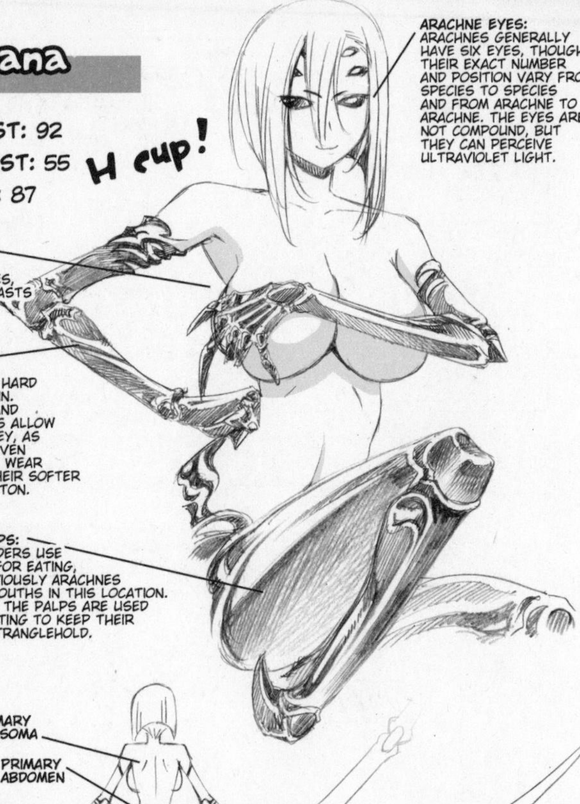

ARACHNE EYES: ARACHNES GENERALLY HAVE SIX EYES, THOUGH THEIR EXACT NUMBER AND POSITION VARY FROM SPECIES TO SPECIES AND FROM ARACHNE TO ARACHNE. THE EYES ARE NOT COMPOUND, BUT THEY CAN PERCEIVE ULTRAVIOLET LIGHT.
ARACHNE BOOBS: HUMANOIDS WITH LARGER BODIES, SUCH AS CENTAURS AND ARACHNES, CAN SUPPORT LARGER BREASTS MORE COMFORTABLY. THE LARGER SIZE ALSO MEANS THEY ARE QUITE HEAVY.
ARACHNE ARMS: THEIR ARMS ARE COVERED BY A HARD EXOSKELETON RATHER THAN SKIN. THIS EXOSKELETON IS STURDY AND EXTREMELY HARD. SHARP CLAWS ALLOW THEM TO TEAR APART THEIR PREY, AS WELL AS CLIMBING WALLS AND EVEN CEILINGS. ARACHNES GENERALLY WEAR ARM COVERINGS TO PROTECT THEIR SOFTER SKIN FROM THE HARD EXOSKELETON.
ARACHNE PALPS: ORDINARY SPIDERS USE THEIR PALPS FOR EATING, HOWEVER OBVIOUSLY ARACHNES DON'T HAVE MOUTHS IN THIS LOCATION. IT'S BELIEVED THE PALPS ARE USED WHEN COPULATING TO KEEP THEIR MATES IN A STRANGLEHOLD.

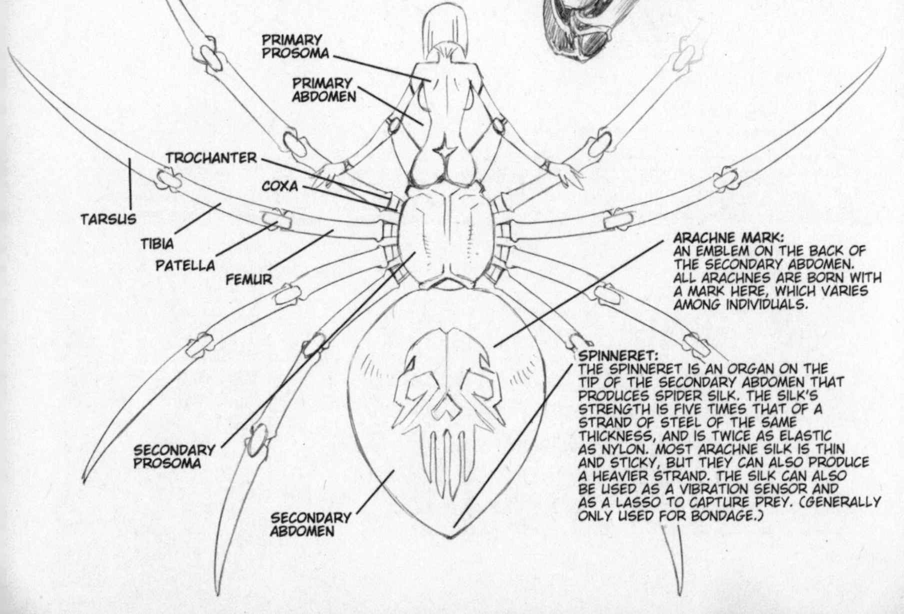

PRIMARY PROSOMA
PRIMARY ABDOMEN
TROCHANTER
COXA
TARSUS
TIBIA
PATELLA
FEMUR
ARACHNE MARK: AN EMBLEM ON THE BACK OF THE SECONDARY ABDOMEN. ALL ARACHNES ARE BORN WITH A MARK HERE, WHICH VARIES AMONG INDIVIDUALS.
SPINNERET: THE SPINNERET IS AN ORGAN ON THE TIP OF THE SECONDARY ABDOMEN THAT PRODUCES SPIDER SILK. THE SILK'S STRENGTH IS FIVE TIMES THAT OF A STRAND OF STEEL OF THE SAME THICKNESS, AND IS TWICE AS ELASTIC AS NYLON. MOST ARACHNE SILK IS THIN AND STICKY, BUT THEY CAN ALSO PRODUCE A HEAVIER STRAND. THE SILK CAN ALSO BE USED AS A VIBRATION SENSOR AND AS A LASSO TO CAPTURE PREY. (GENERALLY ONLY USED FOR BONDAGE.)
SECONDARY PROSOMA
SECONDARY ABDOMEN

SEVEN SEAS ENTERTAINMENT PRESENTS

Monster Musume

story and art by OKAYADO

VOLUME 4

TRANSLATION
Ryan Peterson

ADAPTATION
Shanti Whitesides

LETTERING AND LAYOUT
Ma. Victoria Robado

LOGO DESIGN
Courtney Williams

COVER DESIGN
Nicky Lim

PROOFREADER
Janet Houck
Conner Crooks

MANAGING EDITOR
Adam Arnold

PUBLISHER
Jason DeAngelis

Seven Seas books may be purchased in bulk for educational, business, or
promotional use. For information on bulk purchases, please contact Macmillan
Corporate & Premium Sales Department at 1-800-221-7945 (ext 5442)
or write specialmarkets@macmillan.com.

Seven Seas and the Seven Seas logo are trademarks of
Seven Seas Entertainment, LLC. All rights reserved.

ISBN: 978-1-626920-46-0

Printed in Canada

First Printing: August 2014

10 9 8 7 6 5 4 3 2

FOLLOW US ONLINE: *www.gomanga.com*

READING DIRECTIONS

This book reads from *right to left*, Japanese style.
If this is your first time reading manga, you start
reading from the top right panel on each page and
take it from there. If you get lost, just follow the
numbered diagram here. It may seem backwards at
first, but you'll get the hang of it! Have fun!!

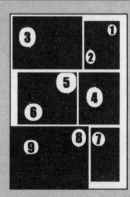